The Public's Business

The Public's Business
The Politics and Practices of Government Corporations

Annmarie Hauck Walsh

A Twentieth Century Fund Study

The MIT Press
Cambridge, Massachusetts, and London, England

This book was set in IBM Theme by To the Lighthouse Press. It was printed on R & E Book and bound by Halliday Lithograph Corporation in the United States of America.

Library of Congress Cataloging in Publication Data

Walsh, Annmarie Hauck.
    The public's business.

    "A Twentieth Century Fund study."
    Bibliography: p.
    Includes index.
    1. Corporations, Government—United States.
2. Corporations, Government—United States—Finance.
3. Municipal bonds—United States.   I. Twentieth Century Fund.   II. Title.
HD3887.W34   353.09'2   77-15595
ISBN 0-262-23086-0

To my parents, as partners:
James Smith Hauck and Ann-Marie Hauck

Contents

Tables

Charts

Foreword

It was about ten years ago that the trustees of the Twentieth Century Fund first took note of a proliferation of public authorities and public corporations in the New York metropolitan area. Further examination revealed that the phenomenon was not merely local but statewide and even nationwide. State and local governments were resorting to the authority device to perform an increasing number of important functions, including regional transportation development, housing development, natural resource management, and economic development. Public authorities were then perceived as efficient and businesslike, relatively invulnerable to the political pressures associated with government bureaucracies. Yet a number of social critics were beginning to question the benefits that communities derived from the operation of these independent, nonprofit agencies ultimately, if indirectly, supported by taxpayers.

Long before the debacle of New York City exposed fundamental weaknesses in the municipal market, the trustees of the Fund recognized the need for a study of these public enterprises financed by tax-exempt obligations. At the same time, they convened an independent Fund Task Force to study the related problem of municipal bond credit ratings, a problem that had emerged in part as a result of the proliferation of tax-exempt bond issues.

Even before the Task Force began its deliberations, an extensive search got underway for a research director to examine public authorities. It was not easy to find someone who had a solid background in public administration and a familiarity with the intricacies of the municipal bond market, along with the independence of mind to make a conscientious and critical examination of both. In Annmarie Hauck Walsh, the trustees found the qualities required for the project.

As a senior staff member at the Institute for Public Administration, Walsh had been, for several years, the director of the International Urban Studies Program, a research project on city governments abroad. She is a professor of political science at the City University Graduate Center and the author of *The Urban Challenge to Government: An International Comparison of Thirteen Cities*. Her research experience had given her insight into the theoretical and practical problems of public administration, and, as a project director and author, she had demonstrated her ability to manage a large research undertaking and assemble its results in book form.

In the fall of 1972, Walsh began her research. Subsequently, some of the concerns that prompted the Fund to sponsor the study became issues of heated controversy, as several New York–based authorities experienced fiscal crises of varying severity. As a result, Walsh's book has even greater topicality now than the trustees of the Fund could have predicted.

However, Walsh's book *The Public's Business* is just what the Fund hoped for—a fresh and iconoclastic examination of one of public administration's most underscrutinized yet important institutions. Guided by a concern for and a keen perception of the public interest, Walsh has produced a clear, readable analysis of the financing, administrative structure, and inevitable political functioning of public authorities. The Fund is grateful for Walsh's dedication and penetrating scholarship. I am confident that her study will be a significant contribution to public debate on a subject of great significance to every taxpayer.

M. J. Rossant, Director
The Twentieth Century Fund

Preface

Neither the title nor the organization of this book immediately suggests that it reflects comparative study. Comparative study of political organization is essential, in my judgment, to discover how organizational characteristics are associated with variations in performance and political outcomes. Therefore, although I have not tried to include in this one book systematic descriptions of investor-owned corporations, departmentalized government agencies, and government-owned and mixed enterprises abroad, these are the foils against which I have examined American public authorities (or statutory corporations) that engage in similar activities.

The purpose of the study is to analyze public authorities. Another, more difficult, purpose is to begin to explore the complex relationships between organizational characteristics, decision making, and resource allocation. How do the structures devised for administering public business and for channeling resources into public investment influence, determine, or limit the political and economic results of governmental programs? This is a hazardous question, requiring proddings into the work of scholars in public administration, political science, economics, and the sociology of organizations. Specialists in each field may object to loose translations of their language, to synthesizing treatment of their work, to loss of precision and detail.

This book deals with government-owned businesses—primarily state and local—that raise capital by issuing revenue bonds in the private money markets and invest it in public facilities. A central premise of the work is that the money markets form a system in which a significant number of public enterprises dependent on them behave in similar ways.

The structure of the book reflects some personal premises about organizational behavior. Formal organizations are products of culture and history. Strategies for institutional change must begin with historical diagnosis, and this is the job of part I. After an introduction in chapter 1, chapter 2 examines how the historical development of popular ideas and political reforms has shaped American attitudes toward public debt and capital investment, toward the involvement of businessmen in government operations, and toward the proper role of government enterprise. Chapter 2 also explains the legal and academic rationales that have shaped government corporations. It ends with an attempt to replace some inherited values and assumptions about the government corporation with empirical premises that should change the context in which they are judged.

Part II describes the impact of the municipal bond market on public enterprise. The cases included show how the characteristics of the financing system, more than any other trait of the public authority, explain its growth. This promotional dynamic is generated by the numerous opportunities for private profits to flow from public authority expansion.

Part III describes the leadership and management of government corporations. It is with the internal leadership and management practices that the crucial strengths of the public authorities lie, together with their challenge to democratic political institutions. Many public authorities provide models of management effectiveness that highlight the comparative ineptitude of state and city governments. The comparison helps to identify specific incentives for productivity that are commonly missing in government but are present in a number of government corporations.

Part IV examines fundamental problems of control and policy that are highlighted by the public authority experience. Chapter 10 demonstrates that only extraordinary political leadership has succeeded in controlling public authorities from the outside. Alternative ways of organizing public enterprise are reviewed in chapter 11, including some European examples and probable changes in the federal government's involvements. Chapter 12 reappraises the public authority and offers recommendations for change.

No government source of data gives a reliable count of public authorities or government corporations. (The appendix deals in detail with this data problem.) The financial community keeps better track of the activity of public corporations. In particular, The Bond Buyer, Inc., publishes reports on the activities of public authorities (as well as other state and local borrowers) in all states. My research materials included a clipping file developed from three consecutive years of *The Weekly Bond Buyer* divided into thirty-five subject categories. In addition, the Securities Industry Association (SIA) maintains data on the borrowing done by "statutory authorities"; SIA provided printouts according to categories that I requested.

The voluminous literature of public administration and related fields was another major source of research material for descriptive data on individual authorities (hundreds of them) and on the history of public finance. The kinds of conclusions I draw sometimes differ from those drawn by other authors, usually because I have asked different questions of the same material. I have used, as well, a large number of documents lacking the individual importance that would justify inclusion in the bibliography: consultants' reports, prospectuses, government documents, statutes, and legal cases, for example. My colleagues and I analyzed over one hundred authority annual reports. Unless otherwise noted, citations of traffic or other business volumes, revenues, and debt volumes in the text are taken from authority annual reports.

We also interviewed members of a dozen underwriting firms. We tried to set up interviews with bond attorneys, but if their appointment secretaries did not invoke privilege, the attorneys did. So we attended several of the professional workshops in which bond attorneys gather to educate one another, and we did our interviewing informally.

We conducted in-depth case studies of the changing role of public authorities in New York State; four Pennsylvania municipal corporations; the New Jersey Highway Authority and New Jersey Sports and Exposition Authority; the Lower Colorado River Authority of Texas; the Metropolitan Council of Minneapolis–St. Paul and the public authorities under its supervision; the Municipality of Metropolitan Seattle; and three municipal corporations in West Germany. I had previously studied French and Yugoslav mixed and public corporations performing urban service functions, and I now spent a week at the Port of London Authority. We conducted additional interviews on public utilities in the states of Washington and Nebraska and on the U.S. Postal Service, and we communicated or met with four former governors. Wherever individuals' statements or judgments are given in the text without footnote, the source is our interviews and correspondence.

The case studies alone have not served as the basis for generalization. Apart from noting unusual characteristics, I have used specific information from the case studies to illustrate (sometimes by exception) patterns confirmed by other sources. These research methods may be considered rough in the terms of science, but I remain convinced that they yield more empirically based insights than quantitative analysis could at the present state of legal and organizational confusion.

The research for this book took two and a half years and the assistance of some indispensable colleagues: James S. Hauck, my father, a retired business executive for whom this study was a first foray into the public sector; Ardith L. Maney, then a graduate student, now professor of political science; and Kim Taylor, then a law student, now an attorney. The book also reflects research done by Guenther F. Schaefer in Germany and by James L. Garnett in Minnesota. The exceptional energy, intelligence, and efficiency of all those colleagues produced much of the factual material on which the book is based. I take full responsibility for the research, having shared the interviewing and designed the specifications for data and documents to be collected. I am also responsible for the conclusions that have emerged from two years of writing in solitude.

I owe debts of gratitude to the Institute of Public Administration, New York, and the City University of New York Graduate Center for support and encouragement supplementary to the sponsorship of the Twentieth Century Fund. Violet E. Lewis, the project secretary, not only kept our appointments straight and our petty cash supplied but also, with considerable discretion, improved spelling, grammar, and style in numerous manuscript drafts. Xenia Duisin and Jonathan Zweigel of IPA's library were indefatigable document searchers, for which I am grateful.

Wallace S. Sayre and Luther Gulick influenced my approach to integrating the study of politics and public administration, and I am indebted to Gulick for his careful reading of the manuscript. R. James Thornton deserves special thanks for his lengthy and detailed comments. Although he will undoubtedly still take exception to some of the emphases of the book, his reflections from the perspective of an institutional broker have informed the final draft. Finally, my family was an important part of the enterprise. My mother, Ann-Marie Hauck, kept the clipping files in order. My husband, John, and elder son, Peter, were asked for and unstintingly gave enormous patience. My younger son, David, was born between chapters 9 and 10 and, quite without choice, sacrificed some mothering.

Annmarie Hauck Walsh

The Public's Business

Our Public Enterprise Heritage

1 Introduction

American government is in business in a big way. Government enterprise in the United States has been growing for over half a century. This trend is distinctly not toward "socialism," as that term is understood in other parts of the world. Socialism entails both public ownership of enterprise and some explicit public policies that are applied to enterprise decisions. In the United States, for the most part, government enterprise involves public ownership without public policy.

Since the births of the Port Authority of New York and New Jersey in 1921 and the Tennessee Valley Authority in 1933, the most common form of government enterprise has been the public authority. Despite enormous differences among their tasks, local and regional conditions, and governmental sponsors throughout the country, public authorities have proliferated in remarkably uniform form. They are one of the few popularly acceptable forms for American government to engage in economic activities.

Public authorities build and run public works of monumental proportions: bridges, tunnels, parkways, great dams, ports, airports, public buildings, industrial and recreational parks. They provide essential services: water, gas, electric power, transportation, training, insurance, and mortgage finance. They have functioned with technical competence, with relative speed, and until recently with little obvious burden on taxpayers. They have rarely been sullied by open scandal or serious mismanagement, so that, overall, their record compares favorably with that of American state and local governments.

Because they are widely regarded as business rather than as political enterprises, public authorities have enjoyed support from groups in nearly all positions on the political spectrum. Public debate on public authorities usually deals with such issues as the relative merits of rail and road transportation, energy expansion or environmental conservation, and whether urban development should primarily benefit the poor or the middle class. Not even the severe critics of specific public authorities have been willing to recommend that they be dismantled and their operations turned over to governments.

From time to time, critics do charge that public authorities are autocratic, beyond the reach of the people, or unresponsive to political officials, but these criticisms focus on the very characteristics that advocates of government corporations regard as virtues. Public authorities provide a relatively independent base of operations for entrepreneurs in the public sector, providing managers with administrative power that is greater than that usually found within the regular hierarchies and bureaus of government. The corporate form of public authorities permits jobs to be done and projects to be completed without the clamorous debates, recurring compromises, and delaying checks and counterchecks that characterize the rest of American government.

The successes of public authorities have, in fact, motivated much of the criticism of them. Critics on the left seek a more purposeful, dynamic, and democratically controlled public sector. Those on the right seek to reduce the scope of government enterprise, or at least to check its growth, and to limit its activities to those that aid private endeavors. In the persistent thrust of American politics toward strategic middle grounds, public authorities have withstood such assaults practically unscathed and continue to claim rights to independent management.

A distinguishing feature of public authorities—and one of the factors contributing to their strength—is that they raise capital from private investors through the money and capital markets to invest in public facilities and services. These corporations engage in activities that produce revenues, usually in the form of prices, fees, or rents collected from the users of the facilities or services that the corporations operate. These user charges may be inadequate to meet the full costs of the corporation, but they form a significant part of corporate revenues that can be saved, invested, or spent at the discretion of corporate management. Public authorities do not levy taxes but retain their own earnings, borrow funds for investment by issuing short-term notes and long-term bonds, and receive government loans and grants.

These ways of getting and spending financial resources make public authorities distinctly different from normal government agencies, which must request funds from annual government budgets. The funds used by government agencies must be authorized and appropriated by votes of elected legislatures and their committees, raised by taxes imposed on the public, and then spent only in accordance with specific, often elaborate, rules and regulations for public finance and accounting.

Government corporations are created by a public statute that defines their powers. They are owned by the government that so establishes them, but they are hybrid creatures, possessing some of the characteristics of private firms and some of public agencies. They are corporations without stockholders, political jurisdictions without voters or taxpayers. Those enterprises operating under the federal government may be titled corporations, authorities, banks, services, or agencies. State and local government corporations are generally labeled public authorities, although they, too, are sometimes called

agencies, commissions, districts, corporations, trusts, or boards. The disparate
titles do not reflect orderly distinctions of organizational structure or funding
methods. This book focuses on public authorities that state and municipal
governments have established with independent corporate status, without effective taxing power, and with access to the tax-exempt bond market.[1] Where
it discusses federal enterprises, metropolitan councils, and foreign examples,
it does so for the limited purposes of clarifying the setting and peculiar characteristics of public authorities and of identifying viable alternatives to them.

Unlike privately owned firms incorporated under the general business laws
of the states, public authorities are restricted to specific types of business activity defined in the statutes that have created them. They usually cannot
merge, diversify, or shift purposes without legislative action. Also unlike private firms, they are generally exempt from property and corporate taxes, and
their bonds and notes entitle investors to interest payments that are exempt
from federal income taxes. Some authorities are empowered to condemn land
or to exercise other police powers—over the use of waterways, for example, or
over the behavior on toll highways or in housing projects. Although authorities frequently enjoy monopoly business rights, they usually are not subject
to the regulatory commissions that oversee investor-owned utilities with monopoly franchises.

In other respects, public authorities are run like private businesses. They
use business-type budgets and accounts, rely heavily on private consultants,
informally let contracts, and control their own personnel systems and pay
scales. Most authorities are run by part-time, business-dominated boards of
directors and full-time managers who need not answer directly to any elected
officials.

Although precise counts have not been made, public authorities are the
only type of independent public institution that has proliferated in the
United States since 1960 (school boards have been consolidated, the growth
of special taxing districts has slowed, and the creation of new municipalities
has dwindled). Their establishment takes a variety of forms. New York and
Pennsylvania, two states with extensive arrays of public authorities, illustrate
different approaches. New York, where all "public benefit corporations"
must be chartered by individual special acts of the state legislature, had 230
public authorities in 1974. Pennsylvania, where cities, towns, counties, and
school districts can create public authorities by ordinances of several different
types (within the terms of general enabling legislation passed by the state),

had 1,872 "municipal corporations" and ten state public authorities in 1973. Over two-thirds of the states use the Pennsylvania method, although none has spawned so high a number of municipal corporations.

At least six thousand local and regional authorities and one thousand state and interstate authorities are operating today (see the appendix). But their growing number is not as significant as their mounting expenditure. The amount of funds raised by public authorities each year has tripled in a decade. State and local statutory authorities alone spend more than $14 billion per year on operations, including interest payments, and they invest some $10 billion per year in new capital facilities. By way of comparison, the capital budget expenditures of New York and California state governments were $893 million and $1.8 billion, respectively, in 1974. Public authorities are the largest category of borrowers in the tax-exempt bond market, raising more money for investment than either all state or all municipal governments. This corporate investment exerts a massive influence on the patterns of development in the nation, an influence that is largely insulated from public debate.

In a democracy, public resources should be allocated among competing projects by open and farsighted political processes. Public authorities, which claim—and are generally perceived—to be free of the narrow and sometimes nasty aspects of American politics, may also escape constructive pressures at work in the political arena. Yet they are inherently political and politicized, a peculiar paradox that represents a failure of public policy. It is the thesis of this book that public authorities that are supposed to act in the general interest of a state, region, or city frequently do not. Because of their insulation, they overemphasize financial returns and reflect or accept the viewpoints of banking and business participants. They bias government investment in favor of physical infrastructures for short-term economic return. Ideologies of laissez-faire, localism, autonomy, and limited politics converge to limit the forms and ambitions of public enterprise, to preserve the power of groups with narrow and specialized aims, and to relieve the enterprises themselves of obligations to respond to broader interests.

The financing of public authorities through the private tax-exempt bond market determines priorities of public planning, shapes criteria for selecting new projects, and affects the pace of public investment. This method of financing encourages higher rates of borrowing, spending, and construction than are possible for programs that must run the gauntlet of the political marketplace. In some cases, the result has been overborrowing, overspending, and overconstructing, but only certain kinds of spending and constructing are promoted and encouraged: projects with predictable financial results for the authority. In focusing on financial results, the authorities tend to ignore costs and benefits to the public at large and sometimes to competing private interests—costs that will not show up on the corporate books.

Although public authority projects are largely exempted from the more arduous tests of the political marketplace, they also enjoy exemption from the tests of the economic marketplace, which involve open competition and require responsiveness to buyer demands. To be sure, most government corporations must produce revenues in order to operate and to pay debt service to private investors, but a lack of competition for their services, tax exemption, and other financial advantages have made it easy, at least for some of them, to charge whatever prices are necessary to meet their costs, without concern for cost control. Other public authorities have been heavily subsidized throughout their histories. In the absence of severe fiscal crisis, even heavily subsidized corporations have been subject neither to public scrutiny nor to politically determined allocations of resources.

American intellectual and political history and tradition have molded the public authority, the controls over it, and the values it fosters. The public authority appears to be among our most creative and admired institutions. Yet the all but impregnable position of these institutions, and the persistent patterns they have demonstrated for misallocating resources, for contributing to waste, for confusing public and private interests, should be subject to scrutiny and correction. The difficulty is that the patterns traced in this book tend to be ignored or taken for granted, receiving little notice or attention from the public, save in rare times of crisis or scandal.

Not all organizations that are called public authorities fit these patterns; there are exceptions. Nevertheless the particular individuals and authorities described here and the controversies in which they have been embroiled indicate the dimensions of a failure in public policy and a tough web of forces that seems to trap us into more of the same. Neither scapegoating nor arguments by exception can lessen the need for fundamental changes in the conduct of a good part of what is the public's business.

The prospects for change depend on what E. E. Schattschneider called the politics of scope. Much of what has been said and written about public authorities in effect limits the scope of conflict involving them, protecting control by dominant insiders by making it extremely difficult to expand the political arena in which they operate. The widely accepted premise that the operations of public authorities should be protected from politics influences the selection of policies and programs and precludes certain changes. This book attempts to identify the policy biases of public authorities as they currently operate and to remove the protective armor that shields them from serving the public interest more fully and effectively.

Certain premises are essential to a fresh evaluation of public enterprise. First, *public enterprise decisions are loaded with social and political implications,* as well as with technical and financial implications. Technical problems throughout modern government are inextricably linked with political problems; solutions desired by one group are anathema to others and may be variously favored or opposed by still other groups, depending on the circumstances. The problems of distributing benefits and burdens in society have no purely technical solutions. Economic theorists and policy analysts have tried to assign weights to various social and political costs and benefits for the purpose of evaluating program alternatives, but it is impossible to determine objectively, for example, whether benefits to one group of people justify costs to another. Only the ox that is gored knows how much it hurts. Many services provided by the public sector are essential to the life of contemporary communities. The power to fix rates is in such cases the power to allocate public resources. The location of highway interchanges affects the social and economic base of towns along the route. The directions and prices of rail transportation determine people's access to jobs. There may be no Democratic or Republican way to collect garbage, but urban conflict has amply demonstrated that legitimate community interests are involved in the distribution of sanitation and all other important public services. The resolution of such problems usually requires bargaining, as well as analysis and information.

Analysis and information have their place in government, contrary to what some fans of unfettered interest group politics maintain. No legitimate interest can be served by misplaced or structurally unsound highways and bridges, rail transit with inflated costs and service defects, cost overruns on housing construction, training for nonexistent jobs, or clerical bungling. Politics, however, is not the only (or even the most prevalent) cause of incompetence. Where politics encourages incompetence, it should be transformed rather than tolerated. To deny that politics has a legitimate role to play in public enterprise is to reject representative democracy and to overrate man's current capacity to devise technocratic solutions to social problems. Hence, openness to democratic political processes is a valid and important criterion for the performance of public authorities.

Second, *ethical dilemmas and temptations to corruption are present in both business and government.* Neither business firms nor public authorities are automatically freer from unethical or illegal behavior than government agencies are. Without pursuing the complicated dimensions of notions of ethics, many of us can agree on minimal standards of acceptable conduct. Where laws are broken, where hidden conflicts of interest subvert organizational purposes, where pursuit of private gain interferes with public safety and with the usefulness of a facility to the public, that line has surely been crossed. The organizational framework of both public and private enterprise, of both government bureaus and corporations, should be designed to minimize opportunities for crossing this line.

It cannot be assumed—as it often is—that public authorities eliminate opportunities for corruption in government. Private incentives are ubiquitous; no man is entirely the organization's man. When private incentives become the dominant ends in themselves and resulting behavior deviates significantly from the formal purposes of the organization, the pathology of corruption is present. In the public sector this pathology takes the form of special favors, personal loyalty, quid pro quo granting of rulings and contracts, and patronage jobs. These practices are also common in business, where they are often not considered deviant. When the qualifications of competing job candidates or products are not dramatically different or are difficult to judge, business executives fall back on personal loyalty, favors owed, and familiarity to fill positions, to let contracts, and to choose suppliers. Business uses a mixture of the merit system and personal patronage as suits its purposes; and conflicts of interest, at least until recently, were seldom questioned in the private sector. Instances of top executives' investing in companies to which their own firm awards contracts are widespread and seldom prohibited. Even kickbacks—while frowned upon—are rarely punished unless they interfere with securities law. Arnold Toynbee has summed up a common European view of the relative ethics of business and government: "One cause of the decline in political morality in America is that this has now sunk to the lowest level of American business morality."[2]

Business executives themselves are deeply involved in politics, although they tend to play down that involvement. William W. Keeler, the chief executive officer of Phillips Petroleum, justified his company's defiance of U.S. policy against doing business in southwest Africa (in compliance with an International Court ruling) by stating that corporate decision making should not be affected by political pressures.[3] At the same time, Keeler had been maintaining personal contacts with the secretary of the interior and had served on government policy committees for twenty years. He admitted that these associations had given him access to information on competing oil companies and influence over government petroleum policy. His political activities were within the bounds of generally accepted business behavior, except for his illegal contribution of $100,000 in corporate funds to the 1972 Committee to Re-elect the President. In earlier years, even this contribution might have been legal.

Private business organizations have—among other purposes—to make money for their employees, stockholders, and other investors. Management normally defines the other goals to be pursued and the means used. Government enterprise differs from private enterprise in that its success cannot be measured in financial terms or defined solely by management executives. The U.S. constitutional system emphasizes equity, due process, and responsiveness to popular preferences. Consequently business ethics are not adequate to prevent corruption of the purposes of public enterprise. "Businesslike" is not an attribute that can be relied upon to evaluate public authorities.

Third, *the form of public organizations significantly affects the policies they adopt and the kind of management they conduct.* Any structure for making decisions encourages certain types of choice and discourages others. Organizational structure screens the kinds of demands that government will consider as legitimate possibilities. Together with culture, class, and popular ideas, organization determines the public agenda. To evaluate public corporations relative to other institutional options, we must search for patterns in the demands that they meet and in the agenda they set. What interests are promoted and what interests are shut out by choice of this form for government enterprise?

Public authorities have been frequently called more innovative and flexible than government. The evidence does not bear this distinction out. Like other formal organizations with tasks to perform, government corporations need to limit the conflict and uncertainty to which they are subject. Within them, executives with business backgrounds and entrepreneurial personalities devoted to getting the job done expeditiously often find the pressures and delays that arise from public debate especially frustrating. The formal independence of the public corporation also makes it more defensive toward external contingencies and attack than a bureau that is an integral part of a government department and an elected administration. For several reasons, then, government corporations may aggravate the normal bureaucratic concern for self-protection.

Public corporations also seek to ensure their own success. When certain projects succeed, they try to expand similar types of projects and to abandon or avoid having to continue more problem-ridden programs. Many public corporations try to "cream," to take over only the richest parts of the public sector. Their motive is not so much greed for excess revenues as a desire for a secure cash flow and an eagerness to avoid difficult jobs and dependence on public appropriations.

These tendencies are variously moderated by the corporation's mission. Some tasks do not lend themselves to creaming and to safe alliances. Some authorities confront difficult assignments—transit, municipal hospitals, or low-cost housing. Such facilities are generally unimpressive as revenue producers, and their users often lack political power. Authorities without allies to defend them tend to move slowly. In contrast, most highway authorities have encountered only minimal opposition, and the alliance of contractors and users that benefits from highway construction could defend them with little opposition. Highway authorities have seldom had to negotiate trade-offs with interests in, for example, rail transportation or environmental protection. The result was relatively fast-growing highway construction. The political influence of groups whose interests are involved affects the behavior of particular public corporations.

The technical specialization required in modern public enterprise tends to work against innovation and adaptability in limited purpose corporations. Construction engineers cannot easily switch over to environmental impact analysis or highway planners to transit engineering. When the task changes, it often requires difficult changes in personnel and leadership and alters familiar relationships within the corporation. Moreover, public corporations have adapted a number of techniques from the private sector to develop internal consensus; and internal consensus, like specialization, works against flexibility.

Rules and routines are an integral part of any formal organization. They emerge from past adjustments to problems. Enterprises that do not have to adhere to simple indicators of performance, such as profit, and are buffered from the more dramatic shifts in political demands tend to be conservative and to rely heavily on precedent. Public corporations, therefore, may be less innovative and flexible than either regular government or the private sector.

Fourth, *the efficacy of management in the public sector is in no way con-*

tingent on market forces. When government corporations are efficient or well managed, their relationship to the marketplace has little to do with that fortunate result. The classic market model assumes that the usefulness of an enterprise's output is reflected in competitive consumer choice—that if the product is useful, consumers will buy it at a price that will be profitable to the producer. Translated into the language of economics, marketing and consumer choice influence profitability, which is the link between production efficiency and consumer utility. Without this link, the concept of efficiency is superficial. "Producer efficiency in the absence of consumer utility is without economic meaning."[4] It would be possible, for example, to organize an enterprise that would be superefficient at producing an item—say, green wigs—that no one wants. (Socialist systems have experienced this problem.) The private sector, confronted by a surplus of green wigs, might resort to advertising to convince consumers that green wigs are chic. Such a use of advertising is not a realistic recourse for the public sector in a mixed economy. Consumer utility in the public sector is a social question, a political issue.

Most public enterprises in the United States produce goods and services under monopoly or scarcity conditions. Production efficiency is an inappropriate goal in those circumstances. Consumers, other than those wealthy enough to provide their own substitutes (helicopter commuting, private beach club, high rental housing, and so forth), have no alternative to the facilities offered by the public agency. The public agency is able therefore to cut costs and to increase internal efficiency at the expense of the potential consumer as well as of the broader society. A quest for production efficiency under these conditions reinforces organizational tendencies to cream and to minimize uncertainty.

Public goods and services have, in economists' terms, significant externalities. They affect much more than the satisfaction of individual users; they affect people outside their immediate market. One political economist concludes that "unrestricted individualistic decision-making in relation to common resources or public goods will lead to the competitive dynamic of a negative sum game: the greater the individual effort, the worse off people become."[5] Familiar pictures of polluted lakes and ten-lane highways that are as congested as their two-lane forebears illustrate this "tragedy of the commons."[6]

To be sure, public corporations may be internally efficient and financially rational while they are protected from competition and financial risks, but in these circumstances they will experience few incentives to be responsive to the needs of their own consumers—who are, after all, a captive audience—let alone to the needs of the larger community in which they operate or to the long-term needs of society. They deal with the public's concerns primarily through their public relations departments. Private companies and government agencies can also be expected to lose their accountability when they are buffered from both political and competitive economic pressures.[7]

An investigation of government corporations, then, is part of a more imposing search for answers as to how the forces of politics, the realities of economics, and the exigencies of effective management can be combined to improve the conduct of the public's business. Considering the impact of contemporary technology on human lives and our high dependence on public manipulation of the environment, this question is central to the quality of life, if not to social survival.

2 Precedents and Preconceptions

Government-owned enterprises, like other aspects of American government, have tangled historical roots that shape their growth and popular ideas about them. These roots are the mixed heritage of libertarian economic theory, moralistic attitudes toward public debt, turn-of-the-century reform movements in state and municipal government, the pragmatic experiments of the New Deal, and reaction against the expansion of government activities that followed.

Eighteenth-century economic thought, popularly termed laissez-faire capitalism, endows current debates on public enterprise with a rhetoric that retains remarkable emotional power in the face of contradictory experience. Throughout the twentieth century, for example, opponents of public electric power generation have based their arguments on premises of classical libertarian theory. In 1907, the National Civic Federation (most of whose members were drawn from the business community) sponsored a voluminous study that demonstrated that the privately owned electric power industry had yielded inefficiency, high prices, and slow expansion of service to new customers. Nevertheless, faithful to economic theory, the federation refrained from recommending public ownership. Active opposition from the National Electric Light Association helped convince it that regulation of investor-owned utilities by government commissions should be tried first and that public ownership should be regarded as a last resort. The resulting regulation by public utility commissions is one of the longest-running unsuccessful experiments in political history. The unsatisfactory aspects of the industry that were identified in 1907 persist today.[1]

Yet two decades later, expressing his opposition to federal involvement in hydroelectric power developments, President Herbert Hoover, vetoing a public power bill, proclaimed: "I hesitate to contemplate the future of our institutions, of our government, and of our country if the preoccupation of its officials is to be no longer the promotion of justice and equal opportunity but is to be devoted to barter in the markets. That is not liberalism; it is degeneration."[2] After another two decades, President Dwight D. Eisenhower echoed Hoover's opinion when he branded the Tennessee Valley Authority (TVA) as "creeping socialism."

Again, twenty years later, the Central Maine Power Company led a publicity campaign to defeat a proposal to establish a state power authority in Maine by stressing that free enterprise was the "American way." The company's chief executive described the proposed authority as "the most radical plan ever advanced in these United States."[3] But, in fact, throughout the United States, 299 private power companies, 1,898 municipally owned electric utilities, 112 state and county power corporations and utility districts, 923 rural electric cooperatives, and 10 federal agencies were in the power business. (The 299 private companies, however, enjoyed 80 percent of the retail sales.) Despite a widespread dissatisfaction with electric service and despite prices that were among the highest in the nation, the voters of Maine defeated the public power proposal.

Curiously, laissez-faire economic theory as originally conceived was more flexible in terms of government enterprise than its twentieth-century advocates recognize. In the year of American independence, 1776, Adam Smith published his treatise, *Wealth of Nations,* which became the bible of libertarian capitalism. Smith argued that good management "can never be universally established but in consequence of that free and universal competition which forces everybody to have recourse to it for the sake of self-defense."[4] The theoretical system that Smith conceived was incompatible with government ownership of economic enterprise, but in dealing with the problems of government, Smith issued a significant caveat:

According to the system of natural liberty, the sovereign has only three duties to attend to . . . first, the duty of *protecting the society from the violence* and invasion of other independent societies; secondly, the duty of *protecting* as far as possible *every member of the society from the injustice* or oppression of every other member of it, or the duty of establishing an exact administration of justice; and, thirdly, *the duty of erecting and maintaining certain public works and certain public institutions,* which it can never be for the interest of any individual, or small number of individuals, to erect and maintain; *because the profit could never repay the expense to any individual or small number of individuals, though it may frequently do much more than repay it to a great society.*[5]

Smith's American followers have generally overlooked this insight that social cost and benefits are more relevant measures than financial profit for certain public services. The fact is that defense, social equity, and public works with limited opportunity for competitive profit seeking—Smith's three categories of exception to the market—can be used to rationalize most government enterprise in the United States. Smith further described government-owned enterprises as "chiefly those for facilitating the commerce of the society, and those for promoting instruction of the people."[6] Two hundred years later, aid to industry, transportation, and education account for between one-third and one-half of all state and local government borrowing.

Although many more qualifiers to the libertarian model of unbridled free market economy have been added since 1776, public corporations have multiplied for pragmatic rather than theoretical reasons, demonstrating patterns of growth that do not well fit any of the theories developed to distinguish the functions of the private and public sectors.[7] But the legacy of classical economic theory is resonant in political rhetoric and in popular criteria applied to public enterprise performance. Even more striking, countertheories have not developed in the United States. With no positive concept of public enterprise, no popular movement for social ownership, American politics has shaped public corporations haphazardly to fit specific, practical problems. Government corporations have no common bent toward decision making in the public interest, and government, for its part, has not sought to guide or control them systematically.

The Origin of American Public Enterprise

Even in its early years, the United States did not maintain the practical separation of economics and politics suggested by the *Wealth of Nations*. All business corporations in the United States territory were originally chartered by government statute. Roughly two-thirds of those chartered before 1800 had quasi-public purposes such as developing canals, harbors, channels, toll roads, and bridges. Governments frequently subscribed to corporate stock, and in some states the chartered corporations reported their expenses to government officials. From the perspective of government, all the chartered companies served the public purpose of regional development. These eighteenth-century business corporations had many of the attributes common to the modern public authority: establishment by government charter, management by a board of directors, capital financing supplied by private sources combined with public subsidies, and specific provisions for government supervision.[8]

Among the earliest companies chartered in the original states were banks. The First and Second United States Banks had federal charters, and the federal government held 20 percent of their stock. In 1791, the government held a majority stock interest in the Bank of North America. In the late eighteenth and early nineteenth century as cities grew, the number of chartered insurance and manufacturing corporations mounted. Like modern public authorities, some of these corporations were exempted from taxation by special law, and in some states government charters dictated their organizational and managerial details or gave them franchises and powers of eminent domain.

At the same time, free services provided directly by the government were developing as an alternative to services for sale by chartered corporations. Some rough "King's highways" and post roads had been laid out in the colonial period, for example, but new states delegated subsequent highway development in the Northeast to chartered highway corporations (there were seventy-two by 1800) that attracted private capital for road building in return for promised payments of interest and dividends. Thousands of miles of toll roads were built by these corporations, and as unfenced land became scarce, the public was left with few travel options. Commercial needs for new east-west routes, with less-assured promise of profits, added to pressures for direct government road building. In 1806, President Thomas Jefferson's secretary of the treasury prepared a national plan for internal improvements on which Treasury surpluses were to be spent, and Congress authorized the first federal highway appropriation. By 1825, highway development by investor-owned corporations was dying out, and state and municipal construction was the rule. Government-subsidized, toll-free roads became the forerunners of the interstate highway system. Subsequently the highway lobby (formally organized by 1902) was to ensure the domination of this alternative until the mid-twentieth century, when the earlier pattern of mixed investment in toll roads was revived in the form of the modern turnpike authority.

Similar changes in the distribution of resources, posing similar problems for the public, stimulated the growth of governmental activity in the management of harbors, waterways, and water resources. At the beginning of the nineteenth century, almost all water supply plants were operated by chartered business corporations; at the end of the century, three-quarters of such plants were government operated.

Wide-open private exploitation of land, timber, and other natural resources had characterized the frontier. Beginning in the late nineteenth century, reduced abundance (relative to population and use) led to the first national forest reserve and government-controlled timber operations. Private timber interests vigorously protested government ownership and operation of millions of acres of forest land. They employed rhetoric similar to that later adopted by defenders of private power, but they subsequently accepted and profited from governmental forestry policies.

The first schools in the United States had begun as chartered institutions (largely parochial). In response to immigration and rising levels of technology, particularly when the family and community no longer constituted a production unit and apprenticeship systems no longer met the economy's needs, governments provided free schooling.

Changing dimensions of resource supply and demand, of technology, of business conditions, and of material expectations, then, influenced the growth of the public sector throughout American history, and they remain the factors underlying the multiplication of public authorities. When these forces mobilize effective political and business demands for expansion of governmental activity, the breakthroughs occur with little public discussion of the purpose or the economic system.

Speculation and Public Debt

In the 1830s, Andrew Jackson argued from a populist perspective that government monies and private monies should no longer be mixed to promote development. It was a time when states and municipalities were brewing such mixes on a large scale. They gave franchises to private companies; they chartered mixed ownership corporations, holding majority stock in some and minority stock in others; and they established public enterprise boards to build schools, water systems, city streets. Several states had revolving funds for purchase of up to two-thirds stock in business firms.

Business corporations were still required to obtain charters from state legislatures. To expedite their charter applications, financiers offered legislators stock and other benefits, so that cozy relationships and conflicts of interest proliferated. The states and localities also were engaged in intense competition to attract development. Locations of railroad spurs, turnpikes, and banks, for example, were critical to the future of a county. Private business expansion obviously affected the local public interest.

The boom created by these partnerships between business and state governments ended with a bang, bankrupting businesses and public treasuries alike, when virulent speculation produced the 1837 financial collapse. The first legislative responses to boom and bust in state government finances were changes to permit the incorporation of business firms without legislative charters, to prohibit the use of state credit to aid private enterprises, and to put low ceilings on state debt. Thereafter corporations became viewed as private businesses rather than as quasi-public institutions.[9] Because states had relied upon borrowing through the private money markets to finance their participation in business, new constitutional limitations on borrowing quickly curtailed their entrepreneurial activities.

The initial legal changes, however, had little effect on the interests that had been benefiting from business-government partnerships for economic development and profit making. The participants quickly found other techniques to replace those no longer available. They shifted their field of operations from state to municipal governments. When official figures were first available in 1843, state debt amounted to $232 million. By 1860, nineteen states had adopted constitutional amendments restricting state debt, and new states admitted to the Union thereafter also adopted restrictions. State debt, which reached $353 million in 1870, declined to $235 million by 1900. But municipal debt, which was only $28 million in 1843, galloped up to $516 million by 1870 and reached $1.5 billion by 1900.

Enabling legislation for municipal participation in business moved west with the railroads. The municipalities subsidized the railroad companies through cash grants, bonds, rights of way, and stock purchases. The railroad companies speculated in land, and local governments joined them. Like the earlier state ventures, many local debts grew too heavy to survive general depressions in the economy, for example, in 1870. Widespread scandals over conflicts of interest on the part of local politicians, coupled with defaults on local debt, stimulated a new round of outrage and constitutional amendments.

These early financial crises caught the participants by surprise, and indignation on the part of the bondholders was dramatic. Pennsylvania had been the richest state and the best known one abroad. Over two-thirds of its outstanding debt of $35 million was held by foreign investors. When Pennsylvania was reduced to temporary insolvency in 1842, English investors were horrified. William Wordsworth, as poet laureate, wrote two sonnets on the peculiarities of the new debtors. In "To the Pennsylvanians" (1845) Wordsworth elegized.

All who revere the memory of Penn
Grieve for the land on whose wild roots his name
Was fondly grafted with a virtuous aim
Renounced, abandoned by degenerate men
For state *dishonour* black as ever came
To upper air from Mammon's loathsome den.[10]

A petition to the U.S. Congress and streams of letters to English and American newspapers by the Reverend Sidney Smith—himself an investor in Pennsylvania bonds—attached a combined sense of sin and rage to material loss caused by business failures:

I never meet a Pennsylvanian at a London dinner without feeling a disposition to seize and divide him; to allot his beaver to one sufferer and his coat to another; to appropriate his pocket handkerchief to the orphan and to comfort the widow with his silver watch, Broadway rings and the London guide which he always carries in his pocket. How such a man can set himself down at an English table without feeling that he owes two or three pounds to every man in the company, I am at a loss to concede; he has no more right to eat with honest men than a leper has to eat with clean men.

Figure to yourself a Pennsylvanian receiving foreigners in his own country, walking over the public works with them, and showing them Larcenous Lake, Swindling Swamp, Crafty Canal, and Rogues Railway, and other dishonest works. This swamp we gained (says the patriotic borrower) by the repudiated loans of 1828. Our canal robbery was in 1830; we pocketed your good people's money for the railroad only last year. . . .

And now, drab-coloured men of Pennsylvania, there is yet a moment left: the eyes of all Europe are anchored upon you. . . . Start up from that trance of dishonesty into which you are plunged: don't think of the flesh which walls about your life, but of that *sin* which has hurled you from the heaven of character, which hangs over you like a devouring pestilence, and makes good men sad, and ruffians dance and sing. It is not by Gin Sling alone and Sherry Cobbler that man is to live; but for those great principles . . . , *principles* (I am quite serious in what I say) *above cash*, superior to cotton, higher than currency—principles, without which it is better to die than to live, which every servant of God, over every sea and in all lands, should cherish.[11]

These lofty principles, "above cash," were invoked to induce cash repayment in full to investors from sources beyond those pledged in the original loans. In essence, a moral dimension was added to the issue of public debts in a well-organized campaign to work up the public conscience—and to put pressure on government officials for satisfactorily negotiated settlements. The campaign used pulpits, pamphlets, the English and American press, and direct lobbying. Although the effort failed to persuade the U.S. Congress to authorize federal assumption of state debts, the rhetoric imputing sin to financial failure had more success. Negotiated settlements became the rule, and imputations of moral responsibility have remained a basic aspect of the politics of public borrowing. Investment in government bonds was never again treated as a simple business deal for which the investor is expected to calculate and assume risk (with proportionate interest-rate compensation), certainly when compared with investment in private sector stocks and bonds.

The defaults on state debts through the mid-nineteenth century had not been the results of conscious choice but of the financial collapse of speculative projects. Later episodes of default on public debt resulted from post–Civil War Reconstruction in the South and from speculative developments on the western frontier. Some of them tempted public officials to repudiate rather than negotiate the debts to carpetbaggers or railroad men. Eastern bankers, primarily New York investment houses, underwrote or held most of both the Reconstruction bonds from the South and the railroad and real estate development bonds from the West. After Democrats recaptured southern governments and populism swept the West, repudiation of public debts had some appeal as regional strategies.

Burdened with debt for that which they did not own or control, forced to deal with representatives of absentee owners, victimized by swindlers or oppressive freight rates, it is no wonder that the farmers and localities of the midwestern states were stirred to revolt. The feeling was partly that of sectionalism. Repudiation of railroad aid bonds provided at least one way of retaliating against eastern capitalists and against the railroads upon whom the farmers blindly pinned all their agrarian troubles.[12]

Some county councils evaded judgments against defaulters handed down by the courts, meeting at peculiar times and places to avoid process servers. Even in this era, however, cities generally negotiated settlements with their creditors. (New Orleans made one notorious settlement of fifty cents on each dollar owed.)

The collapse of real estate speculations in the 1920s set off the next cluster of defaults on public debt. Bonds backed by special tax assessments were providing indirect subsidies for land developers. Developers as residents would vote for special tax assessments to secure loans for water, sewer, and road construction, facilitating the sale of homes to unsuspecting residents of the new subdivision, who then inherited the debt. In 1926, overheated speculation in Florida real estate led to a number of defaults in repayment of this kind of assessment bond.

Both credit ratings and the views of underwriters indicate that the investment community still tends to punish Wisconsin, Florida, and Louisiana for defaults or attempts at debt repudiation of over half a century ago, despite the fact that outright repudiation of debt has been eliminated by the courts. Evidence of the continuing sense of moral responsibility that is attached to public debt is also found in the label that the investment community attaches to revenue bonds to which state governments have made no legal or contractual commitment; the phrase "moral obligation" bonds evokes nineteenth-century concepts of ethical behavior.

Public responses to debt proposals reflect the memory of remote events, frequently making it difficult for cities and states to borrow directly, even when the public favors the investments that borrowing makes possible. Cities and states rely on borrowing for their capital needs, so the evasive device of financing public enterprise through independent corporate entities and nonguaranteed debt has taken hold. This institutional adaptation to conflicting values has been inventive and successful, but the element of public illusion is substantial. The state of Indiana, for example, prohibited by its constitution from all general obligation borrowing, has stamped on its government envelopes: "Indiana, Where We Live Within Our Income." Yet Indiana ranks sixteenth in the nation in per-capita government debt that is "nonguaranteed." (One hundred percent of its state debt is nonguaranteed.)

The Legacy of Reform

Turn-of-the-century political reform movements resulted in laws that still form the framework of rules and practice under which municipal government and public enterprise operate. The reform movements also produced many of the persistent slogans of public enterprise politics.

The Legacy of Rules: Debt Controls   Most of the regulations of state and local borrowing that were designed to cure the scandals of nineteenth-century speculation remain in state constitutions. Prohibitions against giving or lending state or municipal money or credit to private individuals or firms, for example, foreclose the development of mixed ownership corporations. By eliminating the sale of corporate stock to governments, the laws encourage a dependence upon the public authority–revenue bond alternative.

Most state constitutions also contain debt limit provisions today that originated in the nineteenth century. Eighteen states (including New York, New Jersey, and California) require special elections to approve proposals for state general obligation borrowing (issuance of bonds or notes for which repayment is backed by the "full faith and credit"—the taxing power—of the state).[13] One of these states (South Carolina) requires approval by a two-thirds majority of eligible voters. Most of these states do not impose legal ceilings on the amount of debt that can be incurred by special vote, but given widespread voter suspicion of public debt, the special election requirement imposes formidable limitations on the state's ability to borrow.

Twenty-one other state constitutions impose specific dollar ceilings on general obligation debt of state government, tie it to a percentage of property values in the state, or otherwise severely limit the potential for raising capital through state debt. In many of these states, government debt has reached or exceeded the limits, and as a result, each borrowing proposal requires a constitutional amendment. Only a few states have comprehensively modernized their debt provisions to provide for more flexible borrowing arrangements. The Pennsylvania constitution was revised in 1968 to permit borrowing by legislative vote for projects in the state's capital budget, provided that the total debt outstanding does not exceed one and three-quarter times the average annual tax revenues. Mississippi has adopted a similar provision; Hawaii and Virginia have also tied legislative authorizations of certain types to state revenue levels.

Only nine states permit general obligation borrowing by a vote of the duly elected state legislature without a specific ceiling on amounts or requirements for special elections: Connecticut, Delaware, Illinois, Louisiana, Massachusetts, Minnesota, New Hampshire, Tennessee, and Vermont. Of these, Louisiana, Minnesota, and Illinois require special legislative majorities (two-thirds or three-fifths) for borrowing proposals. The debt levels of several of these legislative-action states are nonetheless low. In 1970, in Illinois, Minnesota, and Tennessee, the per-capita debt was under $200. There is no evidence that contemporary state legislatures would rush headlong into profligate borrowing; they have tended to be more conservative than governors in their willingness to build public debt.[14]

Most states still restrict municipal debt to a proportion of property values or require local special elections. Forty-two states use local borrowing referenda for various purposes. State constitutions and statutes also contain detailed regulations regarding terms and interest rates for local government bonds. The restrictions on municipal debt are complex and riddled with exceptions and inconsistencies. They represent a series of ad hoc responses by legislators to diverse problems. The body of regulation of municipal finances that has grown by accretion for over a century has not been subject to comprehensive revision in most states.

Were it not for these encumbrances, public enterprise in states and municipalities would be more frequently undertaken within regular government structures (as it is within the federal government) than in independent authorities. As it is, public authorities fund public projects through nonguaranteed debt. They issue notes and bonds that are not secured by the full faith and credit or taxing power of the state or municipal government—that is, debt not legally the obligation of state or local government. Governments resort to such nonguaranteed debt for two primary purposes: to increase the amount of capital available for public projects and to avoid the archaic constitutional restrictions on guaranteed debt. Revenue bonds issued by authorities do not add directly to the volume of state or municipal debt as measured by the investment community. Hence they expand the total market for governmental securities, attracting more investors than would the straight line growth of state or city debt. They also allow elected officials to escape the political burdens of imposing the charges or taxes that are needed for debt service and operations.

Public officials have increasingly resorted to nonguaranteed debt for corporate projects that are not intended to pay for themselves but are heavily, if indirectly, subsidized by government and its taxpayers. Authority bonds of this type have great appeal because most of them are held to be exempt from all the dollar ceilings, requirements for special elections, interest rate limits, and other constitutional encumbrances on general obligation debt.

The Legacy of Symbols The acceptance of public authorities also owes a great deal to the American political reform movements that have reiterated two central but inconsistent themes: faith in participatory democracy and suspicion of elected politicians.

Reform platforms not only supported debt restrictions, but also called for the elimination of patronage and party machines and a reorganization of governments to incorporate business methods. These proposals reflected the reaction of established interests to urban political organizations that were building power on immigrant votes and to the corporate growth that was fueled by new money during the entrepreneurial partnerships between politics and business that peaked in President Ulysses S. Grant's administration in Washington and in William Tweed's political machine in New York. During the Grant administration, for example, corporate stock was widely distributed among federal officials, including the vice-president. At the state level, "One of Tweed's state senators, catching the full spirit of the occasion, took $75,000 from the Vanderbilt representative and $100,000 from the other side. He preserved the morals of the new politics by voting for the highest donor."[15]

Samuel Tilden, who led the assault on Tweed, was a model mugwump reformer. A wealthy, old-line corporation lawyer and for a short period chairman of the New York State Democratic Committee, he led legal and political assaults that drove "Boss" Tweed into exile and ultimately to jail. Tilden expressed the attitudes of the same economic elite, largely Protestant and professional, that bolted from the Republican nomination of James G. Blaine in 1884. The mugwumps, both Republicans and Democrats, took a conservative view of increasing urban social problems and opposed what they saw as "unscrupulous" new business entrepreneurs, together with the politicians serving their interests. The municipal reform they called for was typified by an old-line businessman who became mayor of Cleveland and reorganized city government on a reputedly businesslike basis while checking the influence of both political machines and corporations.

The next generation of reformers, the Progressives, were sons of the mugwumps, some of them literally so. As Ulysses S. Grant had symbolized the era of political machines and corporate piracy in the White House, Woodrow Wilson, Princeton professor and a founder of "public administration," was the symbol of Progressive reform.

The Progressive movement, which began in the early 1900s and lasted for two decades, was based on an eighteenth-century view of human nature as rational and perfectible. Ethical behavior, it held, would be brought forth by training and through the enlightenment of civilization and would provide the foundation of good government. The educated man of goodwill could be expected to rise above his own narrow interests to perceive and achieve the general good.[16] The restoration of honest democracy depended on the participation of such paragon personalities. "Democracy is at base, altruism expressed in terms of self-government," wrote William Allen White.[17] Direct election of senators on the national level, women's suffrage, initiative, referendum, and recall in state and local government, nominations by direct primary, extension of of the civil service, and city managers for businesslike urban government were Progressive formulas for achieving good government by letting the right-minded participate fully in a political system that had been edging them out.

Although many Progressive reforms were adopted, they failed to achieve the results expected of them. But even if their prescriptions had disappointing effects, their language and ideas have proved remarkably resilient and durable. When a public authority fends off the demands of elected officials today, it still relies on a sense of superiority resting on its alleged ability to bring civic-minded business leaders into public service, to avoid party politics and profiteering. Just as libertarian economic theory provides the rhetoric for nongovernmental control of public enterprise, Progressive dogma supplies the rationale for the autonomy of public authorities and for the business dominance of their boards of directors. One of the inherent characteristics of a symbol is that it elicits an emotional or judgmental response from the listener even in complete absence of evidence about the events referred to. Not only the course of public enterprise politics in the United States but also most of the written works discussing government corporations are tightly woven in the fabric of Progressive symbols.

"Businesslike" and "nonpolitical" are particularly persistent and puzzling components of Progressive rhetoric. How did a sense of the virtues of business and vices of politics grow from reform movements that set out to extol the virtues of enlightened democracy and to excise undue business influence from government? The reform movements alerted the public to the misuses of political power and highlighted the interlocking directorates of commercial and political vice. Muckraking literature and reporting stirred up the basic distrust for authority that was brought to American shores by the earliest immigrants, fired by the American Revolution, evident to Alexis de Tocqueville fifty years later, and rekindled by periodic scandal and reform episodes throughout subsequent American history. In other words, the scandals raked over during the Progressive era reinforced public suspicion of politics and politicians, but the faith and energy of the reformers seeking effective change proved not so contagious. This is another peculiar paradox; it is evident today when public outrage over scandal often fails to be translated into effective political action to correct its underlying causes.

Major influences from the turn-of-the-century reform movements on the subsequent development of public authorities, then, were not renewed faith in direct democracy and belief in the perfectibility of man but a reinforced suspicion of concerted political power and a renewed sense of upper-class business virtue. Laissez-faire economic theory seemed newly justified by the record of great corporate successes between 1889 and 1929. The role of government in that development was discounted and its reputation tarnished.

Corporate Offspring of the New Deal

The American public's sense of business virtue and capitalist efficacy survived the debacles of the 1930s with only minor scars because of the pragmatism of the New Deal and the business-government partnerships of the war years. The New Deal and the war accelerated the growth of economic activities by government, but they did not produce coherent national policies bearing on the relationship of politics and economics. Although Washington promoted the establishment of public enterprises on the federal, state, and local levels, it did so in a form acceptable to traditional-thinking Americans. In his message to Congress accompanying the proposal to create the Tennessee Valley Authority, President Franklin D. Roosevelt emphasized its eclectic and practical character, describing it as "a corporation clothed with the power of government, but possessed of the initiative and flexibility of a private enterprise."[18] When Senator George W. Norris asked Roosevelt for his version of the political philosophy underlying the TVA bill, the President responded, "It's neither fish nor fowl, but whatever it is, it will taste awfully good to the people of the Tennessee Valley."[19] (TVA's origins were nonetheless political; Republican presidents had twice vetoed Norris's earlier bills to establish a public corporation at the Muscle Shoals site.)

The Reconstruction Finance Corporation (RFC) financed many of the public authorities created during the depression. President Herbert Hoover had established RFC, a federal corporation engaged in investment banking, as a means of shoring up the private sector that had been ravaged by the depression. The executives of RFC, with few exceptions, came from private banking, insurance, and corporate law practice. Jesse Jones, RFC chief for thirteen years, was a Texas millionaire with varied business experience (head of a bank, a mortgage company, an urban newspaper, and several building operations and radio stations). Jones was a pivotal representative of the conservative forces in the Roosevelt administration. His feuds with department heads Harold L. Ickes and Henry Wallace reinforced precedents for insulating government corporations from political accountability. Claiming that RFC was meant to be "autonomous," Jones skillfully fended off policy direction over RFC from the Department of Commerce, the Board of Economic Warfare, the War Production Board, and even the president. Jones described Wallace and his staff in the War Production Board as "socialist-minded uplifters" and "long-haired, incompetent, meddlesome disciples."[20] This foe of "socialism" provided $1.5 billion in loans for government-owned, revenue-producing projects, many of them undertaken by wholly owned state and local government corporations specially created to take advantage of RFC financing.

Officials at all levels of government found that by using the public authority device, they could reconcile traditional suspicions of government-in-business with the obvious need for massive public investment. In 1932, the Democratic platform called for an end to deficit financing and a reduction in the national debt. Yet one of the early moves of the Roosevelt administration was to get public works underway throughout the nation by establishing the system of public authority debt. The federal government distributed to the forty-eight states a sample of enabling legislation for state and local governments to use to create public authorities (named, like TVA, after the Port Authority of New York and New Jersey, which thirteen years earlier had been named after the Port of London Authority, generally conceded to be the first bearer of what was to become a common title). In 1934, a personal letter from Roosevelt encouraged the governors to endorse this legislation and to modify debt laws. The RFC and Public Works Administration (PWA) were funded to purchase the revenue bonds of these authorities.

This federal initiative stimulated the growth of public authorities. Nearly half of Pennsylvania's first fifty municipal authorities received federal assistance. Between 1933 and 1935, the state of New York created fifteen authorities, three times as many as it had authorized between 1921, when the Port Authority had been established, and 1933. Eleven New York authorities sold bonds to the RFC or PWA in the early 1930s, and seven received federal public works grants. Robert Moses's empire of highway, bridge, tunnel, and park authorities, the Lower Colorado River Authority (a Texas cousin of TVA), a spa at Saratoga Springs, the Pennsylvania Turnpike, the Hayden Planetarium, the Seattle Street Railways, and scores of rural electrification and irrigation districts throughout the Midwest are examples of public revenue-producing enterprises originally funded by the RFC and the PWA.

By 1948, all but seven states had adopted enabling legislation for public enterprises empowered to sell revenue bonds. Twenty-five of these statutes enabled local governments to create public authorities by ordinance. Postwar federal legislation in specific areas provided grants and loans that further stimulated the development of separately incorporated authorities—to provide housing, urban renewal, airports, hospitals, industrial development, and investment banking for public facilities. More recently, federal law providing tax shelters for investment in limited-profit housing companies and mortgage interest subsidies stimulated the spread of state housing finance agencies.

At the federal level, government corporations multiplied largely in response to war. World War I had first spawned federal corporations in shipbuilding, investment finance, grain and sugar marketing, and housing. (The Panama Canal Railroad, Alaska Railroad, postal savings systems, and power sales from reclamation projects preceded World War I.) Although most of these corporations were liquidated after the armistice, the experience demonstrated the advantages of joint operations and convinced businessmen that federal economic activity could be helpful to business. The War Industries Board and a number of federal corporations had been managed by "dollar-a-year" businessmen to whom President Woodrow Wilson had delegated enormous powers. These men returned to the private sector after the war ended with a practical sense of how business could profit from growth in the public sector. During World War II, "dollar-a-year" men again flocked to Washington. The renewed government-business partnership generated new growth in federal corporations and also developed patterns of government contracting with private corporations.

During World War II, RFC created subsidiaries that engaged in petroleum, metals, rubber, and other defense supply production and distribution. By 1945, there were sixty-three wholly owned and thirty-eight partly owned federal corporations, plus nineteen noncorporate credit agencies and hundreds of enterprises from ropemaking to laundries and supermarkets run by the military. The federal corporate sector was dominated by RFC and its subsidiaries, together with the Commodity Credit Corporation, the Export-Import Bank, and the Federal National Mortgage Association.

Postwar Retrenchment

By 1953, the federal government was the largest electric power producer in the country, the largest insurer, the largest lender and the largest borrower, the largest landlord and the largest tenant, the largest holder of grazing land and timberland, the largest owner of grain, the largest warehouse operator, the largest shipowner, and the largest truck fleet operator. "For a country which is the citadel and the world's principal exponent of private enterprise and individual initiative, this is rather an amazing list."[21]

It was this point that the U.S. Chamber of Commerce, the investor-owned utility associations, and the National Association of Manufacturers used in their campaigns to convince Congress and public opinion that governmental competition with private enterprise was endangering the "American way of life." This campaign coincided with diffuse fright induced by the cold war, the frenzy generated by Senator Joseph McCarthy's hearings, and the publicized alienation of left-leaning professionals in many fields. To these forces, the "privatization" campaign added a specific assumption on which the public authority movement thrives today: that inefficiency is inevitable in government (and in virtually any other activity from which the profit motive is absent). The chamber of commerce proclaimed: "Both enduring economic progress and human freedom depend upon a free market economy. . . . [There is a] built-in inefficiency in government business operations [that] no amount of reorganization or improvement in accounting technique or in personnel selection policy can ever overcome."[22] It recommended that no new government corporations be created and that existing ones be liquidated as soon as possible.

Several congressional committees and presidential agencies became preoccupied with the issue of government competition with business. Their efforts came to predictable conclusions:

Free private enterprise is the best way to organize economic resources for maximum production and diversity to meet fluctuating consumer demand. Private industry produces more effective results by using incentives and keeping costs down while encouraging new ideas and improvements. Government should reduce taxes to increase the private industry base for taxation. Government control does not produce effective results from an economic point of view because it inevitably involves politically motivated decisions, which compete with the profit motive. Government activity should be confined to such fields as foreign relations and national defense.[23]

Hoover Commissions versus Federal Enterprise Former President Herbert Hoover, who headed two postwar presidential commissions on government reorganization, was disposed by temperament and background not only to bring business methods to government but also to attempt to get government out of business. The first Hoover Commission, reporting in 1949, concentrated on internal management practices and found some favorable aspects to TVA. As Senator George Aiken, a member of the commission, pointed out, however, the task force reports to the commission followed so closely the arguments of private interests who were opposing public water resource development that they appeared to ignore the general welfare altogether.

The second Hoover Commission report adopted the premise of inevitable weakness in the public sector: "The genius of the private enterprise system is that it generates initiative, ingenuity, inventiveness and unparalleled productivity. With the normal rigidities that are part of government, obviously, the same forces that produce excellent results in private industry do not develop to the same degree in government business enterprises."[24] The commission presented no assessment of the actual wartime or peacetime performance of the public sector. It recommended that TVA halt chemical research, cut back on fertilizer production, and raise its electric power prices. It suggested that as many other government activities as possible be phased out or reorganized under contract with private firms. The commission also recommended that continuing federal enterprises raise their prices or budget expenditure figures in order to reflect depreciation and other previously nonaccountable costs.

The commission reports reviewed the Alaska Railroad and Prison Industries favorably but urged that the railroad be taken out of the Department of the Interior and incorporated separately.

Senator Lister Hill pointed out that a simple assumption that TVA was socially undesirable had conveniently eliminated the need for study of its record. Commissioner Chet Holifield was also one of the dissenters:

> I must object to the summary, mechanical, and sometimes arbitrary manner in which the Commission's report would dispose of many activities. A similar technique was used in the Commission's report on lending agencies. An effort was made to catalog a multitude of complex government functions and to dispose of them left and right with only the barest consideration. . . . If all the agencies of government heed the Commission's recommendation to emulate the General Services Administration in contracting with private firms for the performance of various government services, the government will be confronted with a much bigger budget.
>
> The incidence of opportunity for private enterprise cannot be determined by adherence to some simple formula that government enterprise is inherently bad and private enterprise is inherently good.[25]

The Hoover Commission did not attempt to consider the distributive effects of policy—who pays and who benefits. For example, even though the elimination of public power plants in the Tennessee Valley would benefit investor-owned utilities, it would raise costs for industries dependent on cheap power. The elimination of TVA's chemical fertilizer programs might benefit fertilizer firms but not commercial farmers. Increases in parcel post rates (also recommended) would benefit the Railway Express Agency but not the heavy parcel post users—corporate and individual. None of these tradeoffs was recognized or analyzed in the volumes of reports by the Hoover Commissions.

Most recommendations of the Hoover Commissions failed in Congress, but some succeeded in the executive branch. The liquidation of the wartime corporations had already halved the number of wholly owned federal corporations; in 1949, the government withdrew its investment from the twelve federal land banks and the Federal Deposit Insurance Corporation. A District of Columbia redevelopment agency and the St. Lawrence Seaway Corporation were added after the war, but the RFC was dismantled in 1954. The RFC functions that survived—those that subsidized the private sector—were reorganized in the Small Business Administration. By 1956, the major remaining federal corporations were those subsidizing farmers and homeowners and removing private risks from banking and trading operations. Budget Bureau bulletins urged transfer, wherever possible, of departmental work to procurement by contract from the private sector.

The Dixon-Yates Controversy   Although he had spent his entire career as a government employee, President Dwight D. Eisenhower entered office with an ideological distaste for public enterprise in general and TVA in particular. At a cabinet meeting, he told those present: "By God, if we ever could do it before we leave here, I'd like to see us *sell* the whole thing, but I suppose we can't go that far."[26] He attempted, however, to put a stop to TVA's growth.

The Atomic Energy Commission (AEC) had installations in the Tennessee Valley, for which TVA was a major power supplier. In his budget message of 1954, Eisenhower proposed to assign new business to be generated by planned expansions of AEC power demand to private utilities instead of to TVA. The Budget Bureau designed an arrangement whereby the AEC would negotiate a contract with a special utility combine headed by Edgar Dixon and Eugene Yates, presidents of two private power companies that were members of the combine, to supply the power for the AEC's new project. The costs of power supplied by the combine would be higher than those of power supplied by TVA, and the combine could not supply power directly to AEC installations. The Budget Bureau proposed that TVA be required to buy the power produced by the combine and to supply AEC from other systems. During the negotiations, Eisenhower refused to reappoint TVA chairman and lifetime executive Gordon R. Clapp, replacing him with a retiring general from the Corps of Army Engineers.

The TVA supporters in Congress opposed the Dixon-Yates contract vociferously, but initially without success. Senator Lister Hill then revealed that the Budget Bureau consultant who designed the arrangement was a vice-president of the First Boston Corporation, which was providing financial backing to the Dixon-Yates combine. Nonetheless the contract was approved. At this point, the city of Memphis, a major power customer, withdrew from the TVA system to build its own plant rather than be dependent on the Dixon-Yates power supply. The AEC thus found itself encumbered by a contract for more power than it could either use directly or market.

In the meantime, President Eisenhower made several public blunders. In its original plans to expand power supply for the AEC, TVA had proposed to build a new plant at Fulton. Eisenhower publicly criticized this proposal as an undesirable expansion of TVA jurisdiction, apparently under the impression that the proposed TVA site was in Fulton, Missouri, rather than in Fulton, Tennessee. He also had stated in early press conferences that the First Boston Corporation consultant was not involved in designing the contract. He then had to retract his previous assertions. In the post-Watergate era, congressional comment on these "inoperative" statements has a familiar ring: "I am getting tired of hearing that the President has been misadvised and misinformed. He is the President of the United States, and if he is being misadvised and misinformed, he had better get rid of some of his misadvisers and misinformers."[27] The president and his advisers, acting on preconceived notions, had failed to examine events and to check facts. In the end, they had to cancel the Dixon-Yates contract and cope with legal suits.

Having discovered its vulnerability to governmental policy shifts, TVA sought and in 1959 obtained from Congress the power to raise capital for new projects by issuing revenue bonds on the private market. Without benefit of governmental appropriations, TVA's Fulton plant was subsequently built, and Memphis rejoined the system.

Contracting Out   During the twenty-two years following World War II, few new federal corporations were established. (A current inventory of federal corporations is shown in chart 2.1.) Federal government corporations are in no way a measure of federal enterprise activities, of which the vast majority are undertaken either by unincorporated administrations, with or without revolving funds, or by contracts with privately owned firms. Administrations are usually federal bureaus headed by a presidentially appointed administrator. Many of them are housed within a cabinet-level department. Others, termed independent agencies, are in the executive branch, in effect reporting to the president. (See the appendix.)

Contracting out of various types expanded so rapidly that federal contract costs now exceed the federal payroll. (President Richard M. Nixon recruited his budget director, Roy Ash, from Litton Industries, a company whose development had been largely dependent on government contracts.) The General Accounting Office has used a broadly inclusive definition of work that may be contracted out to the private sector, and federal contracts with investor-owned companies extend over research and development, manufacturing (mainly of military and space exploration equipment), exercise of regulatory and police powers, project design, policy analysis and legislative drafting, education and job training, management, and even budget functions. This expansion of contracting out has not been paralleled in state and local government. This is in part because government employees in many states have applied political pressure and used collective bargaining to impose restrictions on contracting for work traditionally performed by government employees. These restrictions are written into state civil service laws.

Chart 2.1
Federal Government Corporations, 1976

Wholly Owned Corporations

Panama Canal Company (1903)
Incorporated under federal statute. Headed by board appointed by secretary of the army; chief executive officer is Canal Zone governor appointed by U.S. president with advice and consent of Senate for indefinite terms. Financed by operating revenues and borrowings from U.S. Treasury.

Federal Prison Industries, Inc. (1934)
Self-supporting government corporation housed in Department of Justice. Headed by board of six members appointed by U.S. president for indefinite terms. Financed by operating revenues from fifty-five industrial operations.

Commodity Credit Corporation (1933)
Government corporation housed in Department of Agriculture. Headed by board of six members appointed by U.S. president with advice and consent of Senate for indefinite terms, plus the secretary of agriculture as chairman. Capitalized by federal appropriations; financed by operating revenues and annual appropriations to reimburse net losses.

Tennessee Valley Authority (1933)
Government corporation headed by a full-time, three-member board appointed for nine-year terms by U.S. president with advice and consent of Senate. Funded by operating revenues and appropriations to public enterprise funds. Authorized to issue notes and bonds to private markets.

Federal Deposit Insurance Corporation (1933)
Independent agency within the executive branch of government. Wholly owned since retirement of capital stock in 1948. Managed by board of three (comptroller of the currency and two appointed by U.S. president with advice and consent of Senate for six-year terms). Financed by income from assessments on insured banks and interest on investment in government securities. Authorized to borrow through Treasury.

Export-Import Bank of the United States (1934)
Banking corporation originally incorporated under laws of the District of Columbia and reincorporated under federal charter. Headed by board of five, consisting of president and first vice-president of the bank and three appointed to indefinite terms by U.S. president. Financed by operating revenues and Treasury credit subsidies.

Federal Crop Insurance Corporation (1938)
Housed within Department of Agriculture with capital stock issued to U.S. government. Headed by board of five appointed by secretary of agriculture for indefinite terms. Financed by operating revenues and appropriations to public enterprise funds.

St. Lawrence Seaway Corporation (1954)
Housed in the Department of Transportation. Headed by an administrator appointed by U.S. president with advice and consent of the Senate, who reports to the secretary of transportation. Financed by operating revenues and U.S. Treasury credit subsidies.

Corporation for Public Broadcasting (1967)
Nonprofit corporation established by federal statute. Headed by a board of fifteen appointed by U.S. president with Senate approval for six-year staggered terms. (Federal employees excluded from board appointment.) Financed by appropriations and private contributions.

Government National Mortgage Association (1968)
Housed in Department of Housing and Urban Development. Absorbed some functions of FNMA when it was transferred to private ownership. Headed by a corporate president appointed by U.S. president. Financed by operating revenues and appropriations to public enterprise funds.

InterAmerican Foundation (1969)
Government corporation headed by seven-member board appointed by the U.S. president. Financed by appropriations to the president, public enterprise funds.

Overseas Private Investment Corporation (1969)
Government corporation within the executive branch (absorbed activities formerly in AID, State Department). Headed by eleven-member board appointed by U.S. president, six from private sector (with Senate approval), five from government. Funded by public enterprise funds appropriated to the president and operating revenues.

U.S. Postal Service (1970)
Independent agency within the executive branch. Headed by board of nine members appointed by U.S. president with advice and consent of the Senate for overlapping nine-year terms. Financed by operating revenues and appropriations to Postal Service Fund. First federal agency whose employment policies are governed by collective bargaining.

Community Development Corporation (1970)
Government corporation housed in Department of Housing and Urban Development. Headed by five-member board: HUD secretary as chairman, three appointed by secretary, and general manager appointed by U.S. president with advice and consent of the Senate. Financed by operating revenues and appropriations through HUD.

Board for International Broadcasting (1973)
Independent federal agency supervising Radio Liberty and Radio Free Europe (originally organized as nonprofit corporations). The board of five members is appointed by U.S. president with Senate approval for terms of three years. Chief executive participates as nonvoting member. System financed by appropriations.

Federal Financing Bank (1973)
Government corporation. Headed by board of five Treasury Department officials. Financed by operating revenues and off-budget public enterprise funds. Authorized to borrow through Treasury or from private markets.

Pennsylvania Avenue Development Corporation (1973)
Government corporation headed by a board of twenty-three appointed by U.S. president and including nonvoting officials of other government agencies. Financed by Treasury credits and appropriations and authorized to retain operating revenues.

U.S. Railway Association (1973)
Nonprofit association headed by eleven-member board of whom eight are appointed by U.S. president with advice and consent of the Senate, plus secretaries of treasury and transportation and ICC chairman. Financed by appropriations and public enterprise funds to provide loan guarantees and capital to Consolidated Rail Corporation.

Pension Benefit Guaranty Corporation (1974)
Government corporation headed by a board consisting of secretaries of labor, commerce, and treasury. (Guarantees payment of federal employee basic benefits covered by private plans.) Self-financing from operating revenues (premiums paid by plans) and revolving funds not included in U.S. budget totals.

Chart 2.1 (continued)
Federal Government Corporations, 1976

Legal Services Corporation (1974)
Corporation headed by board of eleven appointed by U.S. president with Senate approval. (Absorbed functions from Office of Economic Opportunity.) Financed by multi-year appropriations.

Mixed Systems

National Academy of Sciences (1863) and affiliates
Established by federal act of incorporation. Headed by a council and president elected by membership. Financed by grants, endowments, and government contracts.

Federal Home Loan Bank Board and affiliates (1934)
Wholly owned, independent agency in the executive branch, with three members appointed by U.S. president with advice and consent of the Senate. Self-supporting from fees and assessments against the affiliates it supervises: Federal Savings and Loan Insurance Corporation, and regional home loan banks, which have capital and stock owned by member institutions (for example, savings and loan associations) and are headed by boards partly appointed by member institutions and partly by the federal board.

Communications Satellite Corporation (COMSAT) (1962)
Incorporated under federal statute. (President appointed first board, which served until stock offering.) Headed by a board of fifteen: six appointed by public stockholders; six by carrier stockholders (communications common carriers), and three by the U.S. president with advice and consent of the Senate. Self-financing from operating revenues.

National Railroad Passenger Corporation (Amtrak) (1970)
Incorporated under federal statute. Headed by thirteen-member board, of whom nine are selected by U.S. president and three by railroad companies owning stock in Amtrak. The president of the corporation is an ex officio member. Authorized to issue new stock to public. Financed by operating revenues and appropriated subsidies through DOT.

Farm Credit Administration (1971)
Independent federal agency supervising federal land banks and intermediate credit banks, which were initially capitalized by government and are now owned by users (cooperative stock ownership). Headed by thirteen-member board, of whom twelve are appointed by U.S. president for six-year terms and one by secretary of agriculture. Financed by operating revenues and appropriations to public enterprise funds.

Rural Telephone Bank (1971)
Mixed ownership corporation treated as a wholly owned government corporation under Government Corporation Control Act until majority of government-held stock shall be redeemed. Housed in Department of Agriculture. Headed by board of thirteen, including department officials and presidential appointees, plus six elected by user-stockholders (commercial and cooperative telephone companies). Treasury funds capitalize bank through purchase of stock.

Consolidated Rail Corporation (ConRail) (1973)
Corporation created by federal statute. Headed by board of thirteen (two company executives and eleven selected by security holders, of whom six are now named by the U.S. Railway Association). Financed by government loans, issue of securities, and operating revenues.

Source: Government manuals and agency budgets and reports. For explanation, see the appendix to this book.

In fact, incentives for efficiency, productivity, and management improvement are weak in that portion of the private sector for which the government is the major customer and in which the cost-plus contract and variations of it are commonplace.[28] Groups that profit from government contracts, however, are among the most vigorous opponents of federal government enterprise. For example, the Consulting Engineers Council convinced the Johnson administration to limit technical engineering assistance rendered to local towns and districts by the Reclamation Bureau and the Soil Conservation Service. A broader lobbying group, the National Council of Professional Service Firms in Free Enterprise, works with five other associations and some five hundred firms of consultants in planning, transportation, management, and other subjects to monitor legislation and to convince officials at all levels that profit-making professional firms should be given preference over governmental, quasi-governmental, and nonprofit firms in providing services to government agencies. These efforts put "free enterprise" rhetoric to work in extracting private profits from government expenditures.

Below the federal level, interested segments of private enterprise have been more favorably disposed toward public corporations because state and local governments exercise less control over public authority operations and leave them more open to private sector influence. State and local public authorities lend themselves to compromises between public needs and private interests. Like federal contracts, state and local public authorities offer a detour around conservative belief systems—a detour that both business and political participants seek for practical reasons. They permit elected officials to claim balanced budgets and conservative economic policies while distributing projects and contracts funded by public debt. In short, the political costs of using the public authority device to get something done are often lower than the political costs of either avoiding the task or taking it on directly.

Professional Blueprints for Government Corporations

Public administration professionals and management consultants are the architects of government corporations. Through their writings, reorganization studies, and professional advice, they have developed and spread the prevailing views on the proper characteristics for government enterprise. Expertise in these areas is far from an exact science, and its precepts owe as much to folklore and history as to empirical analysis of experience. The study of public administration developed from the professionalization of Progressive tenets.

It began with a dichotomy of politics and administration that was consistent with the Progressives' suspicion of politics and admiration for business administration. It sought to make delivery of government services economical, effective, and efficient. Not until recent years was a fourth "E"—equity— added to the list; the equity factor was previously viewed as a matter for political judgment and thus received little attention from specialists in administration and management.

The early public administration theorists flourished during an era in which government activity was expanding dramatically; they sought to define the role of bureaucracy and its relationship to government, which had not been considered by the framers of the Constitution. As stated by Woodrow Wilson and Frank Goodnow, the theory held that politics—through chief executives and legislatures—was responsible for establishing ends; administration— through permanent executive organizations—should provide merely neutral means to those ends.[29] Good administration would involve the apolitical application of technical competence to politically defined ends. The elected representatives of the people, therefore, should have little to contribute to the performance by executive agencies of the tasks assigned to them.

Accountability—particularly the linkage between efficient bureaucrats and elected representatives—was and remains the Gordian knot of public administration theories. One approach to the problem has stressed hierarchy, neat lines of authority leading up through a nationally departmentalized bureaucracy to the elected chief executive. Another approach has relied on business models, seeking decentralized, specialized managements only indirectly accountable to politicians, executive and legislative alike. Modern American political history reflects those two contradictory approaches—by both dramatic growth of executive power and popular distrust of centralized political power.

During the depression and World War II, many of public administration's best scholars worked for government, a number of them in the Office of Price Administration. Subsequently they wrote case studies showing how politics in fact penetrated government bureaucracies and how the ends of public policy making and the means of administration were inextricably interwoven.[30] In the 1970s, however, public administration had still not definitively escaped the circular premise with which it began: that effective and efficient management is incompatible—or at least uncomfortable—with democratic politics. In the extreme, this premise produces autocratic and inaccurate views of history, as in Raymond Moley's justification of Robert Moses: "From the pyramids of Egypt, to the rebuilding of Rome after Nero's fire, the creation of the medieval cathedrals and the reconstruction of Paris by Baron Haussmann, all great public works have been somehow associated with autocratic power. For pure democracy had neither the imagination nor the energy, nor the disciplined mentality to create major improvements."[31] Of course he begs more questions than he answers, conveniently skipping over Greece, avoiding the implications of the fact that Rome's emperors had let it burn down before they rebuilt, apparently disqualifying the interstate highway network and Hoover Dam, and ignoring that the checks and balances designed for American government in no way constitute pure democracy.

More cautious and common use of the same premise agrees that efficiency and democracy are somehow opposites but maintains that some of each must be sacrificed to achieve balance: "Any attempt to weigh the efficiency of the public authority accordingly, must be done with the realization that such efficiency may be attributable in part to the relative freedom of the authority from the kind of electorate or constituency to which regular governments are responsible."[32] This central dilemma of public administration injects ambivalence and indecisiveness into prevalent theories and consultants' advice concerning government corporations.

The Orthodox Theory of Corporate Administration   Between the two world wars, a series of articulate American writers in the field of public administration promoted the concept of the government corporation and defined the attributes it should possess.[33] Preferring the indirect approach to accountability, they considered autonomy the preeminent attribute of the government corporation.

These writers viewed the relationship of the corporate board of directors to the parent government as analogous to that between the boards and the stockholders of private firms, and they cast the legislature specifically in the role of the stockholder, viewing Congress, rather than the executive, as the ultimate source of accountability. Although it had no particular basis in law or practice, this concept of legislative supervision was given wide credence: "Columnist David Lawrence was reflecting a common misconception when he wrote 'basically the RFC is supposed to be an independent agency and not part of the executive department or the White House, but a creature of Congress, as are all other independent boards and agencies.' "[34]

By the 1940s, students of private sector business had observed that the theoretical accountability of corporate management to stockholders had only a very indirect impact on corporate control.[35] These findings did not undermine the analogy for control of the government corporation, however, perhaps because, as the proponents saw it, the more remote the legislative supervision, the better. They sought to protect public enterprise from the spoils system. Consequently most state and local authorities (and, to a lesser degree, federal corporations) enjoy a legal, administrative, and financial autonomy that regular government agencies lack.

Legal autonomy means separate corporate status in law, with the freedom to sue and be sued and to apply for regulatory rulings and so forth without recourse to the Justice Department, a state attorney general, or municipal corporation counsel. This attribute has a considerable impact on the processes by which public policy is made. An authority can bring or respond to litigation as it wishes, unlike a state agency, which can respond to litigation only through the attorney general's office. Sometimes this independence is a welcome relief to beleaguered government executives, when corporate managements bear the brunt of legal battles, leaving mayors, governors, and presidents on the sidelines.

Administrative autonomy for public authorities usually includes freedom from management controls: from the civil service systems and pay scales of parent governments; from central budget administration; from detailed preaudits and some postaudits by government auditing agencies; from government regulations on contracting, purchasing, and price setting. These management controls were applied to government departments but not to public corporations, and the goals of both the controls and the corporate exceptions to them were said to be providing buffers against special interests and promoting efficiency.

Over subsequent decades, the practical usefulness of bypassing increasingly complex and centralized government bureaucracies has enhanced the attractions of the public corporation. As McDiarmid put it, "Rigidity at the center results in paralysis at the extremities, at the very point at which the service is rendered and flexibility needs to be the greatest."[36] Administrative autonomy is more desirable today than when public administration theorists initially proposed it.

One purpose of the public corporation's administrative autonomy was to avoid red tape and endow public ownership with "the elasticity, continuity and efficiency of private commercial management."[37] Of course most of the functions of modern government—from garbage collection to job training, from police to schools—require flexibility and continuing judgment. Until the problems of red tape, rigidity, and weak management are eased within government itself, the temptation of the policy maker dealing with any particular function is to divide government into corporate bits and pieces.

The managerial freedom of public authorities also gives authority executives a free hand to dispense contracts and related business and thus build up substantial support from their steady suppliers of goods and services. The relative freedom of public corporations contrasts sharply with the detailed, often tight controls that are applied to private firms that do business with the government. Federal contractors must comply with detailed specifications as to accounting, hiring, personnel management, safety regulations, purchasing and subcontracting, and other practices. No such detailed specifications are applied to government corporations on any level.

Financial autonomy as defined by the proponents of the government corporation meant both corporate self-support and budgetary freedom. The government corporation was to support itself on its own operating revenues, derived from fees paid by consumers of its services. The early writers on public administration had picked up from conservative economics the idea that dependence on the market would force an organization to behave efficiently. They opposed loan guarantees or subsidies for government corporations because such aids might sustain public enterprises that were inefficient. But this argument reflected a misreading of classical economics, according to which efficiency results from competition among suppliers of a good or service without price controls. Such competitive conditions are largely absent from the public sector. Profits are not evidence of efficiency in a monopoly. Nevertheless today's managers of public authorities argue with remarkable consistency that they are efficient because they are self-supporting. In fact, financial autonomy protects authorities from adjustments of their price policies for public purposes (such as to provide low-cost transit or to ration highway space). It protects them against paying dividends to government treasuries, against dependence on legislative appropriations, and against unwanted public service tasks.

The pure, self-supporting public enterprise that bravely meets the test of the marketplace is a joint product of professional folklore and authority public relations. In reality, it is rare. Even the richest of all—the Port Authority of New York and New Jersey—began life heavily subsidized. It was not able to support itself for most of its first fifteen years when it received appropriations and capital loans from both states. True, the authority cannot levy taxes, but it is eligible for many forms of state and federal aid and local franchises. It has used federal grants for transit, harbor, and airport improvements. Port Authority management has chosen to make the enterprise as a whole self-supporting, but it is not required by law to do so. The misconception that the Port Authority is required to be an economically self-supporting enterprise is, nevertheless, perpetuated in each of its annual reports. According to authority executives, moreover, "the Port Authority has no stockholders, and therefore, no profits."[38] That description of profits evidently excludes net income—$120 million in 1976 after debt service operations and before depreciation.[39] Most of the Port Authority's riches flow from its monopoly control of Hudson crossings and of air travel facilities in the New York–New Jersey metropolis. Insofar as authority management is efficient, its efficiency is not derived from market pressures.

Throughout the nation, housing and urban renewal authorities have always been subsidized. In other fields, indirect subsidies flowing from tax exemption, together with monopoly positions held by most government-owned utilities, make a mockery of the claim that authorities are subject to the test of the marketplace. Most of the recent growth in the public corporation sector is in categories receiving substantial direct and indirect subsidies: housing finance, transit, urban development, sports arenas, hospitals, sewage treatment, and waste disposal. Yet even the directly subsidized corporations often claim that they are self-supporting or at least that they ease taxpayer burdens.

The second element of financial autonomy—corporate freedom from government budgetary processes—was at first justified by the emphasis on self-support, but budgetary freedom soon became a virtue in itself. When federal enterprises were required to send their budgets to Congress for review, the proponents of the pure government corporation believed it would disappear "before our eyes, like the Cheshire cat. Soon there may be nothing left but a smile to mark the spot where the government corporation once stood."[40] In fact, federal corporations have been increasingly subject to policy controls, including the requirement since 1969 that their expenses be included in the unified executive expense budget, without any evident adverse effect on the quality of their management. But nearly all state and local public authorities remain free from budgetary review or controls, determine their own expenditure priorities, and can retain their excess earnings, even if they were initially or are currently subsidized.

The corporate theorists viewed budget decision making as a managerial rather than a policy function, opposing budget controls that would permit the legislature to "invade managerial areas of choice." Of course, TVA relied heavily on legislative appropriations for thirty years. But the corporate theorists persisted in the belief that managements should not have to involve themselves in the political process by dealing with legislators or by cultivating the political support of those whom the authority serves.

As subsidies to public corporations have expanded, their advocates have found it more difficult to oppose governmental control with traditional arguments based upon market forces and economic efficiency. With increases in tax-based subsidies, self-support has obviously become a weak justification for exemption from budgetary control. Justifications for the independence of corporate financial management have therefore shifted to an emphasis on authority obligations to its bondholders. In public corporate doctrine, protection of the bondholders' interests and preservation of authority credit ratings have been elevated to primary principles for fending off government influence. This argument assumes that governmental decisions will be more detrimental than those of authority management to bondholder interests and that bondholder interests should take precedence.[41]

Bondholders' rights to receive timely interest payments and full return of their investment when the public debt matures are legally and practically indisputable, but the notion of rights has been extended to protect the bondholders' ability to sell the bonds profitably (on the secondary market) during their term. Keeping the bond resale value up has justified secrecy in corporate affairs. Robert Moses reacted with characteristic vehemence to a proposal that public authority records should be public records: "The general dissemination of information, alleged to be culled from authority files, which distorts and twists the facts in the interest of sensationalism, would necessarily erode investor confidence in authority operations. This could result in an unwarranted decline in the marketplace of their outstanding bonds and consequent loss to their bondholders. It could also jeopardize the market for future borrowing by authorities."[42] Public corporations questioned in Texas, Washington State, and California were reluctant to release management consultant reports for fear that their credit would be damaged by even the quite ordinary questions raised in the reports.

Bondholder security also limits the flexibility that was purported to be one of the original advantages of the government corporation. For example, while official statements of the Port Authority declare that it is a "direct instrumentality of state government engaged in the performance of governmental functions," prospective bond buyers are repeatedly assured in authority prospectuses that the two states may not "affect" or "alter" arrangements made with the authority.

The concept of bondholder rights has expanded to a point where it seems to encroach upon government ownership. Robert Moses just barely acknowledged public ownership of the authorities that he ran majestically and was sensitive to the wisdom of avoiding identification with any notion of socialism: "The state power authority must sell its bonds to prudent private investors. It must make fair and reasonable contracts. There is no state credit back of its bonds . . . the authority is a business organization, owned by the people of the state, it is true, but using private funds and answerable to the holders of its bonds. To call this socialism is just tommyrot."[43] William S. Callahan, the blustering chairman of the Massachusetts Turnpike Authority, actually crossed the line: "It's none of the newspapers' business. This is not a public corporation. I owe all my loyalty to my bondholders."[44]

Revisionism and Counterarguments   Apart from the orthodox view just described, schools of thought about the role of government corporations in the United States can be categorized as centralist, decentralist, or instrumental.

Centralist theory—stressing hierarchy—has been the dominant thrust of public administration since its beginning. All the major commissions on the reorganization of the federal government have sought to bolster the president's power, to strengthen hierarchy by increasing executive staffs, to incorporate all or most government programs into consolidated departments, and, later, "superdepartments," and to centralize budgeting, purchasing, personnel management, and policy planning.[45] White House staffs and agencies within the executive office of the president have grown continuously in response to this type of advice. Similar principles have been applied to state and city reorganizations. Not until Watergate did the profession (and most political scientists writing about the presidency) seriously consider the potentially negative effects of the growth of executive power and staff.[46]

In his *Congressional Government*, Woodrow Wilson laid the foundation of centralist public administration, arguing that concentrated executive power was an essential component of responsible democracy. He borrowed his concepts of executive power and administrative independence from European parliamentary democracy, leaving behind the concept of legislative ascendancy that is also part of that system, according to which parliaments may readily force the executive to resign and hold elections. Even without this countervailing force, however, the pressures of open politics in a hodgepodge society and the structural checks and balances in American government serve to weaken the effects of most of the reforms that have been devised to centralize power.

Many centralist principles are quite valid: interrelated programs should be coordinated at least to the point where they do not damage one another; budgetary resources should be pooled and the political process should be organized at least to the point where some rough priorities can be developed; special interest pressures should be moderated by general interest leadership (leadership that recognizes some long-range perspectives as well as broad shifts in public interest).

Centralist theory argues for the reintegration of public corporations and other independent agencies into regular departments of government. Centralist theorists were acutely conscious of the problems posed by the independent agencies set up in the New Deal:

Administratively, the President lacked the facilities to handle his vast job. A host of government corporations and other autonomous agencies had been added to the array that had already disturbed President Roosevelt's predecessor; although many of these agencies needed a measure of operating autonomy in their early stages, the result was a widely dispersed executive function precisely when the coordination of program and policy were greatly needed. The President had scarcely any staff assistance with which to manage the federal enterprise. Over 100 agencies presumably reported directly to him. It was humanly impossible, he admitted, to handle the numerous contacts and the mass of detail that confronted him.[47]

During the 1930s, the Department of the Interior proposed to absorb TVA, and only through astute political maneuvering and persistent appeals to congressmen and to President Roosevelt was its chairman, David Lilienthal, able to defeat this plan. As a result of the reports by the President's Committee on Administrative Management in 1939 and 1940, the federal government absorbed many other federal business activities into the framework of executive department supervision. Five years later, Congress established controls over federal government corporations.

The two Hoover Commissions adopted a modified stance, urging a consolidated departmentalization of most government programs but applying the private enterprise model to all "business-type" activities of government that could not be liquidated (the preferred fate). One Hoover Commission report recommended separate incorporation of veterans' life insurance, Washington

National Airport, and the Alaska Railroad. It argued that the Post Office and the Reclamation Service should be permitted business forms of budgeting, financing, and auditing that are ordinarily reserved for government corporations. Commissioners Dean Acheson, James K. Pollock, and James H. Rowe, Jr., dissented from the report, holding consistently to the theory of central controls and rejecting the antipolitical biases of the orthodox corporate theorists: "Business enterprises do not and should not derive any special organizational status from the fact that they are business enterprises and not some other type of governmental activity. Under the Constitution they are in the executive branch of the government. They bear the same legal relationship to the President, the Congress and the total executive branch as do the departments and bureaus."[48]

Decentralist theory differs from the orthodox version of the public corporation in that it does not emphasize "autonomy" for government enterprises; it differs from both corporate and centralist theory in that it is relatively tolerant of political participation in management affairs. The principal exponent of decentralist theory is David Lilienthal, who immersed himself in politics during his TVA years.[49] He badgered and bargained annual appropriations from Congress, fended off hostile congressional attacks, mobilized local and Washington allies to persuade President Roosevelt of his positions, and enthusiastically took on the private utilities in direct and heated battles. Lilienthal rejected the dogmatism of the principal proponents of the "autonomous" government corporation, arguing: "What is required . . . is not a particular type of administrative organization as an end in itself, but certain conditions under which managerial skills and inventiveness are most likely to flourish. These conditions may or may not be present in the case of the corporation as they may or may not be present in the case of other governmental agencies."[50]

Lilienthal believed that TVA's structure provided the federal government with an effective mechanism for decentralizing burgeoning federal activity and conducting regional programs. He foresaw the need to avoid the growth of a massive national bureaucracy that might accompany the growth of federal expenditure. For the most part, American government chose other means—mainly federal grants to state and local governments and contracts with private firms—to achieve decentralization with growth.

In Lilienthal's view, an important attribute of TVA was its responsiveness to the grass roots. Few state and local authorities established since TVA have sought that goal, but in the 1960s community corporations provided a new approach to decentralized development within cities.

"Democracy" and "development" were TVA's official aims. The development goal was pursued by bringing low-priced electricity to modest consumers and to low-density areas that had been ignored by private utilities. "Democracy" meant participation by local groups in TVA projects. Drawing farmers into demonstration projects using TVA electric power and fertilizers, for example, was an effective marketing device; it was also an innovation in community mobilization that a number of developing nations were to adopt thirty years later. Working through state land grant colleges and American Farm Bureau Federation units, TVA sponsored local cooperatives and municipal improvement efforts. It entered into cooperative arrangements with municipal power boards, school boards, state extension services, and local planning commissions to carry out its federally sponsored functions. Ultimately TVA's successful development of local constituencies raised the hackles of the departmental leaders in Washington and encouraged Secretary of the Interior Harold L. Ickes's attack on "corporate autonomy."

Even more unusual was the fact that TVA management considered not only the internal financial results of its projects but also their social benefits and other effects in establishing standards for its own performance. As Lilienthal noted, "The cost of such development work is recorded on TVA's books in the accounting terminology as net expense; but the benefits appear on the balance sheet of the region and the nation."[51] (By the 1970s, TVA was inviting criticism for failing to account for environmental damage in the regional balance sheet. Like all independent formal organizations, TVA experienced difficulties in shifting objectives, in this case from development to conservation.)

David Lilienthal's view of the public authority as a device for decentralizing government and broadening the distribution of economic opportunity has had little impact on formal administrative theory or the public authority movement in the United States. Most writers on public authorities have continued to seek "efficiency," "businesslike management," and "noninterference."[52]

Finally, the instrumental or pragmatic approach to public authorities views corporate functions as infinitely variable and corporate structures as tools available for whatever purpose of government they may serve. The best justification of government corporations from this perspective is their usefulness as management entities, fiscal or legal devices, or political means. Most government officials who actually create new corporate authorities view organizational structure primarily as a means to an end. So do most of the aggressive financial, legal, and management consultants who have in fact invented myriad variations of the government corporation to suit the needs of their political clients. Finance authorities, for example, are means of channeling various government grants, loans, and tax incentives into consolidated backing for bonds issued to private investors. Building authorities are simply alternative devices for funding and constructing public buildings and convenient legal shortcuts around constitutional debt limits, voter resistance to debt, or troublesome municipal boundaries.

Professional Advice to Government   Public corporations are one of the most common forms of new organization recommended to governments by management consultants today. Tailoring their advice to the pragmatic needs of their political clients and usually passing on the orthodox views of the public authority with little fresh analysis, consultants yield to the appealing temptation to solve each new public policy problem by establishing a new institution and giving it a free hand, unencumbered by the persistent conflicts, the biases, and the historical stalemates of existing government agencies. (Unfortunately, the new agencies are also usually unencumbered with effective policy guidelines from government.) A common script—define a specialized problem, seek a purely organizational solution, spin off a government corporation—unfolds repeatedly with different actors and settings. The Connecticut Resources Recovery Authority and the U.S. Postal Service are examples.

When consultants were called upon to study solid waste disposal in Connecticut, they readily identified a problem of scarce resources—in this case, diminishing landfill areas for solid waste disposal. They moved on to design a new organization to manage the problem, briefly outlining a few of the institutional types that might be used: a private utility, the state's Department of Environmental Protection, regional authorities, or a statewide authority. They chose the statewide authority, ultimately called the Connecticut Resources Recovery Authority (CRRA), repeating the familiar arguments that the authority would cope best with the nonpolitical complexities of the problem, raise capital easily, be flexible and adaptable to change, market recycled waste products in a businesslike manner, and provide statewide economies and coordination.

The text of the report did not demonstrate why or how these advantages inhere in the authority form or explore hybrid alternatives, such as a corporate subsidiary of the Department of Environmental Protection. Nor did the report consider whether profits generated by the proposed authority should flow to the state treasury. (As the statute was ultimately drafted, the authority contracts at net cost levels with municipalities.)

The consultants' report also did not mention that the bond issues to raise capital to construct the recommended system could be designed and negotiated by private managing underwriters, including the First Boston Corporation, which had been a subcontractor for the report. Nor did the report state that the system could be built and operated by private contractors and could use equipment purchased from private firms, including General Electric, which had prepared the report. (Projections by both firms were overly optimistic, as community resistance was to limit authority projects.)

The report did acknowledge that the state Department of Environmental Protection could raise capital for the project at lower cost than the proposed authority (using general obligation state bonds issued through competitive bids); but it assumed that a "traditional state agency would lack the rapid yet flexible decision-making capability necessary; and would not be accustomed to selling products on the open market and implementing sophisticated technologies."[53] The report did not deal with the more fundamental question of how government itself—in this case, Connecticut's Department of Environmental Protection, which was then headed by Dan Lufkin, a former investment banker with a very successful record in the private sector— can acquire the capability to cope with technological complexity, shifting conditions, and market opportunities. The apparent assumption of the consultants was that inefficiency is inevitable in government agencies, even when those agencies are headed by businessmen (and, conversely, that efficiency is standard in authorities, even when they are headed by politicians).

Similarly, the volumes of consultants' reports, headed by the work of Arthur D. Little, Inc., that helped the 1968 President's Commission on Postal Reorganization persuade Congress to transform the Post Office Department into the U.S. Postal Service provided little in the way of practical criteria for judging organizational alternatives or for predicting how the new agency would perform.[54] The reports proclaimed without question that an independent postal service would conduct its affairs in a "businesslike" way and "therefore" would produce better, less costly service. The reorganization that took place in 1971 did indeed substitute business patronage for political patronage, but substantial improvements in operations or reductions in costs have remained elusive.[55]

Organization as the Mobilization of Bias

The challenge to public administration to help reorganize American government to improve its performance requires more sophisticated approaches than prevailing consulting techniques. A realistic assessment of public authorities and alternatives to them requires consideration of the policy biases and managerial tendencies of each type of organization in particular circumstances.

The rational model of administration developed by the scientific management school of thought and by much of the administrative-management literature views organizations as closed, self-contained systems striving toward efficiency. A complex organization is, however, an open system for which interactions (political, economic, and social) with its environment are as critical as its internal structure and for which judgments and preferences—of its leaders and their clients—are as important as its official mission.[56] To say that a public corporation has patterned policy biases is not in itself a criticism; it merely acknowledges that the organization behaves in ways similar to those of other organizations with similar expectations and environments. Interviews with a number of authority executives, however, indicate that many take serious umbrage at the suggestion that they have a distinctive approach to problems. They represent themselves as objective. They have largely internalized the values of the rational model of administration, particularly neutrality and efficiency. The proposition that authority executives and their supporting alliances bring other priorities to bear on their work sounds to them like an accusation either that they are not fit for their jobs or that the arguments used to justify the public corporation's autonomy are absurd. Board members, executives, and management personnel in public corporations believe that their organizations are shaped by the orthodox theory. In fact, of course, they are no freer from policy preferences than their counterparts in the private sector, nor can it be demonstrated that they are more predisposed to serve the public interest than elected public officials.

In his classic study, *TVA and the Grass Roots*, sociologist Philip Selznick demonstrates how the friends and allies cultivated by the beleaguered young TVA subsequently shaped its policies.[57] Selznick uses the word "cooptation" to describe the process by which an organization absorbs the viewpoints of leaders and groups whose support it seeks or whose opposition it needs to avoid. The structure and environment of the organization predispose it to respond to selected viewpoints.

The TVA opponents included private power interests, established Washington bureaucrats, and disgruntled senators. Its earliest and most effective sources of support came from local groups, including local components of the Agricultural Extension Services, the American Farm Bureau Federation, and the Farm Bureau agents of the Department of Agriculture. The land grant colleges were at the center of this coalition; TVA recruited staff from and contracted activities out to them. This coalition excluded the interests and agencies representing tenant and cooperative farmers—the poorer and black segments of rural communities. So while TVA initially considered sponsoring self-help cooperatives, subsistence homesteads, and rural zoning, and its statute called for comprehensive regional planning, its pattern of alliances with the agricultural establishment foreclosed the possibility of undertaking those activities. Molded by such political and organizational pressures, TVA became innovative in the power field and conservative in agriculture. Molded by history and the pressures of the money markets, public authorities generally have become innovative in raising money and conservative in spending it.

II Venture Capital for Government

3 The Municipal Bond Market

In recent years, state and local public authorities have raised between $7 billion and $12 billion in investment capital annually, most of it by issuing long-term revenue bonds in the municipal bond market. This method is used by public authorities, large and small, East and West, subsidized and self-supporting, in scores of different businesses. The municipal bond market is part club, part aggressive sales force, and part service system for governments. The conflicts of interest that this triple role imposes on the bond market have been taken for granted for forty years. Only in the mid-1970s are they receiving—probably briefly—some public attention. The media and political officials tend to expect the bond market to act in normal times and in crises as a service to government. The banks and brokers have not educated the public concerning the constraints arising from their dependence on portfolio performance and sales to investors, and the club is losing control of its membership.

The municipal bond market is a loosely organized system for issuing and selling short- and long-term securities of state and municipal agencies of all types. These bonds and notes are, in effect, the IOUs of cities, towns, counties, states, school districts, housing authorities, and statutory corporations. The interest on these securities that is paid each year to the note- or bondholder is exempt from federal income taxes. Hence, the municipal bond market is also referred to as the tax-exempt market. In contrast, the interest paid on federal government notes and bonds is not exempt from federal income taxes; these securities are exchanged in another network called the government bond market. Corporate bonds—the third major type of long-term bond—are also taxable and are exchanged and regulated in the corporate bond market.

The interest rate on tax-exempt municipal bonds is generally lower than that paid on federal or private corporate bonds. A TVA power bond purchased in 1971 entitled a buyer, for example, to receive 7.3 percent of the face value of the bond each year for twenty-five years. The buyer would ordinarily have to include those interest payments in his taxable income. Port Authority and Lower Colorado River Authority bonds purchased in 1971 entitled the buyer to $5\frac{3}{8}$ percent and 5 percent interest for thirty-five and twenty years, respectively, and representative New York and Texas state government bonds purchased the same year both paid 4 percent interest (for thirty and fifteen years, respectively).[1]

The bond issuer, or agency that is borrowing, pays the interest to the investor. Hence tax exemption permits state and local agencies and public authorities to raise capital at lower cost than either federal agencies or private firms and gives public power, transportation, and site development agencies, for example, cost advantages over comparable private businesses. For activities that require large amounts of capital, the savings are substantial both to the issuer and to the investor (who pays no taxes on the income). The U.S. Treasury pays for both these savings through foregone tax collections. The estimated federal tax loss from the exemption on municipal bonds was $4.8 billion in 1976.

Municipal bonds raise funds to construct, repair, and improve all kinds of public facilities. They allow public enterprise—like private business—to build now and pay later.[2] The bonds themselves are certificates, which pledge that the issuer will pay back the money borrowed by the date of maturity and make the specified interest payments periodically through the term of the bond. Most states limit bond terms to thirty or forty years.

Municipal bonds are extremely attractive to certain types of investors. Because of specific features of federal tax law, the tax exemption is particularly valuable to wealthy individuals who can live on relatively fixed incomes, to casualty insurance companies, and to banks. In terms of long-term safety for investment, municipal bonds have been considered by investment advisers second only to U.S. government bonds. With few exceptions, they are marketable before their term is up and can be sold on an informal secondary market at any time before maturity. They are designed for maximum investor choice and flexibility. A single bond issue of $100 million, for example, may be broken down into individual $5,000 bonds carrying different maturity dates (ranging from one to forty years), interest rates, and discounts. Different issues involve different security backing; a buyer willing to assume a greater risk can purchase a bond that pays a higher interest rate (up to 11 percent, tax free, in tight markets of the 1970s).

The Participants

The municipal bond market is neither a fixed place nor a fixed activity. It consists of issuers, bondholders, underwriters, bond attorneys, and advisory services throughout the nation who are engaged in promoting, buying, selling, advising on, rating, or designing municipal bonds.

Issuers   The issuers of municipal bonds fall into three major categories: governments with general tax powers (towns, counties, cities, states, incorporated villages), special purpose districts with limited taxing powers or with earmarked tax sources (school districts, sewer districts, fire districts), and public authorities, or government-owned corporations without taxing power. (Table 3.1 and appendix tables A.3 through A.6 show amounts of bonds issued by these various kinds of agencies.) Governments and special taxing districts usually issue general obligation bonds, legally backed up by their full faith and credit and taxing power; public authorities generally issue revenue bonds, which must be paid back out of the financial revenues of the agency.[3] This distinction usually costs the authorities something; interest rate differentials between general obligation bonds and revenue bonds—both tax exempt—range from negligible to 1 percent. This differential arises from the folklore of the investment community, according to which taxing governments are less likely than revenue-producing enterprises to default. Historical records do not confirm this notion, and the interest rate differential between governments and government corporations has been narrowing as the importance of revenue bonds has been growing (they accounted for 49 percent of all tax-exempt issues in 1976).

Because public authorities repay their bonds out of their own revenues during the life of their projects, banking commentators tend to agree with the proposition that authorities are self-supporting. In fact, authorities derive their revenues not only from sales of goods and services to private consumers but also from lease payments from governments that do levy taxes, and from various loans and grants from city, state, and federal agencies. If authority bonds impose no direct lien on the general tax power of a government, they are called revenue bonds, regardless of the volume of government subsidies that may be backing them. A general obligation bond directly invokes the legal liability of a taxing government, but a revenue bond is often repaid from tax revenues.

Nevertheless the public authority's at least partial dependence on operating revenues to meet its obligations to bondholders makes it much more concerned with financial results than are most government agencies that rely on annual government budgets and legislative appropriations and invest the proceeds of general obligation bonds issued in the name of the state or city itself.

Authority bonds are more tightly controlled by investors and brokers than general government bonds. A state or city treasurer, for example, handles repayment of general obligation bonds, but public authorities usually must appoint an independent bank as trustee to exercise repayment responsibilities

Table 3.1
Annual Municipal Bond Sales by Type of Issuer and Use of Proceeds, 1976 (Millions of Dollars)

	States	Counties	Municipalities	School districts	Special districts	Statutory authorities	Totals
Education	$ 817	$ 200	$ 377	$2,261	$ 208	$ 1,079	$ 4,941
Elementary and secondary	485	153	323	2,254	24	489	3,727
Colleges and universities	270	18	8		176	530	1,002
Other	62	29	46	7	8	60	212
Transportation	1,309	144	400	3	10	720	2,586
Roads, bridges, tunnels	1,121	116	122	3	8	211	1,582
Ports, airports	60	12	240		8	423	736
Other	128	16	38		2	86	268
Utilities and conservation	703	1,026	2,534	84	1,870	3,314	9,442
Pollution control	161	469	549		46	1,062	2,287
Water, sewer	416	459	978	3	595	440	2,893
Other	126	98	1,007	81	1,229	1,812	4,262
Social welfare	1,371	555	510		190	4,121	2,275
Hospitals	95	394	392		92	1,302	2,695
Housing	540	9	52		2	2,272	6,567
Other	736	152	66		96	547	1,597
Industrial		64	148		1	238	484
Miscellaneous	2,833	907	2,015	174	139	1,839	8,002
Total new capital	7,033	2,896	5,984	2,522	2,418	11,311	32,022

Note: Totals may not equal because of rounding. Totals are less than shown in table 3.3 because these columns exclude refunding issues.
Source: Securities Industry Association data.

for their revenue bonds. When a government borrows on its own full faith and credit, investors and underwriters consider that its tax base and court enforcement of its obligation to pay are sufficient protection, for the most part. In order to sell its bonds, however, the authority must sign an indenture agreement—a contract between it and its bondholders—that is administered by the bank as trustee. The terms of such agreements impose conditions on public authorities that are not usually imposed on general government issuers. The purpose of such indentures is ostensibly to protect the revenue-earning capacities that back up repayment. Indentures usually specify what use may be made of authority revenues, the responsibilities of trustees and consulting engineers, authority budgeting and accounting procedures, terms of bond retirement or refunding, required levels of plant maintenance, prices, and limitations on new capital projects. Indenture terms add to costs and narrow the operating flexibility of public authorities, sometimes dramatically. The terms of indentures governing the flow of funds, for example, often include a mandatory sequence in the use of monies, requiring that after reserves reach certain points, excess revenues (profits) must be used to redeem bonds outstanding or to buy up the authority's own bonds on the secondary market (thereby forcing the authority to reborrow for new projects). With interest rates rising, this maneuver is costly. It has involved redeeming bonds that require payment of 3 percent interest, for example, and borrowing new capital at 7 percent or higher.

Although dependence on bank trustees and indentures makes public corporations more dependent on the bond market and less free to determine their own expenditures than government issuers, it also gives them a competitive advantage in accumulating capital. Many institutional investors prefer public bonds that are administered by a bank trustee because they would rather avoid dealing directly with government officials.

Private firms are much less dependent on the corporate bond market than public corporations are on the municipal bond market because private companies have direct access to other sources of venture capital. They can raise cash from the sale of equity stock, for example, or obtain bank loans secured by the assets of the company, like mortgages. Public authorities cannot sell stock or distribute dividends, and most are prohibited by their charter legislation from mortgaging public assets.

For a number of practical business reasons, then, public authorities have become an important component of the bond market. The Bond Buyer, Inc.,

Table 3.2
Municipal Bond Sales by Statutory Authorities, by Use of Proceeds (Selected Years)
(Millions of Dollars)

	1968	1969	1971	1975	1976
Education	$1,204	$ 840	$1,455	$ 1,139	$ 1,079
Elementary and secondary	434	402	460	228	489
Colleges and universities	719	403	968	831	530
Other	51	35	27	80	60
Transportation	1,280	891	1,589	516	720
Roads, bridges, tunnels	581	417	702	162	211
Ports, airports	196	37	410	103	423
Other	503	437	477	251	86
Utilities and conservation	484	313	1,127	2,813	3,314
Pollution control				999	1,062
Water, sewer	351	154	390	523	440
Other	133	159	739	1,291	1,812
Social welfare	818	732	2,427	2,409	4,121
Hospitals				1,307	1,302
Housing	649	486	1,783	555	2,272
Other	169	246	644	537	547
Industrial	374	18	75	200	238
Miscellaneous	330	182	421	3,604	1,839
Total new capital	4,491	2,974	7,099	10,681	11,311

Source: Securities Industry Association data.

publishes a roster of the "Hundred Million Dollar Club," to which member-ship is earned by selling a tax-exempt bond issue of $100 million or more. Nearly half of these big issues sold annually are those of corporate public authorities. (Tables 3.1, 3.2, and 3.3 show the important role of statutory authorities in municipal bond market volume, their share growing from 20 to 36 percent in fifteen years.)

The fundamental interests of the public authority as an issuer of bonds should be threefold: to obtain low interest rates and financing costs, to mini-mize restrictions on its activities within the bounds of bondholder security, and to keep its bonds easy to market. Authority managements frequently compromise the first two aims for the sake of the third, paying higher rates

Table 3.3
Municipal Bond Sales by Statutory Authorities as Proportion of Total Municipal Bond Sales, 1961–1976 (Millions of Dollars)

Year	Total sales	Statutory authority sales	Percentage
1961	$ 8,415	$ 1,693	20%
1962	8,656	2,031	23
1963	10,289	2,584	25
1964	10,619	3,109	29
1965	11,141	2,765	25
1966	11,050	3,303	30
1967	14,319	3,765	26
1968	16,315	4,608	28
1969	11,700	2,985	26
1970	18,082	4,400	24
1971	24,946	7,406	30
1972	23,692	8,014	34
1973	23,910	8,403	35
1974	24,317	7,366	30
1975	30,646	10,910	36
1976	35,094	12,689	36

Source: Securities Industry Association data.

and subjecting themselves to stringent operating conditions in order to be able to raise money quickly whenever they wish.

The ability of the issuer to obtain money on satisfactory terms varies dramatically with size. Small authorities (raising $10 million or less at a time) are at a disadvantage in the bond market. Examples are the municipal sewage treatment authorities that have sprung up across the nation in response to new environmental standards and federal aid. In New Jersey, for instance, over 150 sewer authorities must raise and spend some $2 billion to $3 billion for sewage treatment and disposal facilities in a decade in order to meet state standards. They will obtain that capital through a combination of bond issues, federal aid, and state contributions and use a mixture of tax revenues and sewer charges to pay off the bonds. The sewer authorities proliferated in New Jersey in response to the new financial opportunities. In one New Jersey county, two young sewer authorities sued each other for jurisdiction and rights to state and federal aid. That aid is essential to give them access to the bond market; so, too, is guidance from private consultants.

The Raritan Township Municipal Utilities Authority, created in 1964, illustrates the dependence of small public enterprises on private consultants. By 1970, it still had no project underway, and the estimated costs of its initial proposal, designed with federal planning aid, had tripled. In that year, an energetic lawyer who had been an unsuccessful Republican candidate for Congress a short time earlier acted as the agent for the authority to secure $3 million in state and federal aid and to seek another $3 million from the bond market. Raritan Township agreed to guarantee the bonds, but the rating agency, without offering any explanation, gave the authority a lower credit rating than it gave the township.

The authority's board of directors still could not find an underwriter interested in so small an issue until a young, local company discovered it. Municiplex, Inc., drew up a financing plan, launched a community public relations effort, and selected a New York City firm of bond lawyers. With another underwriting partner, Municiplex designed the bond issue to include both term bonds suitable to institutional investors and serial bonds with varying years of maturity for individual customers. The underwriters negotiated the purchase of the bonds from the authority at 5 percent discount. This meant the authority owed the bondholders $3 million plus interest but obtained $3 million less $150,000. The underwriters sold the first million to a large insurance company and most of the rest to banks, sweetening the deal with "bank float," that is, a commitment that authority funds would be deposited in non-interest-bearing accounts of the bond-buying banks. This banking patronage committed the authority to disadvantageous management of its own funds but provided profits for the underwriters. The underwriters, who had bought the bonds from the authority at a discount, now resold them to banks at a premium (above face value). The insurance company that had bought the first million was a major shareholder in one of the banks involved in further purchases. The bonds paid tax-exempt interest rates as high as 7.9 percent.[4]

The sewer authority was satisfied because it could now get projects underway; moreover, attorneys' fees and underwriting profits were capitalized (taken out of the proceeds of the bond issue) and therefore seemed relatively painless to pay. Clearly the sewer authority sacrificed financing costs and operating flexibility in order to market its bonds; lacking a sophisticated understanding of the system, it did not seek alternative sources of advice or invite competitive bids for its bonds.

The scenario for large bond issuers is altogether different. The Port Authority, for example, has enjoyed a steady supply of New York bank investment and vigorous competitive bidding for most of its issues. Because it has an internal capacity for sophisticated financial planning, it prepares its own prospectuses and promotes its own bonds. Its underwriters have little to do other than make a wise guess for their bids and resell bonds quickly to familiar buyers. Even the first issue in the Port Authority "consolidated bond" series—a new bond type that did not earmark project revenues and was subject to prior liens—was marketed within hours of the initial sale at a net interest cost of 3.066 percent in the tight 1952 market.[5] The authority's own finance director and executive director had toured the nation's banks and bond dealers, making presentations that described the authority's modernized organization and accounting systems and its revenue forecasts. During the 1960s, the Port Authority raised $100 million to $300 million each year from the bond market.

Between 1960 and 1973, the first state housing finance agency (New York's HFA) raised $3.67 billion in long-term funds plus $7 billion from bond anticipation notes (which are rolled over into long-term bonds when projects are constructed). Unlike the Port Authority, HFA does not have an overflow of steady operating income from facilities established and paid for (bridges, tunnels, and airports). Nor does it invite competitive bids or have officers of the largest commercial banks on its board. Nevertheless the sheer scale of HFA financing enabled it to acquire an internal capacity for financial planning and bargaining and gave it easy access to the market during those years. It built up reserves of over $220 million that were not used for debt service in fifteen years of mortgage operations.

Bondholders When authority managers and underwriters assert that public corporations are ultimately responsible to their bondholders, they are forgetting the original concept of the public corporation, in which the elected legislature was to play the role of stockholders in private corporations. Chart 3.1 illustrates contemporary concepts of public authority structure.

In legal terms, however, the rights of bondholders do not correspond to those of stockholders in the private sector. Holders of corporate bonds do not have the right to expect a share in the growth of the company, to hold management to performance standards measured by profitability and dividends, to attend annual meetings, or to cast a vote or proxy for memberships on the board of directors. Bondholders are lenders, not owners. Because the munic-

Chart 3.1

The Structure of a Public Authority

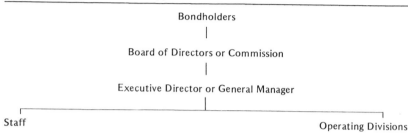

Bondholders

|

Board of Directors or Commission

|

Executive Director or General Manager

|

Staff   Operating Divisions

ipal bond market has been exempt from regulation by the Securities and Exchange Commission (SEC), investors in these bonds have not even been legally entitled to disclosure of specified information about the public agency or government whose bonds they are buying. Bondholders have only the legal right to be paid back with specified interest and to seek damages for outright fraud in sales. Technically they can enforce the terms of bond indentures through the courts, but they rarely do so because of the difficulty of identifying a sufficiently large percentage of bondholders to undertake a class action or group suit.[6]

In rare cases of default—when an authority fails to pay its debts—bank trustees and the original underwriters function as surrogates for the bondholders, working out refinancing and engaging in lawsuits. Public corporations confront no picketing stockholders or troublesome questions at annual meetings.

Bondholders' outstanding long-term loans to state and local governments and authorities now total over $215 billion. The popular image of the bondholder is one of a little old lady with diamond brooches. Actually private households are the second largest category of bondholders, owning slightly more than one-third of that long-term debt at the end of 1975. Commercial banks hold nearly half. Changes in bank portfolios, related to interest rates in other money markets and legal requirements for public investments to back up government deposits, have immediate effects on the municipal bond market.[7] In uncertain times, bank purchases have fluctuated between 30 and 75 percent of the market, but from 1962 to 1972, commercial bank holdings grew rapidly and were largely responsible for the dramatic increase in public debt during that period. Commercial bank dominance leveled off between

1973 and 1975 (see table 3.4). Large bank holdings are clustered in the financial centers of New York City and California.[8]

The third largest category is casualty insurance companies, which hold roughly 15 percent of municipal bonds outstanding. In 1975 all banks and insurance companies together controlled 66 percent of total state and local government (including public authority) long-term debt.

The large institutional investors—banks and non-life insurance companies—are important continuing customers of the major underwriting firms, and their interests are well represented through these agents. Some institutional investors have sufficiently large holdings in bonds of big authorities to maintain direct contact with the corporate management. During the 1930s and 1940s, the federal government's Reconstruction Finance Corporation established a precedent for such direct contact between bondholder and public authority. As a major investor in state and city authority bonds, RFC reviewed authority proposals and required changes in public works planned by state and local corporations. Some institutional investors now enjoy a comparable influence over authorities. Continental Insurance Company, for example, was a heavy buyer of the bonds of New York's Housing Finance Agency and of Metro Seattle. Board members of both have consulted directly with Continental officials about financial planning and revenues.[9] Institutions holding Port Authority bonds have maintained direct lines of communication to authority management.

Similar overlapping interests link many small authorities with local and regional institutional investors. Pennsylvania municipal authority bonds are heavily placed with local banks, for example, and the boards of directors of many of these authorities include representatives of the bondholding banks. Local bankers have initiated new corporations with borrowing power in order to resolve a range of local government problems from sewerage to replacing a burned-down schoolhouse. The same local banks then act as trustees for and investors in the bonds issued by the corporations. Similarly, Seattle First National Bank holds Metro Seattle bonds and is also bond trustee for the corporation and an investment consultant to it.

Underwriters, investors, and authority managers argue that the interests of the bondholders must restrict the range of government control over public authorities. The interests of bondholders are not uniform, however. Households that have relatively small holdings are interested primarily in uninterrupted payment of interest. The usual indenture provisions that require an

Table 3.4
Holders of State and Local Government Debt, 1966–1975 (Billions of Dollars)

	1975	1974	1973	1972	1971	1970	1969	1968	1967	1966
Total state and local government debt outstanding	$235.4	$214.2	$193.5	$177.4	$162.0	$144.4	$133.1	$123.2	$113.7	$105.9
Long-term	217.7	195.5	177.5	161.6	146.2	131.1	122.2	115.1	105.7	99.8
Short-term	17.7	18.7	16.0	15.8	15.7	13.3	10.9	8.1	8.0	6.2
Held by										
Households	81.6	66.9	54.3	47.3	45.2	45.4	46.1	37.0	37.7	40.0
Nonfinancial corporate business	4.5	4.7	4.0	4.2	3.2	2.2	2.8	3.8	3.3	3.6
State and local government general funds	2.6	2.8	2.5	2.3	2.1	2.4	2.2	2.2	2.1	2.1
Commercial banks	103.1	101.2	95.7	90.0	82.8	70.2	59.5	58.9	50.3	41.2
Mutual savings banks	1.5	0.9	0.9	0.9	0.4	0.2	0.2	0.2	0.2	0.3
Life insurance companies	4.4	3.7	3.4	3.4	3.4	3.3	3.2	3.2	3.0	3.1
Other insurance companies	35.0	32.5	30.1	26.5	21.7	17.8	16.3	15.1	14.1	12.6
State and local government retirement funds	1.9	0.8	1.4	2.0	2.1	2.0	2.3	2.4	2.4	2.5
Brokers and dealers	0.6	0.7	1.1	0.9	1.0	0.9	0.4	0.6	0.5	0.5

Note: Because of rounding, components may not add to totals shown.
Source: U.S. Board of Governors of the Federal Reserve System, Flow of Funds Accounts, 1946–1975.

authority to keep revenues high enough to provide for coverage of debt service plus substantial reserves are adequate to protect these bondholder goals. With downturns in the market, of course, bonds that are sold before maturity may lose some of their face value (to someone else's profit), but individual bondholders are relatively unconcerned with these price trends because they tend to hold bonds until maturity.

Institutional bondholders that have large holdings in the securities of certain authorities are concerned with the price of the bonds in the secondary market. This price is affected by a somewhat uncertain combination of national economic trends, corporate assets, and reputation. Moreover, insofar as institutional bondholders also function as suppliers of banking and advisory services to the authorities or as underwriters for future bond issues, they have specific interests in the authority's growth and excess revenues. These interests subject public corporations to some of the pressures familiar to corporate managements in the private sector. The interests of institutional investors have stimulated the growth of public authorities and of authority financial assets.

Underwriters Underwriters are the middlemen between bond issuers (public enterprises raising money by selling bonds) and bondholders (private investors earning income by buying bonds). They distribute most state and local government bonds by selling the securities to investors.[10] These underwriters are, in a sense, the wholesalers of public enterprise securities: they make their profit by selling the bonds at a price higher than they bid for them. This profit, called "the spread," generally ranges from one-quarter of 1 percent to about 2 percent of the face amount of the bond issue.

Brokerage houses, investment banking firms, and commercial banks with municipal bond departments (called dealer banks) underwrite tax-exempt bond issues. The leading underwriters of tax-exempt bonds in general and revenue bonds in particular are the major financial houses headquartered in New York City. These firms have nationwide sales and promotional forces and branch offices in other cities. In financial subcenters around the nation, clusters of firms also serve regional markets: a number of Boston firms deal throughout New England; St. Louis and Atlanta firms have accounts throughout the South; firms in Chicago, Philadelphia, Texas, and California have a primarily regional focus; and so forth. These firms join with participating firms in New York City for underwriting the largest issues in their regions.

Each underwriter has a number of bond-buying clients (which may include a different division of the same bank) to whom it will attempt to sell bonds from a given issue. Some institutional buyers who maintain relationships with several financial firms divide their purchases among members of an underwriting syndicate.

The underwriting industry is remarkably centralized. Syndicates purchasing 55 percent of total new municipal bond issue volume in the nation in 1971 were managed or comanaged by fifteen investment banking firms (including dealer banks). Investment bankers have also become fairly specialized—some with limited types of corporate customers, others with expertise and reputations for deals involving highway finance, pollution control, bond banks, moral obligation bond issues, and so forth. The industry relies heavily on personal contacts, oral commitments, and, thus far, self-regulation.

All bond dealers are listed in the pocketbook-sized *Directory of Municipal Bond Dealers* published by The Bond Buyer, Inc. Their professional association is the public finance section of the Securities Industry Association (SIA). In 1972, the banks in the business established the separate Dealer Banks Association because they took a somewhat different approach to proposed federal regulation of the municipal bond market and had a special interest in lobbying for a revision of the banking law to permit them to underwrite more public authority revenue bonds—the fastest-growing sector of the market. In 1977, the public finance section of SIA gained independent status, putting both types of underwriter in a strengthened Public Securities Association.

The fundamental interests of the underwriter are in spread and marketability. Higher interest rates make the bond issue easier to market quickly and increase the premium at which the bonds can be sold, yielding larger profits to the dealer. High interest rates, at the same time, are burdensome to the issuer. In financial terms, then, the interests of the issuer may conflict with those of the underwriter, although they share an interest in marketability.

Underwriters may purchase bonds from a public agency through either a negotiated sale or competitive bidding. Most general obligation governmental bonds are sold by competitive bidding. Most public authority revenue bonds are sold by negotiation. For a competitive issue, the public agency or its financial adviser prepares a prospectus and circulates it to underwriters with an invitation to bid. Underwriting firms form syndicates under one or two managers to bid on large bond issues. The firms are flexible in choosing other firms with which to form bidding syndicates. Partners on one deal may be competitors on other deals. The individuals representing each firm know each other and rely on personal discretion to cope with the shifting partner-competitor relationships. When firms form a syndicate to bid on a bond issue of a given authority, they often stay together to bid on that authority's future issues.

Shortly before a bid is due, the syndicate members meet and, largely without written research or formal documentation, decide on interest-cost figures to bid. To assess the authority's business, they usually rely on the prospectus or on a presentation by the financial advisory firm and on the informal reputation and credit rating of the issuing authority. Trends in financial markets and soundings of the syndicates' bond-buying customers also influence the size of their bids. The number of bids made per issue dropped from six to three and one-half between 1972 and 1976. The figures of the various syndicates bidding on a single issue are generally very close; none of the bidders likes to be far from the others. The winning underwriting syndicate is the group whose bid represents the lowest interest cost to the issuer.[11] Table 3.5 shows the range of bidding on tax-exempt issues sold during a sample week.

The underwriting firms in the syndicate agree in advance on the division of the issue among themselves, the price at which they will reoffer it, and the number of weeks that the syndicate agreement will run. The one aspect they tend to be competitive about during the initial sales effort is the respective customers to whom they plan to sell their shares of the bonds. Bonds not sold at the end of the agreed-upon syndicate period may be sold on any terms (on the "market"). Generally underwriters do not like to have to hold bonds beyond the duration of the syndicate fixed price. With few exceptions, the bidders judge the market accurately enough to reap net profits on each individual deal.

Unlike competitive bond sales, negotiated bond sales are transacted without multiple bids. The public authority and a managing underwriter simply work out a financing arrangement together. The underwriter then puts together a syndicate to purchase the bonds from the authority. Negotiated sales have tripled in volume since 1969. In 1976, they accounted for 42.2 percent of new issue volume.[12] (Of the ten public authorities represented in table 3.5, seven negotiated with only one underwriter.) The authorities that make negotiated sales are largely those with mixed sources of income. Straight revenue bonds issued by authorities with an established revenue performance from toll highways, bridges, tunnels, and airports are more likely to be open to competitive bidding. Newer, more complicated forms of financing for housing finance and urban development authorities, subsidized transportation author-

Table 3.5
Summary of a Week's New Tax-Exempt Bond Issues, Showing Number of Bids and Range of Bidding

Issuer	Amount (000 omitted)	Winning manager	Number of bids	Bidding range
March 2, 1977				
Omaha Public Power District, Nebraska[a]	$200,000	E. F. Hutton	1[b]	6.01
Mifflin County SD, Pennsylvania	20,290	Rothschild, Unterberg	1[b]	N.A.
Fort Wayne Hospital Authority, Indiana[a]	11,800	Nuveen-Summers	1[b]	6.576
Connecticut Development Authority[a]	10,465	Goldman, Sachs	1[b]	5.990
Hamshire-Fannett ISD, Texas	5,500	Bank of Southwest (Alone)	4	5.422-5.682
Eanes ISD, Texas	2,600	First National, Dallas	5	5.867-6.004
Delaware Valley Etc. CSD, New York	2,500	Nuveen-Reynolds Securities		
North Haven, Connecticut	2,465	Roosevelt & Cross	8	4.395-4.551
Berkeley Redevelopment Agency, California[a]	2,000	UMIC (Alone)	6	5.953-6.200
Deer Park, Texas	2,000	Weeden	7	4.996-5.237
March 3, 1977				
Texas	50,000	Citibank	6	5.091-5.242
Pennsylvania Housing Finance Agency[a]	32,900	Goldman, Sachs	1[b]	6.55
Alexandria, Virginia	14,670	Bankers Trust	6	4.899-4.963
Terrebonne Parish, Louisiana	10,000	Howard Weil-Merrill Lynch	2	5.434-5.505
Marquette Hospital Finance Authority[a]	8,600	Paine, Webber-Ziegler	1[b]	6.67
William Floyd UFSD of Mastics, Etc., New York	3,720	Chemical Bank	3	6.11-6.24
McCreary County, Kentucky	2,850	Nuveen-Johnston, Brown	2	5.920-5.021
Jacksonville, Illinois	2,630	Stern Bros. (Alone)	1[b]	N.A.
March 4, 1977				
Peoria, Illinois	20,000	Smith Barney-Hornblower & Weeks	1[b]	6.24
Aurora, Illinois	10,295	Smith Barney-Hornblower & Weeks		6.24
Illinois Health Facilities Authority[a]	7,650	Goldman, Sachs	1[b]	N.A.
Landis Sewerage Authority, New Jersey[a]	5,800	Bache, Halsey	1[b]	N.A.

Lee's Summit SD R-7, Missouri	2,000	First National, St. Louis-George Baum	3	4.954–5.022
Dupo Waterworks & Sewerage System, Illinois	1,955	Midwest Securities (Alone)	1[b]	N.A.
March 7, 1977				
Illinois	110,000	Northern Trust	2[b]	5.127–5.139
Prima County, Arizona	6,429	Dean Witter	1[b]	N.A.
Arlington Heights, Illinois	6,000	Continental Illinois	3	4.953–5.065
Waseca County, Minnesota	1,250	E. J. Prescott	5	4.261–4.354
March 8, 1977				
West Virginia	50,000	Bankers Trust	3	5.233–5.267
Oregon	19,065	Blyth Eastman	1[b]	5.250
Port of Seattle, Washington[a]	18,250	White, Weld	6	5.348–5.509
Arlington, Texas	10,100	Underwood, Neuhaus	4	5.480–5.767
East Bay MUD 1, California	8,000	Bache, Halsey	5	5.313–5.413
Midland, Texas	6,500	Cullen Central Bank	5	4.946–4.997
Richardson ISD, Texas	5,000	Republic National	5	5.053–5.132
Ulster, New York	4,565	Marine Midland	3	5.73–5.79
Lake Washington SD 414, Washington	4,255	Seattle Northwest Securities (Alone)	1[b]	N.A.
Adrean, Michigan	4,050	First National, Chicago	4	4.596–4.666
East Bay MUD 1, California	4,000	Bache, Halsey	5	4.16–4.296
Crawford CSD, Pennsylvania	3,685	Butcher & Singer	1[b]	5.678
Northern Tioga SD, Pennsylvania	3,620	Rothschild, Unterberg	1[b]	6.102
Miami Valley Regional Transit Authority, Ohio[a]	2,700	McDonald	3	4.830–4.953
Webster, New York	2,100	Nuveen-UMIC	6	6.23–6.49
Tattor Road Municipal District, Texas	1,700	Greer, Moreland	3	6.672–6.872
Barnesville SD, Ohio	1,580	Ohio County	3	5.953–6.108
Arlington, Texas	1,400	Underwood, Neuhaus	2	5.231–5.321

[a] Authority type of enterprise.
[b] Negotiated sale.
Note: N.A., cost not available. Abbreviations—SD, ISD, CSD, USFD, MUD—usually stand for various types of special districts.
Source: *Weekly Bond Buyer*, March 14, 1977.

ities, sports authorities, industrial aid authorities, and educational facilities authorities tend to be negotiated deals, without competitive bidding.

The underwriter for negotiated sales doubles as the public corporation's financial adviser from the early stages of financial planning. He works with a bond lawyer to draft legislation authorizing authority projects and to design innovative indentures that make their financing feasible. While he is working out security for the bonds, he is simultaneously sounding out potential customers to buy them, so that the financing and sometimes legislation governing subsidy commitments and authority activities are tailormade to the needs of the potential investor. The underwriter and the authority then negotiate the interest costs that the authority will bear, determining price, rates, timing, and the terms of the bond indenture.

The relationship involves one clear conflict of interest: the authority relies heavily on advice from the same firm from which it is supposed to wrest a low interest rate. Nevertheless, few issuers have objected to this system. Most feel that the enhanced ability to raise money that results from underwriter advice and promotion is worth the sacrifice in costs and operating freedom.

Bond Counsel Lawyers are an integral (and expensive) part of public enterprise finance. All the participants in a municipal bond issue rely on the legal opinion accompanying the prospectus to ensure that the interest on the bonds is in fact exempt from federal income taxes and that the bonds are valid debts of the public agency issuing them. In framing this opinion, lawyers must make judgments about provisions of federal, state, and municipal law, the internal revenue code and Internal Revenue Service (IRS) regulations, state and local tax provisions, state law on permissible public purposes, debt limits and required borrowing procedures, and terms of public securities. Both federal and state officials have relied largely on the private bond lawyers to enforce their regulations. The IRS, for example, does not check every major issue, although on more complicated deals involving industrial aid or possible arbitrage complications, lawyers may request rulings.[13] Because in a number of states the courts define the right to sue public authorities narrowly, the bond counsel's opinion that a financing deal is valid is often practically final, even if theoretically questionable.

This dependence on bond counsel originated as a response to attempts by some state and local governments to repudiate their debts in the ninteenth century. On the rare occasions when the courts ruled against investors, it was on grounds that fraud or failure to comply with particular laws governing debt made the original bonds invalid. Issuers then began using opinions signed by a handful of attorneys with blue chip reputations to reassure timid investors. The Reconstruction Finance Corporation insisted upon formal legal opinions from select firms on bond issues that it was to purchase, and underwriters do the same today. Originally investors paid the legal fees. Now the issuers pay these fees in the interests of marketability.

In effect, the bond attorney whose approval blesses a new tax-exempt bond issue represents several participants whose interests are at least partly at odds. In a single deal, issuer, underwriter, buyer, and government may rely on this one attorney's opinion that the project is legal, that the debt of the agency is valid, and that the interest payments on the bonds are tax-exempt. It is the interests of the ultimate bondholder that are most clearly at stake, but he is not involved in the original deal and has little or no contact with the bond attorney who lends his reputation to the issue.

Legal work for general obligations of state and city government is largely routine, but the legal tasks involved in issuing revenue bonds for public enterprises are greater and entail private exercise of substantial public power. The lawyer prepares a trust indenture that for three or four decades will control the application of the money raised, the collection of rates and fees, the maintenance of reserve funds, the application of revenues, and the convenants respecting the operation of facilities by the public enterprise. (These provisions are overseen by the bank that is appointed trustee.) In addition, public authority offerings involve the lawyers in working out special security arrangements and sometimes drafting legislation or even state constitutional amendments that create new agencies, new projects, and new financing opportunities. Private bond attorneys for government corporations engaged in urban development activities are increasingly being used as project attorneys to deal with whole schemes, including leases, mortgages, and secondary financing for the facilities constructed by the public corporation. Hence, like the underwriters, bond counsel have specific incentives for encouraging the use of statutory corporations and revenue bonds rather than regular government agencies and voter-approved general obligation bonds for public enterprise. Public authority financings involve a good deal more legal business.

Of all the participants in public enterprise finance, bond attorneys are the least accessible and least cooperative with outside inquiry.[14] Lawyers outside the field seem to know very little about it, for public finance law is seldom taught in law school. It is learned through apprenticeship within the relatively small number of firms reputed to be bond counsel firms. The *Directory of*

Municipal Bond Dealers includes 159 law firms in this business nationwide. Most of those listed work on only a few issues per year—bonds that either are marketed regionally or are issued by agencies within their localities. Approximately twenty firms have achieved the informal status of "nationally recognized bond counsel" with its concomitant opportunity to handle bond issues that will be marketed to large financial institutions and other interstate buyers. Between 1962 and 1972, while bond volume doubled, these firms continued to handle about 70 percent of the dollar volume, and their number did not increase significantly. Clearly, their incomes must have grown substantially.

The bond attorneys' associational home is the municipal law section of the American Bar Association (and local bar associations). They participate in a network of specialized seminars and workshops sponsored by the Practicing Law Institute and the *New York Law Journal.* The content of these workshops and seminars indicates that bond attorneys are mainly interested in promoting the volume of public authority business, getting governmental clients, and keeping the fee structure capitalized and unregulated. In short, they behave as if they were dealing with the private sector.

The primary qualifications for achieving the status of bond counsel are reputation and experience in the municipal bond market. A law firm that aspires to this status seems to need some sort of sponsorship from an established firm. Mudge Stern Baldwin & Todd become a major bond firm by merging with Caldwell, Trimble & Mitchell (an established bond firm in which former Attorney General John N. Mitchell practiced his bond law) to become Mudge Rose Guthrie & Alexander (its title after Richard M. Nixon and John Mitchell resigned from the partnership).

The attempt to establish New Jersey's first bond firm involved a slightly different approach. During the 1970–1974 Republican administration of Governor William T. Cahill, New Jersey concentrated its bond counsel business in Mudge Rose. A young Newark firm, Kraft & Hughes, was also permitted to provide a legal opinion for a state bond issue. Kraft had apprenticed in two of the main New York bond firms—Hawkins, Delafield & Wood and Mudge Rose—and had then served briefly as associate counsel to Governor Cahill. Mudge Rose cooperated in the initiation of its former colleague by agreeing to a joint opinion on one major deal, putting its imprimatur on the prospectus with Kraft & Hughes. This connection was sufficient to secure a listing for the new firm in the *Directory of Municipal Bond Dealers.* [15]

Like underwriters, bond lawyers specialize in certain kinds of deals. Approving opinions shunned by one firm may be obtained from another. John Mitchell's bond firm invented and promoted what became known as the "moral obligation" bond, putting language into state law that made state government indirectly responsible for corporate debt. Another major bond firm, Wood Dawson Love & Sabatine, has been critical of moral obligation bonds, which John Dawson, in the business from 1926 to 1974, feels involve an unjustified avoidance of state constitutional provisions. Dawson's firm also declined to approve revenue bonds backed by open-ended lease-purchase contracts between an authority and a government, but this kind of authority bond is widely approved by other firms. Dawson specialized in public power revenue bonds and the state government securities. (He was instrumental in the reorganization of Louisiana's financing system in 1968.) Other partners in Wood Dawson have been active in substituting nonprofit corporations for traditional statutory authorities and designing joint venture electric projects involving both private and public utilities.[16]

Most local public enterprises are dependent upon specialized lawyers for their form, functions, and financing. Experts in the field of government finance have observed that public corporations are costly to the taxpayer because interest rates for their revenue bonds are higher than those for general obligation government bonds, but they have paid little attention to the extra costs represented by lawyers', trustees', and other consultants' fees. Most authorities incur two sets of legal fees—for local counsel and national bond attorneys—whenever they undertake to issue a bond. Counsel fees are paid out of bond proceeds and impose no immediate hardship on the authority management, but interest is paid on them—together with the rest of the total bond proceeds—over the years. Even when the public agency issuing the bond does not pay the legal fees directly (as in the case of some obligations that bear federal guarantees), it absorbs them ultimately because the cost is taken out of the price paid for the bond.

A survey by the Municipal Finance Officers Association (MFOA) judged that legal and financial advice in 1973 accounted for 81 percent of marketing expenses for revenue bonds, compared with 63 percent for general obligation bonds. Legal fees were 50 percent higher for revenue bonds and 300 percent higher for special assessment bonds (which are increasingly being issued by multipurpose authorities). The costs per face amount were larger for small issues. Local bar associations and some state groups have actually suggested minimum fee schedules, which can be contrarily viewed as attempts at price fixing. Governments have not attempted to set maximum fees or to monitor counsel selection in this field. Some state courts, however, are beginning to hear cases charging that authority bond lawyers have received excessive fees.

No government bond issuer in the twentieth century has attempted to repudiate its debt. Considering the varying standards of judgment among the law firms, it is doubtful that the bond counsel's opinion is the best way of applying federal, state, and local law and protecting the investor from invalid or fraudulent securities. The costs of preventive medicine—fees to a select group of nationally known bond counsel—have probably grown out of proportion to the protection afforded.

The Center for Analysis of Public Issues has concluded that

In simpler bond issues the local attorney plays a minor role that can be fulfilled within a few hours' work. The special bond counsel carries more of the legal burden while agency administrators and financial officials provide major help. Complex bond issues may require more from the local attorney. Both the special bond counsel and local attorney customarily are paid with funds raised by selling the bonds. Paying local attorneys' fees in such a manner is a slipshod, wasteful way to handle public funds.[17]

Four states (New York, Massachusetts, Maine, and Wisconsin) rely exclusively on the opinions of the state attorney general for state general obligation bond issues. Seven others combine a review by the attorney general with the use of outside counsel. In the others, even state government must use private bond attorneys in order to borrow. A New Jersey proposal in early 1974 that the state attorney general act as bond counsel for authorities and other public agencies predictably elicited indignant protest from bond attorneys. They reiterated the need for "expert," "disinterested," "nonpolitical" advice and were backed up by the Securities Industry Association. Both groups argued that any change would damage bond marketability.

In fact, throughout public authority politics and policy debates, the portent of unmarketable bonds is part threat and part self-fulfilling prophecy. The bond market groups can increase interest rates for a particular group of issuers in order to prove their point. The claim that bond attorneys supply a "nonpolitical" source of advice cannot be substantiated. Bond attorneys are typically heavily involved in politics. Two attorneys charged in the courts with obtaining excessive fees from the Bergen County Sewer Authority, for example, were the Democratic and Republican county chairmen, respectively. Similar ties between attorneys serving local public authorities and state and county party politics are found in states across the nation. (I found individual public authority bond attorneys active in local politics in California, Massachusetts, Minnesota, New Jersey, New York, Pennsylvania, Texas, and Washington.)

Special Services   With the exception of a few giants among government corporations, public enterprises depend upon an array of consultants and specialized services, in addition to lawyers and underwriters. The process of issuing revenue bonds generally requires a feasibility report from engineering and economic consultants, financial advisory services, and a credit rating.

The ratings for public enterprise are issued primarily by two private companies—Moody's (owned by Dun & Bradstreet) and Standard & Poor's (owned by Interactive Data Corporation)—which rank state and local governments, special districts, and public authorities.[18] Unrated authorities can negotiate sales only to local institutions at relatively high interest rates. The ratings range from triple A to C. Commercial banks generally require a rate of Baa or better for their investments.

Since 1965, the methods used by the rating services and the somewhat arbitrary effect they have on the public costs of raising investment capital have aroused increasing concern. Particularly unhappy are large cities, a number of them smarting under lowered grades, and U.S. congressmen concerned with the plight of the small, less-known jurisdictions.

The methods of the rating services are indeed somewhat primitive. According to a former director of finance for New York City, the number of issuers rated by Moody's, divided by the man-hours of its analysts, indicates about thirty minutes per analysis.[19] The computation is debatable, but the problems are indisputable: the services do not utilize computer data management; they rely on miscellaneous social, economic, and financial statistics combined with subjective judgment to assess the creditworthiness of a government instrumentality; and they make no effort to take into account the real risk of default by the public agency, its budgeting and accounting practices, or sundry legal factors. They do take into account subjective impressions and atavistic memories. The raters still refer back to southern defaults during Reconstruction and some Populist debt repudiations. One of the anomalies of the system is that the ratings sometimes favor government corporations over regular government agencies (despite the general theory that revenue bonds represent a shift in risk from taxpayers to bondholders). Crime rates and racial tension in Boston and New York City contributed to the lowering of their ratings in the 1960s. In 1973, Moody's brought New York City back to A; Standard & Poor's raised its rating subsequently. Neither noted the city's mounting volume of short-term debt, which was to collapse its financial structure over the following twenty-four months. Moody's maintained the city's A rating until threatened defaults on loans were imminent in the fall of 1975. The ratings merely followed events rather than predicting them. Critics of the ratings system emphasize that it concentrates power over the public sector in a few private firms, that their credit practices increase public tax burdens, and that insufficient information is disclosed to investors. The methods of the rating agencies have changed little while municipal bond market volume has grown from $7 billion to $33 billion annually in fifteen years.

The relationship between the ratings and interest costs is not simple. Authorities with mediocre ratings can reduce interest costs by timing and sizing issues carefully to suit investor preferences. Large institutional investors have their own research capabilities and need not rely entirely on ratings. They determined, for example, that securities of public authorities and governments in New York State performed better during the 1960s and less well during the 1970s than counterparts in other states with comparable ratings.

A simplistic reliance on ratings, or even on rumor about them, is nevertheless not rare. For example, Tennessee contains a high number of small authorities and special districts, which stimulated regional underwriting businesses in Memphis. Memphis dealers expanded, reaching out for clients to urban agencies in other states. By using high-pressure sales tactics, some of them managed to sell public bonds to investors at prices well above the prevailing market. In 1971 and 1972, when instances of fraud were revealed (such as misrepresenting the powers and ratings of a local authority), the Securities and Exchange Commission initiated an investigation with the approval of the underwriting establishment and determined that the Memphis dealers had misled out-of-state buyers about the ratings assigned to local authority bonds. In other words, the financiers in the municipals market had been obtaining their information about credit ratings from the issuers' advisers. Dealers buying into the bond issues did not even bother to open the rating services' directories before making pricing decisions worth millions of dollars.

The private rating agencies have substantial power, and insiders are well aware of it. In his one-man crusade to make the Port Authority embark on mass transit projects, attorney Theodore Kheel wrote letters in 1973 to both rating agencies urging them to lower the authority's rating. The Port Authority responded by privately promising the rating services that it would seek a transit fare increase to keep revenues up. Its October 1973 bond issue, which preceded by one day the demise of the fare increase in Interstate Commerce Commission hearings, sold at a relatively low interest rate; the authority still had its A rating.

The ratings purport to measure relative risk. Since World War II, defaults of public corporation revenue bonds have been few and temporary, but the ratings at the time of purchase were not lower for corporations that ultimately defaulted than for those that did not. During the past thirty years, the Chesapeake Bay Bridge and Tunnel Commission, Chicago Transit Authority, Bi-State Transportation Authority (St. Louis), West Virginia Turnpike Commission, and Evergreen Valley Development Corporation have defaulted in payment of interest or principal. Their ratings ranged from Caa to A at the time of their last issue before default or refinancing. Up to one year before it briefly defaulted on repayment of short-term bank loans, New York's celebrated Urban Development Corporation kept its A rating. The current methods of judgment by the raters overlook many factors that bear on the risk involved in public authority ventures, particularly given the shifting attitudes of the contemporary investment community.

Despite these anomalies and the fact that a great many small jurisdictions are not rated at all, the financial community has testified in Congress against change, and the financial press sees little need for reform. *Barron's*, for example, described a bill submitted to Congress in 1973 that provided for SEC review of rating measures and of the consistency of their application as "an ineffective solution to a largely nonexistent problem." (Other proposals include improvements within the rating services and federal sponsorship of a competing, nonprofit municipal data bank.)[20] Some enterprising segments of the market have organized private insurance systems for the bonds of small municipalities and medium-grade revenue bonds. Several companies (among them an association of bondholding casualty insurance firms) now provide insurance that backs up payment of principal and interest. Purchase of such insurance provides the issuer with a double-A rating. Bondholders can also insure portfolios through these services.

A second group of special service firms that influence public authority financing consists of financial consultants to government enterprises. Some twenty firms nationwide that are not associated with underwriters offer financial advisory services to government agencies. They do not buy or deal in the bonds that they help to plan. Under a consultant's contract, they participate in the authority's capital planning; schedule its borrowing; prepare a prospectus for it; make contacts with potential dealers, buyers, and raters; and help the agency invite and judge competitive bids. Their primary aim is to help the authority raise funds steadily and at the lowest interest rates possible, in exchange for established fees. For example, Wainwright & Ramsey calls the attention of nationwide buyers to whatever small jurisdiction is its current client, trying to get the highest number of bids for its governmental clients in order to get them a low interest rate. Old-line advisory firms of this type are facing tough competition today from two sides: the growth of dealer-promoted negotiated financing and the intrusion of management, accounting, and economic consulting firms into the public authority finance field.

Underwriting dealers also provide financial advisory services under contract to local governments and public authorities. When the issue involves competitive bidding, the dealer-adviser generally refrains from bidding. On a negotiated financing, however, the adviser also underwrites the issue and reaps the profit from the spread between the price he pays to his client for the issue and the price at which he sells it to his investing customers. (The recently established Municipal Securities Rule-Making Board has proposed that financial advisers be barred from underwriting issues they have worked on.)

Whether or not the adviser is a dealer, a public authority project that is to be financed by the sale of revenue bonds involves the design of the facilities to be constructed and determination of their capital costs, an accountant's analysis, engineering and economic feasibility studies, and, finally, a financial plan for raising the money required. All of these steps are carried out for most public authorities by outside consultants. Some states, including New York and California, specify government financing procedure in sufficient detail to reduce dependence on advisory services, but the whole range of consultants' services embraces an increasingly significant portion of the small- and medium-sized authority's planning and decision-making tasks.

The feasibility report—which details engineering, economic, and financial aspects of the proposed project—is a crucial component of every major public authority work that will require revenue bond financing. With few exceptions, the financial community insists that such a report be prepared by consultants outside the public corporation and be included in the bond prospectus prepared by the financial advisers. The criteria used by engineering and economic consulting firms that prepare feasibility reports influence dramatically the priorities and projects adopted by public corporations of all types.

Interlocking Careers

The system of financing public enterprises has grown steadily and functioned smoothly for thirty years despite the absence of formal regulation and the presence of startling conflicts of interest. Executives and financial officials of the public enterprises that issue bonds work closely with various segments of the financial community. The Municipal Finance Officers Association (MFOA), which represents the finance officials of governments and public corporations, cooperates continually with the Public Securities Association, the municipal law section of the American Bar Association, and the New York Municipal Forum to develop united stands before congressional committees, to plan conferences and career workshops, and to clarify and improve bonding procedures.[21] Liaison committees of these four associations meet at each of their respective conventions. (The Bond Buyer, Inc., has published MFOA proceedings.)

Founded in 1906, MFOA has a current membership of over four thousand. Its primary concern is the bond market, although it also deals with other aspects of local government finance. Mainly a membership association for executives of local governments and government corporations, it also includes bankers and bond attorneys as associate members. The associational life of people in this business takes up more time than paperwork. The executives of underwriting firms who specialize in tax-exempt bonds are members of the associations for government and public authority officials, as well as of the typical civic and business groups to which bankers and brokers belong. They frequently participate with public officials in the activities of the Municipal Finance Forums, the MFOA, the International Bridge, Tunnel and Turnpike Association, and the American Public Power Association, among others.

In addition to close relationships among the professional associations for attorneys, underwriters, and public agencies, individual careers cross those lines and help bind the system. Former government agency officials become underwriters and financial consultants, and association executives trade posts. For example, the first director of the Washington, D.C., office of the MFOA had previously done public relations work for the Securities Industry Association (as its director of public finance), had been a local and regional councilman, and had participated in a study of bond options for municipalities and authorities. He subsequently moved to a post with the National Governors' Conference.

Wainright & Ramsey's president previously was associated with a rating service from which his firm now seeks favorable judgments for its clients. Its executive vice-president formerly worked with an underwriting firm. The advisory firm's Miami representative was former auditor of the city of Miami. A member of its staff who advised Metro Seattle subsequently started his own consulting firm and competed for Metro's business. Career interchanges among banks, investment firms, public agencies, and their interest groups promote internal trust to a remarkable degree. At any point in the financing process, indiscretion could cost someone a great deal of money. Raters, for example, do not leak forthcoming changes in ratings, although the change may throw an underwriter's pricing decision out of kilter before the issue is sold.

The club atmosphere reaches deep into public authority decision making. Robert Moses was a member of the club. He likes to tell the story of how he negotiated the establishment of the Bethpage Park Authority (with a board duplicating that of the Long Island Park Commission, which Moses headed) in order to purchase a friend's private golf club by personally dealing with bankers, federal officials, and state legislators with whom he was acquainted. On another occasion, Moses and Morton McCartney, a banker and then head of a division of RFC, personally hatched the financing scheme that enabled the Museum of Natural History to purchase the troubled Hayden Planetarium.[22] Years later, having allocated the underwriting business of half a dozen authorities, Moses was able to raise money for the New York World's Fair by calling in favors from a large number of acquaintances among investors and underwriters. When the fair's creditors received only thirty cents on the dollar, the underwriters worked with others to obtain an IRS ruling that permitted tax deductions of 100 percent of face value if the World's Fair notes were contributed before redemption to the Lincoln Center for the Performing Arts (which had a partner of the underwriting firm on its board).

Personal interaction and informal partnerships of bankers, lawyers, and authority executives making public enterprise decisions are demonstrated by case studies in the following chapters that are drawn from six states. The business of raising money for public enterprise and working out project schemes tends to be conducted by fairly close-knit groups. Those who would split from a syndicate and bid competitively against someone with whom they were formerly in a group are called "guerillas" or "mavericks." Their number is still small, though growing. The underwriters usually trust one another and the raters (because most of their customers do). The specialized press has a good deal to do with the ability to market bonds, and personal contacts with people at *Business Week* or The Bond Buyer can help an issue. As public enterprise expands, however, an overlapping of interests is causing more visible internal friction. (In 1975, for the first time, bond market participants sued each other; some regional investors charged New York underwriters with holding back information on the financial condition of public authorities.)

Public authority finance is an important source of business expansion for underwriters, attorneys, and consultants. Shifting dimensions of federal law and national money markets determine the basic perimeters of tax-exempt borrowing volume. Those perimeters have been expanding for fifteen years. Within them, active promotion by the business seekers in the municipal bond market accounts largely for the dramatic increase in the amount and variety of activities undertaken by government corporations and public authorities in the United States.

The very promotional energy that built the system now threatens to crack it. The more the public enterprises borrow, the greater their debt service burdens for the future, the heavier their dependence on the private sector banks and brokers, and the narrower their range of choice for future activities in the public interest.

4 Money and Corporate Strategy

The municipal bond market has long favored investment in projects with predictable results and in services for which rates of growth in demand and revenue can be readily forecast. Such are the characteristics of the classic public authority projects funded by revenue bonds: highways, bridges, tunnels, airports, docks, dams, and other power-generating installations. The government corporations that limit themselves to this kind of project have prospered; they are, for the most part, self-supporting.

The New Jersey Highway Authority

The New Jersey Highway Authority (NJHA) is a typical toll road enterprise, one of the scores of highway, bridge, and tunnel authorities that influenced land use and development in the nation's urbanizing areas throughout the 1950s and 1960s. The incentive for creating it was financial, and in financial terms it has been an unqualified success. To open its shore areas for recreation to its urban population, the state government had started parkway construction in 1945, but its efforts to fund capital investment out of current tax revenues had produced only twenty miles of highway by 1952. It then established the Highway Authority to do the job. Using revenue bonds the authority completed the basic 164-mile project in three years, and construction cost per mile was about $500,000 less than that of the earlier constructed state portions. The state could have borrowed the money to finish the job itself. But neither the beleaguered state budget officials nor the private financial advisers favored that alternative. As a result of the decision to seek the fiscal advantages of statutory corporations, however, New Jersey has had to make continuing sacrifices.[1]

The first two bond series issued by the NJHA were guaranteed by the state because the underwriters thought the traffic projections in the feasibility reports were weak. The reports, prepared by firms of consulting engineers, included twenty-year projections of traffic and toll revenues on the Garden State Parkway and a capital budget for the authority. (Subsequently, surveys, planning, and construction were also contracted out.) New Jersey voters approved a $285 million state guarantee of authority bonds, which the authority has not had to call upon.[2]

The authority raised its first $150 million in 1953. With the guidance of the state treasurer (because of the state guarantee) and a consortium of municipal bond advisers, it advertised for bids and sold the bonds to the lowest bidder, a syndicate of three hundred financial institutions headed by several national banks. These bonds carried interest rates of 3 percent and 2.75 percent, to mature in diverse batches between 1960 and 1988. Since the authority sold them at a discount, the net interest cost was 3 percent.

In 1954, the NJHA raised another $135 million from state-guaranteed bonds, this time taking only one bid—from the same syndicate. The net interest cost for this issue was 2.8 percent. According to the underwriters' estimate, the state guarantee saved an estimated 1 percent annual interest on the total $285 million over thirty-five years. (In other words, a straight revenue bond backed only by the authority's income might have carried an interest rate close to 4 percent.) The engineers and underwriters had been unduly pessimistic, however, and booming traffic and revenues in subsequent years eliminated investor requests for guarantees.

Even with the state guarantees, the bond lawyers and financial advisers who drew up the first bond indentures required an authority pledge to fix parkway tolls at a level that would produce net revenues of 120 percent of annual debt service. The first prospectus contained an anticipated toll schedule, and the bond indenture determined pricing policies on the only major highway along New Jersey's ocean shore. The indenture also created six special funds into which, in predetermined priority, the authority must deposit its revenues. One of them—the Bond Redemption Fund—is administered by a bank trustee. Two others also were bond-related pools of protected monies. Because of indenture terms on bond redemption and flow of funds, the authority has paid off low-interest loans before they came due. Other covenants in the bond indenture determined the type of insurance to be carried on Garden State Parkway facilities, provided for annual reports to the bondholders, prohibited future mortgages on authority facilities, mandated standards for maintenance, and required that reports by independent consulting engineers justify all future projects and changes in toll structures. In addition to guaranteeing repayment of bondholders, New Jersey pledged not to alter the powers of the authority. Twenty years later, despite the authority's perfect record of debt service, its wealth of excess revenues (with which it built the Garden State Arts Center), and its substantial financial reserves, this pledge still limits state government efforts to integrate transportation structures and finances.

The New York City firms of Lehman Brothers and Hawkins, Delafield & Wood served as financial advisers and bond counsel, respectively, holding onto the Highway Authority's business until the Republicans took over the New Jersey statehouse in 1970. Under Governor William Cahill's administration, two "Republican firms," Dillon Read and Mudge Rose, won those assignments.

The authority exhausted the proceeds of the first two bond issues before construction was completed. It then raised more money by issuing bonds without state guarantee carrying a net interest cost of 3.2 percent, half a percent higher than the previous issue with the guarantee. (The prospectus for these bonds states that they do not constitute a debt or liability of the state or any of its political subdivisions.) An additional sinking fund was added to the authority's accounting structure for these bonds. Later revenue bonds issued by NJHA raised $25 million in 1956, $40 million in 1962, and $24.9 million in 1964. Continual growth in traffic and authority income, well above original projections, made these additions to capital easy to obtain.

By 1970, authority annual income was up to $48 million, and net revenues were over one-and-a-half times debt service, allowing the authority to accumulate capital reserves from earnings. These reserves further enhanced the authority's borrowing power, and in 1971 it went back to the market for $80 million to invest in highway widening and improvement projects. These bonds were sold at a discount that cost the authority $1.52 million of the proceeds. The sale was negotiated without bidding at a net interest cost of 6.54 percent through a dealer syndicate headed by Dillon Read, the authority's new financial adviser. The new prospectus added still another covenant that tolls could not be reduced unless net revenues would remain at least 130 percent of debt service (a "coverage" ratio of 1.30).

At the same time, the authority pursued its general policy of retiring debt before maturity, redeeming $33 million in outstanding bonds ahead of schedule. These bonds carried interest rates that were three percentage points lower than the new bond issue. By 1976, toll revenues were up to $59 million, and the authority received several million dollars in additional income from investments, mainly in U.S. government securities (which pay a higher interest rate than the authority pays out on its own borrowings because U.S. securities are not tax-exempt). During twenty-two years the NJHA has raised $450 million, of which $291 million was outstanding debt at the end of 1976.

In its 1962 prospectus, the Highway Authority pledged to institute tolls in the previously free Essex County section of the Garden State Parkway. [3] The original legislation establishing the NJHA had exempted this section of the parkway from tolls in order to accommodate local traffic in the Newark area. Now, arguing that the lack of an Essex tollbooth was causing congestion on the parkway, the authority gained agreement from the state legislature to permit it to eliminate short-ride, non-toll-paying urban traffic. In exchange, the authority would contribute $13 million to construct a highway department interchange.

In seeking this legislation, the authority relied on an engineering consultant's report predicting that the growth of toll-free traffic in Essex would jeopardize the parkway's earning power and produce an operating deficit. In fact, however, operating revenues from tolls and restaurant and service station concessions had increased from $16.8 million in 1958 to $26.9 million in 1963. (The original feasibility reports had projected them at $19 million in 1963.) The ratio of net revenues to debt service was well above indenture requirements. There is no evidence that legislators looked behind the consultant's warnings to the authority's actual records. Toll-free privileges for local traffic were ended.

In addition to the Essex section, two other sections of the highway had been toll-free. They had originally been built by the state with federal aid and were exempt from tolls under the terms of federal law. The authority tried for over a decade to take over that portion of road; local mayors and state legislators battled against it. The authority repeatedly obtained reports from its engineering consultants recommending takeover, but when takeover was finally included in a federal bill, Senator Clifford Case inserted a requirement into the legislation that the authority build parallel free roads.[4] The authority subsequently dropped the plan, and the section remains free.

In 1969, at the request of the state Department of Transportation, the legislature authorized construction by the Highway Authority of a spur from Toms River to the New Jersey Turnpike. Authority management, opposed to this project, commissioned a feasibility report, which concluded that the spur "cannot meet the test of economic feasibility required for financing."[5] In the meantime, by its own choice and with its own excess capital, the Highway Authority had constructed the Garden State Arts Center at a total cost, according to its own account, of $7.8 million. (Informed observers estimate its real costs at over $10 million.) The center incurred operating deficits totaling about $1.2 million through 1973. (By 1976, authority bookkeeping showed its annual deficits dwindling.)

When a legislative report called for a reduction of tolls for commuters, the Highway Authority argued, successfully, that the discount would impair corporate ability to finance improvements. But consultants' traffic forecasts and feasibility studies repeatedly recommended widening the existing routes. The northern portion of the Garden State Parkway was swelled from six to ten lanes at a cost of $7 million per mile. When the gasoline supply crisis caused sharp drops in automobile traffic during 1974, the Highway Authority had the flexibility to cut back labor costs quickly and ended the year with net revenues only 1.6 percent below those of 1973. (From 1975 to 1976, they jumped up 5 percent.)

The fiscal considerations that were the prime concern of the authority and its consultants clearly excluded a number of public projects and favored others, with some distinct, if unintended, policy consequences. The issue of tolls on the free sections of the parkway has some nonfinancial aspects for which only the local politicians spoke. Local traffic was composed largely of low- and middle-income people driving to work; local interests saw social and economic reasons for keeping these trips cheap. But the perspectives of the financial and engineering consultants and authority management were focused on technical factors: congestion, through-traffic flow, and maximizing operating revenues.

Beginning with Alfred E. Driscoll (who subsequently became chairman of the New Jersey Turnpike Authority), New Jersey governors were frustrated by their inability to get a broad-based state tax enacted until 1976 and by the voters' repeated failure to approve state bond issue proposals. Former Governor Richard J. Hughes, subsequently a partner in the firm that served as local counsel to the NJHA until the Republican takeover in 1970, has explained: "So long as a state, like New Jersey, is deficient in sources of state revenues, it is more than ever necessary to depend on the authority technique to sustain the highway and many other capital facilities of the state."[6] Yet New Jersey governors have repeatedly—and to date unsuccessfully—attempted to bring the excess revenues of the state's three major toll-road authorities under government control. In 1959, Governor Robert B. Meyner proposed to use surplus turnpike revenues to back investment in mass transit. In 1963 and 1972, New Jersey voters rejected state transportation bond proposals for similar purposes. The statute and indentures of the Garden State Parkway hold that its revenues cannot be used for any purpose except highway improvement and debt service. In 1973, Governor William Cahill proposed a bill that would consolidate the three toll road authorities in the state as subsidiaries of a new state transportation authority, providing for payments to the parent authority from excess toll revenues. Authority opposition—thus far successful—leans heavily on the argument that continued autonomy of three separate toll-road corporations in the state is necessary to protect the bondholders.

The Port Authority of New York and New Jersey

The Port Authority has raised more than $3.5 billion from private investors, and it has a financial potential to raise as much as $1 billion more.[7] It issues only revenue bonds, which are amortized from charges paid by the businesses and individuals who use authority facilities. Port Authority bonds are sold to underwriting syndicates through competitive public bidding, usually in $100 million issues. A massive enterprise with over eight thousand employees, the authority's annual budget is larger than the operating budget of either of the state departments of transportation. Its net operating revenues were over $200 million in a bad year (1975) and rose 7 percent the next year. The Port Authority conducts most of its financial planning and legal analysis internally, using Hawkins, Delafield & Wood to provide legal opinions to accompany its bond issues.[8]

The Port Authority's financial structure demonstrates the feasibility of combining deficit-producing public tasks with profitable services in one corporate framework. Its enormous financial success, however, tends to dazzle governmental study commissions and tempt them to replicate it, seldom with the same results.[9] In any case, the authority's early projects—particularly the first Staten Island bridge—were financial disasters based on faulty traffic forecasts. Its first big profit maker—the Holland Tunnel—was actually built by a bistate commission and transferred to the authority in 1931 to give the corporation a credit base. Several of the Port Authority's most lucrative projects—marine terminals and airports—were also not built by it but leased after World War II from city governments that thought they could not raise the capital needed for expansion because they were under tremendous pressure to catch up with backlogs in public services.

The Port Authority's earliest bonds—issued after 1926—were linked to revenues from specific projects. When the authority took over the Holland Tunnel with its growing net revenues, the two states passed legislation enabling it to unify the finances of bridges and tunnels as a group so that losing projects would be supported by the profitable tunnel. (Thus the revenues of the Holland Tunnel provided early debt service for the George Washington and other bridges.) Legislation in 1935 also established the General Reserve Fund, to be fed from revenues of all authority sources and to be maintained at 10 percent of the face value of outstanding authority debt. (At the end of 1976, the fund contained $188 million.) Monies in excess of the General Reserve Fund requirements may be used for any purpose authorized by the states, within the bounds of bond agreements.

In 1952, the Port Authority passed the consolidated bond resolution, under which all subsequent long-term securities have been issued.[10] Port Authority bonds are now uniformly backed by all corporate revenues and reserves. The June 1973 issue of $100 million, for example, was the fortieth series of consolidated bonds, backed by the "full faith and credit of the authority." Revenues from all projects are pooled at top levels of Port Authority accounting, and the revenues from particular facilities or groups of facilities are no longer earmarked as security for specific bond issues. As a result, neither investors nor public officials have much information on or influence over the performance of specific projects and facilities. The Port Authority's facilities now include two 110-story office towers (the World Trade Center), three major airports and one minor one, eight marine terminals (including one for passenger ships), four bridges, two tunnel complexes across the Hudson River, two truck terminals, two bus terminals, two heliports, a multipurpose transportation center, a rapid transit line from New Jersey into downtown Manhattan, and trade development offices in nine cities (including London, Zurich, Tokyo, and San Juan). Authority management has assiduously kept the balance sheets on each of these components confidential, maintaining that consolidated financing renders such figures irrelevant.

Port Authority management argues that although each of its projects must be self-supporting, consolidated financing gives it the advantages of business-like flexibility: "older facilities with established earning power can aid new projects during developmental periods until they reach their anticipated point of self-support."[11] Insisting that its financial structure is based on "a single-enterprise pooling of revenues," authority management argues that "any presentation of net revenues after debt service for individual facilities . . . can only be based on arbitrary assumptions."[12]

The authority has displayed a willingness to sacrifice revenues and even some bond marketability in order to defend the confidentiality of detailed financial data. Because of unclear financial reporting, at least one underwriter has argued that Port Authority bonds were overrated at an A rating: "The Authority does not provide a record of the revenues and expenses of its individual projects, so we have no indication of whether the World Trade Center, the enlarged bus terminal . . . and the proposed mass transit system will increase or decrease debt service coverage. . . . In the absence of detailed earnings of the individual existing projects, and of projected earnings of existing and proposed projects, we suggest that the Consolidated Bonds should be rated somewhat lower."[13] Despite aggregate net earnings that are twice annual debt service, some dealers and investors want classic project-by-project feasibility reports and financial forecasts. In 1973, at hearings before the Interstate Commerce Commission on proposed fare increase for the Port Authority Trans-Hudson transit line (PATH), the authority was pressured to release these figures.[14] Rather than permit subpoena of its acting director to testify on the profitability of other projects, the authority withdrew its application for the fare increase.

No major agency using revenue bonds has (at least through 1975) maintained such massive reserve funds as the Port Authority. But underwriters, investors, and state officials feel a need for more detailed information on individual operations. The availability of such information would not reduce the usefulness of the consolidated multipurpose enterprise as a framework for conducting regional operations. Like conglomerates in the private sector, Port Authority accounting does keep detailed track of financial results by division and by project for purposes of internal planning, budgeting, and control. The headquarters planning department drafts expected budget performance for each division and facility and forwards the information to each facility manager; the staff of each facility keep accounts in specified categories and reports upward to the finance department on standard forms. New projects are started only after feasibility reports explore the financial potential of the individual facility.

The New York State comptroller's office conducted the first detailed audit of Port Authority finances in 1970 and a second audit in 1974. Revenues by specific projects as calculated in those audits are shown in tables 4.1 and 4.2. The figures show that the Port Authority has long permitted lucrative projects to support financially weak ones, such as the old Bayonne Bridge, the heliports, truck terminals, and the bus terminal at the George Washington Bridge. In addition, the authority finances port promotion functions and new project development from overhead allocations fed by the profitable projects. The most profitable projects have been the George Washington and Goethals bridges, the major airports, Ports Newark and Elizabeth, and the main bus terminal.

Clearly, "single-enterprise," consolidated accounting gives Port Authority management a great deal more internal freedom than it would have if financial particulars were regularly available to investors, officials, and the public. For example, several financial analysts have concluded that Port Authority accounting has exaggerated the deficits of the PATH transit line in order to

Table 4.1
Port Authority Operating Revenues, 1969 (Thousands of Dollars)

	Gross operating revenues	Net operating revenues (losses) [a]	Operating revenues after debt service (losses) [a]
Tunnels and bridges	$ 74,327	$ 42,160	$25,445
Holland Tunnel	11,270	2,500	685
Lincoln Tunnel	17,342	7,175	614
George Washington Bridge	33,637	24,716	18,037
Bayonne Bridge	1,701	259	(337)
Goethals Bridge	8,489	6,620	6,044
Outerbridge	1,888	889	401
Air terminals	110,125	48,996	31,068
LaGuardia	25,475	12,450	7,871
JFK	69,335	32,140	20,113
Newark	14,324	4,530	3,529
Teterboro	937	136	(180)
West 30th Street Heliport	35	(163)	(169)
Downtown Heliport	18	(96)	(96)
Marine terminals	28,593	20,386	10,200
Columbia Street	253	217	160
Grain	105	61	4
Port Newark	10,136	6,255	3,506
Erie Basin	1,863	1,303	919
Hoboken	1,468	1,137	602
Elizabeth	7,639	6,490	3,571
Brooklyn	7,130	4,923	1,438
Inland terminals	18,205	7,032	3,863
Headquarters Building	6,031	2,551	2,064
New York Union Truck	563	175	(105)
Newark Union Truck	316	24	(178)
Port Authority Bus	10,550	4,527	2,930
George Washington Bridge Bus	745	(246)	(848)
PATH	11,548	(10,074)	(13,938)
Totals	242,797	108,500	56,539

[a] Net revenues are after deducting both direct expenses and allocated overhead and staff service expenses of the authority but before allocating debt service.
Source: Office of the New York State Comptroller.

Table 4.2
Port Authority Operating Revenues, 1973 (Thousands of Dollars)

	Gross operating revenues	Net operating revenues (losses)	Net operating revenues after interest (losses)	Net revenues after depreciation (losses) [a]
Air terminals	$196,588	$ 82,511	$53,297	$17,834
LaGuardia	42,064	16,078	11,040	4,963
JFK	125,369	57,108	39,149	14,958
Newark	28,501	9,354	3,270	(1,830)
Teterboro	558	389	272	189
West 30th Street Heliport	55	(230)	(240)	(252)
Downtown Heliport	41	(187)	(193)	(193)
World Trade Center Heliport		(1)	(1)	(1)
Tunnels and bridges	84,725	45,565	42,680	35,711
Holland Tunnel	11,754	1,552	1,284	321
Lincoln Tunnel	18,012	6,109	5,299	2,763
George Washington Bridge and Bus Terminal	39,894	28,726	27,164	24,533
Combined Staten Island Bridges	15,065	9,178	8,933	8,094
Marine terminals	34,991	18,201	8,130	(1,978)
Columbia Street Pier	325	53	26	(66)
Port Newark	11,941	6,088	1,825	(2,227)
Erie Basin	739	(113)	(454)	(768)
Hoboken	873	575	268	(161)
Elizabeth	13,135	10,418	7,109	3,847
Brooklyn	5,353	2,130	306	(1,653)
Consolidated Passenger Terminal	2,625	(950)	(950)	(950)
Inland terminals	16,837	4,132	3,724	2,347
Port Authority Building	4,015	1,204	1,153	967
New York Union Motor Terminal	748	207	186	29
Newark Union Motor Terminal	370	12	(11)	(166)
Port Authority Bus Terminal	11,709	2,709	2,396	1,517
PATH	9,246	(17,114)	(24,260)	(27,699)
World Trade Center	30,930	4,399	(3,360)	(9,447)
Totals	373,497	137,694	80,211	16,768
Add: Financial income				20,024
Subtract: Special studies				(632)
Total (net revenues)				$36,160

[a] Unlike the auditor's format for 1969, the 1973 review calculated depreciation on Port Authority facilities (by the straight-line method).
Source: Office of the New York State Comptroller.

strengthen its argument against expanding rail transportation activities. When it purchased the old Hudson and Manhattan rail line, the PATH corporation (a Port Authority subsidiary) also acquired the property on which the World Trade Center was built. If the accounting system had treated PATH and the center as independent enterprises, PATH might have charged sufficient ground rent to the Trade Center to reduce its transit deficits, just as the authority charges its tenants at the airports basic rent plus a share of their gross receipts. If the accounting system had equitably treated them as joint facilities, on the other hand, changes might have been made in the allocation of costs for the PATH terminal in the Trade Center. In short, the accounting systems used for the Trade Center and subway seem designed to increase the net deficits of the rail line (which were a cumulative $220 million through 1975) and to cut the costs of the Trade Center. The state auditors estimate that the costs of the Trade Center are higher than the authority's accounting figures.[15]

The ability of the authority to generate excess revenues that can be reinvested as corporate management chooses made the World Trade Center possible (just as it enabled the NJHA to build the Garden State Arts Center). Some $95 million of Port Authority operating revenues were allocated to investment in the Trade Center, according to state auditors. (No authority operating revenues were invested in PATH.) When a 1968 change in the federal tax law indicated that long-term bonds to finance the Trade Center (which would be commercially rented to private firms as well as to government agencies) might not be held to be tax-exempt, the authority sought bank loans instead. Between 1968 and 1973, it succeeded in obtaining direct bank loans totaling $470 million because it had ample reserve funds and agreed to maintain specified balances in non-interest-bearing accounts of the participating banks. (This agreement was not recorded in the public minutes of the authority that are forwarded to the two state governors. Authority bond prospectuses during those years carried the proviso that bond proceeds would not be used for the Trade Center.) Confronted by the same tax law change, the Massachusetts Port Authority (Massport) abandoned its plans for building a trade center.

Its confidential accounting system gives the Port Authority a degree of freedom found elsewhere only in unregulated private firms. The authority has used this freedom to help it avoid more responsibility for mass transit. In order to utilize this strategy, management resorts to a fundamental contradiction: it claims that the Port Authority is an integrated financial enterprise except for any rail transportation project, and it therefore provides separate financial accounting and calculation of PATH's operating results. Former Executive Director Austin Tobin acknowledges this discrepancy but maintains that it is necessary because of the financial drain inherent in rail transport. The authority asked for and obtained from the two state legislatures a ceiling on authority deficits from rail transportation projects.

Of course, deficits—real or potential—must be closely calculated and provided for, either from surpluses of other enterprises or from tax-supported subsidies, such as state and federal aid. In fact, the authority does support other financially weak projects by such means. Even if running a facility at a deficit resulted in a lasting drop in credit rating, paying slightly higher interest rates might be a calculated trade-off against the opportunity to invest in projects with specific economic and social benefits that may not show up on corporate financial statements. When only private sector criteria of financial performance are applied to the public's business, however, enterprise decision making does not include consideration of such benefits. A broader framework of public enterprise decision making has been very difficult to achieve at the Port Authority, in part because of the accretion of covenants.

A covenant is a provision in the bond indenture approved by a corporation's board of directors that commits the corporation to do or not to do certain things. Insofar as they are incorporated into legislation, covenants may be treated as contracts entered into by the government and may thus freeze policy options. Authority managements maintain that bondholders require stringent covenants, although the bondholders seldom participate with the underwriters and bond attorneys in drafting indentures. Hence it is difficult to determine whether bondholders require definitive covenants or whether skillful authority managements merely invoke bondholders as an excuse to obtain covenants which they seek for their own purposes. These two sources of motivation are usually mixed.

In 1959, in response to proposals by the state governments that the Port Authority finance a commuter railroad improvement program, Austin Tobin maintained that this would damage the authority's ability to raise capital on the private market and would be protested by underwriters and institutional bondholders.[16] To confirm his assertions, Tobin solicited such protests, asking his colleagues in the financial community to express this opinion to the governors. At Tobin's request, a vice-president of First National City Bank called a meeting of investment banking firms that had been syndicate leaders for Port Authority bond issues. Tobin went to the meeting and "urged that in their interests and in the interests of their investors, they stand with me in saying what would happen if the Port Authority ever attempted to pledge its general reserves for commuter . . . cars."[17] At least one of the firms openly disagreed, seeing no insurmountable problem with proposed commuter rail bonds. Writing to another firm in a further appeal for help, Tobin expressed shock that one of their number refused "to stand by customers to whom they had sold Port Authority securities."[18] The plan was dropped and replaced by an arrangement that did not lend the Port Authority's capital-raising capacities to rail transportation. Over the next decade, rail transportation in the port district continued to slide into successive bankruptcies.

The management of the Port Authority has constantly invoked investors as its most important constituency. In this instance, Tobin actually solicited financial community restrictions on the options open to the public agency. When he felt he could no longer rely on his success in the political arena to fend off the unwanted shift in program, he had these restrictions written into covenants.

The long-term bondholder does not really benefit from maximization of authority revenues because he is entitled to receive only the face amount of the bond at maturity. The growth of corporate revenues may raise the price of the bond on the secondary market, but even this link is weak and depends on the overall market's moving upward. The underwriter does have something to gain from restrictions on a government corporation's activities. Provisions that are likely to maximize the corporation's revenues make the bonds attractive to his customers and hence marketable quickly and at a good spread. Underwriters readily acknowledge, however, that if an authority has net revenues that are high in relation to debt service (coverage of over 1.5, for example) and a borrowing track record, it should not need to make unusual covenants. In 1962, when the Port Authority made the covenant limiting transit deficits, its net revenues were over two times the annual debt service. The major benefits of maximizing revenues accrue to the authority itself in the form of increased freedom from political pressures, from government control, and even from specific bondholder controls. With ample reserve funds, the authority can plan projects, weather downturns in business, and generally conduct its own affairs without depending on popular whims or elected officials' budgetary decisions.

The Port Authority has skillfully accumulated and insulated surplus funds in such a way as to minimize actual bondholder controls and to stave off governmental imposition of public and political priorities. The concurrent legislation of the two states and the U.S. Congress that created the Port Authority did not mandate its financial independence. The law enabled the authority to issue tax-exempt securities but also to request appropriations and loans from the federal government and the two states for carrying out projects. The strategies of self-support were astutely defined by the Port Authority's first executives. Its first chairman, Eugenius Outerbridge, and its first general counsel, Julius Henry Cohen, decided that financial independence, avoiding reliance on state credit and tax monies, was an important goal of the organization. (Into the 1970s, the authority was run by men who had apprenticed in its law department under Cohen.) The Port Authority has developed excess operating revenues from current income to transfer into capital investments during a difficult era when older cities have had to resort to the reverse process—borrowing money to meet current operating deficits. In addition, the cities of New York and Newark still own and lease to the Port Authority the properties that produce some of its biggest profits: the airports and docks.

The Port Authority's aversion to involvement in rail transportation has its roots in the early history of the authority, which was created to settle a century-old dispute between New York and New Jersey over control of transportation on the Hudson River and in the harbor. Railroad development on both sides of the Hudson was rapid and haphazard, with each line using separate terminals. The states battled over rail transportation, vying for competing terminals and bickering over regulation of railroad rates. New Jersey argued that rates to the New York side of the harbor should be higher because the rail cars had to be ferried across the bridgeless Hudson. In 1916, New Jersey interests brought formal complaints before the Interstate Commerce Commission to force the railroads to lower their rates to the New Jersey side of the river, arguing that equal rates throughout the port district unfairly imposed on New Jersey part of the costs of the ferry services and of terminals in New York and Brooklyn. The resulting railroad rate case dragged on until 1918, when an interstate commission was established to study the problem.[19] (Ferry service was threatened by ice on the Hudson in the severe winter of 1918.) Two years later, the commission proposed the Port Authority compact. The stated purposes of the new authority were to resolve the counterproductive competition among the railroads by creating a comprehensive transportation plan and to promote the economic well-being of the port cities. The authority was designed to coordinate regional terminals, transportation, and other commercial facilities and to stimulate development of the port district. Somewhat prophetically, the Harbor Commission concluded in 1920 that the "port problem is primarily a railroad problem."

The young Port Authority failed to get the railroads to agree to any integrated freight line and terminal plans. The ICC had ordered "that the great terminals of the Port of New York be made practically one, and that the separate interests of the individual carriers . . . be subordinated to the public interest."[20] But the railroads refused to share common terminals and opposed the Port Authority's construction of a consolidated freight terminal, which lost money for nearly thirty years. Port Authority projects to improve passenger rail travel were authorized by both state legislatures as early as 1927 but were vetoed by New York Governor Alfred E. Smith, who believed suburban commuting to be New Jersey's problem.[21] For nearly a decade after its creation, the authority had thus obtained neither operating revenues nor effective agreements on comprehensive transportation plans for the district. Hindsight tells us that the railroads were shortsighted in their stubborn attachment to unstructured competition. The results were duplicated services, inconvenient terminal locations, inefficient patterns of freight movement, and eventual bankruptcy.

Fifty years later, interstate competition continues to hamstring regional action on rail transportation. Although New Jersey has repeatedly sought Port Authority help to improve its suburban rail systems, it also fears that if the gates are opened to Port Authority rail subsidies, New York City's deficit-ridden subways might drain away the Port Authority's wealth. This fear underlay conflict between the two states over transit plans submitted in the 1950s. The same fear, reinforced by selective pressure from financial backers, persuaded the governor of New Jersey not to support full repeal of the Port Authority's transit-limiting covenants in 1972.

Mass transit is also an unpopular form of public enterprise in the Port Authority and other similar public authorities because it does not lend itself to the type of assessments usually made for the tax-exempt bond market.[22] Rail traffic forecasts cannot easily be translated into revenue forecasts because, after a point, increases in peak-hour traffic for mass transit are associated with increases in average costs and cause a drop in net revenues. Uncertainty in forecasting revenues makes mass transit revenue bonds difficult to evaluate by the methods typical for the authority feasibility study. (Rail transportation did attract more speculative types of investment.) Moreover, a history of bad management in both its private and public sectors has tarnished the reputation of the rail transportation industry in the bond market community. Finally, the need to seek federal, state, and city subsidies for transit introduces uncertainties and contingencies that all public authority managements that have become accustomed to financial independence prefer to avoid. The vicissitudes of New York's Metropolitan Transportation Authority understandably make Port Authority executives uneasy.

The Port Authority has used covenants, then, as part of its broader strategies to maintain financial independence and to protect itself from responsibility for rail transportation and other undesirable arrangements. The Port Authority pioneered in the practice of persuading both states to incorporate indenture pledges made to bondholders into state law, thus transforming them into contracts entered into by state government.[23] In this way, statutes that began as pledges to investors prohibited state regulation of the Port Authority's rate structure, ruled out construction of competing Hudson crossings, and protected all authority facilities from local property taxes.[24]

In 1958, when pressures to plan and develop suburban rail improvements were strong, the Port Authority devised indenture covenants requiring that the authority's board of commissioners personally certify that each new investment would not "impair the sound credit standing of the authority." The two states incorporated this covenant into statutes and thereby agreed, in effect, that whenever their legislatures authorized the Port Authority to do something, it could veto the authorization on the basis of its own internal assessment of the financial attractiveness of the proposal. These covenants, which have been interpreted to require that each project be self-supporting, are inconsistent with the authority's concept of consolidated revenues. If all Port Authority projects must be self-supporting, the authority should presumably be required to supply figures on individual project results to bondholders and state governments. But the authority recognizes no such obligation.

When the states enacted statutes in 1962 that called for Port Authority purchase of the Hudson and Manhattan rail line (renamed PATH) and construction of the World Trade Center, the new covenants promoted by Tobin prohibited commitment of Port Authority revenues or reserves to any other rail transportation projects unless the deficits generated by such projects and PATH together amounted to less than one-tenth the amount in the General Reserve Fund (excluding the other reserve funds) or 1 percent of total bonded debt. Thus, as long as PATH deficits equaled this amount, the authority was absolved of any further rail transportation responsibilities. Tobin had struck a brilliant bargain. In exchange for taking on one rail line, he obtained a protective shield, in the service of keeping faith with bondholders, to fend off any further transit responsibilities.

A decade later, however, as the private railroads went under, pressure for government action to save rail transportation in the region began to mount again. In 1971, the New York and New Jersey legislatures authorized construction of rail links to Kennedy and Newark airports. In 1972, Governors Rockefeller and Cahill announced, with considerable fanfare, an "agreement with the Port Authority Commissioners on a bistate plan of capital improvements" totaling $650 million, to include the rail links to the airports, as well as the extension of rail lines from Hoboken into Penn Station and extension of PATH lines into Union County, New Jersey. This plan, which was also intended to draw on federal airport and mass transit aid, would have vastly improved commutation from northern New Jersey and enhanced New York City's job-holding capacities.

The plan would have entailed rail service deficits above the limits imposed by the 1962 covenants. Port Authority staff, particularly Matthias E. Lukens and Roger Gilman, agreed to it in order to appease the two governors and Authority Commissioners James C. Kellogg and William J. Ronan. Of the manifold press releases and newspaper and magazine articles that described the plan, none pointed out that the existing covenants and PATH bookkeeping precluded implementation. Austin Tobin later described release of the plan as a "grandstand play," with negligible chances of being implemented.[25]

In 1972, however, both states amended the statutes that incorporated the Port Authority's 1962 covenants, making them inapplicable to holders of bonds issued after mid-1973. In signing the amendment, Governor Rockefeller stated that he did so "in order to give incentive to the Port of New York Authority to proceed with urgently needed mass transportation in the metropolitan region." This legislation, however, need not have altered Port Authority behavior until the year 2007, when the last of the earlier-issued bonds would mature.

During legislative battles over the covenants, Tobin had claimed that "without the covenants [we] couldn't have sold a bond for the PATH system or anything else." Port Authority general counsel Patrick Falvey warned that the agency's financial condition was approaching the point where it would be unable to raise capital by the sale of bonds at acceptable rates.[26] At the same time, Port Authority management was assuring the financial community that its financial condition was strong and that the transit plan would not be implemented without substantial subsidy from government and a PATH fare increase. As a result, the authority's bond issue raising $100 million in September 1973 was aggressively bid for and sold at a net interest cost lower than the cost for its June issue of that year. The underwriters acknowledged that the issue was priced ahead of contemporary market levels. In short, at the same time that the Port Authority publicly warned that political proposals posed a threat to its financial structure, it was able to convince the financial community of its superior financial health. Subsequent bond sales and the size of reserve funds indicated that the authority was financially healthy despite a tendency to public hypochondria. When market forces are favorable and internal finances balanced, there is, in fact, little direct impact of covenants on bond marketability.

In 1974, the energy crisis, air pollution problems, and political campaigns in both states finally led New York and New Jersey to repeal fully the statutory protection for the covenants that had limited further Port Authority transit projects. When full repeal appeared inevitable, two authority commissioners resigned (Bernard P. Lasker, securities firm partner and former chairman of the New York Stock Exchange, and Philip B. Hofmann, head of the pharmaceutical firm Johnson & Johnson, who acknowledged that he could not cooperate with New Jersey Governor Brendan Byrne's transportation policy). Another authority commissioner, the late Gustave L. Levy, chairman of the investment banking firm of Goldman Sachs, publicly expressed his opposition to repeal.

The United States Trust Company, as bondholder and bank trustee, brought lawsuits in both states against repeal of the covenants, claiming that repeal was unconstitutional. (Lawsuits started earlier claimed that the covenants themselves were unconstitutional.)[27] Some parties maintained that statutory covenants in public authority indentures are contracts that bind state legislatures, no matter what their effects or content. Others pointed to constitutional law holding that legislatures cannot delegate substantial authority without maintaining continuing controls, that the constitutional protection of contracts must be balanced against reasonable exercise of government power for public purposes, and that one legislature cannot bind future legislatures (that is, that a sitting legislature can alter agreements made earlier). Yet others argued that congressional consent had been needed for what was basically an amendment to the original Port Authority interstate compact. It was hoped that decisions in these lawsuits would provide an answer to a question that is critical to the future of public enterprise decision making: What evidence of real damage or risk to bondholders should be required to limit

government control over authorities? The Port Authority, like other authorities throughout the United States, has been taken at its word when it invokes
its credit rating and pledges to its bondholders to fend off public priorities.
Financial commentators, too, have generally failed to describe in specific
terms the financial damage to bondholders that legislative repeal of covenants
might entail. Their threats to governments are not veiled, however:

In New Jersey and New York, evidently, a politician's word is no better
than his bond. . . . If [they] can act so cavalierly with respect to one group of
bondholders, then all of us in the financial community must make a careful
re-evaluation of all the states' outstanding debt obligations and future debt
financings.[28]

Of what value are any promises made by these two states—particularly in
the already shadowy "moral obligation" category—if the 1962 covenant can
be repealed?[29]

Unfortunately, the courts did not clarify the issues concerning bondholder
damage and public control. In 1977, the U.S. Supreme Court reversed the
judgment of New Jersey's highest court by striking down state repeal of the
1962 Port Authority covenants. In a four to three decision, the court held
that the contract clause of the U.S. Constitution prohibited the repeal. The
opinion does not examine whether investors actually suffered significant
damage, and it acknowledges that the price of the bonds had quickly moved
back up to prevailing market levels. It states without supporting evidence that
the covenants "limited the Port Authority's deficits and thus protected the
general reserve fund from depletion."[30] In fact, they did not limit potential
deficits from nonrail sources, like the World Trade Center, and no actual
deficits had occurred in the total operations, so that the general reserve fund
had continued to increase each year since repeal as it had in earlier years. The
opinion says little about the role of government control but implies that the
majority believed that state governments could and should devise other approaches to their transportation problems than covenant repeal.

Following this decision, new leadership in the Port Authority studied a
move to trade higher investment rates for bondholder consent to financing
rail projects from bridge and tunnel tolls, an option that had been proposed
by an underwriting firm, First Boston Corporation, and supported by a footnote in the Supreme Court decision. Other underwriters are working on plans
to refund authority debt without consent. Major transportation decisions for
two states are thus being made by the court, the underwriters, and authority
management instead of by the elected governors and legislatures.

In the long run, policy makers must still confront the broad questions of public control over public enterprise and the legitimate rights and reasonable expectations of bondholders. These questions have been pending since 1921 when New York City's Democrats protested that the compact creating the nation's first public authority made no provision for surplus profits or other amassed accumulations to be distributed, divided, or apportioned to the states or to the city of New York.

Former New Jersey Governor Cahill noted that Port Authority management ran it "as a business, but it is not a business." Port Authority supporters feel, however, that it should be a business. The lack of expressed public goals, such as regional plans to which authority priorities would have to conform, and the procedures of revenue bond financing encourage the tendency of authority personnel to make authorities act, to the extent possible, like private undertakings. In part as a result, gargantuan office towers took priority over transit improvements, although inadequate transportation is causing firms that might use that office space to leave the New York City area.

The Public Power Systems

Unlike most other sectors of public enterprise in the United States, public power did begin with distinct political and social aims. The public power systems were not created because private systems were unprofitable. On the contrary, private systems were enormously profitable. Private electric companies operated with monopoly franchises, politically let; they charged high rates and serviced high-density areas with low distribution costs. By 1920, many investor-owned utilities were part of huge financial conglomerates, such as the Insull empire, with headquarters in Chicago and subsidiaries across the nation. Public dissatisfaction with these systems was widespread, and regulation by governments spread rapidly. The first public utility commissions, in New York and Wisconsin, began operation in 1907; by 1932, every state in the nation except Delaware had a commission regulating investor-owned public utilities, and all but seven of these commissions had jurisdiction over light and power companies.

Regulation failed to resolve many of the basic problems, and the regulatory commissions tended to be co-opted by the views of the businesses they were supposed to restrain.[31] The public continued to pay high rates for low use, and the availability of electricity in some parts of the nation remained limited. The utility holding companies established rate structures that would pay back the full costs of system construction quickly and pay dividends to several layers of stockholding interests. In their first four decades of operation, the companies did not experiment with the economics of high-volume, low-price sales of electric power.

Public enterprise in the power sector began in the early decades of this century with the explicit aims of competing with the private sector and maintaining a low price policy. Does this early history of aggressive competition and theoretical conflict with the private sector set contemporary power authorities apart from other types of authority that modeled themselves on the private sector? The answer seems to be, less so over time.

Public power can and does undersell private power. (Prices charged by investor-owned utilities average 50 percent higher than those of publicly owned utilities according to a 1975 survey by the American Public Power Association.) The ability to issue tax-exempt bonds, freedom from property and other direct taxes, and absence of stockholders expecting dividends have given public systems substantial price advantages. But over the years, public and private power systems have accommodated each other, increasingly entering into joint ventures and cooperative relationships. The price differential between public and private power is narrowing with the increasing scarcity of hydroelectric sources (water power controlled by dams); with the higher costs of development and operation associated with steam generation (fueled by oil, gas, or coal) or nuclear power generation; and with the obstacles to new projects arising from land-use and environmental concerns. Public power still has some advantages, however, even while prices are rising, because private firms are frequently stymied by consumer and political opposition to new plants and hemmed in by high costs of capital. Investor-owned utilities are experiencing severe difficulties in raising money for new investment, and the price of the power they supply is driving industry out of some cities and regions, particularly in the Northeast. These trends make government power enterprises increasingly attractive political solutions.

Meanwhile, public power authorities are in the throes of an identity crisis. Conditioned to view themselves as socially forward-looking organizations, they increasingly find themselves being accused of unfair price increases and a wanton exploitation of natural resources. Multipurpose aspects of water resource management that are of widespread concern today inevitably affect the corporations that generate electric power. The power authorities began their operations as hydroelectric enterprises damming up rivers. The several uses of a single body of water—for power and flood control, navigation, recreation, water supply, conservation, and pollution abatement—are inextricably overlapping, but federal government cost-sharing formulas (which provide subsidies for the flood control benefits of a dam but not for its water supply benefits, for example) encourage authorities to fragment their bookkeeping for various functions.

The profits are in power and to some extent in water supply, but the pub-. lic is pressing for more action in other fundamentally social aspects of water resource management, such as pollution control. As a result, public corporations and government officials in this field are coming into conflicts that resemble those in transportation. Power authorities are now under political pressure to do more that will yield less in financial terms.

Organizational Alternatives for Power The earliest public electric systems were municipal. California took the lead and had seven municipal power and light agencies established by 1900. By 1930, although two large private companies controlled over half the power generated in California, public systems had won some vicious battles with the investor-owned utilities and were multiplying rapidly. During the 1930s, the federal Public Works Administration provided loan funds for municipal power systems, as well as for federal and state hydroelectric projects, stimulating a rapid growth of public systems. Most public systems were, and remained, profitable, financing substantial portions of new investment out of retained earnings. One of these systems, the Department of Water and Power of the city of Los Angeles, is a highly successful example of an organizational alternative to public authorities: an enterprise that raises capital through revenue bonds but is organized within city government and transfers net revenues to the city's reserve funds.

Another form of public power enterprise is the taxing district. Some of these districts bring in sufficient revenue to refrain from using their taxing powers. The public utility districts of the state of Washington have elected boards of directors and the power to levy property taxes up to limits defined by statute. But several have not levied taxes themselves since the 1940s and in fact pay substantial "in lieu" taxes to local governments. Most of them issue revenue bonds backed only by operating income. (The Port District of Seattle, the biggest public corporation in the state of Washington, also raises money in this way, and its assets are greater than those of any city or county in the state.) The net revenues of the Washington public utility districts range from one-and-a-half to nearly three times the annual debt service requirements. These returns enable them to accumulate substantial reserve funds. In terms of bonded indebtedness, county public utility districts are among the largest public corporations in the nation, second only to toll bridge and highway authorities.

The public utility districts are interdependent with municipal electric distribution systems, with federal government power generating agencies, and with private utilities. For example, the Seattle Municipal Light and Power System is a municipal distributor that purchases power from the federal government's Bonneville Power Administration (BPA) and from two county utility districts. The Pacific Northwest Utility Conference Committee, which has worked out a plan for the expansion of the power sources in that region, includes 104 public power agencies, five investor-owned utilities, and BPA. The public companies have joined together in the Washington Public Power Supply System to issue joint revenue bonds for nuclear projects.

Such public sector combines also have developed in Nebraska, a state in which all electric power is publicly owned. Nebraska's government made an early start in river control for the purpose of irrigation and thereafter added hydroelectric power generation to its established operations. The Nebraska power districts have no taxing powers, relying on operating revenues and revenue bonds for sources of money; they are run by elected boards of directors. These power districts have recently formed a joint operating system to pool production and revenues. The combined Nebraska Public Power District has raised $544 million in bonds to finance a nuclear project on the Missouri River, of which half the power generated will be sold to an investor-owned utility in Iowa and half to public power distributing districts in Nebraska.

In the East, the pioneer in public power was the Power Authority of New York State, created in 1931 under Governor Franklin D. Roosevelt. As is often the case at the birth of a new public agency, debates about its tasks were not resolved, and the New York Power Authority suffered from this defect for decades. At issue was whether the power generated at Niagara Falls and on the St. Lawrence River should be developed by private companies; generated by the public firm but sold cheaply to private distributors, thereby putting public enterprise to work boosting private profits; retailed directly by the public firm to industrial and high-volume users at market prices, thereby maximizing the profits of the authority; or distributed by the public firm to municipalities, cooperatives, and other preference customers to whom the savings would be passed.

Governor Roosevelt's bill establishing the Power Authority cancelled franchises offered to a private company and explicitly called for preference to be given to residential, municipal, and rural customers. The authority produced a series of studies developing the theory that competition from the public sector could encourage the private sector to develop low-rate, high-volume business that would extend electricity to all. Roosevelt gave these concepts national exposure in his 1932 campaign for president when he argued that public power agencies could be the "birch rod in the cupboard," an alternative to or companion of regulation of private utilities. Roosevelt used his experts from New York to develop TVA's power program.

The original board of the New York Power Authority held to this philosophy, but for twenty years it failed to get its own projects underway because supporters of the private utilities and the difficulties of treaty negotiations with Canada repeatedly thwarted its plans. During this period the Power Authority's research and price analyses continued to contribute to the public power movement, but the authority generated no power.

The authority first tasted success under new management. In 1952, Governor Thomas E. Dewey appointed Robert Moses chairman of the Power Authority. Moses quickly compromised with the private utilities, eschewed any explicit social policy governing distribution and prices, and bullied his way to project approvals in his typical entrepreneurial style. Moses himself has described how he and his fellow "realists" took over; he criticizes the Federal Power Commission's attempts to limit the rate of return earned by private firms distributing the public power and rejects the principle of preferential allocation of electricity to public distributors.[32]

Under Moses, the New York Power Authority abandoned its attempt to regulate the retail rates that could be charged for power purchased from it and agreed to sell low-cost power wholesale to the private utilities.[33] At the same time, a rock slide at the Niagara site destroyed a partially completed private project and put the developer in a mood to cooperate with a new source of public investment. In 1954, over twenty years after it began trying but only two years after Moses took over, the New York Power Authority sold revenue bonds for project construction, passing much of the cost advantages of the tax-exempt bonds on to private distributors of electricity. This shift in power policy in New York coincided with the Hoover Commission's criticisms of public enterprise in Washington and President Eisenhower's attempts to clip the wings of TVA.

In 1968, the Power Authority bargain with private power was extended when a public nuclear plant was authorized (by both state and federal governments). The Power Authority bought a nuclear plant begun by the Niagara Mohawk Power Company and, after financing construction, contracted with that company to operate the plant. This arrangement was an attempt to reconcile Governor Rockefeller's proposal that the private utilities develop nuclear energy in the state with Senator Robert F. Kennedy's demand that nuclear plants be built and operated by the state Power Authority at low rates. Under the terms of the compromise, Niagara Mohawk in effect enjoys access to tax-exempt financing. The same firm uses a second pipeline to tax-exempt financing: pollution control bonds issued by the New York State Energy Research Development Authority help finance its pollution abatement equipment.

In 1974, when the investor-owned utility serving New York City, the Consolidated Edison Company, claimed that it could not complete investments in planned projects, no one seriously proposed that the state Power Authority take over its retail jurisdiction, although the authority calculated that Con Ed customers could save at least $50 million per year from its takeover of just one Con Ed plant. The New York Power Authority was authorized to purchase the Con Ed plants in trouble. Con Ed now buys some of its power from the authority at lower cost than it would take to produce the power itself and resells the power to its retail customers. High-cost electricity continues to impose serious burdens on New York's economy.

The New York Power Authority enjoys easy access to new capital even during fiscal crises in New York City and New York State. In 1976, it sold the largest tax-exempt issue ever privately placed, raising $610 million without bids or competitive underwriting. It can undersell Con Ed because of tax exemptions, lack of dividends, lower-cost generating facilities, and inefficiency in the investor-owned utility, whose rates exceed those of nearly all other comparable utilities in the nation. Power Authority rates are not low by national public-power standards, in part because its indenture covenants provide for a high coverage ratio and a depreciation formula designed to provide for amortization in only thirty-one years, although the actual term for its bonds is forty-five years and the national average depreciation period for power plants is seventy-five years. Power Authority bond indentures thus impose more restrictive conditions than are implied by the logic of plant life. Nevertheless, by 1973 the authority was producing nearly one-quarter of the power generated in the state.

TVA Finance   For forty years, TVA managed to maintain the lowest electric rates in the nation and still generated sufficient return to reimburse congressional appropriations and to support flood control and varied regional development projects. Its initial financial policy, based on Henry Ford's theory that a high-volume business would lower prices, featured dynamic rates and aggressive promotion. Rural cooperatives and municipally owned distribution systems, many of them initially aided or sponsored by TVA, received priority in the sale of TVA electricity.

TVA could hold to this policy because the initial investment capital for each of its projects, as for other federal power and water enterprises, came not from bonds but from congressional appropriations. From its power revenues TVA reimburses the U.S. Treasury, at rates of return linked to current interest rates, for government investment in the power system.[34]

Like the Port Authority, TVA utilizes consolidated funding, in that retained earnings from the sale of electric power subsidize a wide range of other activities. But TVA has always reported detailed financial results and provided forecasts by project and by plant to Congress. Although it has to cope with annual congressional hearings, this need to get along with legislators has limbered its political muscles, making it somewhat more adaptable to shifts in public policy priorities than the Port Authority.

The system of capital funding through legislative appropriations was satisfactory until the 1950s, when TVA nearly lost the Dixon-Yates fight; it then sought and received from Congress the power to raise money independently by issuing revenue bonds on the private market, like state and local public authorities (although without their privilege of paying interest that is exempt from federal income taxes). Since 1960, TVA has issued revenue bonds for power projects, requiring legislative appropriations only for relatively minor, nonpower expenditures. For example, of estimated expenditures of $1.357 billion reported to Congress for 1974, only $65 million was derived from federal appropriations and $23 million from other nonpower proceeds.

After more than fifteen years of independent bonding, some changes in authority behavior are discernible. TVA became the biggest electricity generating system in the nation, but public attention to it diminished; it entered a new and more closed corporate stage of organizational life. In the trade-offs leading to passage of the legislation giving TVA bonding power, the authority agreed to a limitation on its service area that the private utilities had sought for a long time. This settlement, together with mounting TVA rates, took most of the remaining heat out of public-private power competition in the region. In the late 1960s and early 1970s, TVA rates rose nearly twice as fast as those of the U.S. power industry at large, although its residential electricity rates were still 40 percent below the national average, and utility rates in the Tennessee Valley remain among the lowest in the nation.[35] In this period, of course, TVA's costs have increased dramatically: interest rates have nearly doubled since it sold its first bond; the cost of coal fuel for steam plants (the era of expanding cheap water power in the valley is over) has risen substantially; and payments to local governments in lieu of taxes have doubled (5 percent of the proceeds from nonfederal power sales is now transferred to local governments).

The Edison Electric Institute and other utility representatives no longer lobby annually to brake TVA expansion. Three huge TVA coal-burning plants have been built with capital raised on the private market, and three nuclear plants are underway, with little objection from the industry. Also with revenue-bond capital, TVA has sponsored two joint ventures with private industry to develop a fast breeder atomic energy demonstration plant. As one business commentator phrased the shift, "TVA has mellowed over the decades and so have its traditional enemies." Private power executives no longer feel threatened by TVA's role as a yardstick to measure their own rates.

Since TVA turned to the bond market, its concern for financial results has increased. For example, it recently resisted the construction of a small bridge requested by a local community and by the House Appropriations Committee because of low traffic forecasts. It sets rates to produce a profit margin (retained earnings) of 10 percent, higher than that of private utilities. TVA may have let its political relationships get too rusty for its own good: One supporter of the agency acknowledged that "through the years since the time that TVA began supplemental financing in the money markets, the TVA board and the Congress may have both eased up on the fine relations and communications they had enjoyed."[36] Increasingly, TVA has encountered opposition to its projects from community groups and environmental associations and construction delays generated by requirements of the Environmental Protection Act and related litigation. (Of course, the whole power industry is experiencing such problems.) Under congressional prodding, TVA is responding to environmental problems. In 1972, it established an environmental research and development program. If the ultimate enthusiasm and results of this effort come close to TVA's chemical fertilizer development programs of earlier days, its contribution can be enormous. But at the same time the authority proposes to purchase huge coal-mining operations to supply its own fuel and has bought an interest in a uranium exploration venture. Groups who oppose strip mining by TVA suppliers are frustrated to find the authority less vulnerable to criticisms channeled through Congress since Congress cannot delay financing of major projects as long as TVA's bonds are salable. Similarly, presidential moves, such as the Nixon administration's impoundment of funds, have little impact on TVA. What began as a multipurpose regional development agency has in effect become a huge power generating system to which other functions are subordinate.

Independent financing is attractive to proponents of rapid construction or development. Although the Bonneville Power Administration is now and will remain an agency within the Department of the Interior, for example, it has successfully sought revenue bonding power from Congress to carry out its part in the Pacific Northwest power plan. In 1978, it begins selling its own revenue bonds through the U.S. Treasury. In the power business, as in highway construction, authorities that use independent revenue-bond financing build more and faster than government agencies that are dependent upon voter approval and legislative appropriations. The legislative process almost inevitably involves delays during which trade-offs, compromises, and bargains may be struck. When the process is too conflict-ridden, delay becomes stalemate, and the parties involved resort to new arrangements (like bond financing) to break out of it. The long-term costs of cutting issues off from political debate need consideration, however, particularly losses in the flexibility and adaptability of public policy.

The Lower Colorado River Authority   The Lower Colorado River Authority (LCRA) is a state authority modeled on TVA. Its origins reflect the events of the depression years, the special role of New Deal encouragement, and the competitive relationships between private and public enterprise that once characterized the power field. Its financing history is illustrative of disparate successful, growing state enterprises.

The Lower Colorado River basin that the LCRA manages is wholly within Texas (and has no connection to the other and mightier Colorado River that rises on the western slopes of the Rockies in Colorado and runs south through four states to the Gulf of California). LCRA's district includes ten counties, but it sells power in forty-one counties in central Texas, including the area around the capital, Austin. During the early decades of the twentieth century, intermittent floods and droughts beleaguered this cattle-raising and subsistence farming region. Controlling the flow of the Lower Colorado River was a prerequisite to further development of the region. During the 1920s, industrial and political interests in the basin combined to explore the possibilities for constructing dams that would control floods and provide a source for commerical power.

Water rights were the keys to power. One local firm accumulated permits that gave it legal control of more downstream water than the river actually produced, much to the alarm of the upstream ("Upper Colorado") interests in sparsely settled West Texas, which would be left with no water rights if the company used its permits to the fullest. At the urging of Lower Colorado business boosters, the huge Insull empire of utility holding companies negotiated to purchase the water rights and to build dams. From 1927 through 1932, apparent corporate controllers of the project, all of them connected with the Insull holding company, passed the project around.[37] In April 1932, when Insull's nationwide financial empire collapsed, work stopped on the first Lower Colorado dam. Some 100,000 holders of Insull stock lost $4 billion, and Martin J. Insull became an international fugitive from justice. These events accelerated the development of public enterprise in the power field and served to tighten controls over investor-owned utilities and over the methods by which holding companies permitted minority stockholders to control the utilities.

In the Lower Colorado region, a local lawyer, the late Alvin J. Wirtz, who had participated in the negotiations leading up to Insull involvement in the dam project, was appointed receiver of the subsidiary that had ended up with the water rights and the partly built dam. He sought out a utility financier to purchase those assets and to organize a new company, which in time applied for a federal loan. The depression had nearly wiped out most private sources of capital, and when both the Reconstruction Finance Corporation (RFC) and the Public Works Administration (PWA) refused a loan to the new company, the stage was set for public enterprise takeover. The determined lawyer, Wirtz, drafted state legislation to establish a public corporation to finish the job: the Lower Colorado River Authority.

For three sessions, the passage of this act was held up in the Texas legislature by opposition from the West Texas portion of the upper river basin, which was being left out; from the private power industry, including Chicago groups formerly associated with Insull and the local utilities in the Austin area; and from those who objected to the considerable profits that the takeover was going to provide for the middleman financier who now controlled the assets. Ultimately, amended to protect the water rights of West Texas, the bill succeeded with vigorous support from local business interests.

The other essential step in completing the dams was arranging loans from Washington for a public project that had been denied for the private project. This region of Texas was then represented in Washington by Congressman J. P. Buchanan, chairman of the House Appropriations Committee, and Congressman J. Mansfield, chairman of the powerful Rivers and Harbors Committee. The RFC head, Jesse Jones, and the PWA's chief counsel, Henry Hunt, bolstered Texas interests on the executive side. Congressman Buchanan went over the head of Secretary of the Interior Harold L. Ickes to President Roosevelt. In 1934, the federal government authorized a loan of $4.5 million for the completion of the renamed Buchanan Dam, and LCRA was launched on its way to what is now a $100 million-a-year power business.

In the early years, LCRA management held to policies similar to those of TVA: engaging in aggressive promotion for extension of electricity, seeking to establish a low-rate, high-volume business, and giving preferences to nonprofit buyers. After proving that it could maintain rates some 30 to 50 percent lower than those charged by the competing power and light companies within the region, LCRA bought them out. It also successfully encouraged the creation of the municipally owned distribution systems to which LCRA now wholesales power, as well as rural electric cooperatives.

Like TVA (and unlike the New York State Power Authority), LCRA put ceilings on resale rates in its contracts (allowing a 6 percent return on a municipal distributor's investment). In 1943, the Texas legislature prohibited limits on retail rates, and since that time, the municipal governments of the region have had an expanding source of nontax revenues from the profitable retailing of LCRA's power. Texas law, unlike constitutions of New York and many other states, encourages municipalities to issue revenue bonds directly rather than obtaining financing through corporate public authorities; thus the retailing units are dependent municipal enterprises, and local taxpayers, rather than authority reserve funds, get the benefits of excess revenues from retail sales.

During the war years, LCRA began selling surplus power to its earlier competitors—the investor-owned utilities—particularly to compensate for shortages. Today, relations between the two sectors are cooperative, and neighboring utilities try to purchase as much LCRA power as they can.

Over its forty-year life, LCRA has constructed or acquired six major dams and hydroelectric power plants on the mainstream of the river.[38] Two steam-generating plants also are in operation, and another is under construction. In 1960, LCRA purchased the irrigation facilities of a private company to expand its water supply operations, which are primarily agricultural and industrial. In 1974, confronted by rising prices and dwindling supplies of natural gas, it began work on a joint project with the city of Austin to construct new coal-generated power plants.

This corporate growth was accomplished with contributions from governments totaling some $33 million (including $8 million from the Public Works Administration, $23 million worth of direct construction by the Bureau of Reclamation, and a contribution from the state of Texas), with retained earnings from the authority's operations of some $75 million, and with capital raised by issuance of revenue bonds totaling $177 million through 1975.

The revenue bond component included a 1954 refunding issue of $27 million, which has been paid off. Subsequent bond issues raised $18 million in 1962, $12 million in 1965, $25 million in 1967, $60 million in 1971, $35 million in 1974, and $60 million in 1976. The authority was operating at a profit, after depreciation and interest payments, within three years of its initial power sales in 1938. Without imposing a single across-the-board rate increase, it had accumulated assets of $99 million book value and depreciation reserves of $41 million by 1970.

LCRA submits a yearly report of its financial results, by activity (it even reports sales by customer account), to its bank trustees (Chase Manhattan in New York and American National in Austin). The indenture terms of LCRA bonds are standard; they include regular transfers to the bank trustees of payments to bondholders and maintenance of debt service reserves covering at least twelve months in advance due (with a provision for excess revenues to be used for early retirement of bonds or transferred to special improvement reserve funds). The authority can issue additional bonds at will (as long as it is caught up with all payments on outstanding bonds) if it receives favorable engineering and counsel's opinions and if its average annual net revenues equal one and a half times (1.5 coverage) the amount needed for annual debt service. The authority further covenants to charge rates that will meet these obligations, to carry specified types of insurance, and to hire engineering consultants for independent review every three years.

For the $60 million LCRA bond issue sold in 1971, the financial adviser was the New York City firm of Wainwright & Ramsey, which wrote the prospectus and arranged for competitive bids from both New York and regional dealers. Bond counsel was a New York City law firm that specializes in public power issues and has advised the authority for decades. For its 1974 bond issues, LCRA, like a number of other authorities in recent years, shifted its business from New York–based to regional firms (an Austin bank and a Dallas law firm). John E. Babcock, an LCRA executive, explained: "For the first time we have used Texas-based financial advisers and bond counsel [as] the first step toward getting out from under the restrictive provisions of the 'priority bonds' trust indenture to allow more flexibility in future financing to meet construction needs." The bond issue was tailored to specific investor preferences, including high tax-exempt interest rates (9 percent) on bonds in the series with early maturity date (1979–1988) that were sold at a premium, allowing tax advantages (in effect, a loss to offset against capital gains). (In other words, the bondholder may receive more of his income from the bond's tax-exempt interest payments and may deduct a capital loss when he sells the bond on the secondary market or redeems it.) A New York–based syndicate of investment bankers underwrote the 1974 LCRA bonds.

Because of rapidly rising costs, scarce resources, and needs for huge capital investment, LCRA, like the power business elsewhere, is now at a financial crossroad. In 1974, a management consulting firm (with a majority of investor-owned utility clients) prepared a financial projection of investment needs for LCRA. Future new financings will be much larger than those of the past. Outside consultants forecast capital requirements of over $780 million (over seven times the LCRA debt outstanding) over the next decade to meet the energy needs of the growing region. Debt service requirements will skyrocket. In 1974, with some internal trauma and external turmoil, the authority imposed the first across-the-board rate increase in its history and was battling with its natural gas suppliers in the courts and with the state's regulatory commission over fuel costs and quotas. The authority has traditionally kept its rates between one-half and two-thirds of those of private utilities, but as LCRA fulfills more of the new investment needs in the area, this differential will have to decline. In general, the price, policy, and perspective differences between private and public power have narrowed. Despite its adherence to TVA's brand of power policy, LCRA views itself as a business enterprise. Like Port Authority management, LCRA management considers reliance on financial results to be its crucial incentive. "We have to be businesslike to support ourselves" said its long-time manager, W. Sim Gideon. The authority is reluctant to be burdened with unprofitable river basin functions. Contrary to academic recommendations, it does not want its jurisdiction expanded to include the Upper Colorado in order to integrate basin management; that area of sparsely settled West Texas would be considerably more costly to serve. For years LCRA avoided undertaking pollution control tasks and supported only modest expansion of its marginal water supply business.[39]

At the same time, LCRA has shown more adaptability than many other public authorities. Its management has shifted with shifting needs. In 1973, it gracefully and strategically agreed to license and inspect septic tanks, a task that management would have preferred to avoid. LCRA dams and related facilities had provided an attractive environment for expensive home development on the outskirts of Austin. This growth now poses serious pollution problems and puts recreational pressures on LCRA's vast acreage of water surface and waterfront land. LCRA management decided that the costs in money and goodwill of undertaking the regulation of sewage disposal from the new developments were a lesser evil than allowing an outside agency to assume this responsibility and perhaps to develop a more stringent pollution control program for the homes and for LCRA plants. As a result, LCRA is now at once the major pollution control authority for its basin and an industrial polluter who lobbies with the federal Environmental Protection Agency and the Army Corps of Engineers for a relaxation of proposed regulations of thermal pollution and disposal of fill material. Authority management sees no particular anomaly in this dual position. Also in 1973, the Texas legislature approved a bill sponsored by a state senator, who soon became LCRA's new manager. The bill allows the authority to charge for the use of recreation facilities. LCRA is now involved in the park and marina business, in addition to the power business and pollution control regulation.

Conclusion

Public authorities have played an important part in creating the infrastructure for our particular patterns of economic development and land use. The relationships between traditional authority financing, managerial independence, and preferred policies for development begin to emerge. The revenue bond as a source of low-cost capital and partnerships with private sector business give authorities countervailing power in their dealings with government. They also establish in those authorities clear preferences for activities with predictable revenue growth. Successful authorities in power, port, and vehicular facilities businesses are diversifying into activities of their own choosing and can, in a variety of ways, escape other activities urged by parent governments. "Financial independence" means, in effect, dependence on the bond market. It is more a management preference and strategy than a legal or economic necessity.

5 Authorities Backed by the Taxpayers

Most highway, port, bridge, tunnel, and power authorities rely largely on income derived from the sales of goods or services to private consumers or to a mix of private and governmental customers, including passengers, motorists, corporate tenants of warehouses, office buildings, and terminals, and consumers of water and power. Those authorities benefit from tax exemptions, but their price structures are the primary sources of revenue used to cover expenses and to secure their debts. Claims of self-support notwithstanding, most other government-owned corporations draw a major portion of their resources or credit from tax revenues. Some were created exclusively to provide services for other government agencies. Many of the relatively recent ones generally rely on government leases, contracts, loans, grants, mortgage cost subsidies, or credit backing.

Lawyers and financial advisers have worked out complex methods of adapting public projects so that they can spin off private returns that are adequate for selling and paying interest on revenue bonds. As a result, government-backed corporate authorities have proliferated in distinct batches that reflect combinations of governmental priorities and bond market preferences. One large group grew in response to post–World War II pressures for municipal construction to make up for depression and wartime backlogs and to accommodate the rapid population growth and urbanization of the 1950s. Statutory corporations could raise capital for new schools, sewers, reservoirs, and so forth more expeditiously than could local governments that were themselves burdened with debt regulations, referenda requirements, and burgeoning debt totals that lowered their credit ratings. Between 1947 and 1957, as a result, the number of public authorities quadrupled nationwide.

During the late 1950s and 1960s, another group of public authorities grew in response to problems arising from metropolitan growth. They provided a mechanism by which programs could operate on a regional basis, unconstrained by obsolete municipal and county boundaries. Metropolitan special authorities proliferated in disparate sizes and shapes and performed scores of services.

Later during the 1960s, authorities were created to issue industrial development bonds (IDBs), which state and local governments use to raise funds for private firms, passing savings of tax-exempt borrowing on to the private sector in order to attract plants and jobs. In the early 1970s, financial advisers developed an adaptation of IDBs to fit the loopholes of new tax law; from 1971 to 1975, the biggest segment of municipal bond market sales was publicly issued bonds to pay for pollution control equipment for private firms faced with new federal and state environmental protection standards. These trends are reflected in the bond sales shown in table 3.2, including the sudden appearance of pollution control activities by authorities, the dramatic drop in industrial funding after the 1968 tax reform, and its gradual recovery through loopholes.

Another trend in recent years is proliferation of state finance authorities that extend mortgage loans for private and semipublic construction projects. Many of these authorities issue bonds that are technically revenue bonds but carry informal government guarantees with ambiguous legal status. Elected officials have turned to these devices—including so-called moral obligation borrowing—for several reasons: they feel mounting pressures on state finance; they are faced with taxpayer revolts that defeat proposals for straightforward government borrowing; they are reluctant to be blamed for unbalanced budgets; and the public has proved tolerant of "backdoor financing." Finance authorities fund dormitories, schools, sports stadiums, hospitals, nursing homes, moderate-cost housing, convention centers, and solid-waste recycling plants. (The sudden surge in this form of housing and hospital finance is evident in table 3.2.) The following cases will illustrate each of these groups of public authorities that are supported by government resources.

Pennsylvania Municipal Corporations

Pennsylvania pioneered in the development of the municipal corporations to build local facilities that proliferated after World War II. In the nineteenth century, Pennsylvania's financial crises and defaults on debt payments had resulted in constitutional revisions restricting municipal borrowing to 7 percent of assessed valuation and putting a ceiling on state debt. By the 1930s, these restrictions were proving to be a straitjacket, particularly in areas where assessed property values were falling. The Pennsylvania legislature therefore passed the Municipal Authorities Act of 1935, which exempted government-owned corporations from municipal debt restrictions. Shortly after passage of this act, over fifty local corporations were established. These early Pennsylvania municipal corporations financed water and sewer system development over the following decade. In 1945, the legislature amended the municipal authorities law to provide the most permissive authorization in the nation for local establishment of public corporations. By 1958, Pennsylvania had twelve hundred municipal authorities, one for every four regular local governments in the state. By 1973, the total was 1,872, financing construction of such facilities as airports, sewer systems, and schools. (See table 5.1.) They had raised a total of $5.745 billion from the bond market. The Federal Reserve Bank of Philadelphia described them as "Pennsylvania's Billion Dollar Babies," even in 1958: "They are not quite governments and they are not private businesses. Paradoxically, they are born of government, yet not directly controlled by the electorate. Nourished by business methods, they are non-profit, have no stockholders and are immune from anti-trust laws. They build public projects using private money. They operate public utilities yet they are not regulated by public utility commissions."[1]

Most of these 1,872 municipal corporations are "lease-back" authorities. They do not operate public services; they simply issue revenue bonds and invest the proceeds in the construction of projects that are desired and designed by the sponsoring governments. They then lease the completed facilities to a single government agency for the life of the bonds. After the bonds are paid off, the title to the facilities is transferred to the government or school district that sponsored the project. During the debt service period, the authority receives its revenues in the form of rental payments from the sponsoring government, which are scaled to cover the interest payments and amor-

Table 5.1
Pennsylvania Municipal Corporations,
May 1973

Type	Number
Airport	25
Parking	89
School	663
Sewer	501
Water	217
Recreation	53
Solid waste	30
Health	25
Others	41
Multipurpose	228
Total	1,872

Source: *Directory of Municipal Authorities in Pennsylvania*, Department of Community Affairs, 1972, and Special Circular 196, Pennsylvania State University, College of Agriculture Extension Service, 1973.

tization of the bonds issued by the authority. The agency usually receives construction bids before the authority issues its bonds so that the authority can precisely tailor rents from government to cover project borrowing costs. The lease-back authority's bondholders have no direct interest in the quality of the project; they are concerned with the security of the rentals paid by the local government.[2]

Lease-back authorities are thus financing devices created for specific government users. They reflect the credit rating of the government that will be paying the rent—out of its own tax revenues plus state and/or federal aid. Sometimes specific tax sources are earmarked for this purpose (for example, hotel or transportation taxes), but usually the rental is simply a general contract obligation of the leasing government.

In their early years, lease-backs significantly increased the costs of local government. The interest rate differential between these authority bonds and comparable bonds that might be backed by the full faith and credit of the local governments that were leasing the facilities ranged from 1.5 to 2.5 percent. Today, as a result of testing and investor familiarity, the interest cost differential for most has shrunk to a negligible margin, but some lease-back authorities, particularly those for commercial ventures such as local parking lots, must still pay substantial added costs.

The most common type of lease-back authority in Pennsylvania is the school building authority. These authorities are chartered by elected school boards but have separate corporate status and are run by their own appointed boards of directors. State education officials closely supervise the design, financing, and construction of school buildings by the school building authorities. School building specifications and financial arrangements are subject to state approval. Rental payments to the building authority come from both school district taxes and state education grants. State legislation provides for a school building authority to receive direct state aid if the school district fails to make the rental payments called for by the lease. Hence the risk to the authority's bondholder is negligible.

School districts with weak tax bases (and therefore no, or low, credit rating) can use the Pennsylvania School Building Authority instead of a locally chartered one. The state authority charges a fee for financing and overseeing construction and sets rentals at 120 percent coverage of debt service. It offers opportunities for economies and concentrated expertise, but it remains a distinct second choice of both local politicians and bond market promoters.[3] Local underwriters and investors prefer to create and fund local authorities, whose boards they can monitor more directly. (In fact, they often sit on those boards.) Local politicians have a more direct influence on construction patronage allocated by local building authorities. Hence school districts refrain from using the state School Building Authority unless they simply cannot afford to establish their own.

Another type of municipal corporation relying heavily on lease-back techniques is the sewer authority. (In 1966, of 353 sewer authorities in Pennsylvania, 237 were lease-back authorities.) The expansion of federal aid for sewer construction and pollution control has encouraged many localities to establish sewer authorities of both operating and lease-back types. Either the renting jurisdiction or the authority itself is eligible for federal grants, an important source of revenues for paying off the bonds.

Lease-back authorities are used mainly for activities that are unlikely to generate profits from user charges. Hence water supply authorities rely less on leases with governments than school building and sewer authorities. As of 1966, of 838 water supply utilities in Pennsylvania, 354 were private, 212 were municipal departments, and 272 were public corporate authorities, of which 90 were lease-backs.[4] Most parking authorities operate their own facilities, but unlike other operating authorities, they do not have monopoly rights, and in many cases the sponsoring downtown commercial groups prefer the risk to be absorbed by the municipality—through lease-back—rather than through the authority and its investors.

Bond Market Promotion   This system of public finance in Pennsylvania has provided enormous benefits to segments of private business. Pennsylvania has more legal firms with municipal bond business and more underwriters' *local* offices than does any other state.[5] The state has numerous municipal authority offerings that are too small for formal credit ratings and for competitive bidding by New York–led syndicates. The local municipal bond business has grown accordingly and has itself influenced the growth of public authorities. Local and regional attorneys, banks, and underwriters encourage local officials to create authorities; they provide the legal and technical expertise to organize the corporations and arrange the financing; and they cooperate with the Pennsylvania Authorities Association to represent authority interests in legislative and public forums. In 1968, when the Pennsylvania Economy League and a state constitutional reform committee recommended that authority lease-back financing be limited, a defense of the technique was most cogently argued by one of Pennsylvania's leading municipal bond underwriting firms, Butcher & Singer (formerly Butcher & Sherrerd).

By its own count, as of January 1973, Butcher & Singer had been the sole underwriter or syndicate manager for 760 municipal authority financings totaling $1.4 billion. Through 1976, the firm had participated in 1,493 municipal authority bond issues in Pennsylvania, totaling $5.6 billion, for the types of projects listed in table 5.2.

Butcher & Singer becomes involved in the earliest phases of developing municipal corporations and guides bonds through ultimate marketing. Local banks and attorneys also can perform these services. In addition to acting as trustees, local banks purchase municipal authority bonds directly as investments. Banks use several techniques to circumvent the prohibition in federal banking law against their dealing in revenue bonds. Technically, for example, Girard Bank of Philadelphia cannot bid on a whole issue of revenue bonds for immediate resale (underwriting). As is common practice, however, the bank did purchase the North Penn Water Authority's entire $3.9 million bond issue (in the form of one large denomination bond) for its own accounts. The bank also was trustee for the authority. The authority agreed to reissue the bond in $5,000 denominations at any later time as requested by the bank, which could then sell the smaller bonds on the secondary market.

In another example, the chairman of the Brandywine Area School Author-

Table 5.2
Summary of Pennsylvania Authority Financing by Butcher & Singer (as of December 31, 1976)

	Number	Amount (dollars)
As Investment Banker		
School	752	1,418,928,000
Community college	7	53,980,000
Sewer	254	482,463,000
Water	161	295,449,000
Parking	48	110,875,000
Hospital	38	713,005,000
Other public facilities	69	1,055,250,000
As Financial Adviser	164	1,507,314,000
Total	1,493	5,637,264,000

ity (a regional lease-back building corporation) is a trust officer of the Girard Bank, and the authority's business is conducted largely out of his desk at the bank. The Girard Bank was instrumental in arranging refunding for the bonds of several smaller school building authorities in order to facilitate the merger that produced the regional Brandywine Corporation.

Recent expansion in lease-back authorities in Pennsylvania has occurred for hospital construction. During the 1970s, cutbacks in federal grants and in private philanthropy for hospitals have created vacuums that the bond market financiers are trying to fill. A concomitant increase in third-party payments (through Medicare, Medicaid, and other health insurance) has provided a relatively stable base for estimating hospital revenues. These payments now indirectly back tax-exempt bonds issued by authorities for construction or mortgage lending. Nationwide tax-exempt financing for hospitals and medical care facilities totaled $2.7 billion in 1976, over 400 percent greater than it was in 1973. All but five states had authorized state or local authorities to assist in this type of financing.

Within one year of the 1971 amendment to Pennsylvania's Municipal Authorities Act that authorized county hospital authorities, seventeen of them were created. Butcher & Singer sponsored public seminars to explain and promote hospital authority financings among investors and public officials. By spring 1973, such authorities had raised nearly $500 million for construction of facilities to be leased to private and public hospitals in the state. In the next two years, the volume of that financing doubled. (The patient cost from interest and depreciation for these financings is estimated at $20 per day.)

Bondholder protections in these lease-back deals are substantial. The directors on the boards of the hospital authorities are, for the most part, bankers and local businessmen. The bond indentures pledge that gross receipts to the authority from the hospital leases will be allocated to debt service. The hospital must pay its costs and cover lease rentals by 120 percent, putting the annual 20 percent excess in reserve, according to indenture requirements. If hospital receipts fall below this level, the bank, acting as bond trustee for the authority, may send in independent consultants to reorganize hospital management or to raise its rates. When the financing is being planned, national accounting firms prepare feasibility reports based on market data. Because of these safeguards, relatively high interest rates, and the participation of local firms and banks, many hospital authority issues have been marketed successfully with only a triple B rating from Standard & Poor's and

no rating at all from Moody's. This success reflects the localization of municipal authority finance in Pennsylvania, where direct knowledge of the corporation can substitute for formal ratings.

These hospital authorities provide only financing; they do not operate any
facilities. The authorities are administered mainly by the trustee banks.
An example is the Lycoming County Authority, created in 1972 to issue
$9,945,000 in hospital-lease revenue bonds. Its board consists of local busi-
nessmen and professionals appointed by the county commissioners, with the
finances actually administered by the Williamsport National Bank. The
authority's architects and one of its attorneys are local; its bond attorneys are
a Pittsburgh firm. Butcher & Singer managed the underwriting, with some
New York brokers joining the syndicate. A large New York–based firm, which
serves as management consultants, conducted the financial feasibility study of
the receiving hospital.

The single deal for which this authority was created looks confusingly
complicated to laymen's eyes, including those of the elected county commissioners who voted to create the authority. Tax-exempt bonds were issued to
finance construction for Divine Providence Hospital, a private, nonprofit corporation in Williamsport. (Third-party payments comprise over 95 percent of
that hospital's cash collections for patient care.) Part of the sum borrowed by
the authority via the bonds will pay interest on the loan itself for the early
years and will pay all commissions and fees for financing. The rest goes to the
hospital's new construction costs.

A religious order rented land to the Divine Providence Hospital Corporation; the hospital corporation subleased the land to the authority; the land
plus construction on it is further subleased by the authority to the county
(at rentals designed to amortize the bonds), which subleased the project back
to the hospital for operation. (Thus the chain of leases runs: religious order to
hospital to authority to county to hospital.) The authority issued the bonds;
the county separately covenanted to provide rental payments to the authority
out of taxes, independent of its rental receipts from the hospital. This sort of
paper circle is a lawyer's and banker's delight. In this case, it provides tax-
exempt financing, without risk to bondholders, to a private institution that
ordinarily would not enjoy it. Municipal hospitals, which could issue tax-
exempt securities directly, often use similar arrangements in order to buffer
the bondholders from risk and to satisfy financial advisers and local officials.
In the Lycoming example, the legal source of the tax exemption is the
county, but although the county has pledged tax revenues to the deal, the

authority bonds are not considered legal obligations of the county, nor do they show up in county debt.

One of the mysteries that has long baffled the handful of commentators who are interested is why revenue bonding by municipal corporations has become so widespread in Pennsylvania. The stock answer refers to harsh debt limits. The state constitution has always permitted exemption from the debt limits, however, for "self-liquidating" revenue bonds issued by regular local governments. Counties and municipalities are now legally empowered to use "municipal nondebt revenue bonds" to finance revenue-producing enterprises. But for several reasons, this form of financing has never become popular.

The apparent attractiveness of government-owned corporations and the wallflower status of town, county, and school district bonds in Pennsylvania have several root causes. Authority revenue bonds were tested first in the courts; once the appropriate legal fictions became familiar, available legal advice favored them, and careful bill and lease drafting nurtured them. The most important legal fiction—that lease-back financing is not local government borrowing but is local government renting—was established in the 1930s.[6] The courts hold that the local government is merely renting a school building or a town hall (from a corporation wholly owned by it), not borrowing money through a dummy corporation. The Pennsylvania courts never actually eliminated the alternative of using municipal "nondebt" revenue bonds, but most municipalities have found the separation between taxes and borrowing (and therefore exemption of the borrowing from debt limits) easier to justify when the "special funds" borrowed are protected by a corporate shell.

In 1954, the courts confirmed the exemption of authority lease-back financing from the constitutional requirements for voter approval.[7] This exemption has allowed local officials to complete local projects and to distribute local contracts without special elections, without taxpayer objections, and without apparent local debt increments. The financial burden of lease-back financing does, in fact, fall on the taxpayer, but very few taxpayers see through the legal fictions and financial complexities that surround lease-back arrangements. Moreover, Pennsylvania students of public administration have portrayed the system as enhancing local control of public services and providing an alternative to state and federal control. One wrote, "In no other field of local government has the possibility of home rule and local administration been so successful as in the operation of waterworks as a municipal enterprise."[8] As that was written, many municipalities were selling their waterworks to specially created corporations and leasing them back.

The advantages that the authority device provides to bond market participants are sufficient to sustain it even in the absence of debt limitations. Indenture provisions (such as trustee takeover in case of default or falling revenues) that are commonplace in authority finance are not permitted by public law relating to regular government bonds.[9] Compared to municipal departments, the incorporated authority allows for greater reliance on outside attorneys and consultants, higher yields and marketability for bonds, greater predictability of revenues that are ensured by rental contracts, and boards composed of businessmen (often investors themselves) rather than elected officials susceptible to turnover. Longer maturities and discount sales, which are not permissible under state law for most government bonds, are allowed for authority revenue bonds. According to several investment bankers, specific income figures from an authority's operations inspire more confidence among investors than do community characteristics such as property values, which are used to assess general obligation bonds.

Constitutional Reform   Over several decades, state review commissions in Pennsylvania have recommended that the securities of public authorities directly or indirectly backed by the general revenues of a municipality should no longer enjoy special exemption from debt regulation. The Committee for Economic Development, the U.S. Advisory Commission on Intergovernmental Relations, the Pennsylvania Economy League, and the 1968 Pennsylvania Commission on Constitutional Review also have criticized lease-back authorities. According to former governor Raymond P. Shafer, "The present state constitution forces the state and municipalities to set up authorities in order to borrow additional money . . . these authorities pay higher interest than would be the case if the borrowing was done on the credit of the Commonwealth or the local government . . . this consideration is forcing the state government and municipalities to spend up to $100 million a year in unnecessary interest charges."[10] In 1967, Governor Shafer called for the elimination of the municipal corporation's advantages over local government and submitted legislation designed to eliminate the state building authorities, concentrating state building responsibility in a cabinet-level department that could serve local governments.

The Pennsylvania Bar Association, the Municipal Authorities Association, and Pennsylvania's banks and underwriters countered with statements stressing the successful history of present systems and claiming superior efficiency of authority management. As lease-back authorities are little more than financing devices, however, and do incur higher financing costs than do governmental alternatives, efficiency in the technical sense is not in fact one of their characteristics. In effect, it is the extent to which they expedite construction and speed up public investment that appeals to their supporters.

One outcome of this debate was a constitutional amendment, approved by Pennsylvania voters in 1968, giving the state legislature broad power to reform local government debt regulation. The legislature did not take action by statute until 1972, when enormous flood damages in the state made liberalization of public finance laws urgent to facilitate economic recovery.[11] Pennsylvania now has the most flexible legal framework in the nation for local enterprise borrowing. Although this legislation greatly facilitates direct municipal borrowing, contrary to expectations it has not weakened the authority system and may, in fact, be strengthening it by providing broader opportunities for negotiated bond sales.

The legislation makes local government debt ceilings a percentage of total municipal revenues (rather than of property tax base only). And even this limitation does not apply to borrowing that is approved by the electorate or borrowing for any project that is self-supporting from its own revenues. The new law also gives other advantages typical of authority financing to local governments themselves. It permits municipalities to establish covenanted sinking funds and more flexible options for terms and forms of bonds and interest paid. The legislation extends maturity to forty years for all types of bonds and permits level annual debt service.

Thus encouraging money raising by local governments, the new legislation also limits the advantages of authorities. Pennsylvania now treats any borrowing by a structurally independent corporate authority that is in fact paid for or secured by municipal taxes via rents, subsidy contracts, or contingent guarantees not as authority debt but as municipal debt.[12] This legislation represents one of the first statutory attempts to sort fact from fiction in the claims of public enterprise to be self-supporting. Moreover, it departs from the special fund doctrine that most state courts have relied upon to exempt public authorities from laws that apply to governments. Authority funds are no longer special funds if they are derived from municipal payments.

The Pennsylvania Department of Community Affairs has broad review powers over borrowing by both local governments and authorities that are supported by rent payments from governments. This provision gives state government a degree of control over authority borrowing previously available only to bond market participants. The law nevertheless protects the interests of outside consultants. The department requires engineering reports, revenue forecasts, and bond counsel approval when it reviews revenue bond offerings for self-supporting municipal projects.

Revenue bonds issued by municipal corporations that obtain no rental agreements or guarantees from tax collecting governments still remain outside this review system. Operating authorities, particularly with regional scope, are expected to continue to proliferate, unfettered and largely unsupervised. More surprising is the fact that lease-back authorities are still thriving as well, accounting for over one-third of all local debt approved by the state's department in 1975.

Moral Obligation Authorities

Early in his first term, discouraged by the defeat at the polls of major bond proposals, New York's Governor Nelson A. Rockefeller was looking for a way to involve private investment in public housing and other state construction programs to fulfill what he perceived as mounting public needs. A series of discussions between bond attorney John N. Mitchell and state housing commissioner James W. Gaynor resulted in the specific provisions that were to authorize the first "moral obligation" bond and to establish the New York State Housing Finance Agency (HFA). Previously, bond rating agencies had refused to assign ratings to nonguaranteed securities for housing construction. Since the 1930s, the bonds of local housing authorities conforming to federal housing acts have been federally guaranteed. HFA offered an indirect and ambiguous state guarantee, subject to legislative appropriations. Bonds guaranteed in this way subsequently became known as moral obligation bonds. The arrangement worked in the marketplace, attracting A ratings and a steady supply of investors. The Rockefeller administration therefore went on to apply the technique to a wide variety of other authority construction programs.[13] Some thirty other states have since adopted variations of it.

The meaning of "moral obligation" is established by the following language in the revenue bond indentures of state corporations and the underlying state statutes:

To assure the continued operation and solvency of the agency for the carrying out of the public purposes of this article, provision is made . . . for the accumulation in the equity reserve fund of an amount equal to the maximum amount of principal and interest maturing and becoming due in any succeeding calendar year on all equity bonds of the agency then outstanding. *In order further to assure such maintenance of the equity reserve fund, there shall be annually apportioned and paid to the agency for deposit in the equity reserve fund such sum, if any, as shall be certified by the chairman of the agency to the governor and director of the budget as necessary to restore the equity reserve fund to an amount equal to the maximum amount of principal and interest maturing and becoming due in any succeeding calendar year on the equity bonds of the agency then outstanding.* The chairman of the agency shall annually, on or before December first, make and deliver to the governor and director of the budget his certificate stating the amount, if any, required to restore the equity reserve fund to the amount aforesaid and the amount so stated, if any, shall be apportioned and paid to the agency during the then current state fiscal year.[14]

In other words, if authority revenues fall to the point where specified reserve funds do not cover debt service for a year in advance, the governor shall transfer general state funds to the authority to bring reserves up to the specified level.

If this constitutes an obligation, it is moral, rather than legal, because, as the HFA bond prospectuses indicate,

Under the Constitution of the State of New York, all monies apportioned and paid to the Agency pursuant to the above quoted provision of the New York State Housing Finance Agency Act, prior to the payment thereof, are subject to appropriation by the State Legislature for such purpose. Accordingly, such provision of the New York State Housing Finance Agency Act does not constitute a legally enforceable obligation upon the part of the State of New York nor create a debt on behalf of the State of New York enforceable against the State under Section 16 of Article VIII of the State Constitution.[15]

The prospectuses further assert that "the Bonds of the Agency are not a debt of the State and the State is not liable on such bonds." These caveats are necessary because the constitution of New York State requires voter approval for state borrowing, and no special elections are held to approve sale of moral obligation bonds. In fact the voters have rejected state bond proposals for projects that subsequently have been financed by moral obligation bonds. During the 1960s, this type of bond comprised the most rapidly growing volume of outstanding debt issued by public benefit corporations in New York State.

The Precedents   Like most other aspects of American public authorities, moral obligation bonds have historical roots. Precedents gave John Mitchell reason to believe that government might be relied upon to honor something less binding than an actual legal commitment.

The federal government had regularly bailed out its wholly owned corporations. A number of federal government corporations are authorized to borrow money on their own, without pledging the credit of the United States, but the financial community takes it for granted that the government will pay investors in case of default. Over the years, the U.S. Treasury has purchased obligations of government corporations that could not be paid off out of corporate revenues, including bonds previously purchased by RFC. (As a result, RFC's record seems better than it actually is.) The technically unguaranteed obligations of federal government corporations are neither included under the public debt ceilings nor subject to fiscal year limitations, but in fact, the federal government has always taken responsibility for debts of its instrumentalities.

There were also precedents for governments to support state and local corporate revenue bonds. Several types of local housing authority bonds are in effect secured by promised federal funds. (As the arrangement is interpreted by Moody's, the U.S. Department of Housing and Urban Development covenants with all holders of local housing authority bonds that it will pay part of the authority's project revenues through annual subsidy contracts.)[16] The earliest bonds of the Los Angeles Department of Water and Power extended a pledge of the city council to commit tax funds to debt service if revenues fell short. (They did not.) More important, since the 1930s, state and local governments have assumed and honored an informal obligation to back up their statutory corporations, even when charters contain no specific moral obligation language. Where defaults have been threatened by public authorities with revenue shortfalls, city and state legislatures have generally voted subsidies and otherwise cooperated with trustees and underwriters in the reorganization and refunding of the corporation. As of January 1975, not only had no state or local government attempted to repudiate its own debts in over half a century, but most had helped to refinance even public debts that were not their legal obligation.

It is not usually feasible for enterprises providing monopoly public services to be allowed to go out of business. Even private firms that provide public services (particularly water and power utilities and transit companies) have been bailed out or bought out when they seemed close to bankruptcy. And throughout the twentieth century, the number of businesses in the United

States that are thought of as public services needing protection from the possibility of bankruptcy has grown steadily. Government action has removed the ultimate competitive risk from larger and larger chunks of the private sector, including utilities, airlines, railroads, defense contractors, farmers, and shippers, as well as from traditional public services and subsidized housing, health, and education facilities.

The phrase "moral obligation" does not appear in New York State's statutes or in the authorities' indentures. It was used by Moody's to describe the provision for the state to fill up HFA reserves and originated in earlier episodes of New York's constitutional history. New York's state constitution includes provisions of the 1874 Constitutional Convention that prohibit state or local governments from giving or loaning credit to any public or private corporation, require voter approval for state debt, and limit local borrowing to general obligation debt subject to specific ceilings.[17] The purpose of the restrictions on the loans of state credit to corporate debtors was to prevent the state from incurring obligations it had not directly assumed. Numerous amendments, however, have allowed gifts and loans for specific types of housing, water, health, and education corporations.

In 1926, a state court held that the state was liable to pay off bonds issued by the New York Water Supply Commission on behalf of an improvement district because the state was closely involved in the transaction. On the other hand, in 1935, the court held that public benefit corporations were separate entities, handling "special funds," free from the debt restrictions of the constitution.[18] In short, although the special fund doctrine frees public authority financing from general constitutional restrictions on methods of incurring public debt, it does not prevent the legislature from subsequently assuming liability; and prior to 1938, the courts could enforce such liability on the state.

When the 1938 Constitutional Convention met, the state had created thirty-three authorities, most of them in the previous five years and many of them in Robert Moses's empire. A series of amendments proposed at the convention were directed at overturning the effects of the earlier court rulings. Moses, who was a delegate to the convention, and the participating bond attorneys were the chief opponents of those amendments. The convention committee examining this issue used the phrase "moral obligation" to describe judicial views of the state's responsibility for authority debt. It warned of the possibility that at "some time or other the courts might possibly decide that the public may be held responsible for the obligations of all these relatively uncontrolled authorities. . . . This would, of course, impose a tremendous potential financial load on the state or city which has created the authority."[19] The convention passed amendments requiring special state laws to create public corporations and prohibiting corporations with both the power to tax and the power to issue revenue bonds (thereby excluding the type of utility in wide use in the West). Another amendment required that tax exemption be granted only by general law, in response to Robert Moses's action in establishing the Triborough Bridge and Tunnel Authority, which was exempted from state income and local property taxes by the terms of its own bond indenture covenants, without underlying legislative authorization.[20]

In 1960, John Mitchell judged that this legal history would accommodate a vaguely specified provision for less than binding state commitment to make good corporate debts, and the ensuing events have borne his judgment out.[21]

The Housing Finance Agency: Booming Banking Business As the Port Authority of New York and New Jersey was the nationwide model for the authority supporting itself on the proceeds of the sale of services to the public, New York's Housing Finance Agency, created in 1960, was the nationwide model for a newer type of authority, a corporation serving as a state financial intermediary, substituting quasi-guarantees, such as moral obligation, and private investments for direct government expenditure. By Moody's count, there were seventy-nine authorities of this type in thirty states by 1975 (including state bond banks, industrial development and pollution control investment authorities, and housing and hospital finance agencies). An association of state HFAs had thirty-five members and was becoming an effective Washington lobby.

Unlike the Port Authority, HFAs are explicitly tools of state government. The first—New York's HFA—was closely monitored by the governor. Its board was dominated by state government department heads, and it carried out its operations partly through existing state government staffs. With the credit of the state standing paternally, if informally, behind it, it borrowed to invest in the projects of other public agencies and numerous limited-profit private firms. By 1975, HFA ranked as one of the nation's largest issuers of tax-exempt securities, having marketed $4.6 billion in bonds and $11.2 billion in bond anticipation notes. Like the Port Authority, it achieved its financial success by selecting projects that promised the safest financial return within its area of activity and establishing direct and accommodating relationships with private investors and other segments of the business community.

Originally HFA was charged with financing limited-profit housing projects through the sale of bonds and the purchase of mortgages. By 1973, the agency had developed a multipurpose wholesale banking business and had become an investment banker for a varied mix of public and private agencies, financing not only housing but hospitals, nursing homes, mental health facilities, youth and day care centers, senior citizen centers, and the state university (see chart 5.1).

A true corporate child of the 1960s, HFA grew into a conglomerate with subsidiaries: the Medical Care Facilities Finance Agency (MCFFA), the Municipal Bond Bank, and the Mortgage Agency. The MCFFA was spun off into separate corporate status at the suggestion of institutional investors, who are more comfortable with an at least superficially diversified portfolio. It accepted loan applications from nursing home companies, hospital corporations, nonprofit medical corporations, and municipal social service districts. Investors with HFA bond inventories would buy more medical facilities bonds under this aegis, although the HFA chairman, executives, and staff doubled as MCFFA personnel, and prospectus terms were parallel. Similarly, HFA personnel doubled as staff for the Municipal Bond Bank, which has not used its authorized borrowing powers. In 1973, HFA's executive director was sworn in as chairman of the New York State Mortgage Agency, known in financial circles as Sonny Mae, stepbrother to the federally sponsored Fanny Mae and federally owned Ginny Mae (Federal and Government National Mortgage Agencies). The Sonny Mae overlap was particularly useful for HFA's relationship with institutional investors. Sonny Mae was authorized to borrow $750 million to buy up old mortgages with low interest rates that banks were stuck with, on the condition that the banks use the proceeds to purchase new residential mortgages paying higher interest rates.

As a result of its record, HFA acquired the power to mobilize enormous amounts of capital. In 1974, underwriters estimated that it could raise capital more easily than New York State, New York City, and most private firms.[22] Even as Moody's began to express discomfort with moral obligation as a source of security, it raised HFA's housing bonds from A to A-1 on the basis of the agency's own resources. According to Moody's, HFA no longer needed moral obligation: "The use of a debt service reserve fund is a standard feature of bond security for HFA programs. However, it is the express intention of the agency not to use this revenue source and to make all programs self-supporting from primary revenue sources. Financial operations of the general housing loan program appear sound; all requirements have been paid from expected and specified sources with no need to draw upon debt service reserves and thus no requirements on the part of the state of New York to make up any reserve fund deficiency."[23]

Part of HFA's strength derived from its sheer scale of financing. It could accumulate vast sums of short-term money to finance projects with notes during construction, issuing long-term bonds only when a project was ready to produce revenues. Such timing eliminated the risk of project noncompletion from consideration in long-term financing. New York's Urban Development Corporation (UDC), which issued long-term bonds for unconstructed projects, had to pay higher interest rates because of the risks of project noncompletion. But it was short-term borrowing that led both agencies into trouble in 1975. The short-term debt was largely ignored by investors and raters, who assumed it could be regularly rolled over into long-term borrowing.

HFA maintains direct relationships with institutional investors, raters, and underwriters. Like the Port Authority, it does much of its own underwriting work, turning to investment bankers only for the actual bond purchase and resale transaction, thus reducing costs and increasing the authority's control over financing. All but one of its issues were negotiated, and the one that used competitive bidding—at the insistence of the state comptroller—carried the highest spread (costing the agency more than its negotiated borrowings). Competitive bidding was not advantageous for HFA because the agency could line up customers for its negotiated issues even before making the initial sale to underwriters. The authority designed the terms, volume, and coupons to suit the ultimate investor, and none of the bonds stayed in underwriter inventories to be depressed by subsequent issues.

Unlike the Port Authority, HFA has no public relations personnel, and before 1975 it received negligible attention in the mass media. Its constituency was specialized and largely financial. Its executives stayed in direct contact with banks and insurance company investors, discussing matters of internal management with them and drawing on their views on the design of financing arrangements.

Paul Belica, its executive director, did not think HFA's responsibilities extended to subsidized public services or deficit operations. "We are not using public funds; public purpose is not our primary concern and if it were, the state should do the job," he said. This statement echoes remarks made by managers of the older public authorities that are further removed from tax

Chart 5.1
New York State Housing Finance Agency Programs, 1974

Program	Statutory authorization	Statutory borrowing limits
1 Middle-income housing		
General housing loan Nonprofit housing Urban rental housing equity loan	Article II, Private Housing Finance Law	$2,100,000,000 (includes $50,000,000 Equity Loan Program authorization)
Capital grant low rent assistance	Article III, Private Hous- ing Finance Law	Total State Appropriation $ 33,228,240
2 Hospitals and nursing homes	Articles 28-A, 28-B, and 44, Public Health Law	$1,950,000,000
3 Community mental health services and mental retarda- tion services	Article 75, Mental Hygiene Law	$ 100,000,000
4 Youth facilities	Title 5-A of Article 6, Social Services Law	$ 100,000,000
5 Community senior citizens' centers	Article VII-A, Private Housing Finance Law	$ 50,000,000
6 State university construc- tion	Article 8-A, Education Law	Controlled by the Master Plan of State University
7 Mental hygiene improve- ment	Facilities Development Cor- poration Act (McK. Uncon- sol. §§ 4401-4417)	$1,050,000,000
8 Health facilities	Facilities Development Cor- poration Act (McK. Uncon- sol. §§ 4401-4417)	$ 800,000,000

Source: HFA Annual Report, 1974.

State agencies acting with HFA	Eligible borrowers	Financial basis	Primary source of revenue
Division of Housing and Community Renewal	Regulated housing companies	Mortgage loan General obligation Lease and sublease	Project State appropriations
Department of Health	Regulated nursing home companies, nonprofit hospital and medical corporations	Mortgage loan	Project and borrower
Department of Mental Hygiene	Regulated mental health or mental retardation services companies	Mortgage loan	Project
Department of Social Services; Community Facilities Project Guarantee Fund	Regulated agencies authorized to provide care for children	Mortgage loan	Project
Department of Social Services; Community Facilities Project Guarantee Fund	Regulated community senior citizens centers and services companies	Mortgage loan	Project
State University of New York; State University Construction Fund	State University of New York and State University Construction Fund	Sale and lease-back	Tuition and other fees paid by state university students deposited in Income Fund of State University
Facilities Development Corporation; Department of Mental Hygiene	Facilities Development Corporation and Department of Mental Hygiene	Sale and lease-back	Fees paid by patients in state mental institutions deposited in Income Account of Facilities Development Corporation
Facilities Development Corporation; Department of Health	Municipalities	Sale and lease-back or lease and lease-back	Rentals paid by municipality

revenues. While HFA's mortgage operations had balanced books, however, the projects financed by HFA were subsidized. Although HFA-financed projects are less vulnerable to cutbacks in federal interest and rent subsidies than are UDC projects, they do depend on diverse sources of state and federal aid for housing, higher education, and medical facilities. HFA's operating revenues ultimately depend upon those public funds.

With its system of multiple housing authorities issuing moral obligation bonds, the Rockefeller administration brought private investment into publicly sponsored housing without federal guarantees for the first time. HFA, UDC, and New York City's Housing Development Corporation (HDC) in effect divided up a housing and development market—with HFA selecting the best sites, strongest mortgages, and relatively moderate-to-high rent scales. Income eligibility ceilings on HFA-financed housing projects rose from $10,000 to $35,000, and the mortgage terms dictated by the agency often escalated with the economic indexes. HFA-financed builders are mainly non-profit corporations and limited-profit housing companies; UDC financed more tax-shelter syndicates and mixed-income projects.[24] New York City's HDC sponsored subsidized inner-city projects.[25] When the state housing commissioner (who also served as an HFA board member) urged HFA to take on the relatively risky Battery Park project (Lower Manhattan redevelopment), the HFA staff balked. Rather than assume that risk and the higher interest costs it would entail, HFA chose to give away part of its authorized bonding capacity.[26] Later, when UDC's financial troubles were mounting, HFA management refused to buy up some of the shakier UDC-sponsored obligations.

Although UDC financed its first middle-income housing projects through HFA, it subsequently used its own bond funds in order to be free of HFA's conservative mortgage policies. Unlike HFA, UDC is an operating development agency, not just a banking enterprise, and its staff, which in time numbered more than five hundred, planned, promoted, regulated, and contracted for construction projects throughout the state, achieving an unprecedented building rate. But the Nixon administration's cutbacks of housing subsidies, the dramatic inflation in interest rates, and local opposition, which delayed several UDC projects, undermined that agency's revenue forecasts. Ninety percent of the units it built depended on federal subsidies. UDC's industrial projects were losing money, and several incomplete new communities had cost overruns and rental problems. UDC's building starts were outrunning its borrowing capacity. By 1973, institutional investors in UDC bonds were sufficiently alarmed to demand appointment of a new financial officer for the corporation. Still, with an A rating, it sold $200 million in bonds in May 1973 despite warnings in the prospectus of shaky financial conditions that would have ruled out any new financing for a private-sector firm. Subsequently, Moody's dropped UDC's rating from A to Baa-1, and the auditing accountants declined to express an opinion on the 1973 financial statement, citing "material uncertainties relating to receipts of required amounts of subsidies."

As UDC's problems grew, the participants in the bond market began to show signs of nervousness about the volume of moral obligation debt in the state. In the fall of 1973, Moody's ventured: "On consideration that New York State's current total *annual* 'moral commitments' alone run up to nearly 10% of its present level of expenditures for state current purposes, further difficult questions arise. . . . Because of the open-ended nature of these commitments, we feel them to be insufficient *per se* to warrant a high investment standing."[27] Nevertheless, UDC borrowed more; in 1974, bankers and brokers marketed a UDC issue of $100 million, part of it at a record tax-exempt interest rate of approximately 9 percent. By the end of 1974, it was clear that the UDC projects already underway could be completed only with heavy state appropriations.

From February 25 to April 30, 1975, UDC was in default on repayment of bond anticipation notes due to banks. When the legislature put together the money package that brought UDC out of default and filled its reserves to the level of annual debt service, it authorized a further fill-up of UDC reserves in 1976. The recovery program, completed in 1977, includes continuing state appropriations, cutbacks in agency staff and program, loans from banks and from state funds, and the creation of still another new state corporation (Project Finance Agency) to buy and refinance some UDC mortgages. The Project Finance Agency—managed by HFA—sold bonds by private placement that were backed by pledges of federal subsidies due on some projects.

Meanwhile HFA found it could no longer roll over its huge short-term borrowings into new long-term bonds (which it had done without difficulty for fifteen years) because private investors were avoiding nearly everything related to New York. Month by month, the governor's office, authority executives, and participating banks cooperated successfully to stave off default on HFA notes (as well as those of three other state corporations) although the state had no legal or technically moral obligation to refinance or pay off those short-term debts. HFA regained access to the market in late 1976 after the state's Build Out Plan provided for completion of its projects in progress and refinancing of all bond anticipation notes. The plan puts a ceiling on all future authority bonds that may be secured by reserve funds to which state appropriations may be apportioned. Underwriting firms played a major role in designing these solutions.

The New Jersey Sports and Exposition Authority Bond market promotion spread moral obligation bonds readily because adding the ambivalent terms to statutes and prospectuses made feasible uncertain projects that otherwise would not stand the test of even the bond marketplace. The New Jersey Sports and Exposition Authority illustrates this effect.

Sports authorities have been a favorite promotional project in recent years. (A Bond Buyer survey in 1976 identified forty-four cities planning new sports, civic, and convention centers that would use tax-exempt bonds.) Promoters and businessmen have joined with mayors, county boards, and governors to persuade the public that government is justified in borrowing money to finance new stadiums even before the expansion football or baseball teams are created to fill them: "Call it civic pride, call it shrewd promotion by profit-minded businessmen, call it an American-as-apple-pie love of competitive sports—all of these serve as the motivating forces that have brought about an astounding proliferation of expensive sports stadiums." [28]

Between 1965 and 1974, sixteen major new stadiums for privately owned teams were built in the United States with municipal bond financing, nine of them by revenue bonds backed by combinations of public and private payment of rents, concessions, or parking fees; earmarked taxes, such as Louisiana's hotel tax; federal revenue-sharing funds (Kansas City); and local appropriations. Yet there is not a publicly owned stadium in the country that is self-supporting if debt service is included, and half do not meet even their operating expenses. [29] By using revenue bonds backed by obscure special tax sources or forms of public credit, stadium promoters have avoided having to convince voters to authorize the direct use of tax dollars and municipal credit for this purpose; and courts across the nation have upheld the pledge of public funds to private profit making in the sports business.

New Jersey's version, a stadium in the meadowlands, ultimately got off the swamp on one wing and a prayer: forecasts of revenues from a racetrack and football by the former New York Giants and the moral obligation pledge "that there shall be annually appropriated and paid to the authority" amounts needed to fill up the debt service reserve fund for the forthcoming year. The prospectus contains the usual caveats: this arrangement is subject to legislative appropriations; the bonds do not create a legal liability of the state. (Mudge Rose provided these statutory drafts and the accompanying legal bond opinions, as it had for the HFAs of both New York and New Jersey.)

Initially plagued by a series of legal suits brought by local environmental and other groups with interests in the North Jersey meadowlands, then confronted by a threat of competition from an authority authorized by New York, and finally battered by Moody's, the New Jersey Sports Authority experienced one of the most difficult births in public corporate history. In the first rounds of litigation, the authority's opponents argued with considerable logic that the project entailed state establishment of parimutuel horseracing without the popular vote to approve betting establishments required by the state constitution; that the authority bond sale would commit state funds in violation of the appropriations and debt provisions of the state constitution; that providing facilities for private sports franchises did not constitute a valid public purpose for condemnation of land or tax-exempt borrowing; that the plan vested broad powers and promised financial gains to a commercial corporation (the football Giants); that the public interest in tidelands is inalienable; and that the project would reduce other state receipts from racetrack taxes and local receipts from property taxes. In addition, Monmouth Park Racetrack brought suit, complaining of unequal treatment under the law and unfair state competition with private business.[30] Although Monmouth and other private tracks pay 9.15 percent of parimutuel pools to the state, the Sports Authority's track pays only 0.5 percent. In the suit, both sides acknowledged ("stipulated") that the authority's operation would hurt Monmouth Park. The Atlantic City and Garden State tracks, which were already suffering declining receipts but had private dealings with state officials underway, did not bring suit.[31]

All of the arguments against the Sports Authority received short shrift in the courts. One trial judge, Judge Morris Pashman, subsequently appointed to the New Jersey Supreme Court, cited Plato on the "profound moral force" of sports and the contributions of pingpong to "rapprochement with Red China"; the court found an overwhelming public interest to lie with the Sports Authority: "Only in the arena can the man in the street get a taste of a better society ... experience the respect for law and justice ... feel the bond uniting him to his fellow man."[32]

Interstate competition and the search for investors posed more difficult problems. Negotiations for sale of the bonds spanned more than nine months of dramatic peaks and valleys. The first set of adviser-underwriters was headed by Dillon Read & Co., a firm generally favored by New Jersey's Cahill administration. In spring 1973, the Sports Authority was authorized to sell only straight revenue bonds; its original statute contained no moral obligation pledge. Moreover, its contract with the Giants gave away most concession income and called for minimal rents, so the economics of the plan depended heavily on the proposed racetrack. Moody's refused to give the authority any rating at all, and Dillon Read found investors wary of the speculative nature of the project. In May 1973, when New York launched its first attack to recapture the Giants, the underwriting firm canceled plans to market a $268 million bond issue at $6\frac{5}{8}$ percent yield.[33]

The redoubtable Sonny Werblin, the Sports Authority chairman, did not give in, nor did his colleague, Adrian Foley, Sports Authority secretary-treasurer and law partner of former New Jersey Governor Richard J. Hughes (and counsel to the New Jersey Highway Authority, as well). They enlisted the support of the state's chamber of commerce and wooed sports and financial writers with visions of the project as a vast multipurpose center, including hotels, soccer, an amusement park, and an indoor arena. To strike back at New York, Werblin opened negotiations with Madison Square Garden tenants, the Knicks and Rangers (New York City's basketball and hockey teams).

Next, Sports Authority management and state officials set out to spur investor interest within the state and to keep the initial contracts intact. Alfred Driscoll, then chairman of the New Jersey Turnpike Authority, agreed to put some $30 million of Turnpike Authority funds into site preparation and access roads for the sports complex. (The following January, when Governor-elect Brendan Byrne threatened to withdraw state authorization for a turnpike extension, Driscoll suggested that authority contributions to the sports complex might be withdrawn in retaliation.) As workmen were laid off at the Sports Authority site, the state's construction unions were brought into the ranks of active supporters (later contributing to Byrne's willingness to go along with the project).

Werblin and Foley asked the Prudential and Mutual Life Insurance companies to commit themselves to purchase a portion of the Sports Authority bonds. Mutual life insurance companies enjoy a relatively low income tax rate and therefore, unlike casualty companies, do not ordinarily invest heavily in tax-exempt securities. Nevertheless Prudential and Mutual had helped bail out the state before—buying into sluggish issues of the Turnpike and Atlantic City Expressway authorities—and were willing to do so again.

Meanwhile, Dillon Read dropped out of the managing syndicate, and the authority signed a new agreement with Hornblower & Weeks-Hemphill, Noyes and Merrill Lynch to redesign the issue and to market the bonds. These two firms were in a relatively good position to move less-than-prime offerings: Hornblower conducts aggressive mass sales campaigns, and Merrill Lynch has a large number of discretionary accounts that can absorb bonds. State treasurer and Sports Authority director Joseph McCrane sought further support from New Jersey banks, which had already committed themselves to the project by extending $50 million in short-term loans to the Sports Authority, payable from long-term financing. They stood to gain more of the state's banking business, diverting it from New York and Philadelphia banks. McCrane could allocate that state business to them.

In September 1973, the authority announced a new financing plan, based on a prior commitment from the two major insurance companies and five New Jersey banks to buy $100 million worth of bonds. The managing underwriters scheduled the sale of an additional $180 million for October, inviting some 250 brokerage firms to participate in this underwriting. They added a mortgage on the public land as security for the bonds, and proposed interest rates now ranged from 7.25 to 8 percent. Other investors were still wary. A bond manager for Salomon Brothers declared: "It's not investment quality." Unable to resist the obvious pun, he went on: "It lacks a track record." Nevertheless, building contractors with bills outstanding agreed to resume work on the sports complex site.

New York had not played its last trump card. Just as both major candidates for New Jersey's governorship began to talk about abandoning the whole Cahill-sponsored project, New York pricked them into state patriotism and at the same time forced another cancellation of the bond sale by authorizing a competing facility. The two states seem to be bidding each other up in an auction for a white elephant. New York's new proposal was to build a sports complex, including two racetracks, in Sunnyside, Queens, over a rail yard. At the governor's urging, authority managers William Ronan and Edward Logue had worked up a plan whereby New York's Metropolitan Transportation Authority would sell the air rights and the Urban Development Corporation would build the structure for the Sunnyside complex.

The underwriters halted their sales efforts for the New Jersey Sports Authority bonds and began searching for additional security to support them.

The moral obligation pledge of state funds to fill up authority reserves was the solution chosen. The sponsors of the project did not even consider the alternative of direct state financing by a general obligation bond issue. The necessary referendum could not have been scheduled until the following November and stood little chance of obtaining voter approval. The resort to public authority revenue bonds backed by the state's moral obligation was explicitly intended to circumvent election procedures and to neutralize a powerful segment of public opinion running against the project.

Governor-elect Brendan Byrne, under pressure from business and labor, lent his support to the sports complex project. A newly elected legislature acted promptly on his request to approve the moral obligation amendment of the Sports Authority legislation. Byrne renegotiated the contract with the Giants, arranging a slightly more favorable deal for the authority. Meanwhile, cost estimates had risen dramatically; the planned bond issue was therefore increased to raise $302 million. On the basis of the moral obligation pledge, Moody's gave the issue a rating of Baa. (Moody's Baa and Standard & Poor's BBB are the lowest ratings acceptable for institutional investment.)

The search for bond buyers began again. This time the authority officials sought a still bigger role for New Jersey banks, and another advantage of using the state's contingent liability came to light: commercial banks could join the underwriting syndicate only if federal banking officials issued a ruling that the bonds involved were not really authority revenue bonds but were general obligations of the state of New Jersey. The U.S. comptroller of the currency stretched these interpretations to the outer limits of logic; his opinion letter of January 1974 stated that, given the terms of the Sports Authority statute and indenture, the state of New Jersey was legally obligated to back the Sports Authority bonds even though the indenture contained the usual disclaimer—a statement that the bonds were not legal obligations of the state—together with the provision for legislative replenishment of authority reserves. This ruling permitted the First National State Bank of New Jersey to become a managing underwriter of the issue and allowed several other commercial banks to join the underwriting syndicate.

Responding to this ruling, local officials in the meadowlands area, who had opposed the project from the beginning, filed new lawsuits in both state and federal courts. In the state courts, they charged that the moral obligation pledge commits the state's credit to the bond issue (in accord with the federal ruling) without the required voter approval. In the federal courts (with a parallel petition to the SEC), they charged that bonds are not, in fact, backed by the state's credit and that the prospectus was therefore false and misleading. These actions failed; the courts upheld the Sports Authority and the reserves fill-up provision. In effect the judicial system took the paradoxical position that moral obligation bonds both are and are not liabilities of the state. The ambiguity of authority finance was enhanced, and the authority received its investment capital. The negotiated sale to the underwriters went through at a net interest cost of 7.47 percent, with lawsuits still pending. After the authority paid off its financing costs and debts, it invested the remainder in U.S. and other securities paying interest rates as high as 8.9 percent.

The New Jersey banks wasted no time in seeking their reward for rescuing the Sports Authority. They persuaded New Jersey's new treasurer to devise a plan to divert more state deposits and investment business to them from the major New York banks. As a result, the New Jersey Housing Finance Agency and the Sports Authority placed their certificates of deposit exclusively with New Jersey banks.

The Sports Authority bonds were difficult to market. When the period of fixed price sales by syndicate members ended, the market price of the bonds took a sharp downturn, and some underwriter-brokers were left with about $30 million of unsold bonds. The free market price then represented roughly a 15 percent loss for the underwriters on the remaining bonds. Over the subsequent three years, however, the price of these bonds rose steadily; in early 1977, they were selling at a premium as high as 110 percent of face value.

The revenue-earning capacity of the sports complex surprised all observers. By the spring of 1977, its income was far exceeding forecasts, and its statutory obligation to pay the state 60 percent of surplus earnings would generate over $5 million for the state in the first year of full operations. The Sports Authority moved, with the governor's support, to gain legislative authorization for it to take over several of the state's ailing privately owned tracks.

Moral Obligation: Fiasco or Fiscal Tool for the Future?   Press coverage of the financial crisis in New York State in 1975 tended to group moral obligation borrowing with a number of dubious fiscal and management practices that had precipitated the difficulties. Five important points seemed to be missing from the commentary:

1. Short-term borrowing, not bonds, however backed, precipitated crisis for public agencies—including New York City government, UDC, HFA, and two other state public authorities.

2. Bond attorney John Mitchell's device—the moral obligation language providing for state contributions to reserve funds—did not apply to short-term notes or to bank loans. Nearly all observers failed to note that the bond market would ultimately have to absorb these ballooning debts.

3. Although nearly all borrowing of all kinds was halted in New York for a time, moral obligation was alive, if no longer popular, in other states of the nation.

4. A new governor and legislature in New York did provide state funds to help pay public authority short-term debt, even though they were under no obligation, legal or moral, to do so. They also responded quickly to HFA's subsequent request for reserves to be replenished by the moral obligation procedure. Pennsylvania and Massachusetts supplied their HFAs with funds when they too had trouble with short-term debt. New Jersey and Rhode Island made moral-obligation payments to authorities, as well.

5. Historically tested solutions to public authority finance problems included guarantees or purchases of bonds or notes by federal agencies or state comptrollers. (Both took place during World War II, with redemption or refinancing in later years.)

Where the moral obligation arrangements have been tested in the courts, with few exceptions they have been upheld. Rulings in West Virginia, New Jersey, Maine, and Pennsylvania confirmed arrangements modeled on the New York statutes (for, respectively, a housing development fund, mortgage finance agency, and two housing finance agencies). In three of the approving cases, the plaintiffs were insiders—an authority board member, a state treasurer, and a bank that was buying the bonds—seeking answers pretested in the courts. The four state courts consistently held that the "moral makeup" clause is an expression of intention without a legally binding effect. Public authority bonds do not constitute a state debt or a loan of state credit; they are authority debt, and a sitting legislature cannot commit future legislatures to appropriate money to fill up authority reserves. But as long as the activity serves a valid public purpose (broadly construed), future legislatures may decide to appropriate funds for the authority's bond reserves just as they may decide to appropriate other kinds of subsidies for the authority. The ultimate security behind the authority debt is a political, not a legal, question. (South Carolina courts have rejected these arguments, striking down authorization for an HFA there.)

The courts have supplied no details on the implementation of the moral obligation provision, and its specific procedures are not so important as most commentators suggest. Indirect government support for authority debt is given in many ways and many places (for example, without a moral obligation pledge, New Jersey's legislature has appropriated funds three times to support debt service of the South Jersey Port Corporation). But the moral obligation provision provides private sector promoters and investors with a psychological assurance that allows them to expand the volume of business that might otherwise be depressed by politicans' and voters' reluctance to support obvious deficit financing. It permits public officials to build now and pay later, to obscure debt, and still to keep a symbolically balanced budget. It allows the public authority to operate without large reserve funds. In effect, it calls for reserves to equal annual debt service (one-to-one coverage) rather than the higher coverage of debt service that is typical of the more traditional operating authorities. Moreover, the specific procedure for filling up reserves need not be used because authorities with the moral obligation language in their statutes also may use a variety of grants, loans, and appropriations to subsidize their operating revenues.

Some members of the financial community spoke out against New York in as fulsome tones of moral indignation as those used by Reverend Smith to condemn Pennsylvania in 1832. Yet the eagerness of underwriters, bond attorneys, and investors to reap profits from expanding markets played as much of a role in causing the collapse as did the ambitions of politicians or authority entrepreneurs. The moral obligation language and similar devices that emphasize the contingent liability of government for public authority debts have vastly increased the rate and scope of publicly sponsored construction, including 260,000 new housing units aided by all state HFAs between 1968 and 1974 and scores of financially marginal projects such as sports arenas and convention centers.

The commission that investigated UDC's problems concluded too quickly that these bonds were "completely discredited." Agencies based on statutes that provide for contingent liability on the part of state government continue to thrive—throughout the United States—including state bond banks and authorities that invest in housing, universities, hospitals, resource recovery plants, and, in Massachusetts, even urban transit. For several types of projects, federal mortgage insurance provides added security for the investor, as in the cases of the Illinois Educational Facilities Authority, the Michigan State Hospital Finance Authority, and the Maine Health Facilities Authority. The U.S. Housing Act of 1974 provides for HFAs to issue taxable bonds with federal guarantees to substitute for tax-exempt bonds with state quasi-guarantees, but the new option has not been used because of bond attorney reluctance to approve taxable bonds and a healthy market for the tax-exempt bonds. One underwriting firm invented still another kind of bond for New Jersey's HFA, using unspent proceeds from earlier moral obligation bond issues to create an insurance fund to invest in federal securities, with the investment income pledged to back up any housing project shortfall. Although the Wisconsin legislature recently revised its constitution to reduce the need for backdoor financing, that state has created three new public corporations to fund construction (Health Facilities Authority, Housing Finance Authority, and Solid Waste Recycling Authority)—one authorized to enter into lease-back arrangements with the state and two permitted to issue moral obligation bonds. Wisconsin actually incorporated the phrase "moral obligation" into the legislation creating its HFA and Solid Waste Recycling Authority: "In any case the joint committee on finance shall introduce in either house, in bill form, an appropriation of the amount so certified to the capital reserve fund of the authority. Recognizing its moral obligation to do so, the legislature hereby expresses its expectation and aspiration that, if ever called upon to do so, it shall make such appropriation." [34]

Nationwide, indirect pledges of state backing do not guarantee success in raising capital, but they do help to get corporate deals off the ground in the public sector, and, in the language of the brokers, they are a method of leveraging public investment—of increasing investment with minimal direct commitment of funds.

The events of 1975 demonstrate that the dependence of public agencies on private investment and the overlapping careers and relationships of market participants induce governments to bail out statutory corporations. Bond market representatives can persuade a state to back up authority bonds by suggesting that if the state does not do so, its general credit will suffer. The financiers convey the impression that the bond market and the facilities that it supports comprise a system that no one in elected office can afford to damage: "Play the game our way, or public investment with private funds will come to a halt." Governors convey this message to their legislatures, with the result that favored projects in every district of the state become linked indirectly to support for the public corporations. The investment community ties together otherwise unrelated transactions in order to influence government decisions. As one financial writer observed, "In light of the recent controversy over the bonds issued by the Port Authority of New York and New

Jersey, there's at least a question among bond dealers as to how good the 'moral' IOU's are."[35]

In recent years, the public has begun to resent such pressures. The pressures are inevitable, however, as long as government remains dependent on banks, brokers, and lawyers who are, in turn, subject to pressures from stockholders, bondholding customers, and other clients. Bankers and brokers cannot be expected to give greater weight to public than to private interests. The weight of these interests is a concomitant of public reliance on private investment. The evolved ambiguity of the public corporation makes it particularly susceptible to these pressures; it is a political subdivision for purposes of tax exemption, an independent entity for purposes of management and freedom from public debt restrictions, and a political subdivision again for purposes of giving investors security when the enterprise is not producing sufficient income. In effect, moral obligation and other forms of contingent government liability for agency debt subject the taxpayers to unpredictable volumes of future expense. They confront the public with bills for debts the public has not promised to pay.

Industrial Pollution Control Bonds

The largest recent area of growth in the municipal bond market is a specialized version of the industrial revenue bond that provides capital at tax-exempt interest costs for private firms. The cost of borrowing is an important factor in capital acquisition or construction. Interest rates can have dramatic effects on businesses, making or breaking them over the short run and influencing general trends in the national economy. The interest rate savings that flow from the ability to issue tax-exempt bonds are important, especially when money and credit are tight and needs for capital expenditure are pressing. Since the eighteenth century, government agencies have viewed the promotion of local development, job creation, and general growth of the economy as important public purposes. Both business and labor organizations actively participate in politics to keep these concerns high on government's list of priorities.

From the railroad aid bonds of the nineteenth century to the regional development bonds of the 1960s, governments have issued industrial revenue bonds to encourage companies to relocate or to expand.[36] Typically, city, county, and state industrial development boards and authorities have issued bonds that financed site development or construction of plants that would be leased to companies during the life of the bond and then transferred to private ownership. In 1968, Congress withdrew tax exemption from bonds generally benefiting private firms. But industrial revenue bonds are still permitted to benefit certain businesses in which both government-owned and investor-owned firms have long been engaged: transportation, parking, docks and airports, water supply, sewage and waste disposal, sports facilities, local gas and electric utilities, residential construction, and land development. The 1968 tax enactments also permit funding by tax-exempt industrial revenue bonds for public banking (including the purchase of private mortgages), industrial projects under $5 million, and purchases of air or water pollution equipment for the use of and eventual ownership by private industry.

The industrial pollution control exception differs from other types of government aids to business. It is not directed at certain types of businesses judged to be especially important to the public interest (such as housing and transportation) nor at businesses felt to be deserving of special help (such as farmers and small firms). Any kind and size of company can qualify; large power companies, metal processors, oil companies, chemical concerns, and paper companies are the most frequent beneficiaries. This public borrowing spree was triggered by the rise in interest rates after 1970, together with pressures on firms to make capital expenditures in order to meet new government standards requiring reductions in the amounts of pollutants spewed forth by industrial processes.[37]

Some conservative investment bankers such as Morgan Stanley and First Boston Corporation eschewed traditional industrial revenue bonds because of their tarnished reputations, dating from nineteenth-century partnerships between government and business. Other firms specialized in such bonds and suffered when this market, totaling $2 billion in 1968, was suddenly cut off by the tax law change. The first probes into the pollution control exception were cautious. Bond attorneys insisted on prior rulings from the Internal Revenue Serivce (IRS), which did nothing with the requests until prodded by Nixon administration officials. The first issue was tiny by market standards. In 1971, Eastman Dillon (a leader in pre-1968 industrial revenue bonds) brought out a $5 million bond of the Allegheny County Industrial Development Authority to buy equipment for a U.S. Steel plant in Duquesne, Pennsylvania. Later, after basic IRS rulings were accumulated, attorneys sent only particularly complicated deals for prior review, and a new boom was underway.

The investment bankers began to promote appropriate enabling legislation in each state. By the summer of 1972, Jim Lopp, first vice-president of East-man Dillon, claimed: "We've been responsible for changing laws in fifteen to twenty states."[38] By 1976, agencies in thirty-eight states were issuing indus-trial pollution control bonds, with Pennsylvania, Texas, Alabama, and Illinois leading in volume. Total sales were reported to be $77 million in 1971, $565 million in 1972, $1.8 billion in 1973, $1.7 billion in 1974, $2.1 billion in 1975, and $2.6 billion in 1976. The tax law exception had grown to exceed the total amount of all industrial development bond financing at its peak in 1968. The system has saved corporations hundreds of millions of dollars (about 2 percentage points of interest costs on each deal) and forged new alliances of investment bankers, corporate executives, and federal, state, and local officials.[39]

These public financings have grown not because of political enthusiasm for cleaning up the air and water but because of bond market dynamics. The leading underwriters, by volume, of pre-1968 industrial development bonds were among the leaders in pollution control (or "environmental") industrial revenue bonds. As the volume of this business ballooned, Morgan Stanley and First Boston abandoned their blue chip restraint from industrial revenue bonds and entered the pollution control market, requiring such refinements as direct guarantees by their corporate customers of the bond issued by the public agency (rather than merely requiring the corporations to guarantee their own lease or installment purchase obligations to the authority).[40] In 1976, six major investment banking firms were managers of an incredible 96.9 percent of the pollution control revenue bond volume underwritten nationwide. Investment trust funds with portfolios of "diversified tax-exempt environmental bonds" were used to attract more investors, and a number of regional underwriters specialized in this type of authority financing. A circu-lar of one Atlanta firm, for example, promises "one-stop" shopping:

> After receiving the financial statistics of your company and establishing that the project is financially feasible, Henderson, Few & Company will then provide you and the Industrial Development Authority with a firm under-writing commitment to purchase the revenue bonds proposed to be issued. With our national marketing systems for guaranteed bond distribution, we as-sume total responsibility for the sale of the bonds. We do not ask your com-pany to provide us with a prospect list unless you prefer to designate a mar-ket place for the bonds to be distributed.
>
> Our underwriting commitment guarantees the delivery of funds to your company. When the amount of the project has been formalized and the general fees and expenses have been determined, we will present to you a firm underwriting proposal reflecting interest rates based on applicable current

market conditions. After your acceptance of our underwriting commitment, we will engage the services of a nationally recognized Bond Attorney who will prepare the documentation required to accomplish the issuance of the bonds. Usually within 45 days the bond issue proceeds will be delivered and made available for the use of your company for the desired project.

As this description indicates, the industrial development authority is the least active of the partners in this three-way arrangement. The government corporations that issue industrial revenue bonds are little more than conduits. First, an investment banking promoter working with a private industrial firm devises the financing arrangement. He then brings the proposal to an industrial development authority. The security that backs the public authority bond in these deals is a lease calling for rental payments by the industrial firm. The bond is rated at the same level as or one notch below the corporate bonds of the firm, and the corporate, rather than the municipal, department of the investment banking firm can manage the underwriting.

Most industrial pollution control bonds are issued by statutory authorities or government corporations. The rest are issued in the name of a city or county by a board or commission set up for that purpose. Scores of county and local public authorities, particularly in areas where one plant dominates the local economy, have been created to issue bonds for a single corporate deal. In these cases, the company that uses the funds is generally represented, by public appointment, on the authority board of directors. Public officials rely almost entirely on explanations and decisions by the private partners in the transactions.

Some other authorities in this finance and leasing business—for example, Ohio's Water Development Authority and Air Quality Development Authority—deal with a number of corporations. Still others are multipurpose authorities that have added the financing and leasing of industrial pollution control equipment to their other business. Texas's Gulf Coast Waste Disposal Authority and New York's Energy Research Development Authority (which finances power facilities and aerospace plants for private firms as well) function in this way. Older industrial development authorities in Alabama, Oklahoma, Pennsylvania, and Tennessee also have taken on pollution control projects in recent years.[41]

Even some of the larger states' public authorities are little more than go-betweens in this business. One of the newest, California's Pollution Control Financing Authority (originally authorized to issue $200 million, which was used up in its first financings for large oil companies), has a full-time staff consisting of only an executive director and his secretary. When this authority requested an increase in its debt ceiling, the state legislature mandated that some of the borrowings be reserved for small businesses. (In 1976, the federal Small Business Administration was authorized to guarantee the base rents from small businesses to the Pollution Control Financing Authority.)

The promoters of the pollution control financings prefer working with authorities rather than with general governments for the usual reasons: less public involvement and quicker transactions. As interest rates spiraled and pollution control standards tightened, the market in pollution control bonds continued upward. Local governments now complain that these company-oriented issues, by absorbing so much of available tax-exempt investment, make financing for public projects more difficult to obtain and more expensive. The Municipal Finance Officers Association, several congressmen, and The Bond Buyer maintain that these borrowings force up interest rates paid on all kinds of tax-exempt borrowings.

The investor who needs tax-exempt bonds can buy industrial revenue bonds paying relatively high interest instead of state and city bonds, which may be viewed as overly dependent on politics and tainted by an association with urban problems. All of these conditions have served to divert tax-exempt investment to private firms. Complex legal questions about how much and what kind of plant equipment is eligible for public financing are the only restraints on abuse.

The industrial revenue bond sector of public authority finance is more shielded from public scrutiny than other sectors of public enterprise. Even the investment banking industry does not have accurate information about the volume and uses of tax-exempt bonds and loans benefiting private firms. Commercial banks structure many of the deals as tax-exempt loans, which do not appear in bond market statistics. The Bond Buyer's estimate of total sales for pollution control industrial revenue bonds issued in 1974 was $2.5 billion; its record of reported issues for that year was $1.7 billion, but such financing may actually have amounted to $3.5 billion according to other estimates. Pennsylvania sources reported that a total of $2.4 billion in tax-exempt bonds and bank loans had been issued in that state alone during 1974. Because of the slightly unsavory history of government investments in and for private companies and because of habitual secrecy with respect to corporate financings, commercial bankers, corporate departments of investment banking firms, and the manufacturing firms benefited have been reluctant to volunteer full information. The public authorities that issue the bonds do not have the staff to prepare full reports. Even the usually uncritical Bond Buyer has asked, "Why should public purpose financing not be public?"[42]

6 Risk, Profit, and the Public Interest

Efforts to attract private investment and to protect it inevitably set limits—some of them salutary—on the uses of public corporations as tools of government. Even the powerful Robert Moses had silent partners who narrowed the options of the public authorities he ran. As Robert Caro describes the decision to locate the Triborough Bridge: "Only the bankers' ideas mattered because it was the bankers who had to put up the money for the bridge. Moses could not, in fact, allow any discussion of the bridge location at all, because discussion generates controversy, and controversy frightens away the timid, and no one is more timid than a banker where his money is concerned. ... There was an alternative—it was just not an alternative that ... Robert Moses would even consider. The city could simply ... wait until it could build the bridge itself—in the place where it should be built."[1]

A question that is seldom answered fully is how many of the limits accepted by public authority officials are useful in terms of public policy and how many simply reflect their too ready desire to please the investment community and thus expand the sheer volume of money that will be made available. The natural interests of private sector participants in the bond market—institutional investors, bond attorneys, and underwriters—lie in maximizing bond marketability and minimizing risk to the investors. But the natural interests of public enterprise should lie in limiting investor risk and increasing marketability only to the extent necessary to raise the capital required for desirable public projects, while at the same time holding down financing costs and keeping as many of government's options open as possible. Public authority boards and managers usually fail to perceive or to pursue the goals of policy flexibility and cost control when they are making financial arrangements. In practice, both public and private participants usually focus on maximizing the money raised from investors, thereby stimulating continuous growth in the volume of public authority activities. The reasons for the apparent lack of arms-length bargaining are several: interlocking careers in the municipal bond market; the folklore surrounding credit standing and debt management; the dynamics of business promotion when the market is ready to absorb tax-exempt securities; the financial and political pressures on elected officials and their limited resources; and the desire of authority managers to maximize their resources, and their limited knowledge of financial techniques.

The public interest also suffers in the bargaining of municipal finance because of several current trends: the scarcity of independent financial advice; the increase in negotiated sales of public bonds; the preference of brokers and investors for public bonds repaid by private companies (industrial revenue bonds), although defaults in this sector of tax-exempt finance are far more common than in any other; skyrocketing interest rates; and the rising costs of getting credit ratings. The sheer variety and volume of underwritings is confusing to all but the experts.

The events of 1975 demonstrate the inequal weight of public and private interests in municipal finance. In the first nine months of 1975, because of investor unrest stemming from New York City's fiscal collapse, states and localities throughout the United States were burdened with $100 million in added borrowing costs. Moreover, some $1.2 billion in planned state and local borrowings nationwide were canceled because of high interest rates, according to The Bond Buyer and the Securities Industry Association. But the municipal finance industry itself was thriving: the total volume of new tax-exempt bond issues in 1975 was the highest in history. (In 1975, $29.2 billion in long-term, tax-exempt borrowing occurred, topping 1971's record of $24.3 billion. The 1976 volume of $33.7 billion set another record.) Public agency borrowing on behalf of private industry through industrial revenue bonds took up the slack in state and local investment.

If the volume of bond business had been low, if the brokers were suffering, and if investor demands for high-yield tax-exempt securities were not sated with industrial revenue bonds, the bond market might not have withdrawn so abruptly from nearly all New York State's agencies or penalized public borrowers in the other states so heavily. The bond market's ability to go elsewhere for tax-exempt business further weakened state and local enterprise. Federal legislation plugging up the pollution control hole in the 1968 tax reforms might thus be a fast and easy means of making fresh funds available to municipalities, states, and public corporations.

Assessing Risk

Before the 1930s, authority bonds were not numerous; hence, unlike general obligation bonds, they have not weathered the test of deep depression. But at least through 1974, they had an untarnished reputation and proven capability to raise enormous amounts of money. Yet in case after case, authority managements cheerfully accepted bond covenants and indentures that imposed stringent restrictions on their operating choices and claimed that the harsh requirements of the private money market made them unable to do what parent governments or local communities wished. The evidence suggests the contrary: that where there is a will, there is a way. The Garden State

Arts Center, the World Trade Center, the sprouting sports arenas, mortgaged nursing homes, state fairs, college dormitories, and other projects favored by authority entrepreneurs have proved feasible for private investment despite complicated arrangements for heavy subsidies.

The restrictive clauses of bond indentures are drafted with an eye to the current marketability of first issues. Such restrictions routinely are carried over into future indentures even when they are no longer necessary to sustain the credit standing of the authority. The accretion of layers of pledges makes some public authority bond prospectuses nearly as complicated as the registration statements required by the Securities and Exchange Commission for private corporations selling stock to the public. And indenture controls are sometimes more detailed than the government budgeting and accounting procedures that authorities were created to avoid.

The key to assessing corporate financial performance is the bottom line; in the case of authorities, the bottom line shows net revenue in relation to debt service (the ratio that is called "coverage"). If the coverage is guaranteed, all the other restrictions are secondary and should be unnecessary to protect investors in normal circumstances. Behind the net revenue–debt service ratio are designated reserves, which are used for debt service only if revenue coverage falls below one (that is, if annual revenues after operating costs are smaller than the amounts needed each year to pay the interest and principal on bonds and notes outstanding). The Port Authority of New York and New Jersey, with coverage of two times debt service and huge reserves, needs to give its bondholders no other protection. The layers of added protection in indentures and covenants help only the underwriters and protect authority management from what it sees as political interference.

Financial arrangements for most public authorities insulate them from even the normal regulatory measures applied to investor-owned corporations. The operations of the municipal bond market are exempt from direct SEC regulation. Indenture provisions governing authority rate setting often preclude government regulation of utility prices. Tax exemption, of course, keeps the Internal Revenue Service out of the public enterprise's books. Private bank mortgages are more stringently regulated than those purchased by public authorities. Public corporations also are exempt from most labor regulations. These freedoms are defended in terms of investor security.

Default   The ostensible purpose of indenture controls is to eliminate the risk of default. But this purpose is not necessarily compatible with the public interest. The taxpayer should not have to provide the investor with risk-free investment opportunities that are more profitable (given the tax exemption) than those available from other investments. Risk-free investments also are available in savings banks, but often at lower yields. In the last fifty years, financial losses by holders of municipal bonds have been nominal in comparison with losses on corporate bonds and other types of taxable securities.

The instances of major postwar authority bond defaults are few enough to be thoroughly familiar to professional participants in the bond market: Evergreen Development Corporation, West Virginia Turnpike Commission, Chicago Transit Authority, St. Louis's Bi-State Development Agency, and Chesapeake Bay Bridge and Tunnel Authority are the sizable cases. But even the investors in these authorities did not lose their capital, as investors in corporate securities in the private sector sometimes do. Nor have the defaulting authorities been forced into liquidation. The usual solutions have been refinancing with some subsidy by government.

In cases of threatened default, the remedies available to bondholders of public authorities are stronger than those available to bondholders of city and state governments. The Calumet Skyway in Chicago is an example of a city government project financed by revenue bonds that could not meet its payment schedule. Its bonds did not carry the remedies that are provided for in authority indentures. Chicago has not made payments on that principal debt for over a decade. The courts have ordered Chicago to raise truck tolls, but no major refinancing has taken place. The skyway revenue bonds carried higher interest rates than Chicago's general obligation bonds because they lacked the full faith and credit backing of city government, and the city argued that this higher yield reflected a risk that the bondholders should assume. Mayor Richard J. Daley resisted pressures on the city to volunteer payments on Calumet bonds from general tax revenues.

If Calumet had been financed by an authority revenue bond (rather than a city government revenue bond), the indentures would have provided for a bank trustee to move in on management sooner, forcing toll increases to cover debt service. A highway authority in default—such as the West Virginia Turnpike Commission—finds the bank trustee supervising financial planning as soon as default occurs. The Chicago Transit Authority (CTA) also fell into default in repaying their debts. The state of Illinois has created a regional transportation authority with taxing powers, which is subsidizing CTA services and helping refund its debts. The state legislature provided funds for additional subsidies, and the trustee bank used sinking fund balances to purchase (through tender solicitation) bonds outstanding at about 82 percent of face value. Investor confidence in forthcoming subsidies has been keeping the price of the remaining bonds on the secondary market up above 75 percent of face value. (A bondholder suit, seeking precedence for debt service over payroll, failed. Many authority indentures actually give bondholders first lien on gross revenues, but a failure to meet the payroll, which stops service and revenue flow, would be self-defeating.) In March 1973, when the Bi-State Development Agency missed payments on transit bonds issued for bus service in the St. Louis region, almost all the participants in the ensuing debate took for granted that some sort of subsidy would be provided. The governments that sponsored these authorities have no legal liability or written moral obligation commitment. Nevertheless, an investment firm charged that the people of St. Louis would "deed away their right to a public transit system unless they are willing to arrange payment of these Bi-State bonds through one means or another."[2] Tax relief was provided.

The odds on the ultimate recovery of substantial portions of capital when a public enterprise is in trouble are good enough to make speculation in the bonds of defaulting authorities profitable, with few exceptions. For this reason, Chicago Democrats who supported an amendment to divert motor fuel taxes to the Calumet Skyway tried to devise an arrangement to prevent recent speculators in those bonds from getting a windfall. (Speculators who buy the bonds at large discounts during default episodes are the owners of record when partial or full payment is arranged. When the Port Authority made payment for the assets of the bankrupt Hudson & Manhattan Railroad Company, for example, speculators who purchased H&M bonds in 1960, six years after bankruptcy, received as much as twenty times their money back in the Port Authority settlement.)[3]

These cases are statistical anomalies; moreover, their defaults are as much attributable to overpromotion and bad judgment by financial houses as by public officials. Optimism is characteristic of underwriters and lawyers who are trying to work out a financing deal; it also can inspire engineering firms preparing feasibility reports. Managing underwriters have been known to request upward revisions of forecasts for prospectuses (in one instance, the engineering consultant and the investment banking firm had interlocking ownership). The traffic and other revenue forecasts prepared by engineering consultants for the establishment of the authorities that have wound up in default invariably turn out to have been inaccurate. The credit rating agencies accepted the reports of lawyers and consultants at face value and did not make independent judgments of legality or of market predictions. In the case of the Evergreen Development Corporation—a ski recreation enterprise that defaulted—Moody's had mistakenly understood that the state of Maine guaranteed all the bonds. And Moody's reduced CTA's rating only after default was publicly threatened.

The Chesapeake Bay Bridge and Tunnel Authority illustrates some of the market forces and miscalculations leading to default. When this authority was first established, a business journalist wrote an article lauding the "self-supporting" attributes of the public authority approach and boasting that "before workmen could lift a finger" on the construction of the chain of bridges, causeways, and tunnels spanning the Chesapeake Bay, the corporation's chairman had to persuade Wall Street, on the basis of studies by outside consultants, that the project was "justified on strictly business grounds."[4] In fact, the regional underwriters who took the bonds to market had a reputation for working out ways to sell less-than-sure investments. In this case, they used a common strategy for marginal cases: dividing up the issue, selling portions at most favorable terms to institutional investors and selling the rest to the public on the basis of the prestige of the institutions that had already bought bonds. The result was three bond series, the first two having first liens on the authority's revenues for repayment of both interest and principal and the third series, which was sold to the public, having a subordinate claim on operating revenues.

The traffic and revenue forecasts for the Chesapeake Bay crossing turned out to have been vastly overestimated; in 1973, net revenues were $10.7 million under projections for that year. Although the holders of the first two series have been paid on time, the third series has been in default since 1970, with $20 million in back interest due by mid-1973. (Series C bonds that matured in 1973 were redeemed in 1977.) In this case, only some bond-holders were protected by underwriter-trustee supervision and by the typical financial controls over authority finance; others were distinctly disadvantaged.

The original underwriting group has been urging the state governments to subsidize a refunding bond issue, which would stretch out existing Chesapeake Bay debt and fully pay existing bondholders. The authority sought an independent opinion from nondealer financial advisers, who argued that the state governments were in no way liable for the debt and were under no obligation to risk their credit in this way. The independent financial advisers could give this opinion from a more objective perspective than could firms that also sold bonds to investors.

New York State's Urban Development Corporation (UDC) was the first of the authorities using the moral obligation pledge to get into serious financial difficulty, but UDC's default was less threatening to investors than the publicity about it suggested. The agency was two months late in paying off one issue of bond anticipation notes. The proximate cause of this temporary default was the refusal of the underwriters to underwrite new long-term bonds for the agency—bonds that had been planned to fund the payment of the notes. UDC did not actually default on any long-term bond payments, and new appropriated subsidies plus new lines of bank credit enabled UDC to meet its debt service schedule. The arrangement will cost New York taxpayers some $650 million for UDC debt service over a decade; it will not cost bondholders (except for those who sold UDC bonds at a loss on the secondary market) a cent.

The Dynamics of Promotion   The thrust of the newer breeds of bond market promoters is to achieve the initial borrowing agreement and to press for government assumption of costs if trouble arises. The Chesapeake Bay Bridge and Tunnel proposal would have faced a tougher test in a political marketplace—if framed, for example, as a joint state government project funded by general obligation bonds subject to approval by the electorate—than it did in the financial marketplace, stimulated by enthusiastic developers on either side of the crossing. This comparison would hold up, too, for lease-back projects in Pennsylvania, for building projects in New York that would not have been successful without moral obligation pledges, and even for toll highways and county sewers across the nation. If voter approval were required, fewer projects would have survived.

The career of Robert E. Toolan, while more colorful than many in the business, gives a fair illustration of how advisers and underwriters in the municipals' market start new trends in the organization of public agencies and government finance and of how their activities spread successful devices from state to state. Toolan has been characterized as father of state bond banks; the first was created under his guidance in Vermont in 1970. (State bond banks are public authorities that borrow to relend statewide to municipalities and local authorities; thus they are state-level versions of the Reconstruction Finance Corporation.) Toolan had earlier designed the bond bank proposal for New Jersey's Department of Community Affairs, but the proposal was defeated there partly as a result of pressure from dealers in municipal and sewer authority bonds whose business might have been displaced by bond bank lending to those local authorities. (Toolan, on the other hand, would have been a managing underwriter for the bond bank sales.) By 1977, bond banks had been established in five states and Puerto Rico.[5] Toolan also took part in early moral obligation financings, including those for New York's Housing Finance Agency, Housing Development Corporation, Mortgage Agency, and Battery Park City Authority.

Toolan's deals reveal the complex trade-offs that make some unlikely enterprises possible. He has negotiated bank purchases of bonds in exchange for authority deposits (for example, for the Miami Airport Authority). He has negotiated to obtain high ratings for untested enterprises (for example, for bond banks). He has sought rulings from the Internal Revenue Service (for example, obtaining a tax exemption for a Tennessee industrial development authority project that was to be leased to the federal government at the time when the federal government was trying to clamp down on this type of exemption). His first deal in California is described in a communication from his firm as "The Financing of Cal Expo: An Impossible Job." In the capacity of financial consultant to the state treasurer, he structured a plan to finance the California State Fair and Exposition with revenue bonds, although it had no chance of breaking even. The plan involved three corporate entities, several leases and subleases, and legislatively appropriated subsidies.

This kind of promotional energy—expended by others as enterprising as Toolan—lies behind the growth of indirectly subsidized activities by public authorities. It swells the growth of negotiated, rather than competitive, public financings because closed negotiations are required to tailor marginal public enterprises for special investor needs.

Promoting the Public Interest

One maxim inherited from the nineteenth century remains valid: politics is biased in favor of overborrowing, and elected officials are inclined to risk the public interest of the future for political support today.[6] A corollary must be added: the private sector is biased in favor of overlending, and the municipal bond industry is inclined to risk the public interest of the future for profit today. (In both maxims, the prefix "over" reflects subjective judgment, of course.) One of the fundamental mistakes of political officials has been to rely on the financiers—whom they perceive to be conservative—to exercise fiscal caution and steady supervision. In the absence of any reliable source of restraint, current borrowing determines larger and larger portions of future allocations of resources.

Mentors of the "pure" or self-supporting forms of public authority have expressed dismay over all the variations that call more clearly on taxpayer support. Several state and local treasurers and comptrollers also argue that only the older, more profitable type of public authority serves the public interest. But the reasoning behind this dogma is not self-evident. If it were accompanied by adequate public information, political accountability, and financial planning, the public corporation could be useful as an organizational tool for many tasks and purposes, either subsidized or not. The restraints on other means of accomplishing the tasks have clearly raised the value of the corporate tool: to finance projects outside debt regulation and executive budgets, to bypass elections, to substitute for unpopular metropolitan government, to subsidize selected segments of the private sector. Lease-backs, regional service corporations, indirectly guaranteed corporate securities, and even industrial revenue bonds of certain types have increased the financial capacities of the public sector substantially. Moreover, virtually every authority that is now self-supporting at one time used taxpayer help. Reasonably balanced public policy requires that even the self-supporting authority accept the notion of financial subsidy in particular circumstances. In many cases, maximizing the financial return from selected services has done a disservice to broader public interests.

Like most other institutions, however, authorities can be abused. The current system of public authority financing encourages governmental agencies to adopt a pace of investment too fast for contemplated repayments, and when the bill comes due to the public, it is unexpectedly high. State and local governments have failed to carry out basic financial and organizational reforms; instead, they have resorted to improvisations—many of them involving authorities—that do not match long-term resources with needs.

The availability of financing for some purposes and not for others has skewed the priorities of government enterprise without regard for the public interest. Financing for the capital construction of universities reflects such distortions of need and resources. College revenue bonds became a favorite instrument of a number of bond houses during the 1960s, when experts predicted continuing increases in students and tuition income. Between 1961 and 1971, the volume of tax-exempt bonds for higher education swelled from under $170 million (nearly all of it in state general obligation bonds) to over $1.3 billion (over $1 billion of that in agency revenue bonds). Two federal departments subsidized debt service or bought into parts of these bond issues. Eleven states created authorities to make long-term loans to public and private colleges. Lease-back and moral obligation financing techniques were piggy-backed for some higher education projects, and both state and federal grants and urban property taxes were channeled into debt service. Favored investments were in dormitories and residential colleges. Bonds were issued through public authorities and backed in part by student fees. But student enrollment slowed, despite the forecasts, and more students chose to live off campus. A surfeit of underused dormitories and some bankrupt colleges have resulted, while inner-city schools and colleges continue to suffer from overcrowded, obsolete classroom and laboratory facilities.

The existing system of authority revenue bond financing also tends to distort price structures, often making fees for public services higher than direct costs require, without any explicit consideration of the effects of prices on traffic or other demand patterns. Covenants that provide for high debt service coverage and amortization spread over shorter periods of time than normal life-of-the-project depreciation rates have this effect. Restrictive covenants limit the options available to authority managements, and competition and public disclosure rarely characterize the newer types of public authority bond sales. Moreover, the issuing corporation often does not have enough knowledge of the market and of the financing alternatives to judge the proposal offered to it. Under such conditions, dealers may find it hard to resist structuring some deals to favor their bond-buying customers. Evidence of blatant double-dealing or illegal practices is rare, but the particular interests of the public enterprise would benefit from more adversary bargaining, more objective advice, and less consensus.

In small jurisdictions, public officials are often at a serious disadvantage. Three New Jersey cases demonstrate the dilemma. In 1973, Gibraltar Securities Co. obtained agreement from the Red Bank Chamber of Commerce that a local parking authority, if created, would help its members compete with outlying shopping centers. With this endorsement, Gibraltar's representative then called on the town council with a "one-stop" proposal, uniting advisory and underwriting services to design, create, and finance such an authority; the proposal included provision for the services of architectural and engineering consultants, whose fees would be built into the bond financing, and a "moral pledge" of town credit behind the revenue bonds. The proposal would have been passed by the town council quickly if one of its members had not been an investment banker in the bond business. Only he was in a position to point out the flaws in the proposal for the town's purposes.[7]

In 1972, when the Gloucester County Sewerage Authority was established, a local reporter in Camden, New Jersey, likened its financing to the selling of a used car. Kidder, Peabody underwrote the negotiated sale and also provided financial advisory services. The advisory fee was $212,000, and the discount in handling $30 million in notes was $150,000; the underwriters would receive additional profits when the notes were refunded with long-term bonds. When interviewed, the Kidder, Peabody representative pointed out that the firm could have collected over $600,000 in discounts if it had recommended earlier permanent financing. But the reporter also consulted independent financial advisers, and when she informed the authority board of directors and the county board of freeholders about far less expensive options that the advisers had explained to her, the chairman of the authority board understandably expressed dismay: "Why should a public authority not be in a position to know about these people? Why doesn't the state provide us with this information?"[8]

Finally, in 1974, the Middletown, New Jersey, Sewerage Authority filed suit against Halsey, Stuart & Co., charging that the brokerage firm received hidden profit in a refunding deal. The firm had issued $35 million in tax-exempt bonds for the authority—which used $30 million to refund outstanding debt. Halsey, Stuart used the remaining $5 million to purchase taxable, federally guaranteed bonds to resell to the authority for investment income. It resold those bonds to the authority at a premium representing an eight to six point markup over what the firm itself paid for the bonds. At issue in the case—still pending in the federal courts in 1977—was whether the underwriter-advisory firm disclosed adequate information to the client. Authority directors had not realized they were buying the taxable securities at a substantial markup from the firm that had recommended the arrangement to them.

Clearly, fortuitous elections of investment bankers to town councils, serendipitous discoveries by local reporters, and litigation after the fact do not adequately protect the public interest.

Directions for Change

In the United States, the public sector poses no serious threat to the private sector. Even federal and state loan and grant programs have not displaced private investment; they have, in fact, expanded the demand for private capital on the tax-exempt market in education, housing, health, transit, water, and sewerage. Federal and state aid programs should be accompanied by technical assistance and, in some cases, regulation to help state and local public corporations make sensible and informed judgments about raising the money that supplements government grants and loans.

Recourse to separate attorneys representing the issuer, the underwriter, and the bondholder, a pattern familiar for private sector issues of securities, would increase the costs, time, and complications of selling public bonds. But the law should permit a far heavier reliance on city and state attorneys. Bar associations, in cooperation with attorneys general, should devise guidelines relating to fees (maximum, not just minimum), qualifications, and the responsibilities of attorneys involved in public financing.

State governments should provide basic advice to counties, municipalities, and local corporations. (Thirty states have programs to assist local borrowing, most of them weak and passive.) Local authorities might be required to use nondealer financial advisers and to submit negotiated financing arrangements to a state bond assistance agency for advance review.

States should develop technical assistance programs for authority (and municipal) debt management to explain long-range constraints on borrowing, to explore alternative methods of financing proposed undertakings, to educate authority officials on the workings of the bond market and the options open to them, to develop data and information systems that permit officials to keep track of the volume and directions of public enterprise debt, and to determine guidelines for acceptable prospectus and indenture terms. Such a program could make good use of the explanatory materials that investment banking firms and the municipal bond departments of commercial banks now provide; these materials are seldom read, much less understood, by managements of small public authorities. The states also should explore the possibilities of providing public finance consulting services on a fee basis.

States may try to build up their advisory capacities by using any of three types of agency: bond banks, with responsibilities expanded to provide advisory and sales agent services; state treasurers' or comptrollers' offices, expanded to assist in planning and guiding government enterprise financing; or separate organizations such as the Michigan Municipal Finance Commission. The existing expertise on capital finance in most states is concentrated in one of these three types of institution. Of course, state advisory facilities would compete with private legal and financial advisory services. But such competition is unlikely to get out of bounds and can be used to equalize sophistication levels in the public-private transactions.

The failure of the courts to clarify the term "public purpose," to systematically reconcile contract rights with legislative prerogatives, and to balance modern fiscal techniques against inherited debt limitations signals the need for comprehensive study and constitutional revision in all states. But the failure rate of efforts at constitutional revision is so high that federal stimuli may be needed to achieve state reforms. Modernized debt limitation must take into account—as it has in Pennsylvania—contingent liability through lease-back and fill-up pledges and agreements, as well as traditional finance by government and government corporations. Regular governments should have greater opportunities to issue revenue bonds so that they do not have to resort to establishing separate corporate authorities, where the option is not otherwise warranted. In addition to debt control reforms like those instituted in Pennsylvania, Louisiana, and Wisconsin, states should consider regulating or limiting the terms of public authority covenants and indentures. They might make certain indenture restrictions (such as limits on authority rate regulation, expenditure, and investment) contingent on revenue levels. Thus, for example, such restrictions might be inoperable if authority net revenues were at least 130 percent of annual debt service requirements and reserves were adequate for debt service for the next twelve to eighteen months.

Basic statutes should create opportunities for merger, takeover, or tapping the excess revenues of public corporations, with specific procedures for protecting bondholders. Procedures for protecting stockholders and creditors of investor-owned corporations permit such changes with relative ease. The limitations that some authority indentures place on corporate powers and functions (preventing, for example, mergers of local utilities) would be untenable in any private business situation and are unjustified in public enterprise.

Finally, public corporations should organize their financial plans in some comprehensive format—whether a five-year capital budget or a system of regional investment plans—for public consideration of priorities. The purpose of this change is to permit a realistic analysis of the long-term effects of the projects proposed on public finance, social welfare, and the environment. Such an analysis, performed on an ongoing basis, should serve to inform the public and to raise the level of the political bargaining that ensues. Whatever the structure of the arrangement, representative government institutions should have some power to force changes in the priorities that are served by public investment. The governmental participants must have some goals, some coherent ideas of what they want from public enterprise, if they are to exercise more influence over its performance.

The municipal bond market has well served the purpose of maximizing the money available for public borrowing from private sources. (And political leaders have asked for little more.) The market's record of honesty and internal rule keeping is good, although perhaps deteriorating with sheer growth in volume, but the weakness of the public sector has made it inadequate as a check on the profit motive. Governments must reconsider their heavy dependence on this market, their inadequate information and virtually non-existent financial planning, and their increasing reliance upon authority managements with goals that are narrower than state and city interests at large.

III | Businesslike Government

7 The Board of Directors

Most public authorities do their specific jobs well. It is their choices of what and what not to do that raise tough questions. The biases that emerge in their project planning and financing are solidly implanted in their governing structures. Public authorities tend to conform in structure to orthodox theory of the government corporation in America. They are headed by boards of directors, which are modeled on the boards of private firms. Unlike directors of a private firm, however, they do not answer to stockholders, and the company cannot be ultimately controlled through stock transactions. Directors in the public sector are usually secure from ouster during their terms.

The boards of public corporations, large and small, are a great comfort and protection to management. The directors enjoy the perquisites of their public directorships, but most of them are busily and successfully employed elsewhere. For authority decisions, directors rely on the recommendations of the corporation's full-time staff, and under normal circumstances they seldom interfere seriously with the management of the enterprise. Directors lend prestige to the organization, often provide specific financial contacts, and, above all, buffer management from the impingements of community interest groups and elected officials. What they do not do is run the enterprise.

Part-time boards and committees are seldom decisive managers, particularly when they are made up of people who are not professionally engaged in the business at hand. Marver Bernstein's classic study of federal regulatory commissions, several studies of congressional committees, and studies of state and local government boards all describe behavior that is also typical of boards of directors of public corporations. Such boards depend heavily upon professional staff for information and for bringing matters to their attention; in some cases, they are scantily informed and seldom do they have time and analyses available to foresee and solve problems of corporate management. They tend to develop internal consensus, to form a common point of view even when individual members may have started out as political opponents or personal adversaries; they typically hold perfunctory formal meetings. "Boards . . . seem quite inappropriate for direct administration of any agency. It is not uncommon in agencies which have boards as policymaking bodies . . . to have most of the policies ultimately generated within the bureaucracy of the agency and to be sold to the commissioners by the administrative head."[1]

The directors of most state corporations are appointed by the governor; the directors of the majority of local authorities are appointed by mayors or town or county councils. They generally do not receive full-time pay but are entitled to fees and allowances for attending meetings and for other work on authority business. Where annual stipends are provided, they are usually in the range of $1,000 to $3,000 although some are as high as $40,000.

Authority directors are usually appointed for fixed and staggered terms. Frequently they are reappointed and thus stay in office for longer periods of time than the mayor or governor or local councilmen who selected them. As a result, they have a distinct advantage over newly elected officials who may be their nominal superiors.

Most authority directors (or "commissioners," as they are variously titled) are private persons not otherwise in government service. Some boards, especially those of lease-back authorities, include a few government officials for purposes of liaison or to add specific expertise to the board, but most boards provide little or no representation of the parent government. A few states have experimented with public enterprise directors chosen to represent specific public interests or constituencies. Representative boards, which are common in Europe, are increasingly found in the West and Midwest. These variations remain a minority. Considering the variety of state law, local politics, and practical tasks affecting public authorities, their governing boards are remarkably alike. Appointments, responsibilities, terms, and conditions of service reflect legal and administrative advice that has traveled across state lines and through the decades. The theory of the government corporation called for directors of a certain type: successful people of high repute and achievement in business. They were expected to serve in positions of wide discretion with secure tenure, to formulate policy on nonpolitical premises, and to be appointed on nonpartisan bases. Some aspects of this ideal have been realized. Most unpaid directors have relatively high incomes and good reputations in the community; most directors on public boards serve for extended periods of time. But the degree to which directors manage the activities of the enterprise is much more limited than theory would have it, and their immunity from politics is apocryphal at best.

The Port Authority Precedent

One of the reasons for the consistencies that do exist is that many authorities have been patterned after the Port Authority of New York and New Jersey. Originally a board consisting of three resident voters from each state, the Port Authority Board of Commissioners was increased to twelve members in 1930, all appointed by a governor and confirmed by their respective state senates. Four of the six from each state must reside within the port district. The law sets no other restrictions or criteria for these appointments to a board that serves six-year staggered terms in charge of public assets of some $3 billion.

During the 1930s, the federal government promoted this type of board, and after World War II, hundreds of highway, port, bridge, tunnel, and other enterprises adopted it. But the pattern was by no means a foregone conclusion when the Port Authority was created. The Port of London Authority (which originated the term "authority" for statutory corporations) is frequently cited as the model New York followed. But the commissioners who headed the London Authority explicitly represented various interests—including representatives of government agencies and members elected by shipowners and other private groups concerned with the port. In 1921, when the New York Port Authority was established, the representational possibilities of its board were an issue in the political struggle between progressive reformers and the old-line party representatives, between business leadership and political organizations built on immigrant votes. Active in the reform movement was the New York Chamber of Commerce. Its president, Eugenius Outerbridge, and his colleague, Julius Henry Cohen, drafted the Port Authority compact, shepherded it through the two state legislatures, and subsequently served as chairman and general counsel, respectively, of the new authority. The compact was actually signed in the "Great Hall" of the chamber of commerce.[2] New York City's mayor, the Tammany Hall Democrats, and New Jersey's Hudson County Democratic organization opposed the compact, and local officials pressed for local representation on the authority board. The chamber's version of "businesslike" corporate leadership, which excluded the local machine politicians, prevailed.

Political strategy—albeit reform political strategy—underlay the nonrepresentational, allegedly nonpolitical public authority board. And political tactics brought the allegedly nonpolitical board successes in the state legislatures in 1921 and throughout the subsequent fifty years. As Cohen describes events in 1921, "For sheer lack of votes we were in for a licking," in New Jersey, when one of their best friends, Senator Joe Frelinghuysen "corralled enough votes to change defeat into victory."[3] Subsequent confirmation of board appointments by the legislatures seldom impinged upon management's choices. Over the years, confirmation by the state senates has had little influence on appointments of Port Authority and other corporate commissioners. The confirmation process does provide some opportunities for legislative discussion, but nearly all approvals have been forthcoming.[4]

In the early years of the Port Authority's operations, Outerbridge and

Cohen spelled out corporate norms, arguing that the confidence of the financial community depended upon its dominance of corporate management. The
relationship between money and the governing board was (and is) direct.
Julius Henry Cohen called the authority's $100,000 annual appropriations
from each of the two states "chicken feed": "We needed millions of dollars.
Hundreds of millions. Through Outerbridge's influence, we made contact
with pretty nearly every one of the leaders in the financial world" and persuaded a number of them to serve as commissioners.[5]

Subsequent attempts by local groups to make Port Authority direction
more dependent on local politics did not prevail against the founders and the
principles they had expounded. In 1947, New York City's Mayor Paul
O'Dwyer suggested that the chairmanship of the Port Authority board of
commissioners become a full-time salaried position (and thus provide some
checks and balances with management). Cohen objected: "The leaders in
commerce and industry whom it was expected would serve as commissioners
would not be attracted to the service. Bankers and businessmen serving on the
board performed their service as a matter of public duty . . . the esteem with
which the Port Authority is held with its superb financial credit is something
on which the public relies."[6] He held that the business dominance of the
board was necessary to convince the financial interests that the Port Authority was not a "socialist experiment." The business press generally maintained
that the Port Authority enjoyed Moody's A rating because of the quality of
businessmen serving on its board.

Five years later, a congressional committee urged that if the authority's
board members were less exclusively experienced in finance, if some of them
had careers in transportation, urban planning, or city government, the public
in the port region would be better served. But most commentators were firm
advocates of the business model of the public corporate board. They pointed
with pride to the Port Authority's directors as "financially and socially prominent men . . . thoroughly experienced in high corporate finance."[7] (The
twelve commissioners also were directors or chief executives of some fifty
investor-owned corporations.) When S. Sloan Colt was selected chairman of
the board in 1961, an editorial (which has the distinct ring of company public
relations) praised him as "one of the most important financiers in the
country, but he finds time to serve as unpaid authority commissioner. In fact,
Mr. Colt has been doing it for 13 years—attending frequent meetings, giving
advice and direction at its best, working steadily in the regional welfare. The
same goes for all 12 Port Authority commissioners . . . [who] concern them-

selves with more than their private interests. This dedication is selfless and hard working without thought of reward."[8]

The image of a selfless group of businessmen dedicating themselves to government enterprise had grown from a political strategy of reformers to an article of faith throughout the public sector. Hence, when North Carolina reduced the terms of its Port Authority board members to match the incumbency of the governor and thus gave the governor a more direct influence on policy, an academic commentator protested that the change "violates the *concept* of a port authority."[9] (The state subsequently switched back to staggered six-year terms.) That concept reflects several tacit assumptions: that businessmen do not represent political viewpoints, that disparate opinions have no place in public enterprise direction, and that elected governors should not take a close personal or political interest in the affairs of state corporations.

Recruitment of Board Members   Through fifty years of board appointments by governors of both states and parties, businessmen, bankers, brokers, and insurance men have dominated the Port Authority board.[10] The board also has included a few real estate men, corporate lawyers, and other professionals, but labor unions were totally unrepresented, as were women, blacks, and members of organized community groups. Only a handful of long-term government officeholders or people active in a local community have found their way onto the board; no elected official was appointed from the New York side for thirty years after 1942. The industries most directly interested in the port and dependent on the Port Authority's facilities—railroads, airlines, bus companies, shipping lines, truck firms, and auto user associations—also have not been represented.[11] Former Executive Director Austin Tobin explains that the last thing he wanted when negotiating a tough lease with airlines was an airline executive looking over his shoulder in his own board room.

Yet Tobin, like most other authority managers, was willing to let bankers look over his shoulder when he negotiated financial arrangements. He did not seem to feel that patronage or conflict of interest ensues when people move back and forth from financial houses that advise on or invest in authority bond issues to positions on the authority's board. In fact, Port Authority management has traditionally placed great faith in bankers. In 1935, for example, according to the Port Authority minutes, the board met with some of the regions' banking firms to discuss the Port Authority's plans to refund its first issue of bonds. Present at the meeting were representatives from insurance companies and banks, and subsequently, directors from each of those firms became commissioners on the Port Authority board. (Except for one two-year lapse, the Port Authority board had had a Bankers Trust officer on it since 1924 when the Port Authority rented office space from Bankers Trust.) One of the representatives at the 1935 meeting, Horace Corbin of the Fidelity Union Trust Company, served on the board from 1948 through 1960. During Austin Tobin's management, the authority's policy was not to do new business directly with banks with which current commissioners were connected, although the authority maintained the deposit levels it had previously established with such banks, and commissioners' banks and firms participated on a normal basis in authority bond underwritings, loans, and investments.

Hoyt Ammidon, the recently retired chairman of United States Trust Company of New York, served on the Port Authority board from 1968 through 1972. United States Trust held nearly $100 million in Port Authority bonds, and in 1972, while Ammidon was authority vice-chairman, plans were made by the board to appoint United States Trust as trustee for future authority bond issues. Previously, the Port Authority had not used a bank trustee. In 1974, when United States Trust brought suits challenging New York's and New Jersey's repeal of the statutory covenants limiting Port Authority transit deficits, the bank could sue in its capacity as trustee for authority bondholders. The appointment of United States Trust as bond trustee for the fortieth and forty-first consolidated bond series had ensured that the covenant repeals would be challenged in court despite opposition by both state governors and by William Ronan, who became chairman of the authority board in 1974. (Ronan prevented the Port Authority's legal department from bringing suit against the repeals itself.) Moreover, because of its trusteeship role, the bank's fees for the legal expenses of bringing the suit were paid by the authority (by decision of Port Authority commissioners). The authority paid over $1 million in fees to lawyers for United States Trust through mid-1976, and those lawyers carried appeals to the Supreme Court against the wishes of both governors and the new authority chairman. Ammidon's participation in both public and private institutions with such interlocking relationships would not have been permitted in regular government. His activities gave an appearance of impropriety to observers from the highest levels of state government.

Over the years, the governors of the two states—with few exceptions—have followed the advice of authority board members and management on the selection of new members. The governors fended off pressures from other groups by reiterating the argument that the creditors must control the board if the money supply is to be maximized. Even the inveterate politician Alfred E. Smith, a Port Authority commisioner himself for two years, appointed bankers and businessmen when he was governor.

Authority commissioners often have been acquainted with one another before joining the board, and more than one sitting commissioner has brought several others to the board. The length of service of Port Authority board members and the frequency with which they are reappointed, even by governors other than those who appointed them in the first place, reflect above all the influence on appointments of Austin Tobin, who spent thirty years as Port Authority executive director. Well over half of the postwar commissioners served more than one term; in 1965, Port Authority commissioners averaged almost eleven years of service, and the chairman boasted nineteen years' service.

Howard S. Cullman, who served on the board from 1927 to 1969, was vice-chairman from 1935 to 1945 and chairman from 1945 to 1955; he developed a particularly close relationship with Tobin. Donald V. Lowe of New Jersey, who served on the board from 1945 to 1969, succeeded Cullman but resigned as chairman in 1959 and was replaced by S. Sloan Colt. Colt served on the board from 1946 through 1968 and was chairman for ten years. He was followed as chairman by James C. Kellogg III, appointed to the board in 1955 and still serving as a commissioner in 1975, although he had retired from the chairmanship. Cullman was a financier with an interest in Cullman Brothers, a family investment firm, and director of three banking and insurance firms; Lowe was president of Lowe Paper Company and director of three insurance companies; Colt was chairman of Bankers Trust Company; and Kellogg was a partner in the brokerage firm of Spear, Leeds & Kellogg (also a chairman of the New York Stock Exchange). Such board chairmen could clearly be worth their weight in gold to an enterprise constantly seeking capital from private money markets. Tobin also valued the way in which Cullman and Colt encouraged other commissioners to support his and the authority staff's proposals and admired their ability to maintain consensus on the board and to assure independence for the management of the corporation.

As the authority achieved stable management and financial prestige, it sacrificed the perspectives of urban planning and local democracy. The low rate of turnover and long service of board members made it difficult for other interests to influence decision making and cemented the Port Authority's co-optation by its banking allies. As one student of the Port Authority board concluded, "the appointment system has prevented the Port Authority's foes from deflecting the organization from its goals."[12]

The same effect occurs in other similarly structured authorities. For example, the directors of the Massachusetts Port Authority (Massport)—representatives of the legal, business, and banking professions (with one labor representative required by statute)—have regularly rubber-stamped the agenda provided by Massport's executive director. While the beleaguered community of East Boston waged battles against Logan International Airport expansion, occasionally engaging in demonstrations and sit-ins on airport runways, board meetings proceeded in peaceful agreement, rarely reflecting the controversy.[13]

High Status Politics   Insulation from community interests and from local conflicts is not the same as freedom from politics and pressures. In his early study of the Port Authority, Erwin Wilkie Bard wrote: "If the hopes of those who founded the Port Authority were to be achieved, it was imperative that they isolate their organization from the corrosive influence of its political neighbors. . . . the Port Authority's selection was untouched by the blight of political interference."[14] Yet the commissioners who most clearly epitomized banking dominance of public enterprise management have also had extraordinary political influence. They have been active, first and foremost, as fund raisers for gubernatorial and national election campaigns. For example, Howard Cullman, born into a socially prominent family of millionaires, was treasurer of several of Franklin D. Roosevelt's campaigns, as well as those of Senator Robert F. Wagner, Sr. His political contacts in Washington remained first rate for over thirty years (President Eisenhower sent him to the Brussels World's Fair with ambassadorial rank). Other commissioners, too, have had direct and personal ties with the governors of New York and New Jersey. Their political influence helps account not only for their appointment to the board in the first place but also for the enormous political power they have exercised with the governors and legislatures on occasions when special efforts were necessary to get what the Port Authority wanted.

Austin Tobin has described the board of commissioners as approximating an "enlightened concept . . . of a directorate . . . responsive to their stockholders." (Of course, the authority has no stockholders, but Tobin uses that term to refer to the public.) In support of this proposition, he points out that "practically every project and recommendation submitted to the legislatures . . . received almost unanimous approval,"[15] and the governors have rarely used their veto. In fact, this record of political success is derived from the reserves of political influence that could be used by the commissioners to back up the political skills of Austin Tobin.

Governors of both states have traditionally appointed new commissioners from their own parties, not because party organizations influenced the governors but because the commissioners were often colleagues of the governors themselves or contributors to their campaigns. The intrusion of politics into authority business is unwelcome to Port Authority leaders only when it consists of counterpressures from local party or community organizations (particularly from politicians in New York City and Hudson County, New Jersey). Arbitrary distinctions between acceptable and unacceptable brands of politics, together with the biases of the financing system, go far to explain why past Port Authority projects have so little served the needs of inner-city residents in the port district. The symbolic distinction between business and politics has served to bias policy toward downtown business and suburban political interests.

When they first assumed office, New Jersey Governors Alfred Driscoll and Robert Meyner each stated publicly that they would improve the balance of representation on the Port Authority board. When Meyner was elected, the New Jersey commissioners were all Republicans, and Hudson County Democrats were pressing for Port Authority action on northern New Jersey's rapid transit problems. At the same time, newly elected Democratic Governor Averill Harriman of New York refused to reappoint some prominent Republican commissioners. The Port Authority leadership feared major changes in its board and its relationships with the governors. At this point, Tobin called on allies in banking and in campaign finance to discuss Port Authority interests with both governors.

Meyner's appointments did replace Republicans with Democrats. Otherwise the new commissioners were no more representative than their predecessors: Wall Street broker James Kellogg, a prominent Democratic contributor and fund raiser in New Jersey; corporate lawyer Thorn Lord, a partner of Richard Hughes (later governor) and himself a candidate for U.S. Senate; and lawyer and bank director John Clancy, campaign manager for Senator Harrison Williams. A fourth vacancy under Meyner's control did go to a Hudson County man, former assemblyman and Hoboken city attorney Robert McAlevy. Subsequently, Meyner appointed Charles W. Engelhard, a businessman who was also a frequent delegate to the Democratic national conventions and an unsuccessful Senate candidate, and W. Paul Stillman, Republican fund raiser and director of a New Jersey bank and an insurance company (who resigned in 1977, complaining that Governor Brendan Byrne's attempts to influence authority policy amounted to improper injection of "political considerations").

The only man Tammany Hall ever selected for the Port Authority board also was a banker. Governor Harriman appointed N. Baxter Jackson (to replace Bayard F. Pope, director of Marine Midland and a prominent Republican fund raiser). Jackson, who reportedly had been recommended by Tammany leader Carmine DeSapio, was chairman of the board of Chemical Corn Exchange Bank. (Pope was later reappointed to the board by Governor Nelson Rockefeller, who refused to reappoint Democrats Moran and Jackson.) Neither of the local party organization candidates—Jackson from New York or McAlevy of New Jersey—lasted beyond one term. (McAlevy resigned to become a state judge.)[16]

In the 1960s, Nelson Rockefeller appointed Bernard J. Lasker, former chairman of the board of governors for the New York Stock Exchange and senior partner of Lasker, Stone & Stern, a prominent Republican fund raiser who played important roles in Nixon's presidential campaigns and in state Republican finance; Gustave L. Levy, senior partner of Goldman, Sachs & Co., investment bankers, and still another former chairman of the board of governors of the New York Stock Exchange, also a major contributor to campaign finance; James G. Hellmuth, treasurer of the state Republican committee in New York, a seasoned election campaigner for Rockefeller at both the state and national levels and a vice-president of Bankers Trust Company; and Alexander Halpern, a fund raiser and head of Citizens for Rockefeller, as well as a partner in a well-known New York law firm.

Consensus in the Board Room   Even commissioners who join the board feeling some opposition to Port Authority policies or some special loyalty to a governor tend to adopt the corporate point of view over time. In most organizations, efforts to "induce consensus between the newcomers and the rest of the organization are comparatively intensive."[17] This process, termed "socialization," meets two organizational needs: the newcomer becomes acquainted with the rules and operations of the firm, and he accepts the values of the leadership, including existing decision-making procedures, to sustain unity. To these ends, new commissioners on the Port Authority board receive careful preparation by the staff. Even before their first meetings, many have been impressed by the reputation of fellow commissioners, by the glamour of the Port Authority's facilities, and by its record of financial success.

Austin Tobin's skill in catering to his board members is admired and emulated by authority managers across the nation. He made sure that service on the board carried publicity and prestige and helped business contacts. The authority's staff tries to protect commissioners from criticism and divisive argument. Although Tobin kept new commissioners supplied with information on particular phases of Port Authority activity that suited their interests, for the most part the commissioners naturally depended on the facts gathered and recommendations made by a generally able staff. As Tobin puts it, while his board was not placid, it was "decent and cooperative." The planning staffs of the Port Authority develop both technical project proposals and development priorities. They present their proposals to the board meetings in finished form, backed up by research and statistics. The commissioners, for whom the authority is an outside interest rather than a full-time job, are seldom in a position to provide an independent judgment on the specifics of most propositions put to them. They therefore tend to absorb the viewpoints of the experts on the authority payroll.

The procedures of board meetings reinforce these tendencies. Austin Tobin readily acknowledges that in meetings of little more than one hour's duration, the Port Authority board has acted on scores of agenda items involving regional transportation, airport sites, bond covenants, and the World Trade Center, and it approves annual operating budgets of over one-quarter billion dollars. The vast majority of formal votes at board meetings are unanimous: "The public board meetings are often lifeless, cut and dried affairs resulting quickly in open ratification of agreements arrived at beforehand in various committees of the Commission. Committee meetings are closed, and while minutes may be available, transcripts of the discussions are not. Consequently, such disputes as do occur within the authority are rarely exposed to public view."[18] Loose debate is not encouraged, nor are new ideas generated. Brief agenda and documents are submitted in advance. Board members themselves have no separate offices, secretaries, or staff, but the executives are trained to give top priority to the commissioners' requests for information and generally have succeeded in keeping them happy.

The press and the public are admitted to full board meetings; the minutes of these meetings are public records and are forwarded to the governors' offices. But "if there is any item that is not settled in the committee meetings, it never reaches the board calendar."[19]

The socialization process in the Port Authority board of commissioners is so effective that, although the authority was born out of interstate conflict, the state delegations on the board have never publicly acknowledged a serious conflict, and governors of both states have chastised the board for neglecting their interests. A Hudson County Democrat who had joined the Port Authority board to represent local opposition reported back to his organization that it was seeing Port Authority problems from too local a perspective.

Other interstate commissions and authorities that provide more direct representation of governors and interested agency heads are usually not so successful in submerging conflict. The Delaware River Basin Commission (DRBC), for example, copes continually with interstate conflicts. This commission is younger and has had weaker staff leadership than the Port Authority. Its board is composed of one official from each of four states (the governor or his representative) and two presidential appointees. The DRBC board mirrors and sometimes resolves interstate conflicts; the Port Authority board blacks them out.[20]

After 1965, some of the factors that contributed to the extraordinary unanimity and insulation of the Port Authority board began to change slowly. Between 1967 and 1970, nine commissioners died, retired, or were not reappointed. In this way, two-thirds of the Port Authority board changed. Chairman Kellogg never developed the comfortable, cooperative relationship with Tobin that Colt and Cullman had enjoyed. Tobin objected to Kellogg's tendency to probe matters of internal management and maintenance. New Jersey appointments of this period tended to be less cosmopolitan, more local, and less prestigious than typical earlier appointments:

Gerard F. Brill (1965–1968): local banker and Jersey City Chamber of Commerce official, actively involved in Hudson County politics, who resigned as a Port Authority commissioner to become a member of the Hudson County Board of Taxation.

William A. Sternkopf, Jr. (1968–1971): vice-chairman of the New Jersey Turnpike Authority, an accountant with government-oriented business who resigned when indicted in 1972.

Walter Henry Jones (1969–1974): former New Jersey state senator and lawyer, indicted and acquitted of bank fraud in 1974.

Andrew C. Axtell (1970–): corporate sales manager and mayor of Livingston, New Jersey, former chairman of Essex County Republican committee.

Philip B. Hofmann: a 1971 appointment in the traditional mainstream, chairman of the finance committee of Johnson & Johnson.

Reverend Victor R. Yanitelli: Jesuit college president appointed in 1972 to replace Sternkopf (and to compensate for the stain of indictments by the example of virtue).

In 1974, newly elected Governor Brendan Byrne added some transportation expertise to the Port Authority board by appointing his transportation commissioner, Alan Sagner, and a transportation industry executive, Milton A. Gilbert. (Sagner, businessman and Byrne's campaign finance chairman, became Port Authority chairman in 1977.)

The New York appointments of this post-1965 period were such traditional types as Ammidon, Lasker, and Levy. At the same time, however, Governor Rockefeller was making the most comprehensive and successful attempt in the history of public enterprise to control public corporations by the placement of personally loyal directors. William J. Ronan was one of these appointments, and his behavior on the board distinctly diverged from the average. As chairman from 1974 to 1977, Ronan debated publicly with New Jersey's governor, attempted to control day-to-day management of the authority, and found himself embroiled in controversy because he became a millionaire in public service and traveled with his wife at authority expense.

Robert R. Douglass was another Rockefeller appointee whose career was largely dependent on his personal ties to the governor. A member of the law firm that was counsel to Chase Manhattan Bank, Douglass, like Ronan, was a former secretary to the governor. Commissioner Jerry Finkelstein, a prominent Democrat and publisher of the *New York Law Journal* and the *Civil Service Leader*, also was a key supporter of Nelson Rockefeller, particularly helpful in campaigns for state transportation bond issues.

The effects of stepped-up turnover and disharmony on the board, aggravated by Tobin's resignation as executive director and Ronan's accession to the chairmanship, made the Port Authority more vulnerable after 1974 than it had been since its earliest days. Deterioration in the stability and homogeneity of the board was dramatic by 1976–1977, when six commissioners were replaced in less than a year due to resignations, failure to be reappointed, and one death. This weakening of the board, together with repeated turnover of the executive director, was accompanied by mounting criticism from the public and hostility from the governors, pressures from which the stable leadership of earlier days had buffered the authority.

Other Authorities from the Mold

Although federal enterprises are as often headed by an appointed administrator as by a governing board, when Franklin Roosevelt's administration recommended authority-enabling legislation to the states, it explicitly suggested the use of part-time corporate boards with fixed and staggered terms like that of the Port Authority. The RFC guidelines for federally funded enterprise reiterated the call for independently appointed multimember boards and produced widespread replication of weak oversight by directors from the private sector. During the subsequent forty years, public authority managers have widely shared Austin Tobin's preference for boards composed of "high caliber businessmen," in the words of a regional water authority executive in Pennsylvania.

Of the thirty public corporations that administer ports in the United States today (including three interstate, seven state, and twenty local corporations), twenty-two use the prototype method of board selection. (Five local port authorities in the state of Washington and two in Texas have elected boards. In the Port of New Orleans, commerce and shipping associations nominate candidates for commissioner and the governor approves the nominations.)

The directors of municipal and county building and utility corporations tend to be appointed local businessmen. (One nationwide survey of 122 authorities showed an average board size of six members; 100 of the boards were dominated by unrepresentative appointed members. Two surveys in Pennsylvania have also demonstrated the predominance of businessmen on authority boards.)[21] Even regional corporations serving several municipalities, each of which sends members to the corporate board, tend to be more representative of the regional business community than of the local governments.

Municipal utility corporations formed by private land developers usually have public boards of directors that are heavily or even totally dominated by the developers and cooperating firms. This type of authority provides public services for new residential subdivisions that lack regular local government or a property tax base. Usually, the residential population must ultimately assume the costs through leases or property tax contributions for debt service. In a successful residential development, the authority may become a thriving concern. The Lower Bucks County Joint Municipal Authority, for example, began by leasing water and sewerage plants from developer William Levitt's firm, which had built them in conjunction with the construction of Levittown, Pennsylvania. Subsequently, the authority purchased the plants (Levitt took back $3 million in authority bonds and controlled a majority of its board). By 1973, the authority's total assets were up to $13 million; today its board includes representatives of the five municipalities it serves, as well as representatives of the developer and local construction businesses.

State highway and turnpike authorities also have part-time boards of directors or commissioners like the Port Authority's. Some of them are salaried—with compensation ranging from small per diems in New Jersey, Maine, and Oklahoma up to $20,000 (and $40,000 for the chairman) in Massachusetts, providing perfect patronage opportunities. (Other toll road authorities with stipends in a salary range are in New York, Pennsylvania, Illinois, Indiana, and Ohio.) Toll road authority boards are small, usually ranging from three members to seven. They typically operate with nearly complete independence from state highway departments.

In 1952, the New Jersey Highway Authority began operation with the state commissioner of transportation as its board chairman (because its original bonds were guaranteed by the state), and its staff was borrowed from his state agency. Early in 1954, Katharine Elkus White, the daughter of a politically active family of New Jersey Democrats, a delegate to national conventions, and a former mayor, was appointed to the three-person authority board, and she became chairman a year later. She was reappointed to a second nine-year term but resigned in 1964 to become ambassador to Denmark. Although she calls herself a politican and has been active in politics all her life, she maintained during her tenure that the commissioners owed their prime responsibility to the bondholders of the authority rather than to the state's Department of Transportation, to the governor who appointed them, or to the state highway commissioner with whom the authority squabbled.

Underwriters are familiar with toll highway operations and evaluate them on the basis of straightforward traffic forecasts; such enterprises therefore can usually count on having continuing access to capital, particularly when their boards defend them against the periodic attempts of governors to tap excess revenues and other resources for broader state purposes. Consequently, highway authority boards have reflected less financial patronage and more political patronage than have other kinds of authority boards.

In twenty-two years, only eleven people served on the three-person board of the New Jersey Highway Authority. In 1974, the board included two members over eighty years of age who had been serving since 1955. When Republican Governor William T. Cahill took office in 1970, he expanded the size of the board from three to five members and shortened the term from nine to five years in order to influence the composition of the board and to distribute some classic patronage. (Cahill appointed John P. Gallagher, a businessman and former head of the Republican organization in Middlesex County, who had been credited with delivering that county's vote to Cahill in 1970. He also appointed a Republican leader from Monmouth County and a former congressman, who was an investment firm executive, to achieve a Republican majority on the highway authority.) Subsequently, Democratic Governor Brendan Byrne sponsored legislation further expanding the board to seven members and appointed a Democratic majority.

In Texas, private wealth and election politics are closely intertwined, and the political establishment is more directly represented on all kinds of public enterprise boards than in the East. The directors of the Lower Colorado River Authority, for example, have traditionally used their political skills and influence to handle controversy and, in more recent years, to adapt to changing circumstances. The original nine members of LCRA's board were appointed by the governor, the attorney general, and the state land commissioner. They included Ralph Yarborough, then assistant attorney general and later United States senator from Texas, as well as several businessmen, a former member of the legislature, a newspaper editor, a mayor, a lawyer, a journalist, and a labor mediator. The governor himself made the subsequent appointments, with senate confirmation, for six-year terms.[22] John B. Connally, who served from 1941 to 1947, later became governor of Texas and secretary of the treasury in the Nixon administration. While on the board, he practiced law in the firm of LCRA promoter Alvin J. Wirtz. (W. Sim Gideon, LCRA's manager until 1973, had practiced in that law firm as well.)

From the first days of the Lower Colorado River development, when LCRA's board voted unanimously not to select Interior Secretary Ickes's choice as general manager, through labor disputes in the 1940s (ending with state legislation prohibiting strikes and exclusive bargaining agents for public employees), to 1973, when fuel crises forced LCRA to increase its rates for the first time and new activities embroiled it in controversy, the board has vigorously and successfully defended the authority in political arenas. Between periods of stress, the manager has enjoyed little interference from his board, which typically tends to favor quick decisions and unanimity on the record.

Like the Port Authority of New York and New Jersey, LCRA has over the years won nearly everything it wanted from the state legislature. Early commentators thought that the borrowing limit of $10 million imposed by LCRA's enabling legislation would hamper the corporation's development, but it has, in fact, caused few problems: whenever the authority needed to increase its borrowing capacity, it had little trouble gaining the approval of the legislature. The approved borrowing level gradually rose to $300 million, and the authority manager, Gideon, felt that his occasional opportunity to go back to the legislature helped the authority to keep in touch with its political friends. In the mid-1970s, however, when capital requirements increased dramatically, the ceiling was repealed, permitting expansion of authority debt without recourse to the government.

Although it includes more active politicians, the LCRA board has not departed far from the Port Authority prototype. As of 1965, the twelve-director board included representatives of seven different banks; of these, six were presidents or chairmen of the board and one was a vice-president. Some of these bankers were also in the ranching business, and two others were full-time commercial ranchers or cattlemen. One insurance agency owner was also a former mayor. Most board members were serving their second, third, or even fourth term. Seven directors had served twenty years or more since 1940, and three since the 1950s. When Governor John B. Connally refilled four terms on the LCRA board that expired in 1966, only two were new additions—one from the National Bank of Austin and the other a union representative. New appointments in 1971 and 1973 included a lawyer, a real estate broker, a businessman-mayor, two ranchers, one banker, and a retired congressman–district attorney.

Representative Boards

The possible variations and permutations in the selection and operation of boards of directors for public enterprise are many, yet the degree of uniformity in American public enterprise is quite extraordinary. The hybrids that do exist include three other types of selection. One names to the board people who hold official government positions, usually executives in departments of state or city governments that are related to the business of the enterprise. These statutory appointments of government officials are called ex officio, because it is the official position (the "office"), not the man, that is entitled to the seat on the board. The second type is appointments that explicitly represent either special economic and social interests in the community or political districts served by the enterprise. The third (found mainly in the

Midwest and Far West), often associated with enterprises that have either active or latent powers to tax, is the directly elected board.

Governments choose these variations when they have an explicit desire to coordinate particular enterprises with related public policies or to enhance local control (for example, in the case of regional corporations). These methods of board selection do tend to let more conflict or debate of public issues into the board room, but differences in the method of board selection have less effect on corporate behavior than differences in method of financing (revenue bonds versus government appropriations, for example).

The statutory assignment of officials to boards of directors is becoming more common as larger chunks of state and local government activity are being turned over to corporations; examples include the Connecticut Resources Recovery Authority, the New York State Housing Finance Agency, the New Jersey Sports Authority, and the Alaska Bond Bank.[23] The Connecticut Resources Recovery Authority has ten directors. The governor, with the advice and consent of the general assembly, appoints four, of whom two must be officials of Connecticut municipalities and two must be citizens unconnected with public office who have experience in corporate or municipal finance (these are the seats for the banking representatives). The statute further specifies that not more than two of these four can be of the same political party. Three other directors are ex officio—the state commissioners of environmental protection, finance, and transportation. The other directors are a state senator, a state representative, and the chairman of the Connecticut Solid Waste Management Advisory Council, who serves without a vote.

The dominance of government officials on the board sometimes limits the independence of corporate management, but corporate wealth can cancel out this distinction as it has in successful state finance agencies. So, too, elected boards behave more like business boards than like legislatures when they are supported by independent financial sources. The behavior of the elected boards of the Port of Seattle and of public utility districts in the states of Washington and Nebraska, for example, is not dramatically different from that of appointed public power boards across the country. These corporations are not in any consistent way more or less involved in politics than others. They are businesses of sufficient size and assets, with money-raising power, to operate with nearly as much independence as public corporations with appointed boards.

On the other hand, corporations that do not have independent sources of money or well-established sources of government revenues tend to confront uncertainty and stalemate regardless of the structure of their boards. Urban mass transportation is one field in which public authorities have typically been plagued with money troubles and have experimented with different management patterns. Nowhere has the authority device resolved the dilemma posed by social and environmental pressures for cheap public transit and rising costs forced by sharp peaks in use, automobile competition, and labor contracts. The traditional business management–fiscal planning techniques of corporate enterprise simply have not been successfully adapted to these problems in either the private or the public sectors.

Metropolitan transit authorities in Boston, New York, Philadelphia, Cleveland, Atlanta, Detroit, Washington, San Francisco, southern California, and Chicago serve central cities and suburban areas; most provide several services, and all of them require substantial tax subsidies from local and state governments to supplement income from fares. The authorities also receive federal grants and operating assistance. The boards of all of these authorities and special districts (except New York) include representatives of the communities that pay the bills. The patterns vary. San Francisco's rail transit agency is, in effect, a special district with taxing powers, dependent on voter approval and headed by a board selected by local elected officials. The board of Massachusetts Bay Transportation Authority is appointed by the governor, but an advisory board representing the cities and towns served has budget approval powers and rights to veto some decisions. The board of Philadelphia's Southeastern Pennsylvania Transit Authority includes representatives of the city and four counties (two each) and a gubernatorial appointment. Regional action can be vetoed by two local representatives; unanimity of the rest of the board is required to override this veto.

New York's Metropolitan Transit Authority is the least representative. All of its board members are appointed by the governor with the advice and consent of the senate; the mayor of the city of New York nominates three of the members for appointment. When the MTA was first established, Governor Nelson A. Rockefeller appointed William J. Ronan to the combined position of board chairman and executive director; with continuing support from the governor, Ronan maintained tight control, even though the MTA lacked independent financial power. Fiscal troubles began to appear in the early 1970s when Governor Rockefeller failed to win voter approval for transportation bonds. Ronan's successor, David L. Yunich, an executive from the private sector, found the authority's management in a shambles and left it in that condition when he resigned in 1976, frustrated by uncertain sources of government support. As a holding company, the New York MTA is the largest urban transit conglomerate in the nation; yet its finances are unsettled and open to new intergovernmental bargaining each year. Its board is charged with policy direction and management control of the Long Island Rail Road Company, the Triborough Bridge and Tunnel Authority, the New York City Transit Authority, the Manhattan and Bronx Surface Operating Authority, the Staten Island Rapid Transit Operating Authority, the Stewart Airport Land Authority, and the Metropolitan Suburban Bus Authority. Yet board meetings tend to be routine, and members are not well informed of issues and options in advance. The MTA board has never gained effective managerial control of the separate authority bureaucracies, nor has it developed any comprehensive system of financial planning. Unfinished capital construction and spiraling operating deficits have resulted. The arrangement of the MTA in New York is the product of a more than half-century search, without success, for a responsive and financially viable structure for providing mass transportation services.[24]

Most other boards of metropolitan transit agencies admit a great deal more controversy into the board room than the classic enterprise boards of directors, in a number of cases usefully internalizing some of the inevitable public debate concerning fares, levels of service, and subsidies. The least representative among these boards suffer the greatest financial uncertainty, with executives having to negotiate directly and sometimes daily with mayors, governors, and legislators.

Metropolitan Councils   Most port authorities, power authorities, transportation authorities, and growing numbers of water, sewerage, and waste disposal authorities serve regional markets that encompass more than one town or county. The boundaries of American local government have proved difficult to change with shifting circumstances. Throughout the 1950s and 1960s, reformers proposed rescaling local government and called for representative metropolitan governments, for the most part unsuccessfully. They therefore turned to regional corporations providing services directly to the public or regional corporations wholesaling services to towns and cities—waste disposal, sewage treatment, and water supply, for example. As one study concluded: "The public authority offers a convenient way of providing for a metropolitan area a service or an improvement which involves more than one regular governmental jurisdiction."[25] As urbanization changed social and economic configurations, therefore, regional and interstate authorities multiplied, allowing old governments to retain their identity, if not their full powers.

Given the propensities and financing techniques of the government corporations, the services carved out of city government were generally those with some potential for financial return.[26] And most of the regional corporations, intermunicipal corporations, and urban county authorities that have resulted have boards resembling the Port Authority model. Some observers argued, however, that the work of a metropolitan district's governing body was policy making and that such an agency should be a political entity controlled by responsible officials. Luther Gulick pointed out that the development of plans and adoption of projects for a region are political, not administrative tasks.[27] Norton Long also noted that "the problem of the metropolitan area is the problem of restructuring the most populated part of American local government so as to give it ability to cope with presently unmanageable problems and by so doing renew its vitality. This is a job of constitution making in the classic sense. . . . Is there or can there be in the modern metropolitan areas the necessary sociological, ethical and political conditions for a vigorous local self-government? Or do we face the necessity if government is to be honest and efficient of TVA-ized regions governed by benevolent replicas of Robert Moses?"[28]

This counterargument dominated a conference on metropolitan area problems sponsored by five New England governors and New York City's mayor in September 1957. The participants concluded that metropolitan enterprises should have direct representation of constituent localities on their governing boards instead of following the Port Authority model, which, they noted, isolates revenues, fragments specialized services from coordinated consideration or representative bargaining, and debilitates local political influence over the urban environment.

Two metropolitan experiments that reflect those arguments are the Municipality of Metropolitan Seattle (Metro Seattle) and the Minneapolis–St. Paul Metropolitan Council (Twin Cities Metro Council). Both adapt some aspects of the public authority to regional policy making, and both have combined an ability to market bonds on the private market with enhanced political access to public enterprise decisions. Metro Seattle was hailed as a pioneer in metropolitan government, but for over a decade it actually operated not as a government but as a single-purpose enterprise with a political board of directors. The Twin Cities arrangement superimposed a regional council over a number of semi-independent public authorities.

Metro Seattle: Evolution from Business to Government It was water that first caused major concern about the viability of the traditional local government system in Seattle. In the decade after World War II, the communities around Seattle grew dramatically, with little consideration of public service needs or environmental effects. Sewage discharges nearly destroyed some of the region's greatest attractions, including recreational opportunities at Lake Washington and Puget Sound. Water supply and public transportation into the city lagged behind growth.

The first proposals for a new regional organization to cope with these problems contemplated a metropolitan government with taxing powers and such responsibilities as water supply, sewerage, transportation, garbage disposal, parks, and regional planning. This aim was gradually narrowed to the one ultimately accomplished in 1958: a single-purpose regional corporation, formally entitled the Municipality of Metropolitan Seattle.

Metro's board is composed not of bankers appointed by the governor but of elected local councilmen from the towns and county it serves. It has nevertheless succeeded in raising money. This success may be partly related to the overlapping of political and business leadership in Seattle. Metro's executives and its public support are closely allied with local business.

The movement for a metropolitan government began with Seattle's united business leadership (composed of local professionals, entrepreneurs, and the middle management of the Boeing Corporation). For many years, these business leaders belonged to a luncheon club where they reviewed municipal projects and chose candidates to support in Seattle's nonpartisan elections to public office. Not since the 1930s had organized political parties challenged this type of civic leadership for control of local government in the Seattle area. The luncheon group and the larger Municipal League sponsored a Metropolitan Problems Advisory Committee appointed by the state governor.[29] The committee included Seattle's business notables (such as Ben Ehrlichman, a leading land developer and chairman of United Pacific Corporation, and James Ellis, a partner in Seattle's largest law firm, who based a successful law practice on involvement in government affairs).[30] C. Carey Donworth, chairman of Metro's board since its inception, was also a member of the original civic committee that fathered the corporation. (He has been elected to nine consecutive two-year terms as Metro's chairman.)

James Ellis (like Alvin J. Wirtz of the LCRA and Julius Henry Cohen of the Port Authority) was first the lawyer-promoter and then general counsel of the new public corporation. Ellis is Metro's internal counsel and a member of its transit management committee. A management consulting report in 1972 concluded that Metro's executive director "relies heavily on administrative advice as well as legal advice from Metro's counsel [Ellis]."[31] At the same time, Ellis's law firm (he remains an active partner) does Metro's outside legal work, including providing the accepted legal opinions for Metro bond issues.

Ellis's political clout and public relations skill have been great assets for Metro. For example, he obtained agreements for sewage treatment rate increases imposed by Metro. Unlike LCRA's increase in power charges to municipal customers in Austin, which generated vigorous opposition, Seattle Metro's price increase elicited practically no attention in the media, being supported by editors who had been briefed in advance. Court action precipitated by Metro itself—through Ellis's law firm—forestalled suits by customers and gained early approval for the rate structure (despite planned diversion of sewer revenue to transit planning).

Another vehicle of business-civic influence over public projects in the Seattle region is Forward Thrust, Inc., formed in 1966 by many of the same organizations that had been involved in Metro's creation. Its president is James Ellis. In effect a nongovernmental institution for setting public priorities, it prepares capital improvement plans and related proposals for bond issue referenda for the Seattle area. Of nineteen proposals, eighteen passed, including one doubling the county debt limit and permitting it to borrow in behalf of municipalities within it. Forward Thrust has designed major park, highway, stadium, and neighborhood improvement bond issues; in 1972, it successfully backed Metro's expansion into public mass transit. Metro's new executive director in 1974 came from Forward Thrust.

Unlike a typical government corporation, Metro was established by popular vote. Its backers lost at the polls in 1958, under attack by groups fearing tax increases and by other interests from the outer suburbs who opposed sharing the costs of coping with city problems.[32] A second referendum succeeded, but the resulting Municipality of Metropolitan Seattle had only sewage treatment and disposal responsibilities and was to be financed like a public authority entirely by the sale of revenue bonds and user charges.

Before the advent of federal grants, government environmental protection standards, and the boom in environmental politics, Metro Seattle pioneered in water pollution control. It has earned a nationwide reputation for its successes in cleaning up Lake Washington and Puget Sound and curing local sewage disposal problems at an acceptably low cost. Within the Lake Washington drainage basin, Metro entered into sewage treatment and disposal contracts with twenty-nine local governments that remain responsible for primary sewage and industrial waste collection systems. Sewage charges under the contracts are calculated on the basis of costs, including reserves mandated in bond resolutions and administrative overhead.[33]

Of the $125 million invested by Metro from 1958 through 1968, federal and state grants supplied only 4 percent—less than the average sales tax paid by Metro to the state of Washington on construction expenditures. Metro residents more than paid the full cost of their new treatment and disposal system, including revenue bond debt service, through sewer charges.[34]

Federal and state aid now supply a growing share of Metro's budget, and federal law is imposing new pollution control standards. Metro's local priorities have come into conflict with federal standards. At first glance, the policy debate looks like a typical case of a public authority evading the tougher, money-losing tasks that government would like it to take on. The issue is complex, however, and West Coast experts generally take the position that Metro is correct. Federal standards define the goals of pollution abatement in terms of specific effluent levels of biological oxygen demand (BOD), a measure of the extent to which pollutants absorb oxygen from the water, damaging the environment for fish and plant life. Reducing BOD requires high-cost secondary treatment (which produces sludge that must be disposed of). But Metro Seattle priorities call for continued extension of primary treatment and filtering and separating the city's storm and sanitary sewers. The public is bothered more by algae and solid wastes than by BOD. Metro has therefore emphasized removal of floating debris and harmful chemicals.

West Coast analysts maintain that the tidal movements of the Pacific make secondary treatment unnecessary at current effluent levels. The dilemma is not unusual; federal standards cannot fit all local preferences and conditions well, but the failure of most localities to take any action on problems with national implications forced the federal government to adopt standards. Metro's experts complain that federal involvement jumped, somewhat simplistically, from zero interest to zero discharge and that the process of formulating standards included no consideration of cost effectiveness. In any case, both the elected officials on Metro's board and the congressional committee before which Metro's staff testified clearly have valid political roles to play in working out policy compromises. The issue has political and technical dimensions that cannot be separated.

In terms of the local goals set for it, Metro is clearly a success. It completed its first-stage ten-year construction program ahead of schedule, replacing twenty-eight old local plants plus raw discharge outlets with four modern treatment plants that cut the nitrogen and phosphorous content of regional effluents dramatically. After ten years of operation, Metro's sewage charges were lower than its original proponents had promised during the referendum campaign, and its interest costs were 12 percent below original estimates. It had achieved clearly discernible improvements in Lake Washington, reducing algae below nuisance levels and reopening beaches to swimming. Raw sewage was no longer being discharged into Puget Sound. Observing these benefits, several communities outside Metro's original boundaries voted themselves in.

Metro has gradually strengthened its political leadership in the region by active involvement in interagency basin planning, and when Seattle's transit systems were deteriorating badly, Metro fought hard and successfully to get responsibility for regional transit. In 1958, 1968, and 1970, Metro proponents submitted referenda regarding Metro's takeover of regional transit. Each time voters defeated the proposal. The required 60 percent voter approval for a transit bond issue was achieved in 1972 after Metro's boundaries had been extended. Metro took over the money-losing Seattle surface transit system and the previously subsidized private suburban bus lines that no one else wanted. It has been reshaping them into a regional bus system with high-speed express service for commuters and coordinated parking interchanges. The American Marketing Association gave Metro the regional award in 1975 as "outstanding marketing organization of the year" for its efforts to increase ridership. Metro's management had the courage to buck its original financial backers, who opposed its expansion into transit. The enthusiasm for nearly impossible public problems, and the willingness of Ellis, Donworth, and other board members to expand public service responsibilities, distinguish Metro from most public authorities.[35] In 1973, a year when controversy was raging over the future of federal transit aid and two major transit authorities elsewhere defaulted, Seattle Metro sold its first transit bonds with ratings of A and AA.

The first transit bond issue in Seattle was a modest one—$14.9 million with maturities ranging only up to eight years. The bonds will be paid off or refunded by 1981. The security behind the bonds consists of a 1 percent motor vehicle excise tax, which the state allocated to Metro, and a 0.3 percent retail sales tax in the county, in addition to transit operating revenues. The state legislature approved the excise tax for a fixed term, after which it will require statutory renewal. This provision was designed to limit Metro's independent financing options.[36] In the meantime, Metro is hoping to build up operating revenues of the transit system, including federal highway aid, U.S. Urban Mass Transit Administration assistance, and state highway funds.

Apart from a loan from its sewer funds to its transit funds in anticipation of tax revenues, Metro's transit financing is separate from its sewerage financing. This separation allows the corporation to deal with new transportation problems without endangering the financial condition of other divisions. If earmarked taxes and government grants are not available to make up for future transit deficits, Metro can fall back on general property tax powers. Like many of Washington's public utility and port districts, Metro is empowered to levy property taxes with voter approval, but it has not used this power. If it did, it could issue general obligation bonds backed by property taxes as if it were a metropolitan government.

Metro continues its evolution from public enterprise to regional government with expanding regional planning activities and authorization by the state legislature in 1977 for it to merge with King County if the voters approve. Metro's promoters originally hoped that it would become a general, regional jurisdiction with broad governmental powers. (Their model was Toronto's federation of local governments.) They have chipped away at popular reluctance with political and public relations skill, seeking fundamental reform in increments, probably the only politically feasible method under the circumstances. They seem not to have fallen prey to the temptation to adhere to the simpler and proven successful role of "businesslike" management of only profitable services.

Minneapolis–St. Paul: Harnessing Regional Enterprises In Minneapolis–St. Paul, the sponsors of metropolitan reform also were part of a tight local business-politics network and took their inspiration from Toronto. As in Seattle, water was the catalyst for institutional change. But like many other older urban areas, Minneapolis–St. Paul already had an array of regional authorities with independent bond financing and jealously guarded, single-purpose policy prerogatives.

The aim of the sponsors of the Twin Cities Metropolitan Council was to reshape all regional public corporations into one pattern, with boards appointed by the Metro Council and capital projects financed by general obligation bonds issued by the Metro Council. In other words, the single-purpose public authorities would borrow through a holding company–parent council, which also named their directors.

When the council was first created in 1967, it took over the Minneapolis–St. Paul Sanitary District (since twice renamed, the Metro Sewer Board and then the Metro Waste Control Commission). It subsequently took over regional parks. Then the transit commission became a partial subsidiary, with its board appointed and its capital budget approved by the council but retaining separate borrowing powers. The airports commission has retained separate authority status but must gain approval from the council for major capital expenditures. The council is also authorized to act as a regional housing and redevelopment authority, operating by contract with municipalities (as an alternative to independent housing or development corporations used elsewhere).

The Sanitary District had been a powerful institution, with legal authority to require the county to collect taxes from any city that might fall behind on sewer charge payments to it. It provided sewage disposal services not only to the two central cities that controlled its board and its finances but also, under contract, to suburban towns. Suburban dissatisfaction with the Sanitary District's service stimulated a movement for metropolitan reorganization. (Crisis —when ground water sources were contaminated by seepage from septic tanks—speeded the reorganization.) As a compromise between full-fledged regional government and continuing suburban dependence on the Sanitary District, the League of Minnesota Municipalities led a campaign for the establishment of a sewerage services corporation jointly owned by the area's local governments.[37]

But Minnesota's leaders concluded that another single-purpose public corporation was not a satisfactory solution for metropolitan problems. Real metropolitan power at that time was vested in the special authorities— sewerage, airport, watershed, parks, and transit agencies—and pending proposals would have added regional authorities for water supply, housing, and refuse disposal. The governor labeled the Twin Cities system, "Government by Special District." The proposal for the Metro Council emerged as a method of both solving the sewage problems and bringing an array of public service corporations and districts under coordinated governmental control. The legislation as first submitted called for the council to be directly elected.

The vision of a competing elected body from the dominant population center of the state frightened the state legislators, however, and the version that passed established an appointed council.

The Twin Cities Metro Council on the surface resembles a typical corporate board in the public sector, although it is slightly more representative than most. As first constituted in 1967, it included a university professor as chairman, four company presidents, two attorneys, a suburban mayor, a minister, two bank executives, and a settlement house supervisor. James Hetland, the first council chairman, was a professor of law who was active in both the Republican party and the Citizens League. He contributed considerably to the council's influence. Its early accomplishments included adoption of a metropolitan sewage disposal plan that was accepted by the state legislature, establishment of a metropolitan parks and open space board, and preparation of guidelines to resolve disputes over airport siting. It persuaded the legislature to increase council powers and to adopt its recommended sewer district law. It vetoed new airport construction next to the state's largest game and wildlife preserve, induced improvements on various projects in the region, including highway, housing, and open space projects, and formulated regional land-use and housing policies that are having some influence on development. A private hospital planning agency was transformed into a comprehensive health-care board operating under the council. Most of these actions are distinctly governmental; they are more directly related to broad public policies than to tightly defined agency operations.

Much of the council's staff came from the former Metropolitan Planning Commission; hence, from the beginning, the council has maintained a relatively comprehensive approach to regional issues. This approach occasionally comes into conflict with the special interests represented by the typical government corporations in the area—the single-purpose builder agencies for sewers, highways, and airports, and so forth. Even so, as one avid supporter of the council points out, "The main trouble probably is in the area of staying close to the people in county and municipal governments. Perhaps with more attention to that the council could have obtained more support from local government for its . . . legislative program."[38] The council leadership became more political after 1971 when Hetland moved from his position on the council into a vice-presidency of the First National Bank of Minneapolis. The second Twin Cities council chairman, Albert Hofstede, was a former Minneapolis alderman, a Democratic replacement by a Democratic governor. Hofstede resigned as chairman to run for mayor of Minneapolis in November 1973 and was replaced by a member of the Minnesota legislature. As of 1975, the Metropolitan Council of the Twin City Area is a body corporate run by a seventeen-member board of directors appointed by the governor (sixteen selected to represent specific districts of the urban region). It levies a property tax, undertakes to plan regional priorities and development goals, issues its own "general obligation bonds," and guides the activities of the single-purpose public corporations in the region. (It also has some control over the capital projects of local governments.) Chart 7.1 gives a schematic summary of the council's reach.

With unusual recognition of the overlapping roles of private firms, public corporations, and state and local governments, Minnesota has given the Metro Council review powers over all these insofar as their projects affect metropolitan development. Some of the review powers have more muscle behind them than others. For example, the council is the official regional planning body to review local government grant applications to the federal government for projects within the region. It has only delaying powers to back up its review of private projects of metropolitan significance; the state legislature can resolve conflicts.

The Waste Control Commission (successor to the Sanitary District) still designs, constructs, and operates the regional treatment and disposal system, collecting fees from municipalities that deliver sewage into the system. The Metropolitan Council has become its second-layer board of directors. (Thus the commission resembles a corporate president's executive committee in the private sector.) The council develops a general plan to which the commission's specific plans are supposed to conform, establishes policy guidelines, approves the commission's capital budget, and issues general obligation bonds to finance the commission's projects.[39]

The Waste Control Commission, unlike its predecessor district and most successful public authorities, is not permitted to build up a surplus from operating revenues. It returns excess revenue, in the form of credits, to the contributing municipalities. As a result, it budgets only for what is needed. (The previously independent Sanitary District had regularly budgeted sometimes as much as 75 percent for excess revenue.) The current arrangement serves to slow increases in customer costs.

The Waste Control Commission assumed the outstanding debts of suburban and city sanitary districts without litigation, increased interest charges, or any other penalty. Minneapolis and St. Paul had used their own full faith

Chart 7.1
Responsibilities of the Twin Cities Metropolitan Council

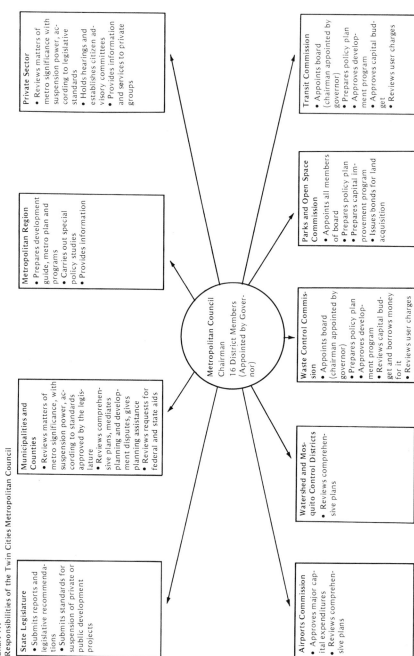

State Legislature
• Submits reports and legislative recommendations
• Submits standards for suspension of private or public development projects

Municipalities and Counties
• Reviews matters of metro significance, with suspension power, according to standards approved by the legislature
• Reviews comprehensive plans, mediates planning and development disputes, gives planning assistance
• Reviews requests for federal and state aids

Metropolitan Region
• Prepares development guide, metro plan and programs
• Carries out special policy studies
• Provides information

Private Sector
• Reviews matters of metro significance with suspension power, according to legislative standards
• Holds hearings and establishes citizen advisory committees
• Provides information and services to private groups

Metropolitan Council
Chairman
16 District Members
(Appointed by Governor)

Airports Commission
• Approves major capital expenditures
• Reviews comprehensive plans

Watershed and Mosquito Control Districts
• Reviews comprehensive plans

Waste Control Commission
• Appoints board (chairman appointed by governor)
• Prepares policy plan
• Approves development program
• Reviews capital budget and borrows money for it
• Reviews user charges

Parks and Open Space Commission
• Appoints all members of board
• Prepares policy plan
• Prepares capital improvement program
• Issues bonds for land acquisition

Transit Commission
• Appoints board (chairman appointed by governor)
• Prepares policy plan
• Approves development program
• Approves capital budget
• Reviews user charges

and credit to obtain low interest costs (a rare economy in public authority circles) for the Sanitary District. Because of its strong tax base, the Metro Council assumed those outstanding bonds with only mild objection from investors or underwriters.[40] Except for the state, no other unit of government has as large a tax base in Minnesota as the Metro Council. It encompasses over half the total tax base of the state. Moreover, Moody's and the underwriters were impressed that the council had substantial business representation and was not affected by local elections; such characteristics inspire the confidence of the financial community.

Regional bonding can even out fiscal disparities among segments of the urban area. Fiscal equalization is a key to fundamental improvements in both the equity and the quality of urban life. It has been largely ignored by U.S. reform movements, although it is a central component of regional reorganizations in, for example, Paris, London, and Hamburg. Minnesota's "fiscal disparities" law, which provides for sharing within the seven-county metropolitan area of 40 percent of all increases in industrial and commercial tax base, represents another step in this direction (if it survives court challenges).

In any case, Osmond Springsted, a local bond consultant for the council, argues that the Metro Council makes better decisions on timing and amounts of bond issues than its component specialized enterprises, which tend to be eager to build big and fast. The council has put some brakes on their borrowing and spending not only to improve the marketability of bonds but also to make sure that the projects are sound.

The Waste Control Commission, which remains an organization composed primarily of the staff of the preexisting sanitary districts, consists of what one knowledgeable commentator describes as "avid pipe layers." The commission staff is oriented to professional engineering; the commission is oriented to maximizing conditions for local development. (Of seven commission members, five are development-oriented local businessmen, two of these "development corporation" executives.)

Villages and towns on the threshold of a building boom press continually for immediate sewer extension. In comparable situations in Pennsylvania, Texas, and California, developers themselves have organized local authorities or utility districts to issue bonds and lay sewers even before subdivisions were completed. In the Twin Cities area, developers—backed by engineers and contractors—must convince the Waste Control Commission of the need for new sewers. They usually make their case successfully; but the commission must then convince the Metro Council that the need is real and immediate and that the direction of development implied is consistent with the regional patterns that the council favors. This requirement has led to delays and a few cancellations of extensions that would have been built had the sewerage utility been an independent entrepreneur.

The Metro Council has injected land-use design considerations, environmental concerns, and social goals into sewer business decisions. The council has delayed or required project adjustments for housing developments in outlying suburbs, in some cases because its general plans for the region suggested that high-density development should not be encouraged in the area in question and in others because the council applied more stringent environmental standards than local officials did, entailing somewhat higher financial costs. In one case, for example, the council vetoed a proposal to save money by running treated effluent through an open ditch, insisting on the use of a covered pipe.

One of the Metro Council's most controversial acts was its announcement of a policy that assigns lower priority in the review of federal fund requests and local project proposals to municipalities whose plans and ordinances do not provide for low- and moderate-income housing. The council pressed new subdivisions that sought sewer extensions and federal sewage treatment grants to review their housing and zoning policies.

The process by which the Metro Council's environmental planning and comprehensive planning departments and its physical development committee review detailed project proposals sent over by the Waste Control Commission is time-consuming, and most of its participants agree that delays and their concomitant costs could be reduced if the board and council staffs worked in closer communication, rather than relying on sequential vetoes, revisions, arguments, and approvals. But the process also reflects some healthy policy politics and a broadening of the range of decision-making considerations. It has avoided the prolonged stalemates that were common prior to 1967.

Metropolitan Enterprise and Politics   Public enterprise and policy politics are inextricably linked. The structure of governing boards together with the financing framework determine public access to debate, availability of information, weight given to nonfinancial factors in project decision making, and the range of values and development goals for public enterprise. The promoters and staff of Metro Seattle have pursued general regional objectives, although for its first ten years the organization was formally responsible only for sewerage, which presented ample opportunities for profit. In contrast, the Port Authority of New York and New Jersey, despite its vast reach, tends to view each segment of its operations as a separate and primarily financial venture, despite "consolidated financing." The effects of one Port Authority project on the revenues of another Port Authority project receive great attention; the effects of Port Authority projects on patterns of development and on environmental, social, and governmental conditions in the urban region receive little attention. Regional planning played a larger part in the organizational aims of Seattle Metro, which had been denied formal responsibility for it, than in the perspectives of the Port Authority, which is formally charged with it.

Financially successful metropolitan public service corporations often engage in narrow-purpose self-optimizing and thereby may "suboptimize" the entire regional system, as Melvin Mogulof has pointed out.[41] However efficiently it may dispose of wastes, a sewer system is not regionally efficient if it stimulates dense development where urban transportation is inadequate and costly, or devalues other uses for water resources, for example. Representative councils have placed greater emphasis on general regional interests that have boards attempting to run public enterprise like a business. Representative councils have not lacked access to the money market when project revenues or tax base provide the foundation for borrowing.

The examples of Seattle and the Twin Cities also demonstrate the gradual nature of effective governmental change in United States political systems. The repeated failure of broad-based metropolitan constitutions at the polls has led many analysts of pluralist politics to conclude that the pursuit of metropolitan reorganization is a political impossibility, that metropolitan reform is the hopeless fantasy of irrelevant do-gooders. But this view is no more than an application of Adam Smith's invisible hand to the political sphere: what we should have is equated with what the political marketplace—a marketplace presumably responsive to effective political demand signals—gives us. In reality, political demands, like economic demands, can be and usually are manipulated for specific ends, public or private. Organizational restructuring changes the relative access of various groups to the decision-making arena and therefore alters political demand patterns. Seattle and the Twin Cities demonstrate not that constitutional reform is irrelevant in American politics but that it requires persistent, politically skilled, incremental efforts by its sponsors and is easier to achieve in the more homogeneous regions.

A Key to the Board Room

The argument against representative councils or boards is that they bring conflict into the board room. But keeping conflict out of the board room means
either excluding significant decisions or considering only a limited number of
sides to public issues. There is a strong case for bringing conflict into the
board room to resolve regional conflicts in an equitable and comprehensive
fashion. The entire board of Metro Seattle, except its chairman, consists of
locally elected politicians, and there is very little evidence that the organization's financial ability or technical integrity have suffered as a result.[42] (In
fact, the primary locus of public enterprise decision making in Metro Seattle,
as elsewhere, is among the full-time executives and outside consultants.) The
elected politicians who serve on Metro Seattle's board are, like most of the
appointed members of authority boards, full-time businessmen. (Their
government jobs are only part-time.) Business dominance seems to be universal. In communities where local political leadership and business leadership diverge (as in in New York), authority boards usually include no local
political leaders. Where the business and political elites substantially overlap
(as in Minnesota and Washington), local political leaders are included on authority boards.

The traditional theories of public authority management hold that the
civic leadership that comprises the appointed board serves the public interest
impartially, directs public enterprise along un-self-serving lines, and keeps the
operation of the authority from being contaminated by politics. The *Handbook for Housing Commissioners* preached that housing authority administration must be put in the hands of "civic leaders whose devotion to the public
welfare is beyond question."[43] Even international development theory has
adopted this idealistic image. A United Nations handbook describes public
enterprise directors as buffers between government and public enterprise
management and recommends that boards not be designed to represent specific interests because such arrangements may politicize the board and subvert
its pursuit of technical efficiency.

Yet bankers who serve on public corporations are no more immune from
subjectivity or susceptible to considerations of public welfare than anyone
else. Nor has the presence of businessmen on their boards rescued public
authorities from politics. Dominance by business is dominance by business
politics.

The political activities of directors of large authorities tend to be those of campaign fund raising and personal advice to governors and other high officials or office seekers. Prestigious "governor's clubs" of campaign contributors include public authority board members, underwriters, and consultants. Chairmen of state and national political party finance committees are found on authority boards. Some state authorities and numerous municipal corporations include people who are active in local political party organizations, particularly county leaders. The prototype public authority board member is a banker who does business with public agencies.

Nothing on the face of these relationships is inherently nefarious. But many business participants in politics portray themselves as above personal interests and opinions. One banker in a gubernatorial "executive club" of major contributors has explained, "We took the position that political leaders need funds. If the good people didn't step forward to support the political campaigns, then the evil people would step in." He went on to reveal his convictions that the majority of the people involved in the "executive club" were "not the type of men who have to buy their way into anything," and that men of lesser wealth would be more susceptible to corruption or more self-serving.

But if public authority board membership offered no personal benefits, it would not be widely regarded as a reward for financial support or political service. In fact, board service can offer opportunities for money making. The long-time chairman of the New York State Thruway Authority collected $35,000 annually from that part-time post and spent substantial amounts of time managing Republican campaigns for Thomas Dewey, Nelson Rockefeller, and Malcolm Wilson. Two other Republican stalwarts on that board—including a former state party chairman—each collected $17,000 annually. Massachusetts commissioners have received even more.

Authorities that pay substantial stipends to board members are relatively few, however. Other indirect opportunities for money making range from legitimate to illegal, with most in an area where "honest graft" shades into "conflict of interest." Authority projects and private real estate profits have been closely linked in most times and places. Illustrations are plentiful. A chairman of the Delaware River Port Authority reaped substantial profits from dealing in land ultimately purchased by that authority.[44] One of Al Smith's appointees to the Port Authority was forced to resign for transmitting inside information to real estate speculators, and Robert Moses altered the location of the Triborough Bridge to increase the real estate profits of William Randolph Hearst. William Sternkopf, the former commissioner of both the New Jersey Turnpike Authority and the Port Authority, is serving a ten-year sentence for conspiracy, bribery, and extortion. According to the U.S. attorney's charges, Sternkopf bought land that was resold to the New Jersey Highway Authority when the Garden State Arts Center was built in 1967. It is not rare for board members, particularly in construction-oriented municipal authorities, to have interests in companies that do business by contract with authorities or whose developments are enhanced by authority investments.

Although contract kickbacks and direct investments in real estate to be purchased for public projects occur in public authorities, they do not turn up frequently. Other more common and acceptable rewards of service in the lexicon of high-class patronage may be summed up under the category of status and enjoyment: association with respected colleagues; expense-paid trips, publicized participation in ribbon cuttings and ceremonies; prestige; and other perquisites of office that accompany service on major public authority boards. As Harold Seidman has pointed out, "Next to top pay levels, heavy sedans are the most eagerly sought-after status symbol."[45] Of course, small authorities do not provide limousines for their board members, but they do supply local prestige.[46] The press relations departments of large public corporations tend to rotate their press releases over the names of various board members. Authority facilities are christened with ceremony, publicity, and tours that put directors in newsprint with other notables. The ego satisfactions and opportunities for activity are particularly important to retired businessmen and politicians at all levels.

The quest for status has even inspired successful businessmen in the state of Washington to go to the trouble of running for election to public utility district boards, which offer no significant direct financial benefits. Following recent enactment of a law requiring such board members to make full disclosure of personal finances, as well as the finances of all corporations with which they are associated, the number of candidates for the office has declined. (Reporting corporate finance data for all the firms of which they are directors is simply too onerous for many of the candidates.)

Board membership also provides opportunities for advancement in one's own career. As one public official with a long career at the crossroads of government and business observes, "I don't know of any bank, insurance company or corporation that isn't politically connected."[47] One of the contact points for that connection is the public authority board. Membership gives lawyers, financial advisers, bankers, contractors, and engineers who participate on these boards enhanced access to potential clients. Bankers benefit from interest-free government accounts, and investment bankers enjoy timely information on bond issues. Board membership also enhances power in the form of opportunities to dispense favors to others: to provide contracts and jobs, to extend privileges on authority facilities, to help the political careers of incumbent officials or their adversaries. Board members of the New Jersey Highway Authority enjoy dispensing tickets to friends and community groups for arts center events, and one reports that acting as impresario for the center is his primary hobby. Board members supply boat rides in Austin, Texas, plane rides in the Tennessee Valley, helicopter rides over the New York Port, and good seats at sports stadiums in a dozen states. Authority directors can occasionally dispense jobs, but they have the security of being able to refuse in order to maintain the competence of public enterprise staff, thereby fending off some of the more troublesome pressures that beleaguer elected officials.

People active in public life invariably belong to several organizations with overlapping purposes. Too often, reformers take as their objective the total elimination of conflicts of interest, as if private goals should or could completely conform to the goals of the organization. Such efforts make it impossible to seek realistic and attainable adjustments, and their failure discredits reform itself. Underwriters, bankers, and others doing business with the public sector should not be excluded altogether from public enterprise boards and committees. If all candidates with real incentives to serve on boards were excluded, board members would be hard to find. The safeguards against conflict-of-interest abuses are public information and balance on the board, both of which are bound to introduce conflict, or at least debate, into the board room.

The law should require that public minutes of board meetings include the debate preceding decisions that are crucial to enterprise growth and that dispense benefits. Appointees to public authority boards should be required to disclose their business and professional affiliations in a form that is not discouragingly onerous. Short disclosure forms should accompany press releases announcing appointments. Board members should periodically list the positions they, and the firms with which they are associated, hold relative to authority bonds, loans, and other contracts.

The statutes that form public authorities should include specific provisions for representation of communities and groups with legitimate interests in authority activities, where this is feasible. The more the corporation depends upon public subsidies, the more urgently it needs political and community representation. Designing and selecting a board of directors should be viewed as a delicate art in which many goals are balanced: maximizing support and resources for the corporation, ensuring responsiveness to legitimate community interests and to the appointing officials, encouraging balanced judgments on authority projects and priorities, and maintaining internal management flexibility and the money-raising ability of the corporation. If bonds are salable, bankers and brokers will sell them, even if they do not have an exclusive hold on the corporate directorate.

8 The Mandarins

Chartered by governments that have weak control over them, supervised by boards paying only intermittent attention, in command of capital to invest and contracts to distribute, the managers of public corporations are in an enviable position. They have access to capital without dependence upon venture capitalists, registration statements for the SEC, stock performance, or mortgage conditions. Bondholders, trustees, and underwriters are usually unconcerned with the day-to-day operations of the authority. The managers enjoy as much discretion over corporate strategy as is granted to presidents of private firms, but the board is seldom in a position to fire them or to force their resignation. Boards of directors have no clear standards of performance to apply to them. Barring evidence of gross incompetence or illegal activity, authority managers are seldom forced out before retirement (and when they are, not by their boards). The manager does not have to show increasing profits, dividends, or stock prices. As long as the authority meets the minimum revenue-producing requirements of the bond covenants and is not involved in a publicized scandal, the manager's job is secure from almost everything except major political upheaval. Moreover, authorities seldom face competition from other firms or the risks of branching out into new products; hence, their revenue trends seldom change sharply from year to year. When steady revenue is assured from monopoly services, it is difficult to evaluate performance beyond minimal technical soundness because comparisons provided by business competition or government budget making are lacking. Revenues are seldom subject to downward pressures, and managers are seldom threatened by upward pressures of other executives. (In 1974, rapid increases in fuel and energy costs caused many authorities operating toll highways, airports, and power plants to experience sharp revenue drops for the first time in their corporate history. But authorities in these businesses had sufficient cash reserves, pricing flexibility, and cutback capacities to weather the change without major internal upheavals, and traffic volume soon turned upward on their facilities.) Finally, management of public corporations can operate in greater secrecy than government and, in many cases, private firms, which must provide information required by public utilities commissions and the Securities and Exchange Commission. Internally, in his relationships with corporate employees and management, the executive director of a public authority resembles the corporate president of a firm in the private sector. He holds consolidated power over personnel, performance, and contracts and is able to take advantage of modern management methods and periodic review by outside consultants.

Public authorities have often been successful in attracting highly motivated and skillful builders, administrators, and power seekers. The opportunity to construct public projects, sometimes of monumental proportions, can be more satisfying for many of these individuals than the pursuit of wealth in private business. The ability of managers to place a personal stamp on public corporations or vast public facilities is greater than that of all but the most extraordinary departmental executives in government. The ideal manager in public enterprise is conceived of as commercial in approach, marked by great initiative and the ability to make decisions, but nevertheless bristling with concern for the public interest and able to negotiate successfully in the political arena. Although reality seldom equals the ideal, many authority managers do display some combination of administrative and political skills.

Many of the powerful personalities who manage public enterprise in the United States have a low tolerance for competition or conflict. They are politicians who do not brook the compromises of day-to-day democratic politics and builders who prefer not to have their blueprints compromised by the requirements of a competitive marketplace. Within the enterprise, they often exercise strong personal leadership reinforced by corporate hierarchy.

The manager of a successful public authority enjoys internal job security; external support from financial groups; the ability to dispense an array of favors for a variety of business interests (such as legal, engineering, construction, and financing firms); control of patronage opportunities, which can be parceled out to political officials (projects in their districts, jobs for their constituents, and so forth); and public relations based on the capabilities of the corporation and the widespread belief that the manager is a particularly honest, competent, and businesslike public servant. The managers of government corporations need not kiss babies and shake hands, beg money for political election campaigns, bargain away half their options in order to exercise the other half, mollify appropriations committees and other legislators or councilmen, or take public positions on general policies that will later limit their strategies. It is no wonder that the public authority managers themselves have made a theology out of corporate self-support and autonomy from politics—the twin foundations of their enviable base of power. As former governor turned authority executive Alfred Driscoll pointed out, "Maintaining and generating income receives constant attention."[1]

The managerial role shifts as the authority evolves. Public authorities go through a kind of organizational life cycle. In their earliest years, they may be run by community leaders who had a hand in their creation. During this stage they are searching for organizational identity, building up goodwill and specific allies, and defining their tasks. As the corporation settles down and completed projects begin to bring in revenues, career public managers take over. Thereafter, in peaceful times, managers are usually recruited from within the organization. In extraordinary times, when the organization encounters unusual criticism or conflict, administrators who are used to having their own way with little interference may be replaced by leaders with stronger community ties or more direct political involvement.

Robert Moses

The most notorious public authority giant is Robert Moses. The monumental biography of Moses written by Robert Caro treats him as a distinct phenomenon of unusual personality and power. But many aspects of his power are common to successful public authority leaders.

Moses was raised in the tradition of civic reform politics and formally trained in its academic offshoot, public administration. Civil service reform and the technical aspects of government reorganization were his earliest professional concerns, but he lacked both the patience of an administrative technician and the flexibility of a candidate for electoral office. (He tried both.) Entering government service as secretary of New York State, young Moses was quickly frustrated with the complexities and uncertainties of state government bureaucracy, and he searched for an organizational framework that would give him more freedom within government. When given the chance to design the State Council on Parks, he assigned himself, as chairman, tenure beyond the governor's term, exempted the council's management from civil service, and endowed the council with independent bonding and land condemnation powers. He used those attributes of the council again when he designed public authorities.

In 1929, when Governor Alfred E. Smith was succeeded by Franklin D. Roosevelt, with whom Moses had already begun to feud, he lost his foothold within the departments of state government. But he kept his protected post in the Council on Parks and continued to build his own agencies with federal help.[2] In 1932, Al Smith took Moses and his aides to Washington to meet Jesse Jones and the rest of the Reconstruction Finance Corporation (RFC) board and senior staff. Thus began a relationship that was to give Moses his independent base of power. Jones said of Moses and his cohorts, "I have seldom met a group as well informed about every phase of the projects that they wanted to promote." Moses calls Jones "one of the really good men of his time."[3]

Moses headed the state's effort to meet RFC's request for programs of self-liquidating projects to absorb federal funds. (Self-liquidation as the RFC used the term meant that user charges were to be imposed to pay off construction debts.) Moses put the building of the Triborough Bridge high on the list of projects and drafted the legislation establishing an authority to build it. Financing the initial costs of the bridge, including approaches and connections, was actually shared with the city, and the mayor appointed the three members of the authority board, one of whom was Moses. He began his thirty-year tenure as chairman of the Triborough Bridge Authority in 1936. (In that year, he also was a delegate to the Republican National Convention.)

Departing from federal guidelines (and from the Port Authority model), Moses consistently tried to combine the positions of chairman of the board and chief executive officer in his authorities. (William Ronan adopted this arrangement when he designed and ran the Metropolitan Transportation Authority, which absorbed Moses's transportation enterprises.) Continuing as the state's liaison to federal public works funding programs, Moses wrote himself in as the only board member of two authorities that were set up to undertake other projects approved for federal funds: the Henry Hudson Parkway Authority and the Marine Parkway Authority. In 1938, Moses became the sole member of the New York City Parkway Authority, which absorbed the Henry Hudson and Marine Parkway authorities and built the Cross Bay Bridge and made shorefront improvements. He successfully lobbied against a state constitutional convention proposal that would have required at least three members for each public authority board. Finally, in 1945, without giving up other posts, Moses became chief executive officer of the New York City Tunnel Authority.

During the first decade of this authority empire formation, Jesse Jones had been the banker and Robert Moses the builder. Authority finances were based on the sale of bonds to the RFC and accompanying federal grants. By the end of World War II, Moses's authorities could stand on their own, and for the next two decades, he was both banker and builder. At the financial turning point in the 1940s, public enterprise faced several choices. Once the original bond issues were paid off, authorities could liquidate themselves and projects could become toll-free as the RFC had originally intended; tolls could continue, with excess revenues flowing into state and city treasuries; or authorities could keep the income flowing into their own corporate reserves and use it (or their credit) to finance new projects, for which they would no longer have to ask elected officials for tax funds, loans, or credit. Moses chose the third alternative and was widely emulated. The RFC and the Public Works Administration went out of business, but, nationwide, very few public authorities "self-liquidated."

Moses's own writings document his personal quest for power, his intolerance of disagreement, and his ruthlessly aggressive strategies.[4] But in constructing his edifice of influence, Moses used building blocks typical of public authority structures: independent financial power, corporate leadership, business patronage, civic reputation, and freedom from the encumbrances of democracy.

Financial Power   The projects for which Moses arranged financing in the 1930s and early 1940s used so-called self-liquidating loans through RFC purchases of authority bonds, Public Works Administration grants to supplement construction costs, and local subsidies for land and approach highways. Later, as Moses merged authorities, he rolled funds over through refinancings and moved funds from project to project until his financial empire was independent of government and reliably attractive to continuing investment from the private money market. Each project and financing led to another.

In 1933, Moses had created the Jones Beach State Parkway Authority, of which he would be chairman, to build bridges, causeways, and highway connections. With RFC financing, this authority began construction of what were to become the Meadowbrook Parkway, the Wantaugh Causeway, the Robert Moses Causeway (which itself eventually led to the construction of the Robert Moses Park on Fire Island), and a highway extension to the north shore of Long Island (which Moses planned to tie into a Long Island Sound crossing for which he pressed, unsuccessfully, into the 1970s). The RFC held the Jones Beach Authority bonds until 1940 and then sold them to the state comptroller. During World War II, the authority briefly defaulted on interest payments, but it repaid the state after the war. Moses's other authorities constantly accumulated and rolled over capital. In 1935, the Marine Parkway Authority sold $6 million in bonds and the Henry Hudson Authority sold $3.1 million; in 1937, the Henry Hudson Authority sold $2 million more. In 1938, the New York City Parkway Authority took over those two authorities and sold $18 million in bonds ($11.9 million to refund and $6.1 million for new construction). In 1935, the Triborough Bridge Authority sold $35 million in 4 percent bonds to the RFC through the Public Works Administration; two years later it sold a new 4 percent issue of $53 million to refund the first and to raise new funds for the Bronx Whitestone Bridge. In 1940, the New York City Parkway Authority merged with the Triborough Bridge Authority, and TBA sold $98.5 million in bonds; in 1945, it sold $110 million in refunding bonds. In the meantime, the New York City Tunnel Authority, which was also later to be merged into the Triborough system, sold $44 million in bonds to the RFC through the Public Works Administration for construction of the Queens Midtown Tunnel, and $57 million to the RFC for beginning the Brooklyn Battery Tunnel.

In 1946, Moses drafted state legislation that merged what had previously been the Triborough Bridge, Henry Hudson Parkway, Marine Parkway, and New York City Tunnel authorities into the Triborough Bridge and Tunnel Authority. That legislation gave TBTA the right to refinance its outstanding debt at any time; this right amounted to a guarantee of the preservation of Moses's power base, because as soon as a surplus accumulated and debts were about to be paid off, Moses could float a new issue and build again.

By the time Jesse Jones returned to Texas and the RFC was disbanded, TBTA was strong enough to go off on its own. To redeem the RFC bonds, it sold a $141.5 million bond issue, later refunded through $215 million in revenue bonds sold to the private market. TBTA had a net operating income of $27 million annually (before investment interest), which, if capitalized at 3 percent with forty-year amortization, would support a bonded debt of $491 million. With outstanding debt of $215 million, TBTA, totally controlled by Moses, had a potential unencumbered capital source of $276 million more. For the next fourteen years, the tax-exempt market took good care of TBTA, until it was merged into the money-losing MTA.[5]

Moses remains an ardent defender of independent financing for government corporations, particularly for what he calls self-liquidating projects. He invoked this policy successfully to oppose legislative ceilings on authority debt and unsuccessfully to oppose the merger of TBTA into MTA. Protesting the merger, he said, "As I conceive it, the Triborough system was created to build self-supporting crossings and other facilities independent of federal, state and municipal budgets and to keep adding to these facilities as traffic increases."[6] In fact, of course, the facilities with which he was involved had received a variety of subsidies from federal, state, and municipal budgets. In addition to bonds and grants, Moses used the federal aid program for highways to finance approaches to his bridges and repeatedly used city funds for land acquisition for authority projects.[7] From his authority coffers, he doled out credit or money for the favorite projects of officials whose cooperation was useful to him, and he withheld investment from the districts of politicians who displeased him. He also used his power to pick up other governmental posts in planning, housing, and transportation and to retain his state and local park positions, a combination of jobs which facilitated his broad land development, construction, and planning schemes.

Corporate Leadership   Having learned the usefulness of being the sole director on his board, Moses insisted throughout his career on complete control of boards wherever he moved. He nominated the candidates that were formally appointed by mayors to sit with him on the TBTA board. For example, on the eve of leaving office, Mayor Wagner replaced Moses's longtime colleague, George McLaughlin, with another old friend, Norman K. Winston. (McLaughlin had served thirty-one years.) In 1965, Mayor John V. Lindsay elicited stinging protest when he departed from the thirty-year-old tradition and, without notice to Moses, appointed his own transportation administrator to take the place of William J. Tracy, a TBTA commissioner who had been reappointed at Moses's request for sixteen years.

In 1954, when Moses agreed to run the New York Power Authority, he insisted on packing the board with his own men. Of long-time Power Authority board members John E. Burton and Hickman Powell, he fumed, "I shall not under any circumstances again serve on any board with these two men," calling them "jealous and vindictive" because they expressed reservations about his reversals of Power Authority policy in order to compromise with the private utilities.[8] Powell was replaced with a Moses colleague, and Burton agreed to an across-the-board staff increase that permitted Moses to bring in his own management personnel.

Subsequently, Congressman Franklin D. Roosevelt, Jr., commenting on Moses's application for federal approval for the Power Authority's plans to develop the St. Lawrence, wrote to Moses:

If it is true that the Power Authority is giving consideration to limiting the distribution of St. Lawrence power to bus-bar sales [wholesale turnover to private distributors], I agree with your predecessor John Burton that it would mean turning over all of this energy to one large power corporation. I would be most grateful if you would let me know what the facts concerning these negotiations really are, and also if you would inform me of the terms of this bond issue, and if you would make public all the terms of the indentures before the agreements are executed in order that those of us who have worked so long and so hard to bring cheap electricity to our citizens may have an opportunity to express ourselves to you and the Power Authority, and in order that the public may make their views known as well.[9]

This issue represented a genuine policy disagreement between private power interests and advocates of government generation of power for distribution to municipalities and rural cooperatives at lower prices. The debate had been going on since the turn of the century through the normal political processes, but Moses criticized Roosevelt's letter as an attempt to "inject politics into the power program, to revive old issues, and to get mileage out of demagoguery."[10] He refused to make public the terms of the indentures or of the contracts to sell the public power. He asserted that negotiation for the sale of bonds was too complex an affair for public discussion, and he suggested that Roosevelt obtain confirmation of the nature of such negotiations from Senator Herbert A. Lehman, pointing out that Lehman Brothers and Harriman Ripley, firms in which Senator Lehman and Governor Averill Harriman had family interests, would be involved in the underwriting. With these tactics and without further opposition on the board, Robert Moses remained the undisputed boss of the New York Power Authority, supervising major development of the state's natural resources for the following nine years.

Like successful chief executives in the private sector, Moses controlled his multiple jobs by developing a network of loyal and competent people on whom he could rely to handle day-to-day decision making and to refer to him only the most crucial matters. Scores of architects, engineers, and administrators spent the greater parts of their careers working for him, many serving in several of the agencies and authorities that he headed.[11] Such a system does not work unless the chief executive has the power to transfer or to fire anyone who is not loyal, not operating satisfactorily with the rest of the team, or not able to accommodate his policy line. The responsiveness that Moses and other authority managers demand is impossible in regular government where civil service managers are protected from firing and political appointees tend to build up their own outside sources of support. Moses's group was like a business management team that could be assigned to different parts of a conglomerate at the chief's will.

Moses encouraged and inspired comprehensive planning in his enterprises. Whenever Triborough or the Power Authority planned a construction project, the plans and blueprints would include a vast array of related public facilities and developments that were not technically under the jurisdiction of the authority itself. In connection with bridges and tunnels, for example, Triborough built parks, made arterial plans for highway systems throughout the New York metropolitan region, and drew up the original blueprints for Flushing Meadow development. (Moses's participation in the 1939 World's Fair was motivated by his eagerness to turn the Flushing dump into parkland.) Developing the Niagara power program, Moses and his staff at the Power Authority developed a plan that included parks, playgrounds, expressways, bridges, and railroad grades. Some of these plans were subsequently carried out by other authorities.

In contrast, government departments must limit their plans and activities to their specific jurisdictions and refrain from impinging on the assignments of other agencies. But apart from specific constraints written into their covenants and statutes, government corporations are free to develop ambitious and broad-based plans. Moses also lobbied and applied pressure, where necessary, for action from other agencies to make his construction influence go beyond the actual charter powers of the TBTA. Neither TBTA nor the Port Authority was explicitly authorized to plan highways. But the plans for both the West Side Highway and the joint TBTA–Port Authority arteries were generated in the offices of these authorities and subsequently adopted as city plans. Moses believed that "the state and city park, parkway, recreation, bridge, and arterial projects in the metropolitan section overlap to such an extent that it is only by coordinating them under one person that any progress can be made."[12]

Business Patronage   Construction is a source of profits to business and of votes to politicians. Unlike TVA and the Port Authority, TBTA avoided building up its own labor force and relied heavily on contracting out. With no requirement for competitive bidding, no restrictions on repeatedly using favored contractors, and no constraints on collective-bargaining methods, Moses negotiated pay and service contracts with a good deal more leeway than even most private entrepreneurs because he did not have to be particularly cost-conscious. He molded a select number of companies and unions into a loyal construction team. He commanded the nearly unbroken support of organized labor throughout his career, managing to negotiate speeded-up construction schedules on favored projects.[13] (Because he had obtained a no-strike pledge, work at the World's Fair site continued throughout a citywide electrical workers' strike in 1962.)

The freedom of public authorities from normal governmental requirements for competitive bidding on contracts elicits repeated howls from government auditors. Only from an office in a public authority could Moses have written to his colleagues in city government that his agency would refuse "to take the responsibility of major repairs and reconstruction of the Metropolitan Museum unless competition is limited to the biggest and best firms in the business."[14] The Metropolitan Museum contract was awarded to the bidder Moses recommended, over the objections of the Contractors Association. Moses negotiated the sales of TBTA bonds without competitive bidding, despite objections by state officials. In 1964, an audit by the New York state comptroller's office concluded that the underwriters' spread on the issues for the Verrazano-Narrows Bridge was substantially greater than any spread that the Port of New York Authority (using competitive bidding) gave underwriters in the same period.

Moses personally negotiated contracts of all kinds, including those allocating bond counsel fees, bank fees, traffic surveys, insurance, printing, engineering, purchasing, and construction business. For the Verrazano-Narrows Bridge, Moses contracted with Madigan-Hyland for engineering services well before the bridge was authorized. Jack Madigan had been a Moses cohort since the depression, when he was a construction supervisor at Jones Beach. The construction contract for the Verrazano-Narrows Bridge was awarded to Turner-Slattery, again without competitive bidding or formal advertising. The contract was written to permit those managing contractors to retain 50 percent of any savings in construction costs relative to budget estimates, in addition to a management fee. Earlier TBTA contracts had been negotiated with the predecessor firm, Walsh-Fuller-Slattery, also on a cost-plus-incentive-plus-fee basis. TBTA was legally a city authority; the charter of the city of New York provides that construction work aggregating more than $2,500 must be performed by a contract awarded through public bidding and that public authorities must follow the city charter, "so far as practicable." Moses simply claimed that special circumstances justified negotiations with selected people.

Only two or three firms are large enough to perform all the steel and erection work for something as large as the Narrows Bridge. For this bridge and the Throgs Neck Bridge, Moses awarded the major contracts to U.S. Steel Corporation and Bethlehem Steel Company. The state comptroller suggested that the authority could stimulate competiton by breaking the jobs down into contracts for each construction phase, with separate procurements, as state agencies do. But Moses opposed this suggestion, and the authority followed its usual procedures in awarding this and contracts for lighting, asphalt, signs, and other aspects of construction.

Moses negotiated leases for the Coliseum (a commercial trade show center in New York City), the Battery Park Garage, and the East Side Airlines Bus Terminal that had no provision for rent escalation and allowed some of the private lessees to make substantial operating profits. By agreement, the net income of the Coliseum in excess of a certain amount reverts to the city, which assembled the land. Hence, the terms of the leases Moses negotiated cut down on the revenues accruing to the city treasury by increasing the profits to private lessees. The Coliseum, financed from TBTA general funds, cost approximately $20 million to construct, including fees to induce the prospective tenants to rent space in the office tower. Although state law limits leases in the Coliseum project to ten years or less, the authority entered into a twenty-year lease with the Federation Bank and Trust Company and loaned $450,000 at low interest to the bank to finance its space alterations. That bank is one of seven that shared the paying agent functions on the Verrazano-Narrows Bridge bonds. (The authority could have reduced costs by using a single bank as the paying agent and taking advantage of quantity discount, but this arrangement would have excluded the smaller banks like Federation.)

Two of Moses's long-time colleagues on the TBTA board were associated with the Federation Bank. William J. Tracy was a director of the bank, as well as a member of an advisory board of Manufacturers Hanover Trust Company, and George E. Spargo, general manager of TBTA until 1963, was on the board of directors of the Federation Bank and Trust Company until 1963. In 1964, Spargo joined the Blauvelt Engineering Company, which subsequently did feasibility study work under contract to TBTA, recommending $200 million worth of improvements on the Queens Midtown Tunnel and the East Side Terminal. Board member George McLaughlin was a vice-chairman of Manufacturers Hanover. Together, Manufacturers Hanover and Federation held 98 percent of TBTA's investment securities, some of which were transferred to Bankers Trust Company in 1963, when Federation resources proved insufficient to cover the amount of securities on deposit.

When, after thirty years of dispensing public authority business patronage, Moses turned his attention and his passion toward the second New York World's Fair, he had little trouble raising funds. (The fair not only appealed to his own taste for monumental events but also generated spin-offs in traffic and revenues for TBTA facilities and new highway and park construction on Long Island. Interlocking TBTA enterprises that fed into the fair grounds included the Bronx Whitestone Bridge and the Queens Midtown Tunnel.) In his typical approach to a new enterprise, Moses edged out the original executive vice-president of the fair and the design committee, brought in a coterie of his own executives, and refused to comply with the regulations of the Bureau of International Exposition; all of these actions contributed to the ultimate financial failure of the fair. Moses marketed World's Fair notes to bankers who had enjoyed and sought more of TBTA's underwriting and related business. Companies that had large contracts for Moses's enterprises, notably for the Verrazano-Narrows Bridge at the time, also were induced to participate in the financing for the fair. Moses represented the fair as financially feasible, and he set out with a determination that it should make a profit. (In fact, he went so far as to oppose cut-rate tickets for schoolchildren.) Nevertheless, as in 1939, fair revenues basically failed to live up to projections, and when its books were closed, it defaulted on nearly two-thirds of its debt. Moses and his team were not accustomed to running enterprises that lacked the safe markets and revenue forecasts of relatively scarce public services. They failed their first real test of the marketplace.

In January 1965, five of the nine bankers on the fair's Finance Committee resigned, complaining about the fair staff's failure to provide them with detailed information about its finances. Moses was not providing them with as much information as they were accustomed to getting from private firms. (The bankers who did not resign were those who had done business with Moses.) Among the bits of information that apparently came as a surprise to the Finance Committee was an employment security contract for Moses as president of the fair, which provided for a deposit of funds to secure payment of his $75,000 salary from 1960 through 1967 (supplemented by an annual expense allowance of $25,000).

Immunity from Democracy Throughout his career, Moses expressed intolerance for the delays that are imposed by open politics and enthusiasm for maximizing development (in the form of speedy construction). Press treatment of Moses bordered on idolatry at times, and in his own statements, he manipulated the symbols of traditional dicta about public authorities: the authority is a fortuitous combination of business management with public ownership "in the best American tradition. It is neither socialistic nor monopolistic, and it is infinitely better than ideological, political warfare"[15]; moreover, "the good citizen builds for the future . . . and his actual accomplishment is what the Recording Angel enters indelibly in the Golden Book. . . .

the great end of life, as Huxley said, is not knowledge, but action."[16] This particular version of biblical virtue reflects values widespread among authority executives: construction is what the recording angel notes, and opposition to construction is surely the work of the devil. To Moses, diabolical obstructionism knew no class or ideology. He described the owners of grand estates over which he built a parkway as a few rich golfers responsible for opposition to a state park, when in fact the large majority of the residents of that area of Long Island were opposed to Moses's plan. When Councilman Stanley Isaacs and other activists in postwar New York City politics tried to halt demolition in slum areas and to add antidiscrimination clauses to public housing contracts, Moses denounced them as undesirable "minorities... who aimed to make and capitalize on political issues. ... Isaacs runs as a Republican among Conservatives and as a Pinko among radicals."[17] When the Tuscarora Indians objected at public hearings to the appropriation and flooding of their land to build Niagara Dam, Moses considered the public hearings to be nothing more than time frittered away and described the Indian leaders as "utterly incredible and clownish."[18] When Moses's successor as head of the New York State parks system suggested that the Adirondack and the Catskill mountain areas should be protected as a natural resource, Moses dismissed environmental conservation as foolishness, huffing, "We need the Adirondacks and the Catskills for controlled mass recreation, however administered."[19] And when one of his successors as New York City parks commissioner pointed out that TBTA should not be a "wandering goose dropping its golden eggs as it pleases" but should comply with reasonable standards of prior notice and review by Parks Department architects, Moses called the new city parks executives "ungrateful amateurs" in interviews dutifully quoted by the press.

Moses was probably ruder, more manipulative, and more powerful than other authority managers. (Massachusetts has several candidates who approach him.) But regardless of the merits of the results, Moses spoke and acted as can only an authority manager—who will never face election himself or require direct support from community groups and other politicians, and who is not accountable to stockholders, competitors, or questioning board members. Moses's ability to bully mayors, state legislators, congressmen, and federal administrators was derived not only from his powerful personality but also from his authority bases of power—financial independence, management control, and business patronage. He reports that Senator Robert S. Kerr of Oklahoma, on entering a subcommittee meeting at which Moses was making a presentation, asked, "Sir, do I have your permission to enter, and can you give me a certificate of safe passage to the chair?"[20] He also records an assertion made by Albert Cole, head of the U.S. Housing and Home Finance Agency, that the agency had "more trouble with Mr. Robert Moses than with any other single individual in all the cities of the United States."[21] Cole asked Mayor Robert F. Wagner to relieve Moses of his control of the slum clearance program. Wagner refused.

A Battle of Authorities Moses held power in the city and the state for some forty years, past an age at which most politicians and administrators have retired. His downfall began when, as chairman of the city's Slum Clearance Committee, he was tarnished by a series of scandals and failures of the slum clearance program that were widely publicized by the press and criticized by federal housing authorities in the late 1950s. Slum clearance contract records, unlike authority transactions, were open to the public once the press decided to look for them. Failure to provide relocation housing for displaced families, unenforced federal regulations, and large profits for project sponsors added up to a dim public record. Under fire for the first time by the press, Moses resigned his positions as city parks commissioner and chairman of the Slum Clearance Committee in 1959, when it became clear that he could obtain control of the New York World's Fair Corporation.

Meanwhile, others had learned to maximize the power opportunities offered by the public authority device. In 1960, Governor Nelson A. Rockefeller began creating, expanding, and increasing the financing of public authorities in New York State. In 1963, Rockefeller asked Moses to step down after nearly forty years as head of the State Council on Parks; he planned to put his brother Laurance in that post. Using a tactic that had worked for him several times, Moses threatened to resign from the Power Authority chairmanship and other state posts as well. He was surprised; Nelson Rockefeller accepted the resignations and remembers receiving only twelve letters of protest.

In the next five years, Governor Rockefeller and his aide William Ronan gained control over transportation finances in the state. As they did so, they closed in on TBTA. In 1967, the voters approved a massive $2.5 billion general obligation transportation bond issue, a vote that gave the governor a financial leeway to plan and to build that had previously been enjoyed only by the independent public authorities. With that resource to apply to the troubled systems in the New York City region, Rockefeller took them over

organizationally through passage of legislation that created a broader transportation conglomerate—the Metropolitan Transportation Authority.

Although Moses had formed the TBTA by merging individual authorities
and had used profits from lucrative bridges to help finance non-revenue-
producing projects, he now opposed those same strategies when Rockefeller
and Ronan attempted them. He fought merger of the TBTA into the MTA in
the press, on Wall Street, and in the courts. He used the traditional arguments
on behalf of authority autonomy: that merger would violate pledges in bond
covenants and law, that the state could not limit or alter the rights vested in
the authority, and that contractual obligations to the bondholders were in-
violate. His teams of attorneys from TBTA, from a bond counsel firm, and
from the law firm enjoying legal business from the World's Fair argued further that a merger would aggravate strike threats, that the TBTA revenue
surplus was more myth than reality, that the motorists (and the highway
lobby) would and should oppose using highway funds for mass transit, that
all revenues of the authority were pledged under the bond resolution, and
that the merger would destroy the concept of the public authority. Losing
the battle in the legislature and in city hall, Moses took to the courts, encouraging the trustees for the bond issues to bring suit against the merger
terms. The litigation was eventually settled by raising the interest rate on
TBTA's outstanding bonds by 0.25 percent. In the combined powers of the
state house and Chase Manhattan Bank, the Rockefeller brothers and their
man Ronan, Moses had met his match. Some commentators have implied that
Chase, acting as bank trustee for TBTA bonds (and headed by David Rockefeller) sold bondholder interests out to expedite the governor's program. This
speculation is not convincing because the settlement was advantageous to the
bondholders and because mergers of authorities have elsewhere been negotiated with no payoff or additional interest to the bondholders. In the absence
of default, bondholder damage is hard to find; the extra 0.25 percent interest
was simply a bonus to the investors, whose repayment in full is safe and steady
in 1977—nine years after the merger.

Ronan subsequently edged Moses out of TBTA affairs, although Moses
continued to receive a salary as a consultant to MTA and continued to promote the Long Island Sound bridge project. In all likelihood, if that bridge
could have been financed through TBTA in the traditional fashion, it would
have been built. The electorate was able to penetrate the barriers around
authority decision making when, and only when, general state funding was

needed to implement the decision and the necessary bond authorizations were voted down.

Port Authority Executives

Austin J. Tobin, a man who shunned publicity and adroitly sidestepped overt political conflicts, was the head of the second huge authority empire in the tristate New York region during Robert Moses's heyday. Tobin and Moses represent distinct personality types each of which has many parallels in the annals of private corporate leadership: Moses the flamboyant conglomerate maker; Tobin the brilliant management-oriented administrator, presiding over a low-risk, steady-growth industry. Nevertheless, they shared common attributes of public authority leadership.

As of 1972, Tobin controlled gross operating revenues of up to $320 million. He had unchallenged command of an organization that was spending some $200 million a year on public project construction and had invested some $3 billion during his tenure. Along with Moses, Tobin had helped to alter the metropolitan region's economy and anatomy.

Austin Tobin spent his entire career with the Port Authority. In 1928, he joined the legal staff; in 1942, he became executive director, a position he was to retain for thirty years. Like many other authority managers, he says that he would not have gone to work for regular government and that he feels a closer affinity for the private than for the public sector. Tobin's major strategy emphasized developing and maintaining strong relationships with the investment community and enhancing the Port Authority's independence through the use of consolidated bonds. He shunned rail transportation as a financial "bottomless pit" and held to the view that considerations of credit and bond marketability should dominate authority decision making. He stressed business management methods and organizational development, particularly after 1947, when he hired Matthias E. Lukens as deputy director.

Tobin had the tenure and concentrated management power to develop an intensely personal style of leadership over the Port Authority and its eighty-five hundred employees. Executives of the Port Authority admired his "charismatic leadership," his integrity, honesty, and efficiency, his role as the guiding force for the entire corporate structure. In 1958, Lukens wrote, "The beginning and the end of management in the Port Authority is leadership and executive direction. These are absolutely crucial for the integrity and loyalty of the organization."[22] More than a decade later, Daniel L. Kurshan, director of administration, who worked with Tobin for decades, amplified this point: "The force of Mr. Tobin's personality and the dynamic character of his leadership has made itself felt through every echelon of the Authority's organization. The nature of his direction has been personal and forceful."[23] Internally, he was a hero, but Tobin's nominal superiors, governors of New York and New Jersey, found him "arrogant," "difficult to deal with," and "impossible," to repeat a sample of their phrases.

Tobin tightly controlled the integrity of the organization by dealing harshly with suspected transgressions and by building a reputation of moral leadership within. He was known for taking swift and drastic action in any instance of corrupt, unfit, or incompetent behavior. (Executives in government hierarchies are bound by civil service and union contract work rules that prohibit swift dismissals, demotions, or even job changes.)

Tobin made good use of the convention that authorities are nonpolitical to fend off patronage pressures from the outside. Because he was so little interested in political influence beyond his own organization's ability to manage itself and its projects as it pleased, his personal involvements with patronage were minimal. He insisted that internal management be free of extraneous influences. For years at the authority, employees circulated a story about a person of note who approached Tobin about a security officer who deserved promotion. Tobin is reported to have answered, "Don't tell me his name or I'll fire him." Tobin did fire middle-level executives who engaged in campaigning for political candidates. To this day he maintains that a "well-run authority has to be completely out of politics," but he readily admits that many of his counterparts in other authorities are heavily involved in politics. Tobin was willing to extend "courtesies" or minor favors to politicians, although he repeatedly denied their right to influence authority policy or personnel decisions.

In his own way, Tobin exercised as much power as Moses.[24] He co-opted commissioners and fended off unwanted suggestions of governors and legislators. He completely rejected the right of Congress to gain access to Port Authority records and to lay down guidelines for Port Authority policy (despite the fact that the interstate authority was created by congressional legislation).

Tobin always insisted that the delegation of management responsibility to him as executive director was crucial to the operation of the Port Authority. In hearings held by the House Judiciary Committee, for example, Tobin maintained that the power to buy or sell bonds was entirely his. He explained that when he provided a committee of his board with lists of bonds bought and sold, the commissioners simply acquiesced, despite their financial expertise. And "they will, sir, up to the time they get a new executive director. . . . They gave me that power because I am capable of handling it."[25] In fact, Tobin did resign abruptly in 1972 when he thought board members were meddling in management.

After Tobin's retirement, the pressures to recruit his replacement from within the authority were strong. The board appointed Tobin's deputy director, Matthias E. Lukens, as interim acting director, but Lukens retired for reasons of health shortly thereafter. A. Gerdes Kuhbach, who had been director of finance since 1962, replaced Lukens, but for two years the board delayed making the appointment permanent. The governors of both New York and New Jersey were interested in appointing a director from outside the authority in order to enhance their control and induce better cooperation in transit improvement programs. Governor Nelson A. Rockefeller tried to have William J. Ronan appointed to the job, but Governor William T. Cahill was not willing to accept someone so closely tied to Rockefeller. After two years of bickering, the board of commissioners of the Port Authority gave Kuhbach a two-year contract as director. His salary was increased from $70,000 to $80,000—above that of all state or local officials except the governors—by decision of a board committee. This decision was not recorded on the public minutes and not readily subject to gubernatorial veto, but under subsequent protest from the governor of New Jersey, the increase was rescinded.

Once appointed, Kuhbach made it clear that authority priorities would not change; his stated goals were to maintain strong financial results and credit ratings. (He once planned to be a bond trader and was trained as a tax lawyer.) Some transit advocates hoped that Kuhbach might take an active interest in rail transportation because he had spent twenty-one years with the New Haven Railroad, working his way up from assistant counsel to executive vice-president before he joined the Port Authority. The financial collapse of the New Haven Railroad, however, had taught him a lesson he did not wish to repeat. Pressure from the governors and new dissensions on the board resulted in his contract not being formally extended in 1976. The stalemate over appointment of a new executive director continued into 1977 when an aide to New York Governor Hugh Carey was appointed executive director and New Jersey Commissioner Alan Sagner replaced Ronan as chairman of the board of commissioners. During the five years Ronan had served as chairman, he had tried to assume management control, but he no longer had the personal support of an incumbent governor (although he was still in close counsel with Vice-President Rockefeller). His construction plans for the MTA (from which he had resigned) were in apparent shambles; he was opposed by some of his fellow commissioners on the Port Authority board; he lacked the allegiance of most Port Authority executives; and he had neither the goodwill of the press nor taste and talent for day-to-day management.[26] Ronan's career of extraordinary authority power was brief relative to those of the old-timers.

The Port Authority passed through five years of unstable leadership which lowered the morale of its executives and encouraged the governors to become more involved in its affairs than they had in decades. The authority bases of power, however, are still intact and offer new leaders an opportunity to restore its strength.

Other Managers

Tobin and Moses may be the best-known giants of the public authority lexicon, but the basic characteristics of management power are repeated in public enterprises, large and small, around the nation. Edward J. King's power and drive brought the Massachusetts Port Authority from rags to riches in fifteen years. It took late-night meetings, extraordinary board appointments, and the determined efforts of two consecutive governors to oust him—over loud protests from his friends, who included bankers, legislators, union officials, and contractors. Both King and William S. Callahan (of the Massachusetts Turnpike Authority) were called "Massachusetts's Moses" by the Boston press. Minnesota press items reflected parallel views of sewer board chief Richard Doughty, calling him a "dictator," a "caesar," a "hard-driving, results-oriented administrator." The Los Angeles Port Authority's Bernard Coughlin has been described as "the West Coast Austin Tobin."

One of the lesser-known powerhouse public enterprise executives is Paul Belica. Executive director of the New York State Housing Finance Authority from its inception in 1960 through 1976, Belica was simultaneously chief executive officer of the Project Finance Agency, New York Bond Bank, and Medical Care Facilities Finance Agency, as well as chairman of the New York State Mortgage Agency. Like his counterparts in other public enterprise conglomerates, Belica is an energetic man with personal ideas about how "his" agencies should operate, and he took considerable pride in their performance. With a varied background in the construction industry and diplomatic service, he admits he would not be attracted to work in regular government agencies. Belica was a worthy state counterpart of Jesse Jones. He developed direct contacts among the financial institutions, fended off unwanted demands from state officials, and maintained an intensely loyal staff. After leading the agency through fiscal crisis in 1975–1976, he resigned when it became clear that HFA had entered a stage of consolidation and dependence on the state government.

Highway and turnpike authorities usually have had stable management. D. Louis Tonti, executive director of the New Jersey Highway Authority, had an international reputation as an effective turnpike authority manager, serving as president of the International Bridge, Tunnel and Turnpike Association and fulfilling consulting assignments from California to Italy. Tonti had worked his way to an engineering degree and through some years of law school. After several years in private transport enterprise, he became assistant to the first executive director of the New Jersey Highway Authority shortly after its creation. In 1955, when the authority was in full operation, he became executive director and held this position for seventeen years. Apart from occasional mild disagreements with board chairman Katharine Elkus White, he was the undisputed boss of the authority. Purposefully using Tobin's strategy, he kept board members generally informed of the activities of the authority but willing to accept his judgment. He too relied on a loyal staff—a public relations director, a comptroller, and a chief engineer whose highway authority careers paralleled his. Making skilled use of outside engineering consultants and legal counsel, he resisted unwanted projects, including proposals for a ferry service at the southern end of the parkway and highway spurs that did not promise to contribute to authority revenues.

Although he likens himself to Austin Tobin, in many ways Tonti's flamboyant personality is more reminiscent of Robert Moses. He developed a patronage machine based on the allocation of construction, legal fees, and financial contracts, and he—like Moses—made one unsuccessful attempt to run for governor. (Also like Moses, he was a candidate lacking political diplomacy. Tonti told one group of mayors from whom he sought support that their jobs were obsolete.) Tonti used parkway revenues for a wide range of what he called "corporate purposes," most notably to finance construction of the Garden State Arts Center, a favorite project for which the Highway Authority had no explicit legislative authorization. A devoted opera buff and classical music fan, Tonti justified the construction of the arts center complex as "developing the recreational potential of land" adjacent to the Garden

State Parkway. Initially described in public as a $1.6 million project, the cultural center ultimately opened with a price tag of nearly five times that amount, all of it underwritten by parkway tolls. Tonti reports that Governor Richard Hughes wanted to kill the project in the early stages (because, in Tonti's words, the governor "did not know the difference between Bach, Beethoven, and the Beatles"). Tonti claims to have persuaded the governor's wife, however, to encourage support for the project. The Garden State Arts Center was to Tonti what Jones Beach was to Robert Moses: a source of personal enjoyment, opportunities to entertain friends and colleagues in style, and seemingly harmless favors. It remained so for subsequent directors who dispense free tickets for events with some fanfare to community groups and with less fanfare to New Jersey politicians.

Tonti's expensive try for the Democratic gubernatorial nomination, together with with his admiration for classical music and its stars, led him to seek personal income beyond that offered by public authority management. Freedom to run the parkway business and rich opportunities for contract patronage provided temptations too great for him. In 1973, he was an inmate of the federal prison camp at Montgomery, Pennsylvania. Together with several other authority executives in New Jersey, Tonti had fallen before the scythes of the team of United States attorneys that prosecuted eight mayors, two state secretaries, two state treasurers, two political bosses, one United States congressman, and sixty other public officials in the state of New Jersey.[27] In April 1972, Tonti was indicted on forty-seven counts, alleging conspiracy with the chief engineer of the Highway Authority to extort money from concerns doing business with the Garden State Parkway. He pleaded guilty to one count, covering $120,000 received from Frederick R. Harris, Inc., of New York, the general consulting engineer for the toll roads from 1966 through 1970, and sums from Automatic Toll Systems, Inc., and Teller & Cooper, two companies supplying toll booths and related equipment. Tonti served twenty months of a three-year sentence.

Leadership Life Cycles

Most public authorities are untouched by overt scandal. The typical life cycle of public enterprise management begins with leadership by the groups influential in the corporation's creation, settles down in its operational stages to professional management dominated by engineering and law, and finds more politicized leadership at times of high controversy when public debate breaks into the enterprise's affairs. The Port Authority itself has followed this pattern—dominated initially by its founders from the New York Chamber of Commerce, managed for thirty years by Austin Tobin, and suffering a flurry of gubernatorial interest and uncertain leadership in the 1970s. The New Jersey Highway Authority was first managed by the head of the state Transportation Department, which had sponsored the creation of the authority, followed by Tonti's long rule, and then by politician John Gallagher, who feuded with a new governor of different party and was forced out of his job before his contract term was completed. (In 1977, when the authority needed an improved image, a professional newsman took over the post.)

In Austin, Texas, the early years of the Lower Colorado River Authority were dominated by sponsor Alvin J. Wirtz and his colleagues. For thirty-seven years, the LCRA was run by men associated with its creation. The first general manager, Clarence McDonough, had been chief of the engineering division of the U.S. Public Works Administration, which was financing LCRA's initial dam construction; he guided the authority through its initial construction phases with the PWA loans. Max Starke, the second manager, expanded the market for LCRA electricity and bonds during fifteen years of rapid growth. After his resignation in 1955, Starke continued as a management consultant by annual contract until his death in 1972. W. Sim Gideon, a former law partner of Wirtz, succeeded Starke as general manager and managed the authority for the next eighteen years. During this period, LCRA was run in a relatively efficient and conflict-free manner and enjoyed steady growth, stable business conditions, and virtually no competition. Decision making was largely concentrated in the general manager's office, as it usually is in small authorities, and LCRA revenues grew steadily although rates charged to customers did not increase. Shortly before Gideon retired, oil price increases and the energy shortage forced the authority to raise its rates. At the same time, the authority had to face higher interest rates for expansion capital and was contemplating controversial proposals for activities in recreation and pollution abatement. To deal with these new pressures, in 1973 the LCRA board chose as general manager Charles Herring, a skilled lawyer-politician with a bent for public relations, who had represented the LCRA district in the state legislature for sixteen years. They also raised the salary for the position to $55,000 annually, making it comparable with the salaries of presidents of private utilities of similar size. Herring's assistant, John E. Babcock, manager of the Environmental-Research Department of LCRA, which includes public affairs and newer, more controversial aspects of LCRA's work, has a background in newspaper work and has served with the authority for over twenty-five years in several capacities. The LCRA management team includes an assistant general manager with experience that also spans the public and private sectors (from city management to utility plant construction). These shifting leadership patterns help explain LCRA's ability to adapt to new pressures.

Metro Seattle is a relatively young organization. James R. Ellis, general counsel, and C. Carey Donworth, chairman of Metro since its beginning, continue to be the core of Metro Seattle's leadership after fifteen years of operation. The executive directors of Metro Seattle were at first professional engineers (most of them recruited from within). In 1975, when proposals that Metro become a general county government were beginning to gain currency, its director resigned to join an engineering consulting firm. After screening nearly three hundred applicants from a nationwide search, the council appointed as executive director a local expert in public affairs, Richard Page, who had been an aide to a mayor and a senator, program director for Seattle's Forward Thrust, Inc. (headed by Ellis), and Metro's director of public services. A shift toward political skills in times of challenge was again demonstrated. Page left in 1977 to become federal transit administrator.

Long-term management by engineers with careers in public enterprise is typical of the smaller municipal corporations, such as Pennsylvania's local public service corporations, New Jersey's sewer authorities, and utility districts in Tennessee and Alabama. The Pennsylvania Municipal Authorities Association, for example, has members who have made lifetime careers in the general management of sewer, water, and construction-oriented authorities. Public enterprise engineer-managers number in the thousands, and many of their names may be seen carved on small sewage treatment plants, dams, bridges, and power plants across the nation. Small lease-back authorities are an exception to the pattern of strong internal management; many are run on a part-time basis by bankers.

Far from being temporary corporations that will go out of business when their initial construction costs are paid off, public authorities show a strong will to survive and to expand. A young organization may be dependent on the prestige of its board of directors or its sponsors to garner money and support, but over time, sponsors, board members, and the community that created the corporation give way to professionalized management and operating routines. When the corporation has developed its own financial resources, its professional staff takes control of policy initiation and defends the organization from outside intrusion. (The board and political supporters may remain important at times of special stress and for providing a protective mantle of reputation and representation.) During public conflicts, the corporation's management can shift to leaders more oriented to politics and public relations, but politicization of management is often short-lived. This flexibility in leadership that allows response to the needs of the organization rather than being controlled by voting trends, political debts, or civil service rules gives an authority greater independent strength than a typical government bureau has.

The stages of leadership are not necessarily sequential or sharply differentiated. They depend upon shifting power relationships among the board, the staff, the chief executive, and outside leaders. They are affected by shifting variables, such as the capital requirements of authority projects, corporate norms, community ideology, dependence on outside groups, and the complexity of services performed. But as the organization becomes more complex and financially secure, power passes to the employed executive and his staff except in times of public crisis. And even those public authority managers who come from active political careers tend to emphasize corporate independence and organizational goals after awhile. The function of the board of directors is, then, to lend sufficient prestige and influence to keep up the authority's reputation in the community.

9 Productivity in the Public Sector

Some twenty-five years before "great society" became a political slogan, Charles Beard pointed out that "every enterprise in the Great Society, as well as the Great Society itself, rests upon administration."[1] The United States Constitution makes no mention of administrative agencies, which are now overwhelmingly the largest component of government. Public debate tends to assume that once programs are approved, a real and effective effort will be made to implement them; subsequent failures to achieve goals are ascribed to errors in the policy itself. Political speeches, the press, and television devote a great deal more attention to whether a dam should be built, whether job training should be funded, and whether the poor are deserving than to contract letting, cost overruns, payroll tie-ups, useless regulations, unnecessary overtime, multiple approvals, and so forth. Yet distortions of goals and diversions of resources have sabotaged a wide range of manpower, health, and community action programs. The failure of American government to deliver goods and services promised by legislative proposals is one of the basic causes of contemporary cynicism about politics in the United States. This failure and the disillusionment it has caused are traceable in part to unrealistic expectations and in part to ineptitude in managing the public's business.

Even the traditional services of government have been so badly managed as to deteriorate in quality while increasing in cost. Government now affects all aspects of the quality of life. It consumes large and growing portions of personal budgets and national resources. State and local government accounts for nearly 15 percent of all employment in the United States. All government purchases account for 22 percent of gross national product. Information as to whether those resources are spent ill or well has become essential to citizens who seek to make intelligent political choices. Managerial incompetence and organizational paralysis have more damaging effects on the public interest than does common graft. The public costs of graft are negligible compared to the public costs of mismanagement, yet government takes elaborate (if unsuccessful) measures against graft and virtually ignores management. The widespread belief that inefficiency is inevitable or universal in government merely provides an excuse not to bother changing the status quo. This evasion carries a high price.

The performance of public authorities and other government corporations illustrates that it is possible for some public jobs to be carried out well and quickly. Of course, the effectiveness of public authorities results in part from their ready access to money and in part to the concentrated power and prolonged tenure of authority directors and managers. Moreover, public enterprises vary greatly. Financing devices that are run from a desk in a bank or a government bureau have few management traits in common with huge enterprises like the Port Authority and TVA. Nevertheless, most operating public authorities manifest some distinctive management patterns that contrast with those of regular government bureaucracies. Public corporations provide stronger incentives for productivity and performance than do state and local governments. As a result, one of the most frequently cited reasons for creating public authorities is to avoid the red tape and personnel of regular government. But productivity and problem solving are at least as necessary for criminal justice, education, and social welfare as for the highways, bridges, dams, and other concrete sculptures that public authorities have fashioned. It is important to understand the contrasts between governments and corporations, not to escape government but to improve it.

Public Mismanagement

In effect, it is comparison with regular government agencies that makes many public authorities seem well managed. The setting in which political executives operate in city, state, and federal government discourages management performance. Government agency heads serve short tenures, averaging roughly two years in some categories. In stark contrast to corporate leaders, these businessmen, politicians, and professionals, appointed to a government post by a mayor, governor, or president, often merely add to their own prestige by a few years' service as political executives and then return to their primary careers. Many of them are ignorant of their agency's procedures, regulations, traditions, and sensitivities when they enter government service and are only slightly less ignorant when they leave. They have little reason to work toward long-range goals that span a number of budget years or to pursue changes that will make current enemies but improve future performance.

The concept of the political executive appointed by the elected official and exempt from the civil service was designed to add flexibility to government leadership and to give the newly elected official the capacity to manage the permanent bureaucracy.[2] But political executives tend to come and go even more rapidly than their elected bosses, and they often have different aims and friends. Their interests put additional emphasis on short-term results.

These problems affect city administrations most severely, though all of American government suffers the consequences of the management failures of city governments because the localities are the service-delivery arms of federal and state government. Many national programs can only be as effective as the local agencies that carry them out. The War on Poverty bogged down in the foxholes of local bureaucracies.

Mayors, governors, and their commissioners naturally try not to alienate large and vocal groups, especially public employee unions and associations. These elected officials often distribute press releases announcing management crackdowns on waste without in fact cutting programs. They reorganize agencies without changing work patterns, and they make long and loud dramas of collective bargaining without imposing management muscle to enhance productivity or cut costs. The news media carry the political announcements but seldom call their sources to account by investigating the underlying facts and effects.

Most city programs have no "bottom line," no profit or net revenue figure or other clear-cut performance standard by which the agency head can be measured. Government agencies tolerate low productivity on the part of employees as long as it does not cause short-term crises and stays within the boundaries of procedural regulations. Even the permanent department head can reap few rewards for special achievement. He tends to measure his success by the size of the budget allocation he can wrest out of the annual budget process. The line-item budget and annual appropriations encourage the department head to spend the full amount allotted for each item and not to look at the possible benefits of shifting expenditures from one item to another or cutting costs. Government hierarchies provide few incentives to meet particular program targets, and performance data are seldom collected in sensible and readable form; as a result, department heads cannot be held to account as effectively in government as they can be in the private sector.

City executives seek short-term, newsworthy projects. The costs and results of those projects are of little importance because the public seldom has the will or the opportunity to evaluate them. The media report on newsworthy projects individually. They deal with budget problems collectively, usually without reference to particular projects. And voters often approve the very projects for which they subsequently defeat funding proposals.

Even when the political executives of city government stay in their jobs and maintain undampened enthusiasm, they generally lack effective control of the organizations they are supposed to run. The civil service is the permanent work force of most state and city governments. Unlike those in many European countries, U.S. civil service systems do not readily offer career opportunities that span more than one jurisdiction. Public employees spend their lives in one government, often in one agency. They rise up the ranks in accordance with arcane and rigid procedures that rely on specialized exams and seniority. Few supervisors are recruited from without or come into the agency with fresh views, executive experience, or special training. Within each city government, clerks become budget officers; teachers become school system executives; sanitation workers become supervisors and district managers. This system can provide upward mobility for talented people, but it can also lead people to jobs for which they are not suited (good teachers often are not good administrators and vice-versa).

The higher ranks of the civil service in state and local government have little distinct management perspective or loyalty to a chief executive. They have seen politicians come and go and are generally hard to impress. Moreover, civil service rules that were designed to prevent arbitrary personnel decisions now protect incompetence and discourage initiative. Most of our civil service systems in their present form offer little job satisfaction to public employees and do not sustain the quality of performance found in many public authorities.

Collective bargaining agreements with unions of city or state employees contain provisions that add to and freeze many civil service regulations.[3] Employees pay union and professional association dues mainly to assure job security. In state and local government, the quest for security has taken forms that directly interfere with productivity, mainly by protecting the employee from all change, even minor shifts in tasks.

One of the mysteries of modern civil service little understood by the uninitiated is the proliferation of job titles. If you have ever been shunted from desk to desk or from phone to phone in a municipal building, you have experienced the effects of overspecialized job classification. Job classification is a core feature of civil service systems. Each class of jobs bears a title that carries with it a set salary range and specified duties, requirements, and promotion examinations. As problems arise, they are broken down into small components that are assigned to different job titles. Hence, job titles tend to multiply, and duties tend to become more specialized. This trend deprives the civil service employee of the flexibility to answer a new question, to experiment, to solve a new problem. His individual judgment and effort have little effect on his tasks or pay raises. The civil service assigns certain duties and pay to the titles of "junior stenographer," "senior stenographer," or "principal stenographer," for example. A "clerk grade 1" cannot do the job of a "clerk grade 2," who cannot do the job of a "clerk grade 3." Overspecialized job classification protects employees against changes in their work assignments. It also deprives them of the opportunity to work as a cooperative team of intelligent individuals in a dynamic, problem-solving endeavor. It eliminates pride in work. Moreover, government bureaus are bound by extensively written regulations that define the powers of each employee, including the executives, and specify program details. "Deputy directors are authorized to conduct conferences, to certify copies of documents, to grant extensions of time" read typical city codes. Swings for playgrounds must be of certain dimensions, and recreation programs must include only specified games.

Political executives wrestling with this system on a short-term basis may make it worse. They write new job titles, for example, in order to enjoy hiring flexibility during the time lapse that a personnel department or civil service board requires to devise new exams for those titles. Two years later, that commissioner is gone but he has left behind a new layer of job titles.

Most collective bargaining agreements include some general statement defending "management prerogatives" but set forth detailed provisions determining assignments, tasks, and programs. In addition to freezing civil service job titles, in some cities these agreements limit an agency's ability to contract jobs out; they specify qualifications for hiring (height for firemen, college degrees for recreation workers, and so forth) and determine how many workers of various classes must be assigned to different kinds of tasks.

Another trend in municipal civil service and collective bargaining is to complicate discipline procedures and reduce the possibilities for demotion or layoff. In order to discipline a subordinate, a supervisor must "bring him up on charges"—by definition, a hostile procedure. The employee may carry his appeal to a civil service board and, in some towns, into the courts, with cross-examination by lawyers. This procedure is very unpleasant for all involved, and most supervisors avoid it. In addition, the probationary or tryout period for city employees is shorter and less effective than that in the corporate sector. City government makes little effort to keep unsatisfactory new employees from joining the protected ranks or to help them become good at their jobs. All of these traits emerge in stark contrast to the internal flexibility found in many public authorities.

At the extremes, the results are appalling. In one city's social services agency, state auditors found supervisors ignoring sleeping employees; staff reading novels during working hours and catching up on work during overtime; impromptu exercise classes and private commerce in the office; and referrals through seven desks to process one form.

Each specialized agency hobbles along its own beaten track, without communication or cooperation with others. Streets are torn up repeatedly for work by different agencies. Schools expel teenagers whom social workers have talked into staying there. Unskilled workers are trained for government jobs from which they are barred by formal qualifications. Small construction projects, such as a playground improvement, may require fifty separate sequential approvals. Contractors' cost overruns are spent before they are noticed by the responsible agency head (although the overruns may be duly entered in as many as a dozen reporting forms). The illustrations are legion.

Many city governments suffer from advanced cases of bureaucratization, a disease that, in less extreme form, is causing problems in all kinds of contemporary organizations, public and private. As hierarchical controls become tighter and more elaborate, as officials devise regulations to cover more and more situations in advance and impersonally, as specialization reduces each job to simple, unchanging routines, people feel less responsibility and less opportunity to use their own judgment and ability. Frustration in turn reinforces emphasis on job security, financial return, low risk, and high leisure. Apathy, goldbricking, and strident demands become characteristic not only of the lower ranks but also of the equally frustrated middle management and professional groups.

Government reorganization merely shifts parts of the structure around. It does not change work patterns or break the cycle of falling performance, responded to by tightening controls, which in turn further depress performance. One student of public organization describes the progressive pathology in this way:

> Organizations composed of multilevel, self-sealing, non-publicly examinable or testable processes will tend to manifest a low probability for learning and experimenting. The low level of learning will feed back to make the organization seem even more difficult to change. Under these conditions, the participants may come to have little confidence in their own organizations. The lack of credibility and sense of resignation experienced by outsiders are now duplicated and confirmed by the insider.[4]

City governments caught in this cycle cannot deliver the goods and services that both the public and the state and federal financiers demand of them. (Private firms can get caught in the same web. Large investor-owned public utilities are among the better-known examples.) Many public authorities and other forms of statutory corporation manage to avoid these difficulties, in part because of their limited size. Public corporations are the size of a single agency of municipal government, a small town government, or a small- to medium-sized business. They suggest a way to decentralize city government —not by neighborhood but by task. But even in their size category, public authorities have fairly good management records.[5]

Authority Management

In order to draw general comparisons among government corporations, investor-owned corporations, and government bureaus, considerable liberties must be taken. There will be exceptions in each category to nearly any statement that can be made. Nevertheless, some tendencies are suggested by available evidence. Most public corporations do implement their activities relatively well, partly because they have maintained—thus far, at least— comparatively flexible and capable management and work patterns. Government corporations leave a great deal more to on-the-spot common sense and to informed human judgment and less to rules and procedures than do typical government bureaus.

Managers are recruited from both within and without the corporate structure and tend to move from department to department in the course of being promoted. Career ladders and lateral movement within the organization are not determined by seniority or specialized testing. Although large public corporations with formal personnel systems use both seniority and testing, they also leave more leeway than city governments do for personal judgment and accommodation to special problems and people. An executive's decision to promote or to shift an employee may be influenced but not forced by test results and years in grade. Even public authorities whose employees are legally part of city, state, or federal civil service have less rigid job classifications and procedural rules.

Management personnel tend to stay with a public corporation for relatively long periods of time, often for decades, but they do not enjoy guaranteed tenure as civil servants do, and they are used to the pressure of high expectations. These men and women also exercise wider discretion over the units in their charge than do civil servants at comparable levels. Public corporations recruit executives from outside the organization at times of change or stress or when the organization is taking on new functions. The search for new people frequently crosses state lines and is conducted through professional organizations, much as in the private sector. Metro Seattle, for example, undertook a nationwide search for a transit department manager, and some of its pollution control executives have been pirated by public corporations in other parts of the nation. In the 1950s, when the Port Authority launched a major reorganization, it hired a number of executives, including a specialist in administration and organization, a professional director of personnel, and a new finance director, from private business. Many of the executives that joined the authority at that time are still there. Housing finance agencies have recruited specially selected people from state government, attracting them with higher salaries and more flexible work opportunities than state government can offer.

In the authority, as in business, the organization of line and staff carries out decisions ratified by the top executives. In government, line and staff are little more than abstract principles; a department head, lacking the power to hire, fire, promote, and shift personnel, to purchase supplies, or to adjust budget items, must engage in persuasion to get the smallest as well as the largest tasks carried out. Persuasion is also necessary in business, of course. In a number of speeches and lectures, Marion B. Folsom, who served as vice-president of the Eastman Kodak Company and as secretary of health, education, and welfare, compared administration in government and business.[6] He compared efforts to overcome opposition from Kodak's advertising and sales department to the establishment of a market research department, for example, to similar efforts in government departments. But the ultimate loyalty of the corporate staff to the top person and the discretionary ability of management to hire, fire, promote, and shift executives puts more economic and psychological muscle behind administrative persuasion in business. Moreover, less momentous changes and routine assignments can be carried out with fewer debates, bargains, and compromises than in government agencies. Public authorities tend to share these attributes of the private firm.

The generally fluid decision-making and communications patterns of public authorities are more like those of small business than like government. For example, in 1960, while a technician on the recreation staff of TVA was flying back to his office in Knoxville, he noticed that the construction of Barkley Dam on the Cumberland River was leaving a peninsula in the middle that would be an ideal recreation spot. Having a long-term career commitment to TVA and ready access to those who could decide on new projects, he brought his suggestion to the head office. A series of decisions, project design changes, and implementing activities involving several different divisions of the authority were carried out with dispatch. (The only serious delay was caused by the need to get National Park Service approval.) The result is "Land between the Lakes," a camping ground with planned nature facilities that receives over one million visitors per year.[7] Such flexibility in decision making and easy flow of ideas and information on practical problems, both laterally between departments and vertically from the man on the spot to top management, are far more typical of corporate structures than of government departments bound by isolated bureaus, tight hierarchies, specified job responsibilities, and revolving-door executives. Where appropriate, management in public corporations also appoints specially selected teams—task forces that bring together members of several departments and people with different (and sometimes warring) specialties. The task force in enterprise cuts across departmental boundaries to devise new programs, to advise on particular sets of problems, or to oversee a construction project without sequential approvals.

Management Surveys and Reorganization   Public authorities put a more conscious emphasis on management techniques than do government bureaus. They assign more internal staff to consider organization and management on a continuing basis, make more frequent use of management consultants, and reorganize departments more often and more easily. One of the areas in which public authorities perform most effectively compared to regular governments is in adaptation to growth. Expanding public authorities ordinarily call in management consultants. Consultants' recommendations tend to be somewhat superficial and repetitious, but they do provide the corporation with ready justification and periodic opportunities to shake itself up and adjust to new problems. For example, in 1972, when Metro Seattle entered the transportation field and its involvement with other governments and community groups was growing because of public interest in pollution control, it commissioned a major survey of its organizational requirements for adapting to growth. Consultants recommended decentralizing the more routine management functions from the top executive, creating a new department consolidating public and governmental relations activities, improving internal communications, and developing task forces and project teams for specific problem-solving activities. The consultants' report reflected a recognition of the speed of technological progress in the pollution control and transportation fields and recommended an increasing use of demonstration techniques in project design to provide for ongoing evaluation and innovation.

Similarly, in 1973 and 1974, confronting rapid increases in expenditures for the development of new power sources and taking on pollution control enforcement and park and recreation functions, the Lower Colorado River Authority hired a consulting firm to develop a series of recommendations to adapt the corporation to growth. Before 1973, LCRA had been a typical medium-sized public corporation, with a low level of bureaucratization—a personal style of leadership by which the executive director and a group of trusted colleagues made most of the decisions, including those that in a bigger business would ordinarily be made lower down (by plant managers, for example). The consultants found that LCRA was operating with relative efficiency even though it had no formal management program and nothing approximating formal financial planning or performance budgeting. But the growth in which it was engaged would require it to adopt new budgeting techniques, decision-making decentralization, and management programs. The authority instituted these changes and at the same time hired new executives.

Authorities are free of much of the ideology and political sloganeering that hamstring government reorganizations. Austin Tobin has stated, for example, "We don't believe in centralization or decentralization in any absolute sense. Some of our activities may be centralized and others decentralized, depending in each case on such factors as public convenience, economy, quality of service, availability of skilled personnel, need for control, and general effectiveness."[8]

The Port Authority's reorganization and preoccupation with business methods began in 1947. In the postwar period, the organization's activities had expanded dramatically, creating management problems like those common in government: divided responsibility for operating results and overcentralization of approval powers. A single operations department managed all facilities. Other specialized ("process-oriented") departments were responsible for planning, negotiating, and engineering. Tobin, confronting growing demands in the realm of public and political relations, was also swamped by internal questions. The reorganization made line departments—such as aviation, marine terminals, rail transportation, tunnels and bridges, and world trade and port promotion—responsible for the operating results of whole categories of programs. Staff departments provide centralized services and advice, as well as control mechanisms and inspections. The staff departments include the typical categories: finance, law, public affairs, and administration (including organization and procedures, personnel, and general services). They also include four departments that have important control relationships with the line departments: engineering, operation services, planning and development, and real estate. This structure reflects an organization that does a great deal of its own financial, engineering, and other staff work. (Most public corporations contract out more of this work.) All supervisors are charged with continuous organization planning. The Port Authority is not a model of efficiency by any measure, but it has shown a capacity for administrative self-correction that is largely missing in city government. (Now the Port Authority could benefit from another fresh and thoroughgoing internal review.)

Conflicts between line and staff units are common in both business and government.[9] Staff departments typically serve other units of the same organization as clients. But the line organizations—running marine terminals, for example—must follow budget personnel and performance guidelines set by central staff. There are natural disagreements between those who run the docks and the headquarters professionals who tell them how to run the docks. In government, such conflicts involve bureau chiefs on the one hand and budget administrators, central purchasing agencies, and personnel departments on the other. In most private firms, the budget, planning, and personnel units are directly responsible to the general manager or corporate president, or his immediate staff. His personal leadership, his arbitration, his preferences resolve conflicts between staff and line. Government relies heavily on detailed regulations and procedures to bind operating departments. In business, central controls are personal and generally more effective. Public authorities' internal managements tend to come closer to business than to government in this respect. To pursue the Port Authority illustration: the director of marine terminals (line) disagreed with a staff department director that a higher level of maintenance should be adhered to in cargo terminals. The line director felt that rents could not support the higher maintenance costs. After negotiations between the two broke down, a quick referral was made to the executive director, who decided in favor of the line director. In government, this kind of dispute is likely either to drag on interminably or to be resolved—without consideration—by the fine print in some set of regulations. Port Authority practice stipulates that "when a department head rejects or ignores [staff] advice or fails to seek it, he must answer to the executive director for any inadequacy of performance resulting from such decision or omission."[10] This approach provides the individual with some scope for personal initiative but discourages arbitrary or impulsive decision making.

Goals, Performance Targets, and Internal Controls   The tensions between staff and line reflect the fact that what is classically called "decentralization" nearly always coexists with some counterpart aspects of centralization. Management consulting firms for public corporations generally recommend as an organizing principle the kind of "decentralization" that is reputed to be the management technique of private firms. Private firms practice administrative decentralization; the boss delegates decision making to lower levels of management but keeps the power to review results and to revoke the delegation. Administrative decentralization is very different from political decentralization, which aims to disperse real decision-making power among independent "bosses" (popular groups, neighborhood officials, or independent organizations). Political decentralization is polycentric. The federal system of government and competitive enterprise markets are polycentric; corporations are not.[11]

For example, top executives in General Motors—described as a model of corporate decentralization by Peter F. Drucker and Alfred Sloan—make detailed decisions on automobile styling, advertising, pricing, capital investment, pollution control, and scheduling in factories that assemble cars for the several divisions.[12] In other words, the administrative or managerial decentralization that large companies and government bureaus are urged to emulate is quite a different phenomenon from the decentralization of social power or decision making that is a subject of public debate in the United States. In terms of the former, the critical difference between corporate and government patterns lies in government's tighter centralization of personnel, purchasing, budgeting, and financial administration, tighter centralization that demonstrably has not produced effective control over management or money.

In any formal organization that sets out to do specific jobs, the more the participants agree on goals, the greater can be the decentralization of their operations. Program accountability can be both decentralized and controlled. The key is the ability to subdivide the broad goals of the enterprise into tasks that can be performed by relatively small groups and can be measured by results achieved. How the operators achieve the results is not subject to detailed prescription. The results themselves provide criteria for assessing performance.

The financial goals of public authorities serve not only as defensive devices to fend off demands from the larger political community for undesired projects but also as operating principles for internal management control. Self-support substitutes for the profit, cost, and return targets that are set by private corporate managements. Net revenue and bond marketability targets can be used as the "bottom line." Both subordinates and superiors can agree about the fairness of performance standards based on such targets. Authority managers are acutely aware of the powerful motivating force of practical incentives. Management consultants have installed accounting classifications and reporting categories in public authorities for internal administrative control. Each unit of the organization may be given a specific job and a certain amount of money to do it. Related expenses, including a proportion of the authority's overhead and staff costs, are charged to each individual facility. Facility managers then make the operating decisions but can be called to account for how the results compare with targets.

Other goals, including nonfinancial goals of course, can and often should be used to ensure coordinated management. Some public authorities have put a high value on maintaining stable price levels. For example, public power corporations that strive to keep power inexpensive and to avoid conflict with their customers postpone rate increases wherever possible and structure financial targets within the limits of revenues, without the continuous attention to pricing policy that is characteristic of decision making by private firms. Other authorities, whose activities are not dominated by sales of services, develop different types of targets. The Triborough Bridge and Tunnel Authority, which had ample revenue and sources of capital, was motivated by Robert Moses's personal construction plans and urban designs. The TBTA management never developed the elaborate internal accounting, financial planning, and control systems of the Port Authority. In fact, Robert Moses came to grief at the World's Fair, which did depend upon projections of income and close cost control, precisely because he failed to emphasize financial performance. Similarly, the management of New York's Urban Development Corporation pursued very specific construction goals (and achieved them with remarkable speed) until the money ran out. According to the experienced builder from the private sector who assumed its chairmanship in 1975, UDC was an efficient builder (but its targets were too high and the nature and cost of its facilities made them difficult to market). Regional planning efforts in Seattle and Minneapolis–St. Paul are developing goals that provide some balanced priorities for authority management.

In addition to design and financial goals, there are operational targets provided by project and services planning. Public authorities in water supply and sewage treatment, electric power, hospital construction, highways, and similar physical development fields do more project planning and scheduling than government bureaus do. Such authorities take service expansion and project completion dates seriously and usually meet them.

In short, an enterprise needs some clear objectives if management is to be both decentralized and purposeful. Unfortunately, narrow financial criteria are among the easiest to apply. Where profit is not an appropriate goal, some mechanism must be developed for public participation in the specification of objectives, through sponsoring governments or other methods, so that goals are suitable both as management incentives and as criteria for public appraisal.

Budgeting and Financial Planning   Every effective major business corporation engages extensively in planning, but both policy planning and financial planning are strikingly absent from American government. The absence of financial planning is part of the reason why financial crisis in state and municipal government so often goes unnoticed until it can no longer be ignored. Even professional finance officials rarely look beyond budget years, and the five-year financial plans required for some programs are treated as little more than rolling compilations of annual budgets. American industry, by contrast, regularly uses five-year plans based on economic forecasts and corporate goals. A single company is likely to use several different types of budgets (capital, research and development, program, and administrative), tying them together with a five-year plan.

A number of government corporations, particularly the larger ones (generally excluding transit authorities), have adopted financial planning methods in the course of reorganization recommended by management and financial consulting firms. Advance projections of capital needs and revenue forecasts are typical in public utility planning. Public authorities that engage in financial planning also use accrual systems of budgeting and accounting, which reflect commitments rather than merely cash flow. (Many governments still budget on a cash basis.)

Government budgets are broken down by narrow procedural categories called line items (specifying amounts for furniture, office supplies, salaries in various classes, vehicle maintenance, rents, and so forth). Business budgets categorize planned expenditure by program, by facility, and by activity, leaving many of the detailed allocations of a program's budget to be determined during the year by the individual plant or division head. Most public authorities use commercial methods of internal budgeting, budget administration, auditing, and reporting. The business-type budgets used by the well-managed authorities are plans of operation with internal flexibility. They include statements of financial condition, descriptions of sources and applications of funds, and expense estimates by major facility or service.

Corporate budgets are often not public documents; they are internal management tools subject to relatively easy adjustment. The manager controls the administration of the budget. Within limits, he has discretion to adjust spending in response to changes in the cost of his supplies or the emergence of unforeseen problems during the budget period. In the corporate sector, if a department persistently overspends or spends unwisely, its head will be redirected or replaced. In smaller, less bureaucratized authorities, when the plant or division manager finds it necessary to change expenditure plans, he simply brings his questions to the executive director. In the larger, more formalized corporations, division managers must fill out specific forms for budget estimates and make periodic reports on them. Changes in these budgets do involve some red tape, but they seldom result in the kind of delay and conflict that are ubiquitous in state and city government, in which a bureau head has to refer even minor transactions relating to a line-item budget to an outside organization, such as a budget office, which applies its own criteria.

Personnel Many public authorities are empowered to establish their own personnel systems. Some toll road authorities hire manual labor referred from county party organizations. Other authorities have used regular government employees, borrowed from governmental departments. Still others hire from private labor markets with no reference to government or politics. But nearly all public authority personnel systems use simpler job classifications than government agencies, retain prerogatives to make exceptions, and place some reliance on personal judgment. Most public authority personnel systems are not layered over with statutory procedures and detailed collective-bargaining agreements that prevent modificaitons in the system and determine how it shall be administered. (Transit authorities tend to be an exception, having absorbed systems from government and the private sector with complicated work rules.)

Authorities generally pay higher salaries than governments. A number of authorities attempt to keep pay scales competitive with private industry, although they cannot provide the top-level salaries, bonuses, and stock options that private firms offer. They establish salary ranges for particular classes of jobs but use them as guidelines rather than as requirements. Government bureaus often must choose one of the top three names on the list of tested eligibles for appointments and promotions. Authorities do not. Even the Port Authority, which has a more detailed, civil service type system than other public corporations, allows its executives to select for promotion anyone they choose from an eligible list to which candidates are added after satisfactory testing. Wherever reasonable, informal tradition calls for taking top persons from the eligible list and respecting seniority.

Reorganizations have shifted the Port Authority personnel system increasingly away from the civil service model toward that of the private sector, marked by job reclassifications, annual salary surveys, accelerated recruitment from outside, expansion of orientation and training programs, and emphasis on organizational development.[13] Administering the personnel system is now the responsibility of department heads and supervisors, not of the central personnel department. The function of the personnel department is to prepare and administer tests, to maintain eligibility lists, and to dispense benefits and plans for the overall system. Competent employees generally have tenure as long as they are performing needed tasks, but when tasks change, staff can be reduced without reference to a civil service board, bargaining agreement, or the courts.

Throughout public authorities, employment has been relatively stable and secure. Nevertheless, the fact that management has some discretion to hire and fire affects the basic relationships within the organization. (In 1953, for example, Austin Tobin summarily discharged several authority police officers who were charged with consorting with a prostitute. This story has become part of the folklore of the organization.) More important, authorities can respond to reductions in revenues by reducing operating costs more quickly than government bureaus can.

Middle management plays a stronger and freer role in the corporate sector than in government bureaus. Middle management provides close and flexible supervision of operating personnel. A strong middle manager permits the department head to delegate decision making and supervisory functions.

Authority personnel systems put more emphasis on performance and competence and less emphasis on routine or automatic rules than does government civil service. Authority systems seem to combine a high degree of job satisfaction and equity with rewards for performance and skill. They add to the convincing arguments for major reform of state and city civil service systems. Traditional organization theory stresses the value of rewarding superior performance. Both unionization and civil service movements have justifiably tried to cut down on uncertainties of employment and dependence upon arbitrary bureaucratic decisions. Public authorities have demonstrated that public personnel systems can take both of these thrusts into account and make way as well for fluid human relationships and individual development.

Collective Bargaining Although union membership and collective bargaining are less common in public enterprise than in the private sector and in city government, organized labor in recent years has played an increasingly important role in public enterprise. In fact, long before regular government departments were recognizing unions and engaging in collective bargaining, the Tennessee Valley Authority pioneered in the development of collective bargaining within the public sector. Unlike regular federal bureaus, TVA was not subject to congressional legislation in establishing working conditions and salary scales. Since the 1930s, the General Trades and Labor Council of the Tennessee Valley has represented TVA's blue-collar workers in labor negotiations. Nevertheless, TVA employees, like other federal employees, do not have the right to strike under the law; employees have been fired for doing so. In its early years, TVA decided to construct dams with its own groups of construction workers. During the years of major construction, instead of using contractors' teams, the authority hired bulldozer operators, steamfitters, bricklayers and carriers, and skilled and common laborers. Employing its own construction workers enabled the authority to begin construction before final designs were completed and to move men and equipment easily from site to site.[14] It also put TVA in marginal businesses serving its employees—housing, health, education, and recreation programs for which it became well known. The authority developed its own apprentice training program, with activities in this field far beyond the scope permitted to any department or bureau in the regular federal government structure.

Most public authorities and corporations contract out major construction jobs; the labor relations involved in these jobs are actually those of the private contractor with the private union. But authority managements have generally emphasized maintenance of good relations with the construction unions. Recently, for example, the New Jersey Sports and Exposition Authority called out vast numbers of construction union members to demonstrate in order to convince New Jersey's governor to authorize continuation of construction programs.

When management and union representatives do meet in adversary bargaining, the management side in public authorities is stronger than that in government agencies, in large part because unions dealing with public authorities cannot use election politics to affect management jobs. Many authorities entered the 1970s without recognizing exclusive bargaining agents for their employees, and even now few confront as strong a union contingent at the bargaining table as do state and city governments. But since 1970, union organization and bargaining in the public corporate sector have intensified dramatically across the nation. Whether this trend will cause public authorities to follow the government pattern or whether they will maintain and develop their own mode of labor relations remains to be seen. [15]

Organizational Development and Work   Many public corporations have adopted contemporary management fads under the rubric of "organizational development," a term that refers to a mixed bag of activities aimed at generating employee loyalty and satisfaction—training, indoctrination, propaganda, schooling, newsletters, company picnics, attitude surveys, togetherness in cafeterias, company logos, flags, history, and song. The purpose is to encourage the staff to internalize an organization's goals so that they serve both the purposes of the collective and themselves at the same time. Organizational development efforts try to make toll collectors, for example, aware that they act as public relations representatives of the authority, as well as being money changers.

The Port Authority has engaged in more organizational development than most other authorities, just as certain firms in the private sector (such as Phillips Petroleum and IBM) have gone further than most others in attempting to stimulate personal loyalty and social conformity. In 1963, Austin Tobin told an international symposium that efforts by top staff to improve attitudes were a distinguishing feature of the public corporation. He stressed internal ideology: "Fulfilling an organizational philosophy demands that most persons in the organization understand and believe in it. And so from the first day of his orientation course, an employee is urged to develop a questioning attitude. Similarly every supervisor, passing as he must through a supervisory and management training course, is encouraged to train his people to develop a questioning attitude and to contribute ideas on how to do things better." [16] Special training, suggestion, and award systems are part of this elaborate effort.

The Port Authority has spelled out its management philosophy on more than one occasion. Democracy within the organization, accountability, clear lines of authority and free lines of communication, absolute integrity and ethics, good pay with maximum career and training opportunities, the goal of port development, and pooling of revenues were the "Things We Live By" at the Port Authority under Austin Tobin's leadership.[17] In addition, the Port Authority expounds principles applying to public relations, community relations, law, engineering, and real estate as part of its formal management philosophy. The principle of teamwork declares that there shall be no internal politics, no favoritism, no front office cliques, no discrimination, and no power playing: "It is the spirit and attitude of staff which springs more than anything from inspiring top leadership."[18] This rhetoric suggests that the Port Authority is quite devoid of both human weakness and human interest. Large investor-owned companies with similar programs spout similar rhetoric. It cannot be taken at face value, but it may accompany the development of relatively high employee loyalty and identity with the firm.

In 1951, writing the story of TVA, John Gunther declared, "Never in the United States or abroad have I encountered anything more striking than the faith its men have in their work." Francis Biddle wrote, "There was a strong community sense, and a profound conviction that the work was created in human terms."[19] Many public authorities have achieved similar successes according to the assessments of their own employees. Their communications are easy, decisions are not delayed, initiative is encouraged, and job satisfaction is high.

Some agencies of government also succeed in obtaining the long-term identification of individuals with agency goals. Esprit de corps is particularly evident in the uniformed or professional services of the federal government, such as the Public Health Service, the Army Corps of Engineers, the Foreign Service, the U.S. Geological Survey, the Bureau of Reclamation, and the Park Service. These staffs are held together with the glue of common training and dedication to professional standards. Their very internal consensus, of course, brings them into conflict with the political executives that try to coordinate them with broader aims.

Over the past two decades, theories of management have been changing, putting more emphasis on appropriate interpersonal mechanisms of control, such as organizational development, task forces, and communication, than on written regulations and hierarchical pyramids. The trends—at their best—free workers to help shape their own jobs. At their worst, they can substitute organizational propaganda for improved working conditions. It is ironic that government management is more dependent on sheer hierarchical power but in effect has less hierarchical power to wield than does corporate management.

Big government has tended to delay solving new problems until the relevant information has been passed up the hierarchy and a decision has been made and passed down (the typical caricature of buck-passing bureaucracy). In many cases, the process grinds to a halt before the solution reaches its intended destination, or the solution becomes frozen in predetermined routines. In most business-oriented organizations, many problems are solved by collegial communication among operators (people working where the job is done). Authorities are more like businesses than governments in that respect. Their problems of coordination are contained by their size and their more fluid communications pattern.

The Search for Productivity in Government

In the mid-1970s, serious suggestions are being made that the only way to salvage city government is to contract work out to private enterprise.[20] The proposals for "privatization" reflect frustration or desperation on the part of those concerned with improving city government, who have quickly become discouraged by the results of experiments in program planning and budgeting systems and in quantitative productivity measurement, two recent thrusts in city government reform. Contracting out has its own inherent weaknesses, however. Federal agencies have found it difficult to control the performance of the companies benefiting from government contracts. The contracts eliminate the incentives of a competitive market and the uncertainties of fluid prices and performance-dependent profits. Many local governments would find these control difficulties insurmountable. There is no evidence that private enterprise is inherently or even usually efficient and effective when it becomes largely dependent on standard contracts from government.[21] In addition, civil service and collective bargaining provisions in many cases severely restrict contracting out by state and local governments.

The proliferation of public corporations represents an alternative reaction to overbureaucratized and overfragmented urban government. The present growth of public corporations is absorbing activities from conventional state and city governments even faster than from private firms that have not remained viable in such industries as transportation, power, housing finance, industrial development finance, health services, and training and communications. Hence, the capacity of public authorities to restrain creeping bureaucratization, to attract strong and capable leadership, and to negotiate labor agreements satisfactory to both sides may significantly affect the quality of

urban life in the next few decades. As they become bigger and more important, as their collective bargaining agreements become loaded with trivia, as
their managements grow old, and as the issues they take on become more
complex, public authorities can lose the advantages they frequently offer.
(New York City's Health and Hospitals Corporation, the U.S. Postal Service,
and a number of transit authorities demonstrate that shifting large, bureaucratized, strife-ridden enterprises to a new framework may not achieve those
advantages in the first place.) The usefulness of authority management
requires reevaluation from time to time and from place to place. Public authorities, like contracting out, cannot be a universal solution to government
failure.

Students of political science have coined the term "bureau power" to describe the tendency of each bureau—whether in federal, state, or city government—to develop its own vested rights, its own political allies, its own access
to reporters, its own ability to influence election of its bosses, its own traditions and mores. Public authorities do not confront internal bureau power—a
fact that is part cause and part effect of the concentrated influence wielded
by their chiefs. But, from a government perspective, public authorities may
be the ultimate in bureau power—satellites that have spun off altogether from
the general government orbit.

In a comparison between city government and public authorities, bureau
impotence is more impressive than bureau power in government. Although
government bureaus have the power to frustrate elected officials, they are
themselves hamstrung by regulations and group pressures. The notorious resistance of civil servants to change, their stubborn clinging to routines, and
their strident battles for job rights are less an expression of bureau power
than a reaction to powerlessness, to the lack of authority to respond with
common sense to the problems that arise in their work and in their community, to the lack of leadership goals, to overspecialization of jobs and agencies. Prospects for improvement are dim if employees do not like their jobs,
cannot use their own judgment, take little pride in the agency's performanc
and have no contact with management; if executives keep parading throug,
revolving doors; if little information passes from top to bottom, from bottom
to top, and from one division to another; and if the power to get a job done
within the organization is hopelessly divided up between operating divisions,
budget administration officers, purchasers, personnel officers, and so forth.
If this analysis is accurate, then some prescriptions for changing city government are reasonably obvious. The less routine, regulated, and rigid an organi-

zation, the more it must rely on training, professionalization, and, above all, leadership to function effectively and collectively.

Government must develop management positions comparable to those in the corporate sector, creating opportunities for careers that are neither as dependent upon the comings and goings of elected officials nor as focused upon private sector definitions of success as those of today's political executives. The civil service should facilitate transfers, broaden its talent searches, and respond flexibly to changing leadership needs. The framework within which men and women are organized for work must be simplifed to reduce the number of civil service job titles, to take arbitrators and judges out of personnel administration as much as possible, to eliminate the adversary proceedings in discipline and promotion that taint relations among workers and supervisors, and to open up systems of promotion. Mayors and other chief executives must be identified and empowered as responsible managers, held to account by the public and the media for representing the management and broad community interest sides of collective bargaining. This perspective is missing from the bargaining table when boards and arbitrators handle the management side or when mayors are so politically beholden to union constituencies as to leave no balancing factor—in fact, no bargain.

Management controls by elected officials and their colleagues should be fewer and more purposeful. Budget administration, personnel administration, and purchasing and contract administration should be drastically decentralized within city government, as financial planning and policy planning are strengthened and centralized.[22] Inter- and intradepartmental task forces and problem-solving groups should be used to design and monitor projects and performance.

Above all, the links between the political officials at the top and the civil servants below them need to be reforged. Political leaders and agency managers must set forth attainable goals for their agencies, clarify what kinds of performance are expected from employees, and exercise discipline when necessary. Developing trust and participation among employees, strength in middle management, and performance auditing go hand in hand for this purpose. Greater staff effort must be devoted to management research, to organizational development, and to the development of performance standards acceptable to both management and employees. Outside consultants should work with inside teams, as they do in the private sector, to devise and to garner support for internal departmental reorganizations and improvements. Agencies should call in outside consultants periodically, if only to stimulate inside questioning.

The federal government can help to stimulate these improvements in state and local government. First, it could put its own house in order—reducing the enormously overspecialized array of federal grant and loan programs that are administered by local governments. Each of these programs has its own set of regulations as detailed and complex as anything the cities have ever invented, and many city and state government departments have become internally fragmented according to the federal grant programs they administer. The federal government could also provide for nationwide evaluation and exchange of information on successful experiments with civil service reform, on organizational development in city government (as in Kansas City, for example), and on the development of performance standards (for example, by California municipalities). Finally, the federal government could sponsor nationwide exchanges for middle and top management jobs in government, ensuring transfer of pension rights and helping to develop local counterparts of the federal executive classes in the top civil service ranks.

Expanding prosperity induces waste; city payrolls swelled throughout the 1960s, even as all the media focused on urban ills. But the shrinking finances of the 1970s should force the issue of management reform. Resistance is enormous; only the leverage of the federal dollar is a sufficiently potent tool to overcome it. The federal government has sowed the seeds for the growth of public authorities. It must do as much to give comparable capabilities to state and local governments.

The conclusion that aspects of internal management by the major public authorities reflect business practices does not imply that the public authority form is inherently businesslike in some superior sense. Other aspects of public authorities are essentially political. The conclusion does reflect the fact that smaller-scale managements with relatively concrete tasks and steady sources of funds find it easier to administer well than the best of urban governments do. There is no evidence that public authorities could excel in administering complex social programs with multiple and ambivalent goals. Improving management in government is likely to yield more practical results than proliferation of government-sponsored corporations.

IV Public and Governmental Relations

10 Harnessing the Energy of Public Authorities

The primary question concerning public authorities today is how to direct their financial and management resources toward broad governmental goals. Government control of its wholly owned enterprises is weak and uneven in the vast majority of cases. Critics maintain that government corporations are beyond the reach of the people's representatives, unresponsive, and in some cases totally irresponsible. Public authorities have invited such charges by stressing their own autonomy. In fact, the term "autonomy" is misleading since it implies the absence of external influence. The literally "autonomous" authority is as mythical as the unicorn.[1] The authority that dodges the pressures of legislators, local officials, or department bureaucrats may be responsive to the governor; the authority that avoids control by governors, voters, and neighborhood groups may cheerfully accommodate bankers, construction unions, or real estate developers.

The difficulties of institutional control are not unique to the corporate sector. Although highway departments fall within the organizational chart of state government, governors and community groups have found it difficult over the years to control them. Public authorities and highway departments share attributes that produce independent power, such as strong leadership, stable outside sources of financing, a construction-oriented mission that attracts friends to the agency, and a substantial supply of job and contract patronage. Local groups protesting highway and other forms of construction in the Boston area have found arrayed against them a collection of difficult-to-reach agencies, including the Massachusetts Bay Transportation Authority, the Massachusetts Port Authority, the Metropolitan District Commission, the Boston Redevelopment Agency, the Massachusetts Turnpike Authority, and the state's Department of Public Works, which sometimes appears to be the most powerful of the lot.

But efforts to make public authorities accountable confront special problems because of legal ambiguity concerning the place of the authorities in government and the desire to keep politics out of the public's business. Writers and consultants torn between what they see as conflicting concern for public accountability and fear of "political interference" draw conclusions that provide little useful guidance, typically calling for enough independence to permit good operations and enough control to limit serious abuses, without clarifying either.

Contemporary mugwumps who run and defend public authorities assume their superiority—as "impartial" experts—over elected officials, equating shifting political priorities with improper pressures. As one authority executive put it, "The reputation of an authority is constantly in jeopardy before the merciless bombardment of local politicians. If an authority is delivering the benefits expected of it, if it is operating efficiently, letting contracts without favoritism, hiring and promoting personnel without political interference, refusing to bow policy-wise to improper political pressures by changing administrations—then by its very nature it outrages political feelings and it becomes fair game of every politician within artillery range. The shooting season is always open."[2] This fearful equation between the policy priorities of newly elected officials and improper pressures produces an impasse.

One student of authorities who set out to criticize orthodox theories of the government corporation nevertheless accepted the premise that corporate "board members are probably as good or better judges of the need for and viability of plant and line extension as would be any officials of the present government"; therefore turnpike authority plans should not require approval that might intrude "upon the authority's competence in business and engineering matters."[3] This premise fails to recognize that most highways (the entire toll-free interstate system) are planned and constructed by government, that highway expansion is a political question with enormous social and economic impact on regions and neighborhoods, and that the technical competence of even the most respectable boards varies.

The concept of "control without politics" ignores the highly politicized context in which the authorities actually operate. The use of opportunities to allocate appointments and projects by an elected official with an eye on building support may occasionally result in malfeasance, but it is also one of the few effective ways for outside officials to influence and restructure authorities.

Another obstacle to harnessing public enterprise to public policy is preoccupation with financial performance. The government officials most frequently involved in supervising public authorities are financial auditors, who reinforce the propensity of authorities and their underwriters to stress internal financial results and thus to avoid mass transportation, pollution control, payment of in-lieu taxes, moderately priced housing, and other community development tasks. Such traditional financial assessment is clearly an inadequate framework for evaluating and supervising such authorities, many of which either receive direct appropriations from tax funds or depend upon indirect taxpayer subsidies—mortgages, third-party payments for medical treatment, governmental rentals, loan guarantees, and so forth. Governments have not however, devised coherent alternatives.

Another form of control of public enterprise that has inherent limitations is regulation. Typical recommendations call for ever more detailed formal regulations, without coming to grips with the basic questions: control by whom? for what purposes? to what effect? Formal regulations do not add up to purposeful control. One of the most independent public corporations in the nation—the Port Authority of New York and New Jersey—is theoretically subject to a far wider range of legal controls than the average authority, whether state, local, or interstate. The Port Authority is subject to three major types of veto; all resolutions enacted by the board of commissioners are subject to gubernatorial veto; all requests for new projects, powers, and duties must be authorized by two state legislatures; and any taking of property requires the consent of the landowning municipality, compliance with local zoning, or use of local government to condemn land on behalf of the authority. The authority is subject to legislative investigations by committees of two state legislatures and the U.S. Congress. Both states have the right to undertake audits of the authority's internal books and other documents whenever they choose.

In practice, such regulations constitute the rules of a political game. The leaders of the Port Authority have played the game skillfully, relying heavily on the authority's contacts in the financial community, the influence of its commissioners, and its considerable monetary reserves. They usually have achieved their goals and received broad grants of power. But the Port Authority is not entirely out of control, nor do most of its actions frustrate the intentions of the state legislatures and the governors. The authority has retained the basic support even of the governors who are most frustrated by some of its actions, and it has been able to get what it wanted from the legislators, sometimes by playing one state against the other, sometimes by playing the governors against local leadership, and throughout by putting its own resources against opposing sources of support. Opportunities for greater access to authority decision making on the part of elected officials are there, but for the most part elected officials have not had an overwhelming interest in utilizing them, and the authority makes it difficult for them to do so. The Port Authority can insulate certain key points of its decision processes, particularly feasibility reports, plans and project designs, and bond covenants.

Authorities, like any other organization operating in or near the public sector, are constrained to bargain. They cannot long afford to be seen as rigid or stubborn but must develop the capacity for external bargaining, as well as the internal mechanisms for protecting themselves from conflict. Bargaining of course, involves compromise, and the nature of the compromise may reflect varying degrees of success in achieving the leadership's goals, depending partly on internal skill and partly on the skill of those who would control them.

In order to succeed, measures to make public enterprise accountable must reflect two considerations. First, control of an organization is not one-dimensional but rather a function of the competitive resources of various groups seeking to influence the agency: the governor and his staff; competing executive agencies; legislators; bond market participants and other private business interests; the leadership and the internal bureaucracy of the authority itself; and neighborhood representatives, local officials, and other organized interest groups. Second, influence over an organization does not increase with the number of specific formal controls imposed on it but depends instead upon the ability of outsiders to break into organizational decision processes at key points. This point needs clarification. The ability to break into organizational decision processes depends on access, interest, and resources. Access is partly a function of formal controls. Legal requirements for public hearings, for gubernatorial review of minutes, for annual reports, for legislative approval of projects, and for compliance with local zoning regulations provide opportunities for outsiders to have a voice in the corporation's activities and decision-making processes.

Interest is partly a function of the saliency of particular issues. The access provided by procedural regulations is meaningless if the questions at stake do not attract outsiders to attend hearings, to read the minutes, to analyze reports, and so forth. Legislatures tend to give perfunctory authorizations, for example, for projects that require no commitment of budgeted funds. Interest is also partly a function of motivation. Even if an authority's decision making does not raise questions of prime importance to the public or to the official, a politician in search of an issue—or a private citizen—may become concerned with the overall scope and direction of authority activity. Personal motivation ("publicity seeking," to those opposed) has accounted for special efforts to study and influence authorities by state senators and assemblymen, congressmen, comptrollers, and attorneys general in a number of states. These efforts tend to be episodic, but they may result in new legislation, new rulings, or at least written reports that can raise the level of public education on the subject.

The third component of the ability to break into the organizational decision process is resources: staff, time, information, and expertise. Even when they have access and interest, for example, public officials lacking familiarity with the specialized jargon of bond market finances and lacking independent advice on the effects of alternatives upon state credit ratings have found it difficult to counter the arguments given to them by insiders. No state legislator has the staff that is necessary to deal in any coherent and intelligent way with annual reports from public authorities. Even governors usually lack the resources to use their veto powers effectively. Governors seldom assign staff to review authority boards' agenda and minutes consistently.

The key points in authority decision processes—points at which access, interest, and resources can make a difference—are often not the powers, programs, and personnel decisions commonly subjected to political determination under the heading of "policy." They are, rather, more specific—some of them typically classified as "administrative"—projects that may seem modest at first glance but may lead to expansion and proliferation: specific bond issues that, through their covenants and other characteristics, establish a framework for future activity; feasibility reports that set targets for organization programs; specific sources of information and types of planning that define the options open for the future; appointments that reinforce traditional authority priorities. Project proposals, bond prospectuses, feasibility reports, and planning methods are key points in decision processes for the purpose of effective control. If these are put beyond reach by being classified "administrative," or unsuitable for political "interference," government leaders have little chance of guiding the directions of government enterprise.

The Rockefeller Regime

New York State tends to dominate any discussion of public authorities in part because the state and its subdivisions have accounted for over one-third of all revenue bonds issued in the nation. From 1958 to 1974, the role of the state authority ("public benefit corporation") expanded in New York far beyond that contemplated in other states. New York has set precedents for state corporations, as Pennsylvania has for local and municipal corporations. Public authorities collectively are the most important single sector of public finance in New York State.

When the Republicans turned over the state house in Albany to the Democrats in 1974—after sixteen years of uninterrupted control of state government—the outstanding debt of statewide public authorities in New York was well over $12 billion (having grown from only $129 million in 1962), nearly four times the general obligation debt of the state. Through lease-purchase agreements, moral obligation pledges, and other arrangements, the state was indirectly liable for two-thirds of this amount. The long-term debt of HFA alone was higher than the voter-approved debt of the state, and long-term debt would more than double to liquidate outstanding short-term debt. Fourteen other authorities had interest-free loans from the state totaling $275 million, and the state had written off another $150 million in appropriated state loans. Finally, annual state appropriations to meet operating deficits of public authorities were running at close to $150 million and were going to more than double to keep UDC and MTA in business.[4]

Arthur Levitt, the state comptroller, called public authorities the "fourth branch of government,"[5] but in fact, Nelson Rockefeller as governor controlled most of the authority power created during the 1960s.

New York State has a more fully developed array of legal regulations controlling authorities than any other state in the nation. It keeps an inventory of all public benefit corporations within its jurisdiction and an organized collection of the annual reports and operational audits. Authorities that owe the state money by virtue of unpaid first-instance appropriations (start-up money from the state) or other appropriations from the legislature submit their budgets to the finance committees of the senate and assembly and to the executive budget office. (Seldom, however, have they been asked to make changes.) The state comptroller approves all bond issue interest rates and has full audit powers. Nevertheless, throughout the 1960s, both the comptroller and state legislators expressed persistent frustration over the growth of authorities. Governor Rockefeller, on the other hand, succeeded in using them for his own purposes. He and several of his immediate staff discussed the general outlines of the new financial gimmicks, kept in direct contact with the managers of the major state corporations, approved their ambitious construction plans, and were aware of their financial weaknesses. (Rockefeller was specifically aware, for example, that HFA's short-term debt fully obligated its authorized long-term bonding capacity and that UDC would require fresh state funds. He intended to see them through.) To this day he views results that seem to be egregious errors to some observers and taxpayers merely as the price of getting things he wanted built, things that he believed the state needed. "Let's not talk as if we are running a bank," he told the commission investigating UDC's financial collapse. "We are running a social institution to meet the people's needs."[6] This is a rare recognition of the fact that government enterprise is not necessarily to be equated with business.

Goals for Controls   Purpose, direction, goals, and priorities are central to the concept of control. Random exercise of controls without purpose may have nuisance value and may keep authorities on their guard against malfeasance and procedural irresponsibility, but it cannot deflect public enterprise from its own goals, plans, and favored projects. Rockefeller's plans were rivaled in scale and scope only by those for the region envisioned in earlier years by Robert Moses. The overall development plan for downtown Manhattan, for which more than $6 billion has been committed, was conceived and promoted by the Lower Manhattan Association, while David Rockefeller, chairman of Chase Manhattan Bank, was its first president. The plan's components—all of which the governor supported enthusiastically—included the World Trade Center, Battery Park City, renovated docks, and a major urban renewal area. To serve these developments, a new Second Avenue subway route, extension of rail service to the Newark airport and outlying areas of New Jersey, reconstruction of the West Side Highway compatible with the development of Battery Park City, and a helicopter landing were planned. Rockefeller intended downtown Manhattan to be the site of an office space boom, and he sought to provide appropriate transportation to the offices. The project components of the plan were assigned to public authorities. The Port Authority played a central role (PATH, World Trade Center, docks, and the air landing), and New York's MTA, UDC, and Battery Park City Authority were also to be involved.

In addition to these visions of Lower Manhattan, Nelson Rockefeller had particular development goals for New York State. His desire to create a major state university, his housing and later health facility construction plans, and his desire to make Albany architecturally respectable provided the interest, the incentive, and the direction for rapid expansion of revenue bond finance and public authority construction during the 1960s.

The governor used authorities in part to bypass the tradition-bound Department of Public Works—whose architects had a reputation for making all kinds of construction resemble prisons and an operative style that was, in the governor's words, "impossibly bureaucratic." Rockefeller could build faster and more to his taste if he bypassed the regular state department set up for that purpose. His authorities could pay standard architectural fees to outside consultants, higher fees than state departments are permitted to pay. Through the Dormitory Authority, HFA, and UDC, he could build without the annual legislative appropriations and the multiple approvals from diverse government agencies normally required for public construction programs.

Construction for the public benefit corporations reached such volume that at one point in the mid-1960s it was slowed because the various corporations were competing for available construction contractors working in the state.

The authority system also permitted the governor to escape from the requirement of voter approval for state borrowing. He did ask the voters to approve as much borrowing as legal and political realities seemed to permit, but they turned down many of the proposals that were put to them. In the years just before Rockefeller took office, for example, they rejected, for the second time, a $750 million highway bond issue; it was subsequently passed after being substantially reduced in amount and altered in content; also in 1956, voters rejected for the third time a limited-profit housing bond issue for $100 million. It squeaked through in 1958, but other low-income housing proposals failed. Rockefeller set up the Housing Finance Agency in part because he could not raise the massive amounts of money that he wanted channeled into housing construction through bond elections. Then, in 1961, a proposal to guarantee bonds in the amount of $500 million for higher education was defeated for the fourth time. The legislature also rejected a higher education financing plan. Then the governor and his advisers devised an arrangement for channeling tuition into a special State University Construction Fund, which served as a reserve for borrowing by state corporations. In 1965, the voters rejected, for the fifth time, a low-income housing and slum clearance bond proposal; Rockefeller responded by establishing the Urban Development Corporation. In 1967, the voters approved Rockefeller's transportation bond issue for $2.5 billion, which provided the basis for authority takeover of the Long Island Rail Road, but subsequent transportation bond issues were defeated. Clearly, Rockefeller could build faster and richer with revenue bonds issued by public authorities, even if those bonds were ultimately backed by the state's credit, indirectly or through subsidization of operating expenses. He could borrow first and make the legislature pay later.

Rockefeller had another compelling reason to rely so heavily on authorities: his "pay-as-you-go" political slogans and the normal difficulties of balancing a budget, particularly in a state with an aging urban and industrial base. In 1962, state law governing accounting methods was changed to eliminate the requirement that advances to authorities appear in the budget. The fiscal profile of the Rockefeller administration would have looked significantly less pay-as-you-go were it not for this change and other innovations of authority finance.

Governor Rockefeller knew what he wanted for the state, and he had learned during his wartime experience in the federal government that "an important quality of the corporation is its adaptability to the needs of different situations."[7] The governor's secretary, William Ronan, had presided over the massive 1956 state study of public authority devices, and investment bankers and bond lawyers could be depended upon to work out the details of new public benefit corporations for the state.[8] From time to time, as specific problems confronted the governor, he used the same mechanisms to resolve them, minimizing the difficulties coming from the legislature, the public, and the budget. He turned to the authority form to finance mental hygiene facilities (after horrible conditions in state institutions were publicized); to compete with the New Jersey Sports and Expositions Authority; to establish a fund to help thoroughbred horse breeding in the state of New York; to raise tax-exempt capital for private construction, particularly for industry, private hospitals, nursing homes, and colleges; and to plan new prisons (after the Attica Prison uprising). Table 10.1 lists the state public authorities in New York as of 1975. Half of them were established during the Rockefeller administration.

How the Governor Exercised Authority Power   Relying less on formal regulations than on an astute use of personal power, Rockefeller managed to overcome the obstacles that have limited executive power over authorities in nearly all other cases. The resources and strategies that permitted him to do this are basically threefold: skillful use of a wide network of people who were personally known and loyal to him; independent contact with the financial community and advisers with sophisticated understanding of its markets; and expansion of subsidized authorities, combining financial dependence with the rhetoric of autonomy.

The entrepreneurs of many of New York State's authorities of the 1960s differed from public enterprise mandarins of other times and places in that they owed their public careers in the state to the governor, Nelson A. Rockefeller: these included Edward J. Logue (Urban Development Corporation and its subsidiaries), Paul Belica (HFA and its affiliates), Alton G. Marshall (UDC, Sports Authority), William J. Ronan (MTA, Port Authority, Power Authority), Charles J. Urstadt (HFA, Battery Park City), and William A. Sharkey (Dormitory Authority). Central to this network was Ronan—bright, blunt, totally unbeholden to anyone but the governor, and every bit as ruthless and impatient with the normal procedures of democracy as Robert Moses ever was. Beginning (like Moses) as a scholar of public administration who had

Table 10.1
New York State Public Authorities, 1975[a] (Thousands of Dollars)

	Total assets	Bonds and notes outstanding	Gross revenues
Transportation and transit			
Buffalo and Fort Erie Public Bridge	$ 17,329	$ 2,585	$ 3,185
Capital District Transportation	9,528	10	5,603
Central New York Regional Transportation	8,247		4,616
East Hudson Parkway	87,067		6,374
Jones Beach State Parkway	91,388	7,101	12,689
Lake Champlain Bridge	2,583		409
Long Island Rail Road	219,702[b]		119,052
Manhattan and Bronx Surface Transit Operating	17,224[c]		123,605
Metropolitan Transportation (MTA)[d]	481,703[b]	55,115	29,966
New York City Transit	267,136[c]	203,077	526,123
New York State Bridge	75,812	23,835	7,762
New York State Thruway	1,318,373	780,015	126,392
Niagara Frontier Transportation	72,267[b]	2,000	23,059
Ogdensburg Bridge and Port	27,229[b]	860	907
Rochester-Genesee Regional Transportation	10,137	590	8,089
Staten Island Rapid Transit Operating	1,934[c]		1,711
Thousand Islands Bridge	6,770	345	1,626
Triborough Bridge and Tunnel	980,333	276,460	162,016
Port development			
Albany Port District	16,153	3,813	871
Port Authority of New York and New Jersey	4,053,556[e]	1,964,574	490,107
Port of Oswego	4,774[b]		357
Commerce and development			
Energy Research Development[f]	20,689[b]	9,660	3,286
Environmental Facilities Corporation	44,005	35,372	367
Industrial Exhibit	3,955	2,599	551
New York Job Development	82,180	81,066	1,683
Power Authority of the State of New York	2,755,160	1,640,230	155,731
United Nations Development Corporation	60,397	55,200	685

Table 10.1 (continued)

	Total assets	Bonds and notes out- standing	Gross revenues
Finance and housing			
Battery Park City	212,306	200,000	
Dormitory	2,521,762	1,889,532	3,383
Facilities Development Corporation	115,920		53,788
Higher Education Assistance	20,289		79,261
Housing Finance Agency	5,671,120	5,245,712	8,659
Medical Care Facilities Finance Agency	122,670	116,960	434
Municipal Assistance Corporation			
Municipal Bond Bank			
Project Finance Agency			
State of New York Mortgage Agency	404,645	384,395	21,889
State University Construction Fund[g]			
Urban Development Corporation	1,359,244	1,167,358	81,328
Sports and recreation			
Bethpage Park			
New York State Thoroughbred Breeding and Development Fund Corporation	198		1,098
Market centers			
Central New York Regional Market	1,180	148	265
Genesee Valley Regional Market	2,349	1,342	369
Totals	21,167,044	14,149,954	2,067,296

[a] Based upon the participation of the governor in appointments to authority boards; excludes corporations appointed by municipal and county officials.
[b] Cost less depreciation of certain facilities.
[c] Does not include cost of facilities to New York City.
[d] Does not include investment in Long Island Rail Road, which is shown separately.
[e] Does not include Commuter Car Program being financed under state-guaranteed bonds. At December 31, 1975, this program had assets of $103.6 million invested. Outstanding bonds totaled $83.6 million.
[f] Formerly titled Atomic and Space Development Authority.
[g] This agency does not include financial statements with its annual reports.
Source: New York State Comptroller's Office: figures given for authorities that submitted them for 1975.

conducted serious research on public authorities, Ronan was one of the few people who understood the uses and implications of public enterprise growth in the 1960s. He also understood that formal regulations were no more than opportunities, having concluded that past governors had failed to assign staff to monitor authority programs and operations. Ronan was the first head of Governor Rockefeller's program office, and he made that office the training ground for staff who were subsequently placed throughout New York's public authorities, which opponents tagged the "Holy Ronan Empire." Ronan himself left the governor's office in 1966 to become chairman and chief executive officer of the Metropolitan Commuter Transportation Authority (subsequently MTA, which, following the guidelines of his earlier report, was absorbing half a dozen other regional transportation corporations); later he moved to both the port and power authorities.

Ronan's dependence on the governor was thorough and personal. An academic dean prior to his association with Rockefeller, Ronan received his first gift of $75,000 just prior to his appointment as the governor's secretary in 1959. In subsequent years, Ronan's financial standing was enhanced by loans from the governor, which were, over time, translated into gifts reportedly totaling $650,000 when Ronan resigned from the MTA and agreed to spend part of his time in the unpaid position of chairman of the board of the Port Authority. Many years before, Mayor William O'Dwyer had wanted a salaried chairman for the Port Authority, someone who could devote time to supervising the staff. He got nowhere with this effort to adjust the Port Authority charter, but Nelson Rockefeller could achieve the same end without changing the law simply by paying Ronan personally. Ronan was put on a family-controlled payroll, as well as collecting $12,500 a year from the Power Authority.

Belica, Logue, and Marshall, like Ronan, had close and direct ties to Governor Rockefeller. Logue had achieved a considerable reputation for his work in urban renewal and housing construction in New Haven and Boston. Rockefeller induced him to migrate to New York State to head the newly organized Urban Development Corporation with its extraordinary combination of independent powers. The board of directors of UDC was not empowered to appoint the chief executive officer. Logue was appointed directly by the governor and was promised that UDC would have power to override local zoning, a promise that the governor exercised extraordinary political muscle to keep; at one point he warned legislative leaders that he would "take away their judgeships" if they failed to muster votes for this provision. In addition, to "help Logue relocate in New York," Rockefeller made him personal gifts in 1968 totaling $31,389 and loaned him $145,000, of which $100,000 was outstanding in 1974. Rockefeller had great faith in Logue—too much, as it turned out. Logue was a master builder with neither a head for finance nor a talent for marketing. Rockefeller says he relied for financial supervision on George Woods, chairman of UDC's board and former director of First Boston Corporation, which was participating in UDC financing. In fact, Woods never had control over Logue or the agency; Logue corresponded directly with the governor and his budget director. Two months after Democratic Governor Hugh Carey took office in 1975, with UDC in serious financial difficulty but with an outstanding record for speedy construction, Logue was forced to resign. He was subsequently absorbed into the payroll of Rockefeller's Commission on Critical Choices. Rockefeller and Logue had shared an energy and enthusiasm for getting things done and an impatience with costs and other obstacles. Both men had grand visions and admit to little interest in cost controls.

Paul Belica also made use of his personal contacts with the governor, even to avoid involvement in one of Rockefeller's favored projects (Battery Park). For the most part, Belica had little difficulty in working with a board of directors dominated by state government commissioners, because he had direct access to the governor. But when Rockefeller was preparing to leave the state house, Belica foresaw the difficulties of coping with a board of shifting gubernatorial appointments; he therefore had the structure of the board changed so that it was dominated by long-term outside appointments like the more traditional public authorities. HFA grew to conglomerate status (as did UDC and MTA) with the overlapping appointments and shifting assignments that characterized authority controls in the Rockefeller years.[9] When state commissioner of housing Charles J. Urstadt left the HFA board and state government to take over the Battery Park City Authority, he was replaced as commissioner of housing by a former staff member of HFA. One of the private members of the HFA board was Richard Aldrich, Nelson Rockefeller's first cousin and an investment banker (who had also received gifts of money from the governor).[10]

The UDC board also included Rockefeller associates, among them Alton Marshall, who had served as the governor's executive secretary and later became the president of Rockefeller Center, Inc., and a board member of the New York Sports Authority. (In 1970, Nelson Rockefeller forgave a total of $306,867 in accumulated loans to Marshall.) In addition, UDC was provided with a business advisory council that co-opted many of the business clients of the corporation and included several long-time Rockefeller supporters, such as labor leader Harry Van Arsdale, real estate developer Robert B. Tishman, and the governor's brother, banker David Rockefeller.

William A. Sharkey, director of the Dormitory Authority since 1971, originally joined the Rockefeller executive staff as a program associate under Ronan. He replaced Clifton C. Flather, who had managed the authority since 1944. The governor's office considered Flather too reluctant to use the new financing techniques to build the state university system.[11] Sharkey led the Dormitory Authority into Rockefeller-style financing and rapid constructions, maintaining close contacts with Ronan and others from the governor's program office, including one state official who subsequently became an investment banker with whom the Dormitory Authority dealt.

Another alumnus of Ronan's program staff is Richard Wiebe, who had previously been a member of Ronan's research staff at the Hults Commission. Wiebe says that the purpose of the Hults Commission report was to show that authorities were not necessarily independent entities. Wiebe moved with Ronan from the commission to the governor's program staff, to MTA, where he was comptroller, before returning to state government as director of the Office of Planning Services. He was also a board member of UDC. While Wiebe was serving with Ronan in the program office, they designed the East Hudson Parkway Authority to overcome a specific problem: a county parkway system needed capital improvements but did not have the funds to make them. In 1960, the new authority took over the revenues from the Saw Mill River and Hutchinson River parkways (net, about $2.5 million per year) and used them to legally justify first-instance appropriations from the state of up to $52.2 million.[12] Ronan and Wiebe did not seriously expect that the East Hudson Parkway Authority would be able to issue its own revenue bonds or to pay back these appropriations in full. In effect, they set up a method by which tolls could be kept on facilities that had long since been paid off, and first-instance appropriations by the legislature would front for what was in effect a capital grant for highway maintenance. The state resorted again to authority gimmicks for highway repairs when the legislature refused to approve an appropriation for resurfacing state highways, for which the administration had already let contracts, counting on proceeds of a bond issue that was defeated by the voters. Looking for another way to pay for the improvements, the governor submitted the "pothole bill" to the legislature, which passed it, authorizing the New York Thruway Authority to issue bonds to pay for resurfacing state highways that were outside the thruway system.[13]

(John A. Tiesler, then executive director of the New York Thruway Authority, had also served on the governor's executive staff.)

In short, while making the traditional patronage appointments of bankers and other participants in campaign activities and state financings, Rockefeller also made a practice of appointing his personal staff and associates to authority boards and management. These people shared his administration's goals and his willingness to adapt the techniques of authority finance and management to almost any practical problem.

A public authority's relationships with the financial community usually provide the authority with a secure base from which to deal with governors, mayors, and legislators. In New York, the governor's relationships with the financial community provided him with a secure base from which to create and control public authorities. Rockefeller and his advisers had their own contacts on Wall Street. They were able to raise the moral obligation debt over $6 billion because the financial community and bond lawyers were confident that the Rockefeller administration would bail out the bonds should they ever be in trouble; they also had confidence in Rockefeller's control of the legislature, which would have to be persuaded to vote for appropriations if the authorities encountered financial problems. Rockefeller's advisers were skillful in taking advantage of variations in investor interests and in the types of security that could be provided. Rockefeller remains convinced that he could have arranged for new financing sources and program cutbacks without crisis or default by UDC, and some backers concur. But during the critical year of UDC's mounting troubles, he was no longer in the state house, and his successor—with eyes and ears turned to election campaigns—lacked Rockefeller's understanding and control of the situation.

Rockefeller and Ronan liked to exempt the authorities that came under their personal control from normal regulations. In 1974, fourteen state corporations with boards appointed by the governor, all of them Rockefeller administration creations, were outside the scope of New York State's Public Authorities Law. Despite its dependence on the state's indirect pledges of credit and federal and state aid, UDC was exempted from legal budgetary controls; it was not required to submit decisions to the governor for review; in fact, not even its own board of directors reviewed its budget. A confidential task force reported to Rockefeller's successor, Malcolm Wilson, with restrained understatement: "UDC's staff appears to operate with considerable degree of autonomy. While UDC's board of directors, which includes four ex officio members from New York State government, has been an active board,

its concern seemed to have been more directed to individual project development questions than to broad policy matters, especially the problem of
funding the program. Because of its public authority status, the corporation
has not been subject to scrutiny normally given to other state agencies."[14]
Similarly, the exact nature and amounts of subsidies to MTA were largely
beyond the understanding of the public, the press, and most legislators.[15]
Without any formal arrangement establishing what part of the deficit would
be assumed by what jurisdiction and with such confused accounting procedures that Senate Finance Committee staff members threw up their hands in
confusion at MTA budgets and reports, Ronan spent the taxpayers' money in
large amounts with little interference. He ignored MTA's operational and
management problems, showed no interest in cost control, and pursued new
projects with near abandon. He could do so because he was confident of personal backing from the governor.

For investment capital, MTA depended mainly on legislative appropriations and New York State general obligation bond funds. With what one
legislative critic has called "fiscal foolery of the first instance,"[16] the legislature loaned the authority seed money with which to purchase the Long Island
Rail Road and to start other projects and subsequently voted to pay off the
loan from state bond funds, translating the loan, in effect, into a permanent
appropriation—a startling parallel to Nelson Rockefeller's habit of loaning
people money and later forgiving the loans.

The $2.5 billion transportation bond issue for which the Rockefeller
administration gained the voters' approval in 1967 was to be allocated through
the new state Department of Transportation (DOT), which would coordinate
the various types of transportation development in the state. But Rockefeller
exempted Ronan from having to channel MTA's requests for state transportation funds through the DOT. Ronan could not be bothered dealing with a
state transportation commissioner (who collected little more than half
Ronan's salary), and the governor was closer to many of his authority executives than to his state government commissioners. Ronan also was able to
dodge his obligations to appear before the budget director to justify MTA's
appropriations requests.[17] He searched for profit-making projects to supplement revenues coming in from TBTA facilities so that MTA might issue its
own bonds. (It was authorized to use moral obligation backing.) He tried
unsuccessfully to build the region's fourth jetport and the Rye–Oyster Bay
Bridge crossing Long Island Sound that Robert Moses had been promoting for

decades.

Despite MTA's continued dependence on government finance, Ronan took maximum advantage of authority independence and confidentiality. Local officials complained that proposals for the new bridge, for Stewart and Republic airports, and for other facilities were shrouded in secrecy until the last possible moments. In early 1974, the New York State Assembly passed a special bill requiring the MTA to give local governments information on projected highway and transportation plans. In the meantime, even when asked to approve an MTA capital budget in excess of $100 million, New York City councilmen had found it difficult to get information on the Transit Authority's operating costs and problems. Ronan made the state comptroller go to court to get clearance to audit Transit Authority operations. (Ironically, the court cited the Hults Commission study directed by Ronan as authority for the comptroller's power.)

The Limits of Authority Power   In 1973, as the governor was leaving New York for Washington, the authority system he had developed was on the verge of serious trouble. It had grown beyond the scale of effective personal control and was being overtaken by economic events. Despite his prowess at pulling funds from all levels of government, Ronan got out of the MTA just in time to avoid fiscal reckoning. He had repeatedly told skeptical reporters that he would have enough money to finish the jobs he started, including the elaborate complex of planned projects involving the Second Avenue subway, a new tunnel under the East River, and subway extensions in Queens County. Within a few months after taking over MTA, his successor, David L. Yunich, announced halts on project construction. For the second time in twenty years, capital funds for constructing a Second Avenue subway were diverted, this time after parts of the tunnel had been dug.

Other Rockefeller-inspired authority projects also were in trouble. The World Trade Center was in operation, but it was widely criticized as a power glutton saved from financial disaster only by what the state's comptroller termed an outrageous lease with the state of New York that drained private real estate in the downtown business district where the vacancy rate was higher than it had been since the 1930s.[18] At the same time, UDC was losing nearly $1 million per day, and projects not already committed were being halted. Yet several times through June 1973, the UDC enabling legislation had been amended, at Rockefeller's request, to expand the corporation's power and to lessen state controls.[19]

The elected governor of a state is an appropriate leader to guide state corporations into chosen tasks. The Rockefeller administration did this with skill but made a serious mistake based on the widespread misconception that the financial community can be relied upon to be cautious, conservative, and informed about the financial condition of the corporations to which it loans money. During the 1960s, the brokers had replaced the voters in New York as the ultimate brake on public debt; the brokers had proven a good deal more generous than the voters, but the game now provided diminishing returns. Moving into Albany in January 1975, a newly elected governor confronted forty-three state authorities with debt over $14 billion and a projection of income and expenditure that contemplated outright appropriations of $1.9 billion to public authorities in the state over the following five years. According to the estimates left by the prior administration, eleven public authorities would need continuous support of operating costs; twenty had first-instance appropriations that they could not pay back, and no end was in sight for other state aids and credit guarantees. In fact, the financial burdens authorities imposed on the state were to become heavier faster than those projections indicated.

Into the 1970s, the Rockefeller administration failed to foresee that its housing plans were overambitious and vulnerable to cutbacks in federal subsidies; that its dormitory construction plans overshot student demand; that its construction and financing plans for health and mental hygiene facilities were vulnerable to manipulation by the private entrepreneurs who ran the institutions thus made profitable; that the unsettled method of subsidizing transportation authorities, requiring new bargains to be struck between state, federal, and local budgets each year, would become an intolerable drain on political and financial resources. Dormitories had vacancies, and mental health facilities had more beds than qualified staff could handle. The governor and his network of authority entrepreneurs did not notice these developments. Nor did the authorities' financial backers. In June 1973, David Rockefeller was still publicly outlining the ambitious plans for the Lower Manhattan of the 1980s, and UDC and other authorities had found markets for new bonds. The system was vulnerable because of the general weakness of forecasts made by feasibility studies, exaggerated by the optimistic ambitions of project sponsors and financiers; an underlying dependence on uncertain federal aid for all the programs involved in housing, health, and transportation; the sheer volume of construction and debt reached in the state; and rapid changes in the economy of the nation. Decline in the market for operating authority revenue bonds (accompanied by rapid increases in costs of new borrowing) in 1974–1975 was partly a case of supply and demand: the supply of New York bonds was greater than nationwide investor demand, which was increasingly turning to other kinds of tax-exempt securities. Investors were becoming reluctant to overload their portfolios with securities from one state, even before New York City's pains from overborrowing and UDC's troubles became front-page news.

Late in his administration, Governor Rockefeller compounded the difficulties in his attempt to gain voter approval for a new $3.5 billion transportation bond issue that would allow him to allocate highway and transit funds across the state, would indirectly facilitate his claim to budget surpluses, and would purchase support from unions, politicians, and local groups wherever favored projects were funded—thus solidifying his control over the state's politics even if he resigned the governorship. The bond issue might also have enabled MTA to build a revenue-producing bridge and a sports complex over rail switching yards. Without it, MTA was in every bit as much trouble as UDC, although, because it had not issued bonds on the private market, MTA and Ronan confronted galloping subsidies rather than "threatened default" and therefore were not subjected to the bad publicity that plagued UDC and Logue.

To win support from transit proponents for the 1973 bond election Rockefeller and Ronan bargained away the goodwill of the financial community by agreeing to total repeal of the bond covenants that had stalled the Port Authority's rail transportation program, which the two state governors had announced the year before. Repeal served only to undermine the confidence of the investment bankers that they could rely on state government to support authority debts and pledges generally. The business press tied the concept of "moral" in moral obligation bonds to the ethics of keeping covenants (repeal of a covenant was equated with violation of a contract and was struck down as such by the Supreme Court). As a result, Port Authority revenues continued growing, but other authority financings in the state were depressed. Even well-managed agencies lost their marketability because of the psychological reactions of investors. Although the original covenants had been unnecessary and unwise, in agreeing to repeal them the governor contributed to the alienation of the financial community and received nothing back in the bargain.

The Marketplace of Controls

The Rockefeller administration's relations with public authorities were unusual in that they involved the application of concentrated political power to explicit policy goals. Ordinarily, the governor's office is just one of many forces—other executive agencies, the legislature, federal and local governments, the courts, political parties, and interest groups—that compete to influence the direction of the public enterprise. In fact, the area in which competition does characterize most public enterprise is that of government controls. Legal controls generally fall into several categories: powers of appointment, supervision by executive agencies, legislative action, court review, and local approval powers.

Powers of Appointment   Theoretically, the public corporation is responsible to the officials who appoint its board. But the power of appointment—even if entirely unencumbered—is inherently limited by the facts of political life, by the pressures of patronage, and by the traditions and expectations that surround it. The power of appointment can be used to build up personal influence in public enterprises, but it is more often used to reward persons or groups from whom an official needs or has already obtained other support or favors. Governors and local officials exchange authority appointments for campaign finance, policy support, service to the party, banking or legal advice, or other kinds of service, most of them unrelated to the work of the enterprise itself. Although a governor or mayor may add to his electoral power by handing out authority positions to campaign contributors and party fund raisers, he seldom gains control over the decisions of the enterprise that way. (Even ex officio boards are seldom harnessed as theory would have it, to serve comprehensive state policy. State policies are rarely sufficiently explicit to elicit so direct a response.)

Expectations that are built up over the years make it difficult for an appointing official to depart from certain types of appointees who have their own interests to pursue. The orthodox prescription of independent, business-like boards for government corporations also influences the making of appointments. And the authorities themselves bring pressures to bear both directly and through their own allies on appointments and on appointees. Appointment is, as a result, a complex pattern of exchanges that limit the options available to the appointing official. Moreover, appointments traded for political support sometimes backfire. A governor or a mayor shares in the public blame when his appointees are caught receiving kickbacks for public construction. In one twelve-month period, governors of New Jersey, Oklahoma, and Illinois confronted embarrassing charges leveled at officials and contracts associated with state public authorities.[20]

Local and county corporations have caused similar problems. In the case of New Jersey's Bergen County Sewer Authority, for example, the county party committees controlled board appointments that are formally made by the county board of freeholders. Freeholders were tarred with some of the results when the chairman of the County Republican Committee (Walter Henry Jones, also a former state senator and a Port Authority commissioner) collected substantial legal fees from the Sewer Authority from 1960 through 1967. In 1969, Nelson Gross, the new chairman of the County Republican Committee, became the authority's local counsel, and in the subsequent two years he collected more than $220,000 in fees from the Sewer Authority. Gross and board members of the Sewer Authority were subsequently both sued and indicted.

Staggered terms complicate the efforts of incoming officials to gain control of authorities through appointment. Throughout his term, Massachusetts Governor Francis W. Sargent battled with Massport, generally unsuccessfully, while pro-authority lobbyists marched in and out of the state legislature with great effect. They even persuaded a legislative committee to exempt Massport from compliance with air pollution control regulations until EPA threatened to cut off funding for the state's program. Gradually, as vacancies appeared, Sargent appointed individuals concerned for the effects of authority construction on the surrounding community and environment. Not until the end of his term were his appointments a majority on the board.

Packing the board is a strategy that has seldom worked without backfiring. It has only short-run payoffs in any case; with the passage of time, the new board tends to become ingrown, and in any case, it will not belong to the next elected official who takes over. Outgoing governors frequently fill highway authority boards with their own party colleagues, depriving newly elected officials of the patronage positions. These officials can respond by expanding the membership of authority boards. Recently, for example, Governor Byrne of New Jersey—a Democrat—sponsored legislation that expanded the New Jersey Highway Authority to seven members. Its executive director, John P. Gallagher, a former Republican county chairman and earlier patronage appointment, then became a determined public advocate of keeping authorities "out of politics" in order to protest the bill. With a straight face that must have been difficult to keep, he defended what he termed the authority's insulation from politics and protested: "This is a case of politics degrading public service." Gallagher portrayed himself as a fighter for the integrity of the authority and argued that strong political influences on the Highway Authority would undermine the confidence of its investors and bondholders. Governor Byrne's bill to expand the board also elicited indignation from the Republican leader of the state senate, Alfred Beadleston, who labeled it a "political grab" for control of the highway agency.[21] But Beadleston had supported an earlier bill—submitted by Republican Governor Cahill—that had expanded the Highway Authority board from three to five and had made way for Gallagher's appointment. Byrne was the third consecutive governor who struggled unsuccessfully to get New Jersey's turnpike and highway authorities to cooperate in broader transportation policies.[22]

The political struggles that result from efforts to control authorities are costly in time, resources, and power. Governors are occasionally motivated to make these efforts, but municipal and county councils seldom even try. The power of appointment to authority boards and staff rarely carries with it policy control.[23] Chief executives find the power of appointment more useful than not, but they usually cannot rely on it to enable them to influence the direction of public enterprise or to coordinate the policies that the authorities carry out, particularly where independent financial powers prevail.

In a few cases, elected officials are empowered to veto decisions of an authority board. Where that prerogative exists, it has had much less effect than one might predict. The usual procedure for veto calls for minutes of authority board meetings to be forwarded to the appointing official; decisions reflected in those minutes take effect if he does not veto them within a set period of time. But decisions that an authority wants to shield from veto simply do not appear in the minutes; they are made "in committee" and recorded in staff documents. Authority minutes do not even include full budget statements. Moreover, the volume of minutes is often beyond manageable proportions: they are scattered among leather-bound books in state libraries, cardboard cartons in executive departments, and out-of-reach files in state houses. When a governor's attention is drawn by special circumstances, the threat of veto can get him what he wants, and continuing nuisance vetoes have stymied authorities for a time, but governors agree that the veto power does not give them consistent or continuing control over authority activities.

Supervision by Executive Agencies   A statute or executive order may assign the supervision of public authorities to the executive agencies of a government. For example, authorities may be required to submit their budgets to the budget office or budget division of state or city government. Or the comptroller's or treasurer's office may have specific powers to audit authorities' operations and to approve their bond issues. The attorney general's office may have powers to review prospectuses and may hold residual responsibility for challenging acts of public corporations as unconstitutional or illegal. Another bureau dealing with local governments generally may also be charged with the entire question of public authorities and municipal corporations. Finally, a regular line department of government, such as transportation or housing, may have particular coordinating powers over the authorities operating in its bailiwick.

Budget controls   Most authorities have been permitted to maintain and spend at will the proceeds of their own revenues, including revenues derived from tax collections. They submit budgets for prior approval only when they are requesting special appropriations, and only the portion of the budget that would call upon legislative funds is examined in detail. New York has gone further than other states by requiring that all authorities with outstanding loans, appropriations, or other special or appropriated state funds submit budget reports to the state budget director and to the legislative committees on finance.

Long-term state capital budgets hold potential for coordinating the public finances of public authorities, but those budgets are usually treated as little more than rolling year-to-year forecasts. State authorities make their actual borrowing and budgetary decisions internally, and the boards of directors do not often review these decisions in detail. State and city practice contrasts with that of the federal government, where, according to the terms of the Government Corporation Control Act (31 U.S.C. 841), both the budget office and congressional appropriations committees scrutinize budgets of government corporations.

In any case, budget officials have little incentive to battle over the figures from authorities that have independent sources of funds. Even the few government budget analysts who are well versed in authority finance seem to act for their own purposes, not necessarily for those of the governor or mayor or for broad state policies. Frank Collins was chief of the public authorities unit of the New York State Division of Budget until his death in 1974. He designed the Ogdensburg Bridge and Port Authority, which developed and ran a number of facilities in his home town area. He was instrumental in obtaining land from the Department of Mental Hygiene to transfer to the Ogdensburg authority for creation of an industrial park; obtaining authorization and finance for that authority to install roads, water, sewage, electricity, and gas in the industrial park in order to attract industry; absorbing the local airport into the authority's collection of port facilities; obtaining state appropriations for the marine terminal and the development of the port by the authority— all resulting in increased employment and local payrolls. These achievements demonstrate how far the application of the authority form can be stretched, for the Ogdensburg Bridge and Port Authority has never been able to issue its own revenue bonds, has always operated on a deficit basis, and, at its current revenue level, would require some 1,700 years to repay the state's first-instance appropriations.

Audits   Auditing today involves more than a review of bookkeeping and the legality of financial procedures. In the years following World War II, private accounting firms moved into general management consulting and then into policy analysis. Auditors now make judgments about the efficiency of managements (internal audits of operations) and the effectiveness of programs (performance audits). The U.S. General Accounting Office (GAO) has adapted business auditing methods to government. Headed by the comptroller of the United States and responsible to Congress, GAO is empowered to settle and adjust the accounts of regular federal agencies. In the process, its auditors can question individual items of agency expenditure or disallow them. Where the auditing agency conducts what is called a "preaudit," it can actually prevent an expenditure from being transacted.

In 1927, the Supreme Court held that government corporations were free from direct accountability to the Department of Treasury and the General Accounting Office.[24] As a result, with a few exceptions, corporations did not submit their annual accounts to GAO, even though President Roosevelt issued an executive order directing that they do so. By the 1930s, the number and freedom of the corporations had aroused concern in Congress, and GAO became one of the first central agencies to try to assert authority over TVA, objecting to the authority's independence from auditing and accounting controls. In the meantime, the Budget Bureau was trying to bring the administrative expenses of government corporations under its supervision. In 1945, Congress resolved this conflict by passing the Government Corporation Control Act, which provided for annual GAO audit reports on government corporations to be submitted to Congress and for legislative appropriations of authority expenditures above and beyond corporate operating revenues. The latter provision means that a federal corporation can retain its own revenues and spend them according to its own budget with only congressional review, but any additional funds that the corporation requires must go through the normal appropriation procedures. The act permits the corporations to submit business-type budgets and to maintain their own accounting systems on an accrual basis.[25]

The federal act has provided for systematic auditing, accounting, and reporting for over thirty years without major change. It does not stultify corporations with rigid procedures; it provides a useful model for state governments that are ready to organize control over their corporate enterprises. Despite their basic hostility to government corporations, officials in Eisenhower's Bureau of the Budget concluded that the controls were satisfactory: "Experience under the Government Corporation Control Act has clearly demonstrated that it is possible to maintain essential Presidential and Congressional supervision over government corporations without impairing the financial and operating flexibility required for the successful conduct of governmental programs of a business nature."[26] Chart 10.1 summarizes general federal practices of financial control over corporations and public enterprise revolving funds (like the Alaska Railroad).

GAO now audits most government corporations annually, commenting on their financial condition. Over the years, this auditing has settled into fairly constructive relationships (debates continue over its restricted access to files of the Federal Deposit Insurance Corporation). GAO reports that the accounting systems of major federal corporations compare favorably with the best found in private industry. The corporate audits usually recommend particular improvements in management or finance that may be subsequently instituted by Congress or by the corporations themselves, and from time to time they uncover serious problems of mismanagement.

The Government Corporation Control Act also provides for Treasury control over corporate deposits, securities, and investments. The Treasury Department can approve the form, denomination, maturities, and rates of government corporation bonds but does not control timing and decisions to issue nonguaranteed bonds. The public debt limit applies only to specifically guaranteed obligations of government corporations. When the pressure of the debt limit becomes too great, Treasury can direct the corporations to issue

Chart 10.1
Financial Controls over Federal Government Corporations and Public Enterprise
Revolving Funds

	Corporations subject to Government Corporation Control Act	Revolving funds subject to Budget and Accounting Procedures Act
1 Budget		
Form:	Business-type budget required	Business-type budget required
Provision for repayment of capital funds or payment of dividends:	Occasionally	Not usually
Operating expense limitations:	Occasionally	Occasionally
Administrative expense limitations:	Occasionally	Not usually
All costs shown:	Generally	Generally
2 Audit		
Type of audit:	By GAO in accordance with generally accepted principles and procedures applicable to commercial corporate transactions	As determined by GAO and internal audit staff
Subject to GAO disallowance:	No	Yes
Frequency of audit:	Every three years	As determined by GAO
3 Accounts		
Principles and standards:	Developed by corporation	Developed with GAO
System subject to approval by:	Corporation	GAO
Nature of system:	Accrual	Most on accrual
4 Financing		
Fiscal year limitation on capital appropriations:	Varies	Varies
Use of receipts for operating expenses:	Yes	Yes
Use of receipts for capital expenses:	Yes	Often limited
Need for legislative authorization for individual construction projects:	Generally no	As provided by existing law
Charges reflect costs such as interest, depreciation, and overhead:	Generally yes	Not usually

Chart 10.1 (continued)

Interest paid on net government investment:	Generally yes	Generally no
Authority to sell nonguaranteed obligations to public:	Can be authorized by law	No
5 Operations		
Restrictions:	Specific statutes and regulations applicable to corporations	Statutes and regulations applicable generally to executive agencies and civil servants
Sue and be sued in own name:	Yes	Usually no
Litigation handled by:	Corporation or Depart- of Justice	Department of Justice
Property acquired in the name of:	Corporation	United States
Contracts made in the name of:	Corporation	United States
Limitations on authority to make contracts:	Regulations and statutes applicable to corporations	Regulations and statutes applicable to agencies
Claims settled by:	Corporation	GAO and administering agency

Source: U.S. Office of Management and Budget. Entries are based on general federal practices to which there are exceptions.

and sell nonguaranteed obligations outside the federal ceiling. Such issues resemble moral obligation bonds; although they evade the statutory debt limit, the federal government is generally considered ultimately responsible for the obligations of federal corporations.

The relationships of the Treasury and government budgeters and auditors with federal government corporations should be emulated in state governments, most of which have no parallel arrangements for centralized borrowing and commercial auditing. The continued exemption of federal government corporations from regular budget procedures does sustain substantial differences between the operations of such corporations and those of government bureaus. It frees an enterprise from administrative bargaining during the stages of budget preparation and from rebargaining throughout the processes of appropriations and budget administration. On the other hand, the requirement that corporations submit their budgets in advance to Congress prevents them from engaging in the kind of secrecy typical of state and local authorities. A statement of income and expenses from specific corporate activities must be included. Congress may approve a corporation budget by failure to act or may revise the budget. Congressional committees do review corporate budgets regularly, but Congress usually approves them without difficulty.

The guidelines that GAO has issued for auditing government organizations are easily adaptable to the state level.[27] Only a handful of states have attempted to apply GAO procedures. Review by the New York State Comptroller's Office is the most thorough. The public authority division of that office is a permanent entity responsible for analyzing the financial reports of all statewide authorities and conducting occasional full-scale performance audits according to the principles set forth by GAO. Most states require authorities to submit annual reports to state auditors, but they do not specify the form and content of the reports or assign staff to study them.[28]

Authority executives tend to be defensive with respect to audits and to auditors' recommendations for operational improvements. Moreover, even an auditor as determined and informed on the subject of public authorities as New York's Arthur Levitt, who has held office since 1955, is only one of several officials who must compete with the powers of authority entrepreneurs, the governor, other state agencies, the legislature, and the courts to influence the directions of public enterprise. Levitt opposed the use of moral obligation authority financing but was not willing to sue the governor to prove it unconstitutional. He has submitted legislative proposals to limit public authority debt and to intensify controls over public authority activities, but few of his proposals have been enacted.

In Nebraska, the auditor has mandatory review power over bond proposals of specified authorities, but he has seldom altered borrowing arrangements. To interfere with arrangements proposed to provide hundreds of millions of dollars for public projects is everywhere a hazardous and unlikely choice. Moreover, despite the professionalism of auditors and accountants, several audits can yield different conclusions. As auditing has moved into areas of efficiency and program effectiveness, policy issues have become more and more involved in the auditing process. The financial bias of auditing procedures becomes questionable when applied to overall policy.[29] Evaluation requires knowledge about objectives and intentions, about an organization's past and present lines of activity, and about its constituency and clientele. As comprehensive auditing considers a broader range of performance questions, it begins inevitably to raise issues that affect legislative and election politics, the aims of various interest groups, and the plans of the enterprise itself.

Line departments   Most federal government enterprises are technically components of a cabinet-level department. In the 1930s, this relationship—like that between the corporations and the budgeting and auditing agencies—became the subject of major disputes. The secretary of the interior resented TVA's exclusion from his department and its direct access to the president. Agreeing with the precepts of the President's Committee on Administrative Management, he joined with GAO and some of TVA's congressional opponents to urge "departmentalization" (that is, incorporation of the authority into the Department of the Interior). Although TVA remains unattached to any federal department, Washington's regular bureaucracy did prevent TVA-style regional authorities from being established elsewhere in the United States.

Corporations that are organized within federal departments have special status to protect their independent financing arrangements. They are exempt from departmental reorganization plans, for example, and the secretary cannot transfer their powers. The federal Commodity Credit Corporation is an incorporated revolving fund whose operating functions are entirely carried out through the Department of Agriculture, where it is located. This wholly owned government corporation was originally chartered under Delaware law in 1933 and reincorporated in 1948 within the Department of Agriculture, with its authority vested in a board of directors of which the secretary of agriculture is chairman. The Commodity Credit Corporation's price-support activities are not intended to be self-supporting. The department reports the corporation's operating deficit at the end of each year (between $2 billion and $4 billion each year during 1971-1976), and the losses are reimbursable through appropriations. For other departmental functions, appropriations must precede expenditures.

The St. Lawrence Seaway Corporation is a wholly owned government corporation created by congressional act. By treaty, this corporation divides the toll revenues from the locks and channels of the St. Lawrence Seaway with the St. Lawrence Authority of Canada. The corporation submits an annual report to the secretary of transportation and issues its revenue bonds to the secretary of the treasury. To avoid toll increases that the secretary of transportation determined were likely to reduce seaway traffic and to harm dependent regional economies, interest payments on the revenue bonds were deferred and subsequently foregone. (The private market would have termed this "default.") Further subsidies will probably be required to meet the authority's bond redemption schedule after 1978. Such flexibility has been rare at the state and local levels because authorities are isolated from departments of government that might develop comprehensive pricing policies and because of the more rigid requirements of private revenue bond financing and related corporate pricing.

The Massachusetts Department of Transportation, for example, in the early 1970s developed statewide priorities that included limiting expansion of automobile and airplane traffic at Logan International Airport and integrating several authority projects with state transportation plans. The secretary of transportation and four new board members of Massport agreed that it would be advisable to seek looser terms of agreement with Massport bondholders so that borrowed money could be used for such purposes as soundproofing schools in the communities near the airport and so that the city could levy taxes on private businesses at the airport. They achieved neither aim. The department sponsored bills providing for the governor's approval of Massport bond issues over $1 million and Department of Transportation supervision of the authority—bills which failed in the legislature. Federal law and experience demonstrate that corporate activities can successfully be integrated into broad department policy plans such as those envisaged in Massachusetts without sacrificing the advantages of independent management, but authority politics and allies make these changes difficult to achieve.

In a number of states, departments of state government supervise county or municipal corporations; a number of state environmental protection departments, for example, have various approval powers over sewer authorities. In Pennsylvania, state education department approval is required for all stages of school building by municipal corporations. State education officials are in a position to develop and apply a broad plan of school development. The overseeing departments usually lack comprehensive goals to apply to authorities, however, and the individual authorities often have support from local politicians and businessmen that enables them to circumvent the state department. Such support has made many local housing authorities independent of state and city housing departments, for example.

Pennsylvania has strengthened its Department of Community Affairs; a unit within it monitors municipal corporations throughout the state. Each Pennsylvania municipal corporation must file an annual report with this department, but the reports do not provide much operational information.

The department does have an inventory of municipal corporations. Its regulatory responsibility is to apply the provisions of the state's general enabling act, the Municipal Authorities Act, through perusal of the annual financial reports filed with it; the review is not as thorough as the special performance audits that are used in New York. (Such audits would be impractical in a state with some two thousand public authorities, in any case.)

These examples are extraordinary. In most state governments, no department even maintains a comprehensive listing of active public authorities, their officers, members, and addresses, let alone information on financial transactions. The Securities Industry Association has more data available on state and local public authorities than have state governments.

Legislative Power   Traditional prescriptions for public authorities called for legislative control over major policies. But major policies of most public authorities emerge incrementally from a series of very specific financial and administrative decisions that are largely beyond legislative reach. From the moment of a public authority's creation—the passage of the statute or charter that describes its activities, powers, and responsibilities—legislative control diminishes rapidly. The core of legislative power over government agencies is the power of the purse, and agencies not subject to it are rarely held continuously and intensively accountable. Legislatures have specific powers over public authorities, but their application is inherently limited.

Legislative action to create the authority by special statute and to define its powers provides the major distinction between public authorities and nonprofit corporations, which are privately chartered under the terms of general law. The enabling act and the special statute that create each authority define its powers, its mission, and the specific formal regulations that are to be applied to it. The relevant statutes may be detailed and systematic or vague and chaotic; most are somewhere in between. The public corporation cannot, according to legal theory, engage in activities not enumerated or implicit in its statute.

The first issue to be decided by the legislature in the creating or chartering process is whether an authority or government corporation should be established for the purpose specified. The basic tendencies of legislative politics make the pressure to create the corporation overwhelming in most cases.[30] The formula language supplied by the bond attorneys and investment advisers suggests that construction projects, with all the business and benefits that they spin off, will impose no immediate cost on the taxpayers. Such proposals are usually backed up by the governor, the mayor, and local business interests.

Of the states with a significant number of local authorities, only Maine and New York require special acts of the legislature to set up each public corporation. Elsewhere, state enabling acts permit counties and municipalities to create authorities. The terms of charters drafted by municipal councils might impose some constraints on the authorities created, but these charters tend to be vague and standardized. Statements of purposes for special act authorities are more precise but still leave considerable leeway. Some of the language of the Port Authority compact suggests that the authority is a general planning agency and regulator of rail transportation.[31]

Many original proponents of government corporations viewed the limitation of corporate life span as an essential and sufficient control. They assumed that when the initial debt was paid off, the authority's life would end; its facilities could be used free of charge and be managed by regular government agencies. Public corporations very quickly discovered how to circumvent the application of this requirement by spilling their funds into new projects and extending their debt. In Pennsylvania, local authorities chartered under the Municipal Authorities Act of 1945 are limited to debt outstanding of fifty years unless their charters are amended; authorities with outstanding debt have had little difficulty in obtaining such amendments, but at least a public council (of whatever government established the corporation) reviews the situation. Other statutes limit total authority debt, prohibit borrowing after the original project, or tie corporate debt levels to some index, such as local property valuation or corporate income, but these are exceptions. Legislation has also set a limit on the interest rates that authorities can pay on the securities they issue, but when that ceiling is under what the market will accept, amendment is more the rule than the exception. Authorities can be subject to statutory rules governing contract bidding and bond sale procedures. (About half are required to sell bonds by competitive sale rather than by negotiation.)

The amending power usually resides with the legislature that created the authority. (Some locally chartered authorities can be altered only by state law, however.) In theory, then, legislatures hold the power of life and death. The amending power has been used to increase specific controls over authorities (for example, to add executive veto power or to specify financial reporting procedures), but legislators more often than not reject such proposed changes, viewing them as attempts by the governor, mayor, or comptroller to cut into supervision by the legislature. The theoretical ambiguity as to whether public authorities should be accountable to legislators as their "stockholders" or to executive agencies that might coordinate them with other government units fuels such competition. Moreover, the amending power is restricted or encumbered with respect to bond-issuing corporations. Statutes typically prohibit taxing, abolishing, merging, or otherwise affecting the powers of the authority as long as it has bonds outstanding. Insofar as part of the legislation is worded as a covenant, the courts consider it a contract with the investors not readily subject to amendment. (Clearly, however, if the parent government or a new agency assumed corporate debt or guaranteed its payment, amendment would not impair the heart of a public contract with bondholders.)

The authority system as a result does not contribute to the flexibility of government over time. On the contrary, the corporations form a rigid structure that becomes riddled with anachronisms. The case of New Jersey's three toll road authorities is illustrative. Several recent proposals to merge them in a broader framework would adapt transportation policy and finance to current conditions, including rising demand for pollution control, swelling subsidies for mass transportation, and the need to conserve energy. None of the proposals survived in the legislature, and if they had, they would have been subjected to litigation of uncertain outcome. In a variety of utility businesses, too, statutes are needed to effect mergers of municipal corporations that are too numerous and too small to make efficient use of public resources. In the absence of any measurable damage to bondholders, it is difficult to explain why a merger or changes in task should require payoffs of extra percentage points in interest. The private sector has generated a variety of well-tested methods for merging corporations and forming conglomerates; state and local legislatures should be able to make changes in the structure of doing public business—where such changes would be useful—without long-drawn-out battles and bondholder payoffs of dubious necessity. Federal law reserves to Congress a modified form of amending power to facilitate changes in the status of government corporations. As long as the bondholders' claims to payment of interest and principal are protected, bondholder rights should not be used as an argument against modifying the structure and power of state and municipal corporations. If the same level of legal ingenuity were applied to these problems as to devising new financing schemes, corporate flexibility and bondholder interests could certainly be reconciled.

The courts have held that public authorities have only those powers that have been granted by statute, but they have generously interpreted general grants of powers as permitting a wide variety of projects. Not all authorities must come back to the creating legislature to undertake new projects or move into new areas.[32] Many have the power to plan, to finance, and to construct or to acquire a project with little public notice and no formal government action. Even authorities without general grants of power often plan and undertake new works by categorizing them as extensions of existing projects. The municipal and county authorities—and all utilities—have the widest latitude to operate without approval. Bridge, tunnel, and turnpike authorities have limited powers to build new projects without some kind of approval, but even they can generally plan unlimited extensions (such as widening a highway from four to ten lanes or adding tubes to tunnels) without returning to the legislature. The New Jersey Highway Authority managed to argue successfully that the Garden State Arts Center was simply an extension of its existing powers to utilize land along the parkway.[33]

In any case, when a corporation requests authorization of a new project from the legislature, the legislature is confronted with a single project request (a new highway spur running in a certain direction over a selected route and of preestablished size and financing). Authority planning and scanning processes have already ruled out alternative routes, alternative modes of transportation, alternative financing or pricing policies, and so forth. The authorities maintain that they have carried out a scientifically determined program of regional planning or contracted for sophisticated feasibility reports, drawn upon the best expert advice, and so forth. State and local legislatures are in no position to reorder the planning. Project planning is a key point in the decision process that is beyond the reach of legislative controls even when an authority has to return for specific project authorization. The difference between the general authorization for the World Trade Center in Lower Manhattan and the specific decisions on design, size, and cost that were made subsequent to that authorization illustrates the limits of legislative approval. Recently, a New Jersey court ruled that the Turnpike Authority had misled the public by proposing one route for a new spur at a public hearing and subsequently selecting a different route.[34] Usually, authorities enjoy a high success rate for legislation proposed by their managements, except for those seeking to merge local activities into regional enterprises. Metropolitan authorities tend to experience local opposition.

Legislatures, local officials, governors, or other public officials can initiate legislation to direct an authority to do something. For example, the New York and New Jersey legislatures have enacted bills authorizing the Port

Authority of New York and New Jersey to provide rail services to its air terminals, and legislatures of other states and cities have authorized authority tasks never carried out. Authority managements simply failed to implement the projects in the years immediately following, using delay, legal tactics, and financial change to avoid compliance.

Arrangements for automatically covering authority deficits sometimes prevent legislatures from exercising even normal powers of the purse. In Massachusetts, for example, two authorities operated under provisions calling for automatic coverage of their deficits out of legislative appropriations (paralleling arrangements for the U.S. Commodity Credit Corporation). In other places, particularly in the Midwest and West, earmarked taxes flow directly to particular authority deficits.

Congressional committees do have closer relationships with some federal corporations than state legislatures have with public authorities. Even since 1960, while TVA no longer must ask Congress for capital appropriations, TVA executives testify annually to subcommittees conducting budget reviews. A single appropriations subcommittee in the House of Representatives, which has been dealing with TVA since its beginnings, scrutinizes the budget closely. For 1974, for example, TVA was asking for the relatively trivial sum of $43 million in government funds out of a total expenditure budget of $1.36 billion. But the committee grilled TVA officials thoroughly on decisions to raise electricity prices, methods of calculating rate of return, adequacy of pollution control and environmental research efforts, and local criticism of TVA's shutdown of a small wooden bridge.[35]

One of the most effective attention-getting techniques of legislative control is the special investigation or hearing. Such efforts focus resources—staff, time, and information—on authority activities, but in limited, usually one-shot, campaigns. The most famous legislative investigations have featured clashes between determined committee chairmen and strong-willed authority entrepreneurs. Legislative investigations have subjected some authorities to in-depth study, wrested information on authority operations from their normally private hiding places, and subjected authority management to severe criticisms. But most authority entrepreneurs have emerged from this process whole, if somewhat bruised.

Only five years after it was created, TVA was the subject of a bitter investigation by a joint House and Senate committee when the former chairman of its board hinted at corruption after President Franklin Roosevelt forced his resignation. The ousted director had denied the president's right to inquire into TVA affairs, claiming the board was responsible only to Congress. A year later, the committee finally issued a report rejecting the charges and exonerating TVA's management. During the next fifteen years, TVA's involvement in public power versus private power controversies subjected it to almost continuous battles in Congress. As a result, Lilienthal spent more time politicking in Washington than administering in the valley, as indicated by a typical entry in his journal: "Ever since I came back to work late in April I have been traveling back and forth to Washington, trying to get legislation through to authorize the Tennessee Electric Company purchase. In a way it has been nothing more dignified or important than lobbying, and not congenial to me at all, although the men we have been working with are really fine men, Congressmen Sparkman and Thomason, and of course, the grand old man himself, Senator Norris. But I am impatient to be doing many other things."[36]

In 1941, Lilienthal locked horns with Tennessee's Senator Kenneth McKellar when TVA refused to change the project plans and site for Douglas Dam. McKellar resented his defeat on this issue and subsequently made a habit of submitting amendments to reduce TVA's managerial independence. Although McKellar's amendments were never enacted, they were a legislative nuisance, costly in time and bargaining over a number of years. Douglas Dam itself was completed in less than thirteen months, reportedly setting a world record for construction speed. After the war, the president reappointed Lilienthal chairman of the TVA board over the objections of both senators from Tennessee (contrary to the tradition of senatorial courtesy), and the appointment was confirmed easily by the full Senate. Like Lilienthal, most authority entrepreneurs express discomfort with the rough and tumble game of open legislative politics, yet they are frequently good at it.

Legislative investigation is a potentially destructive device that unsettles authority management and can absorb enormous amounts of time with minimal results. It is nevertheless an essential power of last resort. Congress or a state legislature is occasionally the only forum in which local groups who oppose some authority action can find a hearing. In many cases, local political influence has been more effective channeled all the way through Washington, D.C., or through state capitols than through the formalized procedures available for local participation.[37]

In the early 1960s, the House Judiciary Committee began an intensive investigation of the Port Authority, and a senate commission in New Jersey opened hearings close on its heels. The House Judiciary Committee (chaired by Emanuel Celler of Brooklyn) challenged the secrecy of Port Authority

planning and finances. When the legislators discovered that the major decisions of the Port Authority did not show up in the minutes of the board
meetings (on the public record), and when the authority management failed
to produce requested documents, the committee brought proceedings against
three authority officials, including the board chairman. Austin Tobin stood
trial for contempt, while board members waged a publicity campaign against
Congressman Celler.[38]

The Celler committee investigation took place at the peak of the Port
Authority's reputation and credit rating. But opposition was beginning to
mount. Morris County was opposing its designation by the Port Authority as
the only reasonable site, according to authority planning criteria, for a fourth
jetport. New York City's mayor was urging the legislature to require the Port
Authority to pay property taxes wherever its operations generated surplus
revenues. And political leaders on both sides of the Hudson River were pressing for the Port Authority to share in the cost of commuter rail service. The
Port Authority turned to business for support in resisting these pressures. At
Tobin's request an array of bankers communicated with state officials, municipal officials, and federal agencies. The Newark Association of Commerce
and Industry, major Newark banks and insurance companies, and even the
Brooklyn Chamber of Commerce in Celler's home jurisdiction joined the
battle. Enormous press coverage reported at face value many of the typical
themes of Port Authority public relations: that the authority was above politics, that the businessmen who ran its board should not be subjected to political questioning, that its planning was on a technical and professional basis
and should be kept internal to the agency to avoid political interference, and
so forth. The voices on the other side seemed small by comparison. Congressman Peter Rodino asked in committee hearings: "Do you mean to tell me
that this problem [rail transportation] so important to the state of New
Jersey and to the public would be abandoned and the public would know
nothing about the discussion which took place purely because some commissioners had a strong feeling against it?"[39] The answer on the record is "yes"
and remained so.

Legislative investigation has proved crucial to reveal obscure but important
authority activities. The 1970 legislation drafted by the Nixon administration
to reorganize the Postal Service was ambiguous on the question of whether
the service would continue to get capital funds from the U.S. Treasury or
might issue its own revenue bonds. (Other federal agencies borrow competitively through the Treasury or use their own fiscal agents to organize under-

writing groups.) It turned out that the insiders involved in the creation of the Postal Service had formulated a plan for issuing revenue bonds through a negotiated underwriting. James Hargrove, senior assistant postmaster general, was appointed by President Nixon on the advice of presidential assistant Peter Flanagan, formerly (from 1947 through 1969) vice-president of the investment banking firm of Dillon Read. Hargrove had been treasurer of Texas Eastern Transmission Company (Tetco), a long-time corporate client of Dillon Read (and a corporate contributor to Nixon's 1968 campaign). Hargrove's first task was planning a Postal Service bond issue to be sold without Treasury guarantee to the private market on a negotiated basis. The syndicate that subsequently managed the underwriting included Dillon Read, Kidder Peabody, and Salomon Brothers. Kidder Peabody lacked prior experience in government bond deals, but the chairman of its board, Albert Gordon, had made substantial campaign contributions to the Republican party for the 1968 presidential elections.[40] Salomon Brothers, the leader of the managing syndicate, was the underwriting firm of which William Simon, then deputy secretary of the treasury, had been a partner.

Hargrove saw clearly the business advantages of Postal Service revenue bond financing, although it was more costly to the government than the ordinary method of borrowing from the Treasury or issuing guaranteed bonds. In a speech to the Investment Bankers Association meeting in Florida on December 3, 1970, he pointed out that if a private sale of Postal Service bonds without Treasury guarantee were not arranged, the investment banking industry would not get the business. He urged them to rate the bonds highly, and he stated that the bonds carried an implied government guarantee; although the U.S. government "might allow Lockheed or Penn Central to fail, it would never let the Post Office go without meeting its debts." In effect, he was saying that the Postal Service bonds could be sold at a higher profit because they were nonguaranteed corporate bonds, but at the same time underwriters could tell their customers that the bonds were really backed by the government. Representatives of other investment banking firms agree today that without the general belief in an implicit guarantee by the U.S. government, the bonds would not have been salable. This is a federal version of moral obligation.

In a Postal Service memorandum, Hargrove estimated legal fees for revenue bond issue at no more than $10,000. The ultimate arrangement with Mudge Rose Guthrie & Alexander reportedly provided for a bond counsel commission of more than six times that figure. In 1971, having been alerted by a

GAO auditor to questionable issues involving proposed Postal Service financing, Congressman Morris Udall, chairman of the House Subcommittee on Postal Service, asked his staff to conduct an investigation. When the committee called for government witnesses to explain the financing arrangement, William Simon and James Hargrove appeared. They maintained in familiar slogans that the goals of reorganization were to put the Postal Service on a "business basis" and to eliminate the last "vestiges of politics from decision making in the department." Hargrove further claimed that the discipline of the marketplace would force the Postal Service to meet its obligations and would induce efficiency and that such discipline would be felt only if it did not have Treasury backing. Congressman Udall pointed out the patent nonsense in that argument, which implied that Postal Service management needed to be brainwashed in order to be efficient.[41]

Reorganizing the Post Office Department "removed it from politics" only in the sense that it became much more difficult for the congressional committees to control. (Before the reorganization, the House committee was particularly influential.) The first board of governors of the Postal Service came from the nation's business leadership, and the executives came from industry as well. They had little respect for congressional criticisms. Despite the committee's findings and questions, the bond sale did take place, and the Postal Service made no personnel shifts. Subsequently, it has not manifested increases in efficiency or decreases in dubious practices. The total number of Postal Service employees was reduced (while new public service jobs were being financed by Congress to offset high unemployment). Executive salaries were increased. The first postmaster after reorganization, a former corporate executive, collected consulting fees from firms doing business with the Postal Service. Prices increased, but the service failed to become self-supporting as mandated by the 1970 statute. GAO audits highlighted continuing management weaknesses.[42] In sum, the private interests in reorganization of the Post Office seem to have been better served than the public purposes.

At the state level, investigations by legislative committees into authority activities have been even less effective. New Jersey's Autonomous Authorities Study Commission, for example, operated from 1968 through 1972. In a series of hearings in 1968 and 1969, it took testimony regarding the Delaware River Port Authority, the New Jersey Highway Authority, and other state corporations. In 1971, it organized the bistate legislative hearings, with New York, that considered Port Authority finances. The original purpose of the chairman of the commission, Assemblyman Kenneth T. Wilson, was simply to prevent authorities from continuing to use their excess funds for purposes not intended in their original enabling legislation. Subsequently, through consultants' investigations of corporate documents, including vouchers, he became concerned about management particulars, such as legal fees to politicians and the weak qualifications and attendance records of board members. In Wilson's words, "Authorities are created by part-time state legislators who don't know what an authority is and don't know what they have created, and having created it they abdicate all responsibility for the work that it carries out. The authority then falls into control of its executive director because of an incompetent or uninterested board of commissioners, and the executive director ends up wielding a tremendous amount of political power and project discretion."

According to Wilson, New Jersey Highway Authority manager D. Louis Tonti personally tried to persuade him to drop hearings; Governor Cahill asked him to postpone them. Others, including some fellow Republicans, also urged him to stop the investigations, but he reports, "They could not get to me as I was a school teacher. If I were a lawyer in a law firm or an employee of a corporation or in almost any other positions, these pressures might have been effective, but what are they going to do: telephone my principal? I have tenure as a teacher." In the end, his opponents changed the boundary lines of Wilson's assembly district to include East Orange and part of Newark, eliminating part of West Orange, where his strength lay. He did not return to the legislature. One of the commission's accomplishments, legislation establishing veto power over the New Jersey Highway Authority, was given to a reluctant governor: the gubernatorial veto provision was passed over Governor Hughes's veto.

At the same time, New York State Senator Samuel L. Greenberg, a Democrat, prepared several reports on authorities despite limited access to information (the Republican party controlled the legislature, and the minority members and their staffs were not given the reports and budgets submitted by statewide public authorities to the Republican chairman of the committee). Senator Greenberg's report, appearing some five years before the trouble with debt volume became evident, included recommendations for monitoring the amount and financial standing of moral obligation debt. The report dropped into the state legislature like a rock into a bottomless pond, however, and the senator retired to Florida. (Wilson and Greenberg illustrate that there is no Republican or Democratic way to cope with authorities; legislators of both parties deal from weak positions.) The great majority of state legislators have only the vaguest idea of the activities of public enterprise within their districts. The public seems to view legislators not as the stockholders of public corporations but, in Clinton Rossiter's words, as "committees, subcommittees or lone wolves, who have coaxed their inquiring noses beyond the limits of political decorum and constitutional practice."[43] Part of the problem is the chronic weakness of state and local legislatures throughout the nation. California's legislature, reputed to be in far greater control of its own business than most and less a tool of the governor or of a party majority, has kept a tighter rein than most on the development of public corporations within the state. Most state legislatures, however, have neither the committee staffs nor the follow-up capacities to serve as overseers—much less as anything analogous to stockholders—of the enterprises that they create.

The Courts   The courts contribute to the ambiguity of controls over public authorities. (The specific effects of judicial rulings on public enterprise in the courts of fifty states are beyond the reach of this study.) Litigation relating to authority activities is multiplying, but judicial interpretations of public authority powers tend to be permissive. The courts are important participants in the complex game in which legislative, executive, and community groups contend for control over authorities, but they have failed to produce clear guidelines or rules. The corporate right to sue and be sued is useful to the enterprise, however. It means that authorities can control litigation involving them without relying on state or municipal attorneys and procedures. It is more difficult for taxpayers and public interest groups than for bondholders and their agents to challenge authority actions. The courts have seldom given standing to taxpayers and other general public interests trying to bring suit against authority expenditures or building plans. (Environmental protection groups have had more success than others.)

Judicial decisions determining the status of public authorities are inconsistent. As one judge has commented, "The legislation is mostly ad hoc, a wilderness of special instances, so policy considerations to some extent control us in deciding whether particular statutes which do not mention authorities do or do not apply to them."[44] When asked whether administrative control statutes apply to public authorities, the courts have generally held that authorities are not subdivisions of government. But in confirming the tax exemption of authority securities and property and the access of authorities to government credit and funds, the courts have repeatedly ruled that authorities are arms of government. For the most part, the courts have exempted commercial activities of authorities from local property taxes, even where the public corporations are collecting rents from private tenants. Municipalities must rely on agreements with authority managements to pay sums of money voluntarily "in lieu of taxes."

On the question of public purpose, the courts have been sufficiently permissive to make nearly everything that legislatures have authorized corporations to undertake legitimate public enterprises. A broad definition of public purpose, together with the special fund doctrine, which holds that government funds kept separately for earmarked purposes are exempted from normal treasury procedures and debt management regulations provides the legal basis for the public authority system. The language of one of the earliest cases upholding authorities seems particularly influential: "It is never an illegal evasion to accomplish a desired result, lawful in itself, by discovering a legal way to do it." [45] Most courts have made practical and permissive decisions with respect to lease-back arrangements, moral obligation borrowing, industrial revenue bonds, and other current extensions of public authority activities.

Suits involving questions on the frontiers of authority enterprise development are often brought as test cases by insiders. An attorney general may bring a test case in conjunction with an authority or with the authority's underwriters, on the advice of bond counsel, in order to test the legality of the bonds before they are offered for sale. For example, Pennsylvania in effect filed a lawsuit against itself to determine whether its Housing Finance Agency could sell tax-exempt bonds to finance Pennsylvania builders and thus stimulate private construction. [46] Test cases on industrial development bonds for pollution control were brought in a dozen states. Few surprises turned up. In one, the leading municipal bond firm in Washington State brought a test case to determine the constitutionality of a state law authorizing the use of tax-exempt revenue bonds to finance industrial pollution control facilities. The state supreme court ruled that the publicly issued tax-exempt bonds to finance pollution control facilities for private companies violated the provision of the state constitution that prohibits a gift or loan of public money or credit to industrial associations, companies, or corporations. [47] Similar cases have been decided the other way in other states: public authorities using the moral obligation arrangement to float bonds were held to be separate entities created for a public purpose; thus they did not lend the state credit illegally even though they financed private housing or hospitals, and their debt could not be equated with state debt. Courts in West

Virginia, New Jersey, Maine, Wisconsin, and Pennsylvania have confirmed that moral obligation debt is not a direct liability of the state and is therefore legal, although not approved at the polls.[48]

The potential for greater court intervention in authority control is real. It would be enhanced if states codified their public authorities laws and brought some order to the regulatory provisions that the courts might apply. In the meantime, local groups trying to prevent land from being taken on the basis of either property law or environmental impacts are turning increasingly to the courts for assistance in resisting authority decisions.

Most public authorities are exempted from the normal controls of state public utility commissions and their counterparts, although some states allow the public to appeal to the courts to review rate changes. Pennsylvania's local authorities are not subject to state public utility commission rulings, for example, but the courts may hear complaints about the "reasonableness or the uniformity" of prices, as well as the adequacy, safety, and reasonableness of services. Power authorities for the most part are subject to licensing requirements of the Federal Power Commission or state counterparts, and some of them are subject to rate regulation that more often than not grants requested increases. Transit operations that cross state lines are subject to ICC regulation, and the Federal Highway Administration now rules on interstate toll changes after court review.

Increased involvement of the courts in policy and pricing decisions seems to parallel general failure of elected leaders to make difficult decisions, failure that may be pushing more and more public authority issues into the courts. But the courts are simply not well suited to making broadly based policy decisions that affect land use, urban economics, tax costs, and even international relations.

Local Governments and Community Groups   The major effect of the public authority movement on local governments is to cut down their power. Most effective controls on authorities come from state government, and states have used the authority form to shift powers out of towns and cities into state-controlled regional authorities. This movement of public service management from local government to statutory corporations has prompted very little local protest, partly because the public services that authorities provide tend to be those in which the public takes little interest under normal conditions. But the public does take interest in authority activities that affect prices and land. Until relatively recently, authorities made relatively few price increases.

In the early 1970s, toll and bridge authorities that had been collecting revenues for years after the original facilities had been paid off and power authorities that had survived decades without rate increases were startled by the local response to price adjustments.

Land is one of the last vestiges of local control. In many cases, an authority must rely upon the municipality to make appropriate zoning clearances or to exercise powers of condemnation needed to provide land for authority projects. Cities and towns have defended these powers staunchly. More public authority proposals go down to defeat under assault on local land-use grounds than in state legislature debate. A local government's control over the disposition of land may give it leverage to bargain for in-lieu taxes and changes in authority projects.[49]

For the most part, however, municipal governments seem to lose more control than they gain from the authority movement. References to "municipal" corporations or "county" authorities are somewhat misleading because most of them are set up according to specifications of state legislation and are supervised by state governments. In addition, a number of state authorities—particularly with regional impact—have taken over local government services. For example, the Massachusetts Parking Authority was set up as a state agency empowered to construct a purely local parking garage in the city of Boston. But only one member of the authority was appointed by city officials, and the authority seized by eminent domain one-third of the Boston Common. (Its chairman, consulting engineer, and two lawyers were later indicted for larceny in connection with the construction of the garage.) Authority facilities often cut out of city budgets the services that yield revenues from user charges and add costs to city budgets by contributing to traffic problems, policy problems, fire hazards, sanitation burdens, the need for access routes, and so forth. The authority solution to regional problems tends to amputate from local governments only the revenue-producing services, isolating revenues from heavily burdened city budgets and leaving cities with the expensive services. Where the cities have to contribute to authority deficits without controlling their costs, the taxpayers have lost control over the expenditure process.

The pressures of regionalism generated by urban growth have been inexorable. Regional authorities do permit the existing local governments to survive, but the decisions of scores of regional corporations are very difficult for local citizens to follow, certainly more difficult than those of a general metropolitan government would be.

There are four major types of change in patterns of public enterprise management that warrant consideration: dependence on voter control of public enterprise; running enterprises through regular government departments; mixed ownership and intergovernmental boards, as used in Europe; and increasing federal government involvement, particularly in finance.

Voter Power

Many commentators on authority financing have urged that control over public borrowing be returned to the voters. Even some financial advisers and investment bankers who have made it their business to guide governments into the byzantine arrangements of contemporary authority finance, largely in order to avoid delays, expense, and negative results of popular elections, admit that as citizens they would prefer that all government debt be subject to voter approval.

State comptrollers and treasurers argue that commitments incurred without the approval of the people should not continue to mount and that the only way to halt them is to revert to the safeguards of regulation by state constitution. A treasurer of the state of Georgia phrased the argument emphatically: "I deny the right of any backdoor financing to place a direct lien upon the tangible property of the citizens of this state without a vote of those citizens. This is exactly what is happening in . . . lease rental agreements between the state or the local government structure and the authority itself."[1] Those pursuing reinforced constitutional control are opposed to independent authority financing. State and local governments, they say, should issue only general obligation bonds approved at general elections or subject to legal debt ceilings, with bond funds allocated through governmental capital budgets and profits retrievable by government treasuries. Public authorities should be permitted to borrow outside the laws applying to state and local debt only for projects that are in fact fully self-supporting from user charges. If this advice were implemented, authority investment would level off. The growth of public enterprise in partially and indirectly subsidized services would halt; public investment in these sectors would be dependent on special elections and bonds approved by special taxing districts.

This approach is fraught with monumental difficulties. The original constitutional mandates for voter approval of capital projects and borrowing were based on democratic faith that the electorate could and would wisely exercise its power of choice. Lessons of history cast doubt on the faith that

Progressives put in techniques of direct democracy, however. The influence of big organizations—corporate and governmental—over social and economic aspects of life has increased so enormously in both scope and complexity that meaningful public choices can seldom be expressed in "yes or no" questions. By the time such simple choices are presented to a voting public, the range of options has already been screened and narrowed by the combination of or-ganizations, officials, and culture that determines the contemporary agenda of public questions. Moreover, few citizens are willing or able to stay reasonably informed about the complexities of modern urban life and government. Few can apply the time and have the knowledge needed to dissect a general policy question into its internal fact and value organs. Robert Dahl, one of the more optimistic assessors of contemporary democracy, has pointed out that "the number of individuals that exercise significant control over the alternatives scheduled is . . . only a tiny fraction of the total membership."[2]

Those who do vote on these issues have been confronted with borrowing proposals that have become larger and larger in recent years. (The largest on record is Ohio's $4.5 billion proposal of 1975.) The voters have little chance to assess the projects likely to be funded from these huge amounts. Even the more explicit bond proposals put before the voters provide only general descriptions of the type of activities to be funded. Once the aggregate amount is approved, the actual bonds are issued at the discretion of the state or city officials, and the money may be spent during a decade of shifting priorities. The funds raised by the sale of bonds are held in capital budget revolving funds or similar treasury categories, and monies are often not committed to specific projects for several years after the amount of debt is authorized at the polls. Then the actual allocation may be made by executive fiat, within the terms of the bond proposal, and in the format of capital budgeting over which legislatures and legislative finance committes have minimal control. Occasionally, substantial portions of large bond issues of state governments remain unspent five or more years after the borrowing was authorized by vote.

The choice presented to the voters at the time of the referendum gives them little opportunity to react to priorities among alternative kinds of projects (such as highways or transit) and no opportunity for participation in key decisions—choice of site, project implications for future urban land use, distribution of services between ghetto residents seeking access to jobs and suburbanites who have them, alternative investment possibilities (such as housing or health care). All of these are determined outside the voting framework;

what the voter sees is a compact, difficult to read paragraph at the bottom of a ballot.

In short, a formal vote on substantive issues is seldom a very meaningful public choice. At best the electorate can only ratify (or not) the options favored by particularly influential groups and historical biases.

Far fewer people bother to vote on state and local issues than on candidates in national elections. It appears that closeness to the home does not necessarily make an issue salient to the average voter. Moreover, public opinion research suggests that the choices most voters make are based primarily on preconceived notions and fragmentary information.[3] The vote cast for bond proposals is lower than the total vote cast in local elections generally. Substantially fewer than half the eligible voters register their choice in state bond elections, and some major decisions are made by fractional majorities. In 1973, when voters rejected the Trinity River canal project in Texas, the seventeen-county area comprised one million eligible voters; the bond proposal was defeated by a margin of 21,000 votes, with a total of 253,000 ballots cast. Some state constitutions require special majorities—for example, 60 percent of votes cast for certain types of bonding programs in West Virginia and two-thirds of the vote in some local referenda in California. The requirement of special majorities, given small voter turnouts, further skews the arithmetic of marginal approvals and raises serious questions about what and whom the vote represents.

The Supreme Court has ruled that its one-man, one-vote mandate need not be observed in electing officials of special purpose bodies, such as special districts and public authorities, that do not perform "governmental" functions. A federal court held that the directors of a California water district could be elected by property owners where other residents were not permitted to vote. The voting system in that case provided for proportional voting based on property values owned, so that one company cast 37,825 votes.[4]

Increasing reliance on electoral control of public enterprise might result in a preference for the "special district" over the public authority or the growth of enterprise within government departments using capital borrowed by city or state. California provides one of the leading examples of reliance on a combination of tax-supported special districts and departmentalized enterprise. The magnitude of California's revenue bond borrowing (nonguaranteed debt) is modest compared to that of other states of comparable size (see the appendix). The nonguaranteed debt of the state of New York

Table 11.1
Importance of Nonguaranteed Debt in California and New York, 1972
(Thousands of Dollars)

	California	New York
Total long-term state and local government debt outstanding	$17,648,296	$24,295,261
Percent increase, 1962–1972	106%	86%
State government long-term debt	$ 6,132,093	$ 7,943,900
Percent nonguaranteed	12%	63%
Local government long-term debt	$11,516,203	$16,351,361
Percent nonguaranteed	34%	23%

Source: U.S. Bureau of the Census, 1972 Census of Governments, vol. 4, Government Finances, no. 5, Compendium, tables 46,48.

was nearly seven times that of California in 1972 (see table 11.1). California relies more heavily than eastern states do on voter participation in the expansion of its enterprises, and its voters have been more willing to approve debt for specific development-oriented operations than voters in the East.

The California state constitution provides that the legislature cannot delegate to special purpose corporations the activities traditionally performed by municipal governments, with the exception of irrigation, reclamation, and drainage districts. Otherwise local utilities are set up by local vote, not by state law. To issue bonds, a municipal utility needs the vote of two-thirds of its electors and often an annual tax to pay debt service. Corporations providing light, water, power, heat, transportation, and other services have been subject to municipal regulation of prices and rates or placed under the jurisdiction of a municipal public utilities commission.

California's Revenue Bond Law, enacted in 1941, permits all types of political subdivisions to issue revenue bonds through either a public vote or a special act of the local legislature. Several jurisdictions can get together to issue revenue bonds, and many such groups have formed to set up lease-purchase financing of joint projects (circumventing the two-thirds vote required for general municipal debt; regional revenue bonds require only a simple majority).

The state government is required to obtain a majority vote at a referendum for state debt proposals, and the secretary of state is required to mail a ballot pamphlet to each voter giving pro and con arguments on the project to be financed by proposed bonds prior to the election. State government has made modest use of revenue bonds and contingent liability (as of 1974, California had not used moral obligation devices for borrowing), and California's securities are currently favored over those of New York.

The special district as an alternative has its own occasional abuses—not the least of them being proliferation. California's special districts are exceeded in number and total expenditures only by those of Illinois.[5] But California has relatively few authorities in the sense of corporations without taxing power, governed by independent boards of directors, and relying on revenue bonds to raise capital.

The most dramatic abuses of voter power in special districts occur when the interested citizens are too few to justify election. Local utility districts provide some extreme examples. In California, Texas, and Pennsylvania, subdivision and other real estate developers establish special districts or utility authorities in any of several ways: by petition (signed by themselves and their colleagues representing the initial landowners); by election (again by themselves and their first buyers who may also be investors in the development company); or by local council charter or special state statute. The new special district or utility can raise cheap capital by issuing tax-exempt notes and by voting to increase long-term debt to be paid off ultimately by the permanent residents of the completed subdivision or (in some Texas authorities) by the taxpayers of a central city, which ultimately annexes the territory of the new suburban subdivision. In the meantime, the developer finances the basic services for his subdivision but avoids the burdens of private loans and commercial interest rates and in some cases sells the tax-exempt bonds to himself or his company.

Neither resort to the legislature nor resort to election has controlled these abuses. Where elections are required, small electorates can approve large bond issues. In 1972, in fifty-nine water district bond elections in the Houston-Galveston area, 887 voters approved $216 million in debt. In one of these elections, a single voter approved a $4 million bond issue. Only five of the fifty-nine elections involved more than ten people, and fifty-four of the fifty-nine bond issue proposals were passed unanimously. In one Texas municipal utility district in 1977, sixteen voters decided that eventual residents would assume debts up to $55 million.

Special legislation may involve even fewer participants. For example, in Harris County, near Houston, over a hundred utility districts have been created by bills introduced by two state legislators in two sessions. The special districts were designed by bond attorneys, and their statutes are virtually identical. The statutes exempt each district from normal regulation and name its initial board of directors. With few exceptions, the legal advice regarding the water districts was provided by Houston attorney Cyril J. Smith of Smith, Rowe, Fisher & Hay. (That firm, along with two others—Vinson Elkins, of which John Connally was a partner, and Fulbright Crooker & Jaworski, of which former special federal prosecutor Leon Jaworski was a partner—dominate legal opinions for Texas water and utility districts.) An observer of the Texas political scene has provided an explanation for the recourse to districts and the shift from those approved by election to those approved by legislation:

With careful planning, a realistic promoter could turn a waste land into a vast community with funds obtained from the sale of public bonds. There would be no need to worry whether his credit was solid enough to obtain bank loans or whether he would be able to repay the funds obtained from other people through the sale of public bonds. If the enterprise failed, the water district, not he, was obligated to pay off the bonds. There were, however, problems with the private use of water districts. It was a lot of trouble to arrange petitions and elections. The provisions for court hearings and such created grave danger that the enterprise would receive more attention than the promoter wished. During the 1960s more and more of Cyril Smith's clients opted for the municipal utility district rather than its counterpart [the water district].[6]

Local sources report that special legislation to create a utility district costs the developer $2,000—half for the lawyer and half for the legislator who sponsors the bill—plus regular legal fees. The causes of this cannot be diagnosed as party organization politics or cured by business leadership, for it is business leadership that mans the political machinery.

The water district conspirators have not been obtaining their legal advice from sleazy shysters, but from the cream of the Texas legal establishment. And the conspirators themselves are hardly disreputable types. . . . They are a pretty awesome social and political force. Since that force operates mostly in the shadows, it is very difficult for the average person to estimate accurately its scope and strength. But the water district conspiracy does provide a valuable clue.[7]

Texas law (which prohibits branch banking) supports the proliferation of independent small banks that buy the bonds. These independent banks and respectable law firms have traditionally been represented on the boards of special districts and public authorities in the state.

The requirements of elections to create and govern public enterprise sometimes has a braking effect. In the 1960s, throughout the United States, election campaigns for metropolitan government and water fluoridation demonstrated dramatically the negative tendencies of referenda with low voter participation. In many such elections, opponents were typically able to defeat a program simply by generating fear and uncertainty where the public lacked solid information about the program and its likely results. Inclinations to defeat an issue are also manifested by participants in municipal bond elections. Public opinion surveys have shown that people favor extension of government services but oppose extension of financial burdens.[8] From 1926 to 1976, the proportion of borrowing approved in each year's municipal bond elections declined from 76 percent to 58.7 percent, with variations from year to year. The record low of 29.3 percent was in 1975 (when Ohio's $4.5 billion proposal was defeated). Total volume of tax-exempt borrowing, however, hit a record high in 1975, giving testimony to the success and growth of nonvoted revenue bond financing. On the average, voters have approved just over half of the amounts asked for.[9] Public authority borrowing proposals do not experience these cutbacks.

Success at the polls varies with the objectives of the proposal. Returning to a dependence upon narrowly based elections would reduce public investment, especially in such sectors as social services, education, and low-income housing.[10] Roads, bridges, tunnels, water supply, sewers, and other utilities—the classic revenue bond services—are much more popular with voters. (These are also the projects that are likely to generate their own income for debt service. Some states still subject them to voter approval.)[11] In 1973, industrial pollution control bonds that required voter approval also earned high approval rates, though benefits from these projects accrued primarily to private firms in heavy industry.

State and local elected officials, both Democratic and Republican, tend to support higher rates of capital construction by government than do the voters. Some officials charge that low voter support reflects the irresponsible tendencies of those who dominate low-turnout elections. Of course, governors and mayors are more aware than the average voter of the needs for capital facilities. And elected officials can also derive special advantages from the construction of public facilities that generate business for contractors, construction unions, engineers, bankers, lawyers, and other groups active in campaign finance and other aspects of politics, without the restraints imposed by requirements for current taxes or appropriations. The near-invisibility of public corporation debt provides officials an opportunity to seem conservative while actually increasing government activities and capital expenditures.

In short, the ruling out of authority end runs around bond elections would have a conservative effect overall. In particular, it would slow the growth of public capital expenditure for public health facilities, transportation services, sewage treatment, school buildings, and subsidized housing. Investment priorities would tend to be more responsive to popular fads: for example, in the early 1970s, bond issue elections favored industrial development projects over housing. The groups who prefer special elections as a means of political decision making also may seek programs that elections tend to defeat. And devices adopted in the name of participatory democracy often do not actually distribute power more widely. Theories of democratic means must be revised to fit the actual psychological and social profile of the citizenry and the tasks of modern government. Calls for a total elimination of nonvoted debt seem bound to fail because neither the practical pressures for investment in public projects nor the negative impact of voting patterns is likely to change in the short run.

Rather than tightening public debt regulations in order to outlaw subsidized corporate revenue bonds, reform might ease debt regulations in order to reduce the appeal of the public authority device and make it easier for general governments to raise the funds themselves. The Pennsylvania constitutional revision, for example, and similar changes pending in Ohio, facilitate investment by elected governments and reduce procedural nuisances that do not substantially broaden meaningful public participation in decision making. Governments need reasonable borrowing powers and should not be forced into using obscuring debt within independent corporations. Within broad debt limits, based on a percentage of the full and varied tax base, state and local legislatures should be able to issue both general obligation and revenue bonds without special elections. The executive should submit an annual financial plan that shows the burden of debt service and the allocation of investment by agencies and corporations, by program types, by specific areas served, and by groups benefited, in a form suitable for reporting in the media and consideration in the legislature. Only this kind of public information can help shift the initiative for influencing public investment processes from private to public groups. Special elections on special issues have not served that purpose. The issue of public debt should be subject to informed discussion in the normal course of campaign and legislative politics.

Departmental Enterprise

GAO has long contended that agencies within regular departments of government can effectively carry out business-type programs. Federal experience with the Alaska Railroad, Washington National Airport, housing mortgage credit operations, four major electric power producing bureaus, and scores of enterprises within the military departments bear out this judgment (see the appendix and chart 10.1). Special adaptations of departmental practices can give agencies some of the advantages of public authorities or government corporations (for example, through use of revolving funds into which both subsidies and operating revenues can flow and which can be used without fiscal year budget limitations). State and local agencies that wish to issue revenue bonds on the tax-exempt market can be given particular characteristics that will assure investors of their permanence and the integrity of their finances. The Maryland Environmental Service, for example, was granted "perpetual existence" by statute. It is an instrument of the state, operated within a state department, but its three senior officers form a board of directors to approve issuance of revenue bonds. It can borrow, enter into contracts, and receive fees in its own name, but the department head retains the right to approve policies.

Similarly, municipal utilities have more independence than have agencies with non-revenue-producing activities. In some instances, employees in revenue-producing agencies within governments are exempted from some civil service procedures. Throughout the western states, local governments issue revenue bonds, particularly for municipal utilities, without pledging the full faith and credit of the government yet without the use of independent corporations. (Since 1968, Pennsylvania municipalities also may issue revenue bonds outside normal public finance restraints.) In fact, the issuer of the first reported revenue bonds secured solely by net earnings was not an authority but the city of Spokane, Washington, which borrowed for its waterworks in 1897. Municipal electric and water distribution systems may set up depreciation reserves and bond service reserves into which revenues flow before surplus earnings are drawn off into general city budgets.

Like government corporations, departmental enterprises can operate in regional markets. The Los Angeles, New York City, and Detroit water departments are large-scale public enterprises that service their own cities, as well as surrounding towns and counties. They raise capital by issuing general obligation water bonds or governmental revenue bonds, sell water wholesale by

intergovernmental contract, and distribute it retail within their own jursidic-
tions. City budgets can reflect the income and expenditures of the water
departments.

In fact, a wide variety of agents can conduct the public's business: separate
agencies within the state, city, or federal government; bureaus that are
components of broader departments of those governments; mixed corporations with combined private and public ownership; regulated or franchised
private corporations; government contracts with otherwise unregulated
private firms; and hybrids of these forms.

The California Water Project illustrates an effective partnership of federal,
state, and city departments. Lacking the political clout of the Texans and
promotional flair of Robert Moses, California's planners and engineers of the
mid-1930s had failed to sell authority bonds to the Reconstruction Finance
Corporation or the Public Works Administration. Instead, the Federal Bureau
of Reclamation built the Central Valley water supply project under the
federal reclamation law and with federally appropriated funds. In 1959, the
state authorized the California Water Project, an aqueduct system running the
length of the state, to distribute the water produced by the Central Valley
project. The state Department of Water Resources planned, built, and operates the system, selling the wholesale water allocations by contract to both
public and private distributors, who pay the net costs of the system. It first
delivered water to southern California in 1972. Money raised by state sale of
revenue bonds is not mingled with other state funds but is deposited in a
special fund, supplemented by some earmarked taxes and state receipts and
by some monies raised by state general obligation bonds.

One of the California Water Project's major customers is the huge Metropolitan Water District of southern California, a wholesale distributor. Its
member municipalities retail water to consumers or make arrangements for
private or public agencies to do so. The Metropolitan District's board of
directors includes at least one director from each member agency, plus
additional representatives proportionate to assessed valuation available for
district taxing purposes. Voting power is weighted.

One of the retail distribution systems is the Los Angeles city Department
of Water and Power. This forty-year-old municipal system is part of the city
government of Los Angeles. (The 1974 movie *Chinatown* drew on the department's colorful history and crucial role in the development of the region's
land.) Its combined operations of water supply and electric power distribution
are self-supporting. It issues departmental revenue bonds and maintains its

capital monies and operating revenues in separate special funds. It is managed by an expert technical staff, and it employs the accounting systems used by private utilities. Although its staff is under civil service, the department has its own union wage scale. Is is supervised by a board of five commissioners appointed by the mayor of Los Angeles with the approval of the city council, but the general manager provides concentrated direction. The city charter prescribes in detail the independent powers of the department. It has retained a high credit rating even though the city can tap its excess revenues with the consent of the board.

European Variations

The forms that public and quasi-public enterprises take are more flexible and varied in Europe than in the United States. Numerous European enterprises feature representative boards of directors and governmental controls over project priorities, excess revenues, and public subsidies.

In West Germany, public corporations are concentrated in banking, transport, energy, and utilities.[12] Table 11.2 shows the importance of public corporations in total West German business volume and the levels of government involved. (The figures in the table are twenty years old, but later data have not been collected. According to German authorities, however, the approximate shares of the market have not changed significantly. An insufficiency of data on public corporations is obviously not a problem unique to the United States.) Community and regional corporations in West Germany are heavily involved in transit operations, utilities, ports, markets and other wholesaling services, banking and credit, and home construction.

Like U.S. public enterprises, those of West Germany are not products of socialist movements or of explicit ideologies of public ownership. Since the feudal lords ran profitable enterprises and medieval cities provided services essential for local trade and commerce, certain economic and administrative activities—particularly warehousing, ports, and markets—have been considered governmental responsibilities. The growth of modern public enterprise is closely associated with the development of private capitalism. During the late nineteenth century, Germany industrialized rapidly and the national government took part in providing infrastructures for expanding national commerce, particularly for capital-intensive industries such as railroads and mining. The relationship between private and public sectors in Germany at this stage was based on mercantilist principles. Major expansions in government economic

Table 11.2
Percentage Share of Public Corporations in Total Business Volume in Various Sectors of the Economy in West Germany, 1954

Sector of Economy	All levels of government	Percentage of governmental share by level of government (all levels equal 100 percent)		
		National government	Länder (including city-states)	Community and regional corporations
Agriculture	0.6	66.7		33.2
Forestry	77.5	3.2	50.5	46.2
Fisheries	12.5	20.0	60.0	20.0
Subtotal agriculture	7.9	7.7	48.1	44.2
Coal mining	39.4	100.0		
Other mining	21.7	53.8	46.2	
Energy (including combined utilities and transit corporation)	73.0	12.1	26.1	61.8
Steel and metal industries	16.5	100.0		
Heavy equipment	3.0	86.4	13.6	
Automobile industry	19.6	100.0		
Oil industry	1.9	100.0		
Subtotal industry and manufacturing	9.6	41.9	21.7	36.3
Wholesale	2.5	45.8	0.8	53.4
Banking and credit	61.0	14.0	46.0	40.0
Home construction	20.0	1.0	9.0	90.0
Transport and communications	67.1	89.4	3.3	7.3
Total (all government economic activities of public corporations)	8.9	52.7	14.3	33.0

Source: Willi Albers, "Öffentliche Erwerbseinkunfte," in *Handwörterbuch der Sozialwissenschaften*, Göttingen, 1960.

activity took place precisely when private enterprise was fast growing. (While German government was providing capital for industrial investment, sources of private capital in Britain were financing similar investments in the United States, such as those for the development of privately owned railroads.) In Germany, this expansion of government investment also encouraged the development of public banking.

Like American public authorities, German municipal and regional corporations are run by strong, business-oriented managers, and below the managerial level, the civil service and other procedural regulations of government do not apply. Also like American public authorities, the corporations experience pressures for patronage or favoritism (such pressures are found in nearly every political system known to man), and they manage to fend off the most destructive of these pressures, at least to the extent of minimizing interference with operations.

Most West German public corporations, however, are more closely tied in with the governments that own them than are standard American public authorities. Elected local officials usually choose the governing board or sit on it. The sponsoring government controls the basic finances of the corporation. And the corporations themselves enjoy greater flexibility for merger, growth, diversification, and other adaptive functions than do public firms in the United States. In German cities, for example, local transit and utilities corporations often merge; the profits of the utilities operations thus absorb the deficits of the transit operations.

An example is the Stadtwerke Mannheim, which was, until 1973, a conglomerate of four corporations: two transit companies, one utilities distribution operation, and one power and water enterprise. Although it was incorporated, it was under the direct supervision of the Mannheim city government. Its managing council was appointed by and overlapped with the city council, and its net profits or losses appeared in the city budget. But its manager ran it as a business enterprise, and each of the subsidiary companies had a good deal of operating independence.

The manager of Stadtwerke Mannheim is a business executive of high standing, who has managed to triple the volume of services without increasing the number of employees, partly by computerizing operations. The utility segments of the corporation produce a sizable profit, and the transit sections have run up large deficits. To some extent, electric and gas rates have reflected transit deficits. The manager was not happy with this arrangement—which he called a distribution of "welfare payments" because utility rates subsidized the transit fare—but the company had no trouble obtaining funds for capital investments and other needs.

In 1973, a new regional transportation conglomerate of which the city of Mannheim is a major shareholder took over the two transit companies. The Mannheim city government organized a new corporation, with a board appointed by but more independent from the city council than that of the old Stadtwerke Mannheim, to run the other two enterprises. The new board includes employees of the corporation, giving internal management an important role in direction, but the city's mayor remains chairman of the board, the usual arrangement in wholly owned municipal corporations. (No bond covenants or other financing agreements limited the options for reorganization.)

Except for transit, public enterprises in West Germany are profitable. Regional and municipal utilities corporations make significant contributions to the revenues of local government. Cities have their own utilities corporations, which purchase power or water wholesale from regional enterprises. Nearly all the municipalities and counties of West Germany own savings banks or other banking institutions, such as home finance corporations. Municipal corporations also provide markets, warehouses, port services, fair grounds, recreation facilities, auditoriums, stadiums, hotels, and restaurants.

German municipal corporations differ from their American counterparts in their method of financing. They raise capital from three sources: their own revenues, often fattened by price policy and by accelerated depreciation;[13] grants or loans from government; and commercial borrowings from government-owned banks. The West German government provides no special tax exemptions for borrowing by public corporations; West Germany has no tax-exempt bond market, and it taxes the interest on bonds and other securities of German public corporations just as if it were earned from the securities of private firms. Nevertheless, German public enterprise has never had difficulty raising capital. The government that owns a public enterprise is assumed liable in cases of financial difficulty; special moral obligation provisions or other methods of establishing contingent liability are thus unnecessary. Being government organizations, public corporations are considered among the safest investments in the nation. Because much of their capital comes from savings bank loans, and because the savings banks themselves are municipal or county institutions that give some priority to public investments, the public corporations enjoy a steady source of capital.

Municipal and county savings banks in Germany are legally permitted a 5 percent rate of profit; profits exceeding that amount are transferred to the owning municipality or county. Savings banks throughout the country tend to keep their profits at the 5 percent level in order to avoid the transfer and to keep the costs of local credit as low as possible. If a bank operates with a deficit, the county or city that owns it is obligated to fill up its reserves.

Other types of public corporations transfer their net profits or net losses directly to the regular budget of the county or municipality that owns them. Still others, particularly the intergovernmental regional enterprises, are controlled through membership voting or shares of ownership held by the several local governments and other public corporations that participated in creating the enterprise. None of these forms of governmental control of public enterprise finances seems to interfere unduly with the internal management of the corporation. In fact, as a result of pressures from local politicians for profitability, consistent with price policy, German corporations seem to have more concern than most American public authorities for holding down costs.

West Germany has dealt with urban growth largely through regionalization of public enterprise, experimenting with a grand variety of corporate arrangements to provide for regional functions, generally without disturbing the traditional boundaries of local government. For example, water supply is a local concern, but in German as in American urban areas, needs for water have outgrown local sources. The local governments in the Stuttgart region have therefore formed the joint Regional Water Resources Corporation. Some hundred public entities—cities, counties, towns, and other public corporations—own the corporation collectively (in this case, no shares are issued). A membership assembly governs it, with votes distributed in proportion to agreements to purchase water, measured in allotments. The members buy the allotments, or drawing rights, and proportionate levies are collected from them. In theory the corporation is run by an executive committee chosen by the membership assembly, but in practice it is run by the managers—an engineer and a business executive. The mayor of Stuttgart is chairman of the committe, but the managers feel they are fully in charge of corporate operations.

Unlike local banks, which have created subsidiary businesses such as home construction firms, and unlike the diversified Stadtwerke Mannheim, the Stuttgart Regional Water Resources Corporation is a single-purpose corporation limited in law to providing its members with potable water at the least possible cost. It has no taxing power and must cover costs through the price at which it sells water to its members. The member governments provide investment capital through subsidies and long-term commercial loans. Operating costs are covered from the wholesale price of water.

This structure provides a means of handling political debates in an appropriate arena—the membership assembly where conflicts over the division of allotments (and therefore of costs and water rights) among the city and outlying towns are resolved. It protects the permanent staff from debilitating overinvolvement in political conflicts without eliminating representative leadership.

Although the structure and legal base of public enterprise in Britain are quite different from those in Germany, being, among other things, more centralized, British public enterprises also show greater responsiveness to government policy than U.S. public authorities do. For example, the Port of London Authority (PLA), on which the Port Authority of New York and New Jersey was reputedly modeled, differs from U.S. port authorities in that it not only owns the port facilities and leases docks out but actually employs the dockworkers, providing the loading and unloading and related services directly to shipping companies. As a result, the PLA participates in the more trouble-ridden aspects of port management, including longshoremen-union disputes, automating the docks, and unpredictable revenue trends. The Port Authority of New York and New Jersey wants no part of such activities. The British government has specified the lines along which labor disputes are settled and ordered the PLA to provide lump sum payments (the "golden handshake") to workers forced into early retirement by automation on the docks. The PLA management expresses the characteristic distaste of authority leadership at having to fulfill such social functions of public policy, but it is accustomed to these impositions and has modernized the London Port despite what some might call government interference.

Since 1970, the PLA reports to the British Department of the Environment. Its board, previously twenty-eight members, some of them nominated by shippers and other user groups, now consists of fifteen appointees of the departmental secretary, including four authority management executives. New management is decentralizing commercial operations. Financing methods have also changed. For many years the PLA raised capital through debentures sold on private money markets. The debentures imposed no specific conditions on authority expenditures. The PLA also received government harbor loans, which were tied to specific projects (and were available for private enterprises as well). The London Port is no longer operated for profit, and the authority depends mainly on the government funds. The departmental secretary has powers of approval over important harbor development projects, and British law has made PLA responsible for pollution control in the port and on the River Thames. The pollution control responsibilities must be financed out of the overhead budget without special government funding. The authority is developing long-term pollution control standards for effluent discharges and is required to enforce them against commercial and industrial enterprises along the river. (The enterprises can appeal the PLA decisions to the Department of Trade and Industry.)

Unlike the Port Authority of New York and New Jersey, the PLA does not operate airports. The British Airport Authority operates five and has turned deficits to profits in the first decade of its existence. It raises its capital directly from the government and (like the U.S. government's St.Lawrence Seaway Corporation) can adjust repayment schedules according to cost pressures and price policy.

Throughout Britain, electric power and water boards provide services through forms of enterprise management that are internally similar to American public authorities. But the government also sets pricing policy, and the board members tend to be local government officials and professionals with lifetime careers in public enterprise rather than businessmen or bankers.

Another example of public enterprise in Europe is the Italian Institute for Industrial Reconstruction (IRI).[14] It was created in 1933 to serve much the same purpose as the U.S. Reconstruction Finance Corporation. IRI has grown into a gigantic holding company that invests in public services, has been a major factor in the development of southern Italy, and competes with American-sponsored multinational corporations in buying up shares of local Italian companies. It is a multisectoral enterprise that engages in management, production, and finance in numerous industries. Some of its operations parallel the jobs done by public authorities in the United States, particularly constructing and operating toll highways.

IRI's leadership comes from a central institute with a relatively small, high-powered staff that formulates policy for the series of holding companies under it. It uses profits as a yardstick for performance but bases its accounting on longer and broader assessments of returns from a project than might be acceptable to private enterprise groups concerned exclusively with their own short-term financial returns. Its financial analyses take cognizance of external or social effects, and it is required to pay 65 percent of its annual net profits to the government. The Italian government provides subsidies through an endowment fund for the costs of noncommercial activities, such as maintaining unprofitable shipping lines, that the government has declared are in the national interest. The consolidated bonds that IRI issues do not carry a formal state guarantee, but the Italian version of moral obligation is the general belief that the state would prevent default.

In France, the Paris transit company (Régie Autonome des Transports) provides transit services throughout its urban area, drawing on subsidies from three levels of government to compensate for its substantial operating deficits. In that respect, it is similar to U.S. transit authorities. Legally an independent public authority of a commercial nature, it is run by an intergovernmental board of twenty members, including an appointed corporate president and representatives of local governments, national government departments, and employees, together with five private members, appointed for special competence. Paris transit's management submits an annual budget, which is balanced and includes a suggested fare structure to meet costs; it nearly always proposes a fare increase. If government fails to approve the fare increase, public subsidy is allotted to cover the resultant deficit in the operating budget. The government subsidy is divided by a fixed formula among the national government, the city of Paris, and the region's counties (*départements*). The national government supplies capital funds for expansion projects but channels them through a regional planning and investment agency that weighs priorities among different local governments, corporations, and projects (transportation, housing, water and sewer, recreation, and so forth) in the region.

All of these European counterparts of American public authorities have problems as well as advantages, like any complex organization. But they do illustrate a variety of methods to adjust public enterprise to social needs, to modify profit criteria, and to provide for subsidized services. When a government forces an enterprise to undertake activities that are inherently unprofitable or to provide certain services at price levels below cost, regular arrangements provide for a routine infusion of tax-based funds. Conversely, when a public enterprise operates at a substantial profit on the basis of arbitrarily fixed prices and distributed monopoly rights, the government generally has devised some method of either changing the enterprise's price policy or using the resultant profits. Insulation from regular governmental institutions is not a prerequisite of orderly enterprise management.

The sudden and apparently unexpected collapse of New York's Urban

Development Corporation in 1975 and the reaction to it would not have occurred in Britain, France, or Germany for four reasons. First, planned projects would not have ballooned so far out of line with government's ability to finance them, because nothing comparable to bond market lending and promotion is available to inflate enterprise borrowing. Second, in Europe, housing subsidies are not subjected to the dramatic fluctuations that accompany changes in administrations and political party control in the United States. (UDC's revenue forecasts changed drastically because of sudden cutbacks in federal housing subsidies.) Such abrupt changes in public housing finance policy do not take place in Britain even with shifts from Labour to Conservative governments, despite the common generalization that American parties are closer in outlook than British parties. Third, the liability of the government for committed debts of a public corporation owned by it is not subject to question in Europe. And fourth, government lending institutions in Europe provide an alternative to the necessarily fickle judgments of bankers and private investors.

Federal Influences

To a considerable extent, the rapid growth of public authorities since World War II, the ballooning debt of these and other state and local government bodies from 1960 to 1975, and the kinds of facilities in which funds were invested are consequences of federal government actions: various banking regulations; historical terms of federal aid; specific legislation permitting expansion of public power generation; reclamation or flood control projects; federal programs aiding and stimulating local hospital, sewer, and housing construction; and operating subsidies for state and local housing and transit corporations. Of course, the tax laws above all have shaped public enterprise in the United States. In 1976, the IRS renewed an attempt to bring investment by public authorities to a complete halt by preparing regulations that would eliminate tax exemption from all enterprise operations that are not subject to close control directly by state or municipal governments. The draft regulations have been criticized by congressmen and would have to survive attack in the courts to have widespread impact, but the IRS continues piecemeal battles against the growth of authority financing by claiming that specific cases, such as community development authorities and a state university, do not qualify as political subdivisions of state or local government.[15] At minimum, this effort is likely to render the bond attorneys more conservative (less innovative) in their opinions on authority financings in the near future.

The municipal bond market is the only major securities market that has operated outside the scope of the Securities and Exchange Commission's routine regulatory jurisdiction. It has succeeded in doing so by being relatively responsible and politically alert. Those public interests that the unregulated tax-exempt market may place at a disadvantage are diffuse and largely uninformed; hence, they are an uneven match for the active participants who benefit from the status quo. It is only the staggering growth in the volume of capital raised for public enterprise that has called the freedom of the municipal bond market into question. Among the recurring proposals before Congress in recent years (in addition to limitations on tax exemption) are provisions for alternative, taxable bonds; federal regulation of the municipal securities market; easing of the banking law restrictions on revenue bond underwriting by commercial banks; and creation of new federal financing corporations to expand alternative sources of capital for state and local enterprise.

The public authorities have maintained a relatively low profile throughout the elaborate lobbying and intra-alliance maneuvering on these issues. The underwriters' groups, state financial officials, and the Municipal Finance Officers Association have been surrogates for the authorities throughout most of the struggle, although the public authority associations have done some backup lobbying where necessary.

The expansion of public enterprise has been so closely tied into the private bond market that advocates of public power, public transit, public port development, and so forth are loath to consider specific changes that might upset this system, even though they may be disposed in principle to favor reform of taxes, securities, and grants-in-aid. The congressional committees that deal with these issues also are decidedly cautious. All of the available testimony comes from insiders and raises issues involving complex questions of comprehensive tax reform, securities regulation, and urban aid.

Tax Reform Beginnings   The exemption of state and local securities from federal taxes dates back to early U.S. tax history. The federal government exempted the United States Bank from state taxation on the grounds that the power to tax involves the power to destroy.[16] Using this precedent, over the course of the nineteenth century, states and municipalities succeeded in winning exemption from federal taxation for their bonds. In 1913, the Sixteenth Amendment to the U.S. Constitution empowered Congress to collect taxes on incomes "from whatever source derived." But Congress has continued to exempt state and local securities from the income tax by legislation.[17]

In the early 1920s, in the early and late 1930s, in the mid-1940s, and again in the late 1950s and the 1960s, tax reform groups mounted vigorous campaigns against this exemption. They consistently maintained that the exemption impairs the application of progressive rates of taxation, encourages misapplication of state and local government resources by establishing financial incentives that are unrelated to policy priorities, causes a hidden transfer of wealth from the average taxpayer to rich investors in bonds and to project beneficiaries, drains savings from taxable capital investments, and costs the U.S. Treasury a great deal in lost taxes.

The supporters of tax exemption have argued primarily that taxing interest payments received from municipal bonds would add to state and local borrowing costs, increase the burdens on regressive property taxes, and inhibit public investment. They also have argued that change would destroy the federal system and that tax immunity for state and local government, and their corporations, is so deeply rooted in the Constitution as to have survived the Sixteenth Amendment. The battle has always been waged in a small arena —two or three specialized congressional committees. Until 1968, supporters of tax exemption kept all reform measures from reaching the floor of Congress.

The Port Authority and Triborough Bridge and Tunnel Authority have been the two authorities most visible in the tax debates. Austin Tobin was one of the founding fathers of the Conference on State Dissent, a coalition of state and local government officials that was formed in 1938 to resist Treasury Department assault on the tax exemption. In 1972, he was still a major national spokesman on the subject, leading discussions at the Municipal Finance Officers Association annual conference. Robert Moses also participated, consistently providing a colorful, if overdramatic, assessment of the issue: "The entire structure of tax exempt government and quasi-public authority debt is now threatened by the congressional search for new revenues and by the normal popularity of soaking the rich."[18]

In any case, by the mid-1960s, support for broad tax reform was widespread. It focused on the example of Mrs. Horace Dodge, a wealthy widow portrayed as living in luxury and paying no taxes on a $1 million annual income from municipal bonds.[19] Another impetus to reform was the revival of the industrial revenue bond, a revival that was causing the U.S. Treasury to incur staggering tax losses and hurting northern states which were losing industry to southern states where public agencies were lending to private firms in large numbers.

Since the financial debacles of the nineteenth century, most state constitutions had prohibited the lending of credit or granting of money by governments to private persons or corporations. Exceptions for certain public purposes—notably housing—had been common, but in the 1960s, efforts to attract industry to depressed areas cut broader roads around the restrictions. As of 1960, thirteen states had authorized public agencies to issue tax-exempt industrial development bonds (IDBs) and use the proceeds to aid private industry. By 1968, thirty-eight states had legislation providing for IDBs. Where counties and municipalities were not permitted to issue these bonds, incorporated authorities were created to do so. Using these arrangements, diversified investment banking houses brought the benefits of tax-exempt financing to their private corporate clients: $82.5 million for Armco Steel Corporation, $60 million for Sinclair Petro Chemical, $80 million for West Virginia Pulp and Paper, $75 million for Georgia-Pacific Corporation, $130 million for Litton Industries, and so forth. One port authority in Oregon borrowed $140 million to construct facilities for a Japanese-owned aluminum company. That figure exceeded the total net debt of all Oregon municipalities.

In Pennsylvania, a new class of municipal authorities was created for this kind of borrowing. These local authorities issued revenue bonds and paid them off from lease-rental payments made by private corporations. When the bonds were paid off, the title to the facilities constructed passed to the private firm, which had in effect purchased a new plant at low cost by gaining access to tax-exempt borrowing. This type of financing attained such volume that, by the late 1960s, it was cutting into the funds available for regular public purposes. In 1968, the volume of new IDB financing was $2 billion, and the Treasury Department projected annual federal tax losses of $200 million from bonds of this type.

The game had been overplayed, and even some of the fans deserted. Objections to runaway IDB financing came from some of the groups that had previously fought any limits on tax exemption: the Investment Bankers Association (predecessor of the Securities Industry Association), the municipal law section of the American Bar Association, and the Municipal Finance Officers Association. In 1968, the Internal Revenue Service ruled against the IDB tax exemption; the SEC claimed that the bonds were fundamentally private sector financings that should be subjected to its registration requirements; and Congress for the first time supported the Internal Revenue Service on the issue. By statute, it excluded IDBs from tax exemption.[20]

This quick breakthrough took place because the bond market participants lost their cohesiveness. Underwriters that specialized in IDBs were reaping huge profits. Other underwriters and financial advisers specializing in traditional state and local government financing were finding it harder to attract investors. State and local finance officials and public authorities were confronted with high interest rates and sluggish markets for other types of borrowing. Representatives from various states, including New York, Massachusetts, and Illinois, complained that they were losing jobs in a "second war of the states." Several trade union organizations protested the shift in jobs to nonunion states. The catalyst was a serious threat of more drastic tax reforms in the form of a proposed minimum income tax written into the draft tax bill pending in the House in 1968.

The 1968 act eliminated the tax-exempt status of public bonds to construct facilities for privately owned companies, except for issues of up to $1 million or for enumerated purposes.[21] By the first half of 1969, the volume of that kind of financing had dwindled to $8 million (compared with $640 million in the first half of 1968). This shift dramatically demonstrates the effect of the tax laws on public investment patterns. One of the purposes for which the act maintained tax exemption was construction of facilities for industrial air and water pollution control equipment. Chapter 5 described how this execption came to be an enormous loophole: by mid-1974, the volume of public authority and local government tax-exempt funding of that kind of pollution control equipment for private industry equaled the 1968 total of all IDBs.

Authority financing for private projects raises a host of unanswered questions, but it is only part of a broader pattern by which our peculiar version of a mixed economy makes provisions for private profit in nearly every public undertaking, from providing for the indigent aged (through profit-generating nursing homes) to raising capital for essential public services.

Taxable Bonds for Public Purposes   In 1968, the bond market coalition permitted the first incursion into the municipal bond exemption. The next year legislation that passed in the House of Representatives included a minimum income tax (as well as a maximum). Investors would have to pay taxes on part of the interest on public enterprise bonds insofar as they were not otherwise paying a set proportion on their total income. Uncertainty about the effect of this legislation, together with the underwriters' strategy to show that they could retaliate against change, produced a temporary drop in the municipal bond market that was described in the financial press and in congressional hearings, partly for political effect, as a "collapse of the market."

Uncertainty is threatening to a system as dependent on precedent, experience, and instinctive personal judgments as the bond market is. Moreover, the very complexity and obscurity of the system make uninitiated officials cautious about tampering with it. Opponents of reform warned ominously in committee hearings of massive capital market restructuring and interest rate dislocations that would ensue from the House bill. The minimum tax (as applied to public sector bonds) died in the Senate. After this near success by the tax reformers, the municipal bond market alliance intensified its lobbying and public relations activity. In 1972, the Institute for the Retention of Tax Exempt Bonds was organized to promote the idea that "tax exemption had been one of the strengths of the American way of life."[22] The members of this association are underwriting firms, bond attorneys, and institutional investors. The director was formerly a member of an underwriting firm and a public relations official of the Investment Bankers Association. In 1973, the Municipal Finance Officers Association opened a Washington office.

As of 1977, tax reform of state and local borrowing provisions remained on the legislative agenda, in part because of the enormous growth in the total volume of projected capital investment needed in the public sector. Some observers doubt that the traditional tax-exempt bond markets can generate sufficient investment to meet these needs. Many sources of investment capital do not gain advantages from tax-exempt interest payments; pension funds and life insurance companies, for example, have other legal sources of tax exemption and therefore seek the higher interest rates obtainable from investment in taxable corporate and federal bonds. Meanwhile the costs of unabated growth in tax-exempt securities to the U.S. Treasury continue to mount. (The Treasury Department estimates the federal tax loss from the exemption as ranging from $2.9 billion in "tax aid" for fiscal 1972 to $4.8 billion for fiscal 1976.) Tax costs clearly exceeded the savings from tax exemptions enjoyed by the state and local borrowers. In other words, the federal government loses more in foregone taxes than state and local enterprises save from borrowing money at lower interest rates. As specific federal programs provide guarantees for tax-exempt local agency borrowing, they create securities stronger than U.S. government bonds.

These facts have prompted proposals for a compromise in the form of a taxable bond option.[23] Under this compromise, state and local governments would have the choice of selling bonds on which the interest is taxable. These bonds would carry higher interest rates and therefore cost the borrowing agency more. The federal government, however, would directly reimburse the public issuers—authorities and governments—for some percentage of the interest costs. The municipal bond coalition is divided on this proposal, and it therefore stands a chance of being enacted into law. The taxable bond option may be a means of expanding the municipal bond market by attracting new investors, such as the pension funds, while giving the banks and brokers a larger share in the future growth of public enterprise than they would have if such growth were more dependent on direct federal aid. Many of the larger financial institutions with diversified clients and strong capital positions foresee added sources of business from marketing taxable municipal bonds. By the mid-1970s, debates before the Senate Banking Committee and the House Ways and Means Committee centered on the ideal size of the subsidy rate for taxable bond options; suggestions ranged from 20 to 50 percent of interest costs.[24] The taxable bond options that were authorized in 1974 for use by housing finance authorities (with federal subsidies and guarantees) remain unused, but other bills to provide guarantees and subsidies for taxable municipal securities for other purposes have been introduced, and a number of city mayors have indicated a willingness to sacrifice tax exemption for credit guarantees.

Banking Laws and Regulations   Bond market participants also are divided concerning the application and amendment of banking laws. Since 1933, federal law has prohibited commercial banks from underwriting revenue bonds—as opposed to general obligations of states and municipalities.[25] For over a decade, without success, the Office of the Comptroller of the Currency has urged Congress to eliminate this provision. In some situations, however, administrative officials can effect what Congress refuses to legislate. As the official responsible for enforcing the banking laws on nationally chartered commercial banks, the comptroller of the currency can make administrative rulings that permit the banks to bypass the provisions of the law. For example, comptrollers have tried to include public authority revenue bonds in the category of "general obligations of the state or political subdivision of a state," thus erasing, for purposes of federal regulation, the distinction between general obligations and revenue bonds. Such rulings are based on the argument that "if the largest commercial banks cannot underwrite revenue bonds, competition in the bidding is artificially restricted and costs to taxpayers may thereby be increased."[26] This argumant makes little sense, of course, when the ruling is applied to those negotiated public authority issues on which there is no competitive bidding.

In 1966, the investment bankers brought an action against the comptroller of the currency to restrain him from bypassing the law in this regard. The district court decided against the comptroller.[27] Since then, however, the office has ruled that the moral obligation language, providing for legislative fill-up of authority reserves, transforms revenue bonds into general obligations in the terms of the banking legislation and therefore permits commercial banks to bid for the underwriting business of agencies like the New Jersey Sports and Exposition Authority and New York's Housing Finance Agency.

In recent years, commercial and investment bankers also have disagreed over what form regulation of the municipal bond market should take. The investment banking firms and brokerage houses are more willing to accept a regulatory structure under the supervision of the SEC, with which they already deal in connection with private corporate financings. The dealer banks do not want to be subjected directly to SEC regulation because it would add an entirely new regulatory hierarchy to the bank examiners with whom they already must cope. In late 1974, a widely publicized scheme whereby Vietnam veterans who had been prisoners of war were induced to invest their back pay in Florida IDBs and other scandals involving nursing home revenue bonds stiffened the determination of the Securities and Exchange Commission to extend regulation over the municipal securities business; the SEC outlined types of information with which an investor must be provided when public authority and other tax-exempt bonds are offered to him. In 1975, Congress ended a long era of reliance on unregulated gentlemen's agreements in the municipal bond market by enacting a compromise combining mechanisms for industry self-regulation with SEC supervision. The resulting Municipal Securities Rule-Making Board, comprised of representatives of the underwriters, is drafting rules on procedures, such as disclosure of information on the borrowing agency and record keeping.[28]

Federal Credit Institutions   Federal aid in the form of grants and loans has always been a major alternative to raising capital by issuing state and local bonds, but for the most part the two systems have been complementary.

Federal grants and operating subsidies have actually expanded the capabilities of public authorities to issue revenue bonds in such fields as housing, health, and pollution control.

Signs of revived popularity for the corporate form in federal affairs are also emerging. During the Nixon and Ford administrations, new enterprises established by the government included the Overseas Private Investment Corporation, the Community Development Corporation, Pennsylvania Avenue Development Corporation, Pension Benefit Guaranty Corporation, Amtrak, ConRail, and the Rural Telephone Bank. These corporations are more complementary than competitive with the private sector; the Community Development Corporation, for example, set up in the Department of Housing and Urban Development, can guarantee bonds issued on the private market by public authorities for the development of new towns and urban settlements.[29] Some other proposals, however, would compete directly with municipal bond underwriting. Bills for this purpose were submitted in Congress to create a rural development bank, a national development bank, an urban development bank (Urbank), the Federal Financing Bank, the Environmental Financing Authority, and several others able to loan directly to state and local authorities and other agencies, some in the manner of the Reconstruction Finance Corporation. For example, the Environmental Financing Authority (authorized but never activated) was to purchase water and sewer bonds throughout the country, reducing the dependence of county authorities and municipal corporations on bond attorneys and underwriters.

Congress has created a Federal Financing Bank (FFB) whose purpose is to coordinate demands for funds that were previously scattered over a wide number of specialized federal borrowing programs. The legislation as passed does not establish new lending programs. The corporation is under the general supervision and direction of a cabinet-level secretary—in this case, the secretary of the treasury—and has a five-man board of directors of which he is chairman. The bank is authorized to buy or sell any obligation that is issued, sold, or guaranteed by another federal agency. The bank itself needs Treasury approval for the sale of its own bonds, which may be issued to the private financial market or to the Treasury itself. It can buy bonds of any local public agency that are already guaranteed by a federal agency if doing so will reduce the borrowing costs to the local authority. But the FFB is really more an attempt to coordinate federal credit assistance than a program to buy local enterprise securities. It also remains a voluntary device; other federal agencies that issue revenue bonds, such as TVA and the Postal Service, can choose either to issue them directly, with Treasury approval, or to use the FFB. The FFB thus provides an opportunity for government corporations and other agencies to coordinate or consolidate their bond issues. It is a counterpart, at the federal level, of state bond banks that attempt to consolidate capital borrowing by local issuers.

The FFB permits the government to integrate federal and federally assisted borrowing programs with overall economic and fiscal policies—in other words, to consider raising capital for federal enterprise as part of the overall system of public finance. This kind of perspective is more urgently needed at the state level. In a sense, this federal bank is designed to reduce the situations in which individual agencies and corporations raise capital at higher interest rates than the Treasury itself would have to pay, just as state and local authorities often raise capital at higher interest rates than state and city general obligation bonds would involve.

The Securities Industry Association and the Municipal Finance Officers Association lobbied successfully against a provision that would have enabled the FFB to buy the taxable municipal bonds that might be issued if a taxable bond option law were to be passed.[30] Underwriters have been particularly opposed to the proposed Urbank, which could purchase state and local agency securities. This corporation might be a new lending institution for the expansion of public enterprise and city capital budgets—a comprehensive alternative to complete dependence on the investors and brokers in the municipal bond market. The need is obvious. When the investment community no longer considers a public enterprise a viable investment, its projects and mission deserve independent evaluation; if judged in the public interest, such enterprises could be financed with federal loan guarantees (through the federal Community Development Corporation, for example) or with direct federal loans through the proposed Urbank.

Other Federal Influences Other possibilities—some useful, some not—for shifts in the patterns of public enterprise are hovering on the federal horizon. Investor-owned power companies (through the Edison Electric Institute) are seeking federal guarantees for utility bonds, which would take some energy out of public power authority growth at a time when the interests of many consumers lie with public power. Full federal insurance of all government deposits in the banks, a recurrent proposal, would cut down on bank investments in public authority and other tax-exempt bonds because many of these investments are required now as security against uninsured state and local deposits. The federal Urban Mass Transit Agency's funding decisions will affect fare structures and new project plans for transit, port, and other regional authorities across the nation. Medicare and Medicaid allocations determine the volume of hospital authority fundings. Proposed health insurance schemes will affect those fundings as well. Proposals to ease the restrictions on IDBs (despite their current high volume) could expand authority aid to private industry even further in the late 1970s, particularly in the form of job development and industrial development authorities investing in industrial parks and related facilities.

Overall, federally assisted credit (such as loans with federal guarantees and tax-exempt bonds and notes) accounts for more than 25 percent of the economy's private credit flows. Federal officials have noted, with considerable chagrin, that public authorities have used much of this credit assistance to borrow and have then paid off their debts with additional federal subsidies, such as grants and loans for specific programs. The U.S. Office of Management and Budget calls this the "double dip" and would like to end federal aid to agencies that use it to pay off tax-exempt bonds or, conversely, to eliminate the tax exemption for revenue bonds backed by income that includes federal subsidies. This change might halt the proliferation of county sewer authorities that combine financing from tax-exempt bonds with federal pollution control grants and loans.

In the United States, public authorities are usually treated as aspects of state and local government. However, the intricacies of the federal system are such that what appears to be a wholly state and local form of enterprise is dramatically dependent upon decisions taken at the federal level. The proliferation of public authorities as a result of the New Deal was not a unique set of events but rather an example of the way in which the federal government continues to determine the range of permissible authority functions and to influence the scale and direction of authority investments, acting with little forethought or consistent policy direction. The combination of federal stimuli and bond market promotions has had a far greater influence on the growth of public enterprise than the decisions of state and local legislators who vote public authorities into existence.

12 Reappraisal

Public enterprise has thrived in the United States because, with few exceptions, it has proved satisfactory—indeed profitable—for particular segments of business and government. Promotion from business has spurred the growth of borrowing, enterprise, and investment on the part of state and local governments and their corporations. All of the resulting public activities directly generate jobs and income in the private sector, particularly in banking and brokerage, in legal, engineering and financial consulting, and in construction. The most rapidly growing sectors of government enterprise are designed to reduce the risks and to strengthen the profits of nongovernmental entrepreneurs in scores of businesses: manufacturing firms forced to reduce polluting effluents; nursing homes and hospitals; sports arenas; tax-shelter and other limited-profit housing ventures; utilities distributing electric power, gas, and water; colleges and specialized training firms; research and development, communications, and transportation industries; and all their suppliers. While individual authorities sometimes compete with some specific businesses, they aid many more.

The operations of government corporations are profoundly political. They have a direct and dramatic impact on the directions of urban development, on the allocation of public resources among regions and groups, on the uses made of rivers, parks, watersheds, and city centers. This impact is the stuff of policy politics. Public authorities tend to be co-opted by the banking and business interests with whom they work. This co-option is the stuff of interest group politics. The appointments of public authority leaders, and sometimes their contracts, are related to election campaigns and to the quid pro quo of candidate support. These relationships are the stuff of party politics. Although the spoils system has never played as large a role in corporate operations as it has in regular government operations, it is clearly present, particularly at the upper levels of authority management.

On this issue, public authorities are subject to both unrealistic praise from their own staffs and unrealistic criticism from opponents. The idea that the planners and managers of government corporations can be divorced from politics, politically neutral, and yet effective is utterly inconsistent with the characteristics of enterprise, public policy, American politics, and human behavior in organized groups. Corporate managements are not to blame if they fail to meet such unrealistic expectations. (They do, however, attract criticism when they act unduly suspicious of outside comment and when they protest too much regarding their own objectivity.) Acceptance of the fact that public authorities and their leaders are inevitably embedded in politics is a necessary first step toward developing a realistic approach to the problem of accountability. David Lilienthal addressed this point in his personal journals:

> There are, of course, all kinds of politics. Administrators and technicians, however high minded their purposes may seem to them, cannot piously abjure party politics, and then indulge in their own variety. "Taking care of the boys" at public expense is an evil in any guise whether it is on the basis of personal friendship, business or social ties, or some amateur political notion about an elite of brains (self-selected), a kind of Phi Beta Kappa version of Tammany Hall. . . . The usual forthrightness of Congressmen is wholesome compared with the holier-than-thou attitude toward politicians of those who occasionally practice their own personal brand of politics.[1]

If "nonpolitical" is a criterion of public authority evaluation that must be discarded, so too is "businesslike." Both terms are devoid of useful and specific meaning in this context. The superior virtue of business participation, of civic leadership, of private investment is a fundamental assumption in popular American political theory that skews evaluations of the public interest and limits the opportunities for equitable representation of nonbusiness points of view.

Woodrow Wilson, a founder of progressive public administration, as well as a reform politician and the president with perhaps the greatest influence on American ideology since Thomas Jefferson, preached the virtues of competitive business and the survival of the fittest: "Put all the business of America upon the footing of economy and efficiency, and then let the race be to the strongest and the swiftest. . . . Are you not eager for the time when the genius and initiative of all the people shall be called into the service of business? . . . to see business disentangled from its unholy alliance with politics?" Yet even Wilson warned: "The business of many of those corporations which we call public service corporations, and which are indispensable to our daily lives and serve us with transportation and light and water and power,—their business, for instance, is clearly public business; and, therefore, we can and must penetrate their affairs by the light of examination and discussion."[2]

Newspapers, radio, and television news departments, as well as specialized journals, report the news and editorialize about the work of public authorities in idealized terms, siding, in most cases of conflict, with corporate managements rather than with public officials and communities. Media commentary is loaded to the point of tedium with allusions to the "nonpolitical," "businesslike" characteristics of public authorities, labels that seem to reduce the space available for the presentation and analysis of hard facts. When the commentary turns critical, it is often equally unenlightening and unrealistic, failing to reflect, for example that first-class expense account travel by executives, secrecy for project plans and finance, and personalized selection of contractors are common business practices. If public authorities are expected only to be businesslike, these practices are likely to accompany the more desirable management techniques.

The interlocking directorates of public enterprise, banking, construction, and brokerage businesses simply extend patterns that are familiar in the private sector. Representatives of investors with stock or other interests sit on the boards of directors of private firms. Certainly bankers, brokers, and other businessmen with an interest in public enterprise cannot be castigated for serving on the boards to which they are appointed by a governor, mayor, or town or county council. Some of them should be expected to exercise more discretion than they have in the past about clear conflicts of interest, but the entire subject of "conflicts of interest" in the literature and practice of American business and politics is a welter of contradictions and confused values.

The idea that government institutions will be better the more they emulate private institutions operating in a free market is rife with internal contradictions. In any case, practical evidence of market failures in particular sectors was readily available by the first decades of the twentieth century. Although, in practice, both business and government moved rapidly away from unfettered competitive markets, Americans have never given up their faith in them; both the American people and their leaders have represented dramatic changes in business practice and growth of government intervention as minimal adjustments or responses to temporary aberrations.[3] One adjustment—regulation of business by independent commissions (in the fields of transportation, communications, food and drugs, securities exchange, power) —is a combination of limited public control and continued private management. The public authority represents another adjustment—a combination of private control and public management.

American politics, like American economics, has extolled the pursuit of self-interest by individuals and organizations in the context of a free marketplace of ideas, interest groups, and votes. The participants in the municipal bond market and on the boards of public authorities are merely acting out the American dream. Individual scandals and scapegoats obscure the underlying and persistent weakness that produces them. American government and society have failed to develop a consensus on the values and patterns of behavior appropriate for those who participate in public institutions. Americans do not believe in the public interest. When government corporations (or other agencies, for that matter) assume the aspect of runaway horses, the cause is more often the absence of any rider in the saddle at all than the superior strength of a determined beast. The first requirement of effective political control of public enterprises is recognition that political control is desirable and that it can be combined with management skill.

Concepts of financial, legal, and administrative autonomy for the public authority have influenced the forms used in the conduct of business in the public sector, freezing the legal and organizational options that are considered feasible in American government and depriving American public enterprise of the flexibility and variations of form and finance that are available in Europe. These ideological straitjackets make it difficult to develop satisfactory ways of financing deficit-producing public services, such as mass transit, for which the classic public authority form does not work. At the same time, efforts to implement corporate autonomy have failed to insulate corporate entities from outside pressures and internal preferences. On the contrary, the uniform legal and financial structures of public authorities have simply given the upper hand to certain pressures and preferences and screened out others. Although the thousands of corporate entities established by state and local governments throughout the United States are legally separate, indeed unrelated, the municipal bond market has knitted them into a system with clear interdependencies and common tendencies. Both their legal separateness and their kinship in the revenue bond market limit the ability of public authorities to plan and to make investment decisions according to comprehensive and flexible criteria suitable to broad regional and national goals.

The public authority planning process is shaped by financial dependence on private markets, a dependence ironically created by the concept of authority autonomy. Authority planning tends not to consider the impact of corporate policies and projects on the national or local economy (public and private) or on the environment—physical, social, and political—within which the corporation acts or even on other public agencies. The public authority planning process emphasizes financial returns to the single corporate entity. It produces a significant bias in favor of overstating the returns and understating the costs of chosen projects, especially when the costs are external to the corporation that is financing the particular project (falling on the surrounding community, on other programs, on private businesses with whom the public authority may compete, or even on future generations). Corporate managements tend to avoid or at least to resist the cost burdens of projects that have small direct returns but possibly significant indirect returns. Hence general taxes ultimately bear the burden for some of the costs of both profitable and nonprofitable corporate projects.

The independent sources of money on which public authorities rely encourage them to borrow too much, too fast, when demand for investment in their bonds is healthy and abruptly deprive them of funds when the conditions of the bond market are unfavorable. Splintering public investment into separate corporate portfolios makes it impossible for government to engage in coherent financial planning.

On the other hand, the administrative decentralization achieved in fact by public authorities and by some federal government corporations has had salutary effects—particularly on their management and operations—that become apparent in any comparison with regular government agencies, especially agencies of state and local government. Stable and talented executive leadership, internal emphasis on management improvement, performance incentives, and decentralized operations are the important characteristics of public authority administration that stand out in contrast with general government and contribute significantly to the effectiveness of public authority operations. (Of course, some public corporations are badly managed and some government agencies are well managed, but the exceptions, too, confirm the importance of these four attributes.) In short, efforts to bring more balanced direction, more comprehensive planning, and more integrated public policy control to public enterprise must not eliminate the administrative attributes that this and every other sector of government need. The crucial dimensions for designing public institutions are not political-versus-business-like. They are policy leadership-cum-management skill.

The orthodox model of the government corporation posited "self-support" as a stimulus to efficiency, somewhat paradoxically transferring Adam Smith's free market model from private business to public business. Somehow the strokings of the invisible hand would bring forth efficiency from the separate and free operations of self-supporting government corporations, as it was supposed to do with private enterprise. In fact, throughout American history, the private sector has readily perceived and enjoyed the benefits flowing from government franchises, tariff protection, contracts, insurance, and subsidy. Both external government diplomacy and internal government policies on the utilization of natural resources (from land grants to oil depletion allowances) have provided a framework for U.S. economic development. Nevertheless, as Gary Wills has put it, "Though the businessman did not live by his theory of laissez-faire, it was all the theory he had. He pretended to live by it, and often thought he did. Besides, though the theory was abandoned when it was to the businessman's advantage to abandon it, it was religiously adhered to and trumpeted when that led to his advantage."[4] Perhaps more important, legions of politicians and students of government have continued to believe that American business lives by laissez-faire and, contradictions aside, that when business needs help or supplement from government, the public sector itself should conform to the laissez-faire model as closely as possible.

Federal government corporations and a growing proportion of state and local public authorities do receive government funds, some directly through grants, loans, and appropriated subsidies, some indirectly through insurance schemes, third-party payments, loan guarantees, leases, and contracts. Even those that are self-supporting in the traditional sense (with operating revenues derived from nongovernmental consumers sufficient to cover operating expenses and debt service) are subsidized by tax exemption, monopoly franchise, public land, or selective use of police powers. The public authority that operates monopoly services or enjoys competitive advantage from cost subsidies can obtain high financial returns—not because of efficiency but because of favorably structured market conditions. Efficiency in the internal operations of public authorities is directly related to the administrative attributes of leadership, continuous management improvement, performance control, and administrative decentralization rather than to economic determinism. Those attributes are no more prevalent in public authorities without direct subsidies than in those with direct subsidies. Administration is an art in itself, not a stepchild of economics.

Policy Biases of Public Authorities

Public authorities as a general class of organizations—government-owned corporations chartered by statute, without stockholders, directed by a separate board, and reliant to some significant extent on revenue bond financing— show some common tendencies: to borrow and to build with minimal delay; to select projects more conducive to generating net financial revenues than alternative means of providing public service; to rely on established methods with predictable results; and to emphasize physical rather than social targets. These tendencies reinforce one another.

Public authorities seldom encounter the political and constitutional constraints that normally slow the process of borrowing by regular government.

Authority financial planning involves continually rolling over funds, translating short-term debt into long-term debt, pouring operating funds from one project into security to borrow for new projects. Some proponents of the authority form regard avoidance of delay as its major advantage. And yet delay provides for debate, for consideration of many sides of a question, for compromise and caution. Avoiding delay is desirable when the public need for services is urgent and resources for investment are continually expanding. It is undesirable when demand is not expanding (leaving underused dormitories, declining ridership, overpriced housing) or when resources contract (as when the bond market simply slammed the door on agencies in New York State in 1975, in the absence of compensating public sources of investment). Moreover, reducing delay in public construction favors development over conservation. (Obstructionism is the most effective tool of groups promoting environmental protection and others who oppose construction of dams, power plants, and highways.) Public authority preferences for physical goals, revenue-producing projects, and demand forecasts also favor development over conservation.

Public authorities are free from interests and pressures from parts of a state or segments of a community that do not benefit directly from proposed physical construction. For example, in river basin development, a regional corporation can ignore the interests of the upstream source areas and favor those of consumer areas; in transportation development, competing needs of segments of the public not served simply do not penetrate the authority planning process.

The preference for profitable projects that is born of revenue bond financing, business boards, and internal yearnings for organizational autonomy favors highways over rail transportation, water supply and power production over pollution abatement and recreational use of water resources, school building over expansion of student counseling, sports arenas over open space, industrial parks over small business assistance, and middle-income and luxury housing mortgage finance over rehabilitation and low-income housing construction. Only additional infusions of government subsidies or rules offset these biases.

The principles of the bond market insist that financial considerations should determine policy. Thus, when Ivy Baker Priest became the treasurer of California, she opposed proposals for federal credit assistance agencies because they would go beyond the ordinary credit requirements of private bankers and would allow government policy or political considerations to "set priorities among borrowers." She considered inappropriate any attempt to set criteria for public investment that might be unrelated to credit.

Credit criteria seldom address the question of whether there are better ways of obtaining the desired result. Hence, public authorities conduct only a very limited kind of planning. Project planning is focused on servicing projected future demands; the projections simply depict a continuation of past trends into the future. Any planning process that focuses on demand forecasts, whether of air or auto travel, water use or electric power consumption, even sewerage and waste disposal volumes, basically facilitates and accelerates current trends. Austin Tobin reflected the planning techniques of most public authorities when he observed: "Our own planning in the field of arterial highways for the New York metropolitan area accepts the fact that the structure of our surging metropolitan area today is being shaped almost entirely by the motor vehicle. In airport planning we make the basic assumption that air transportation will become the dominant means of long distance travel."[5] This kind of planning assumed and then contributed to the demise of the railroads throughout the United States.

In highway development, a new road generates new growth along its route. This growth in turn generates increased traffic on the road. The growth and the traffic provide the basis for planning additional lanes or, by similar steps, new tubes for a tunnel, second decks on a bridge. Quantitative traffic studies show that more lanes generate more traffic, which in turn generates more plans. Thus, the four-lane scenic road that Alfred Driscoll proposed (and the Highway Authority built) to allow families to take Sunday drives to the long sweep of New Jersey's ocean shore and beaches has grown into a ten-lane superhighway, spawning population explosions and industrial growth in the shore counties and damaging the resource the road was planned to show off. The concomitant erosion and pollution surprised communities unequipped to handle the water supply needs and wastes of new growth. In some former beachfront towns, high tides now lap the sea wall (built at state and federal expense), and in others, multistory condominiums have their supports planted against the sea wall. County sewer authorities have been established to cope belatedly with some of the wastes; a county "economic development authority" has been created to cope with others—by issuing industrial development bonds for pollution control equipment on private plants. Needless to say, the planners of this scenic road foresaw none of these consequences.

Unforeseen consequences flow from other types of authority construction. In Boston, within a dozen years, Logan International Airport's annual passenger trips increased from three million to nine million, cargo grew by nearly 500 percent, and the number of employees doubled. The airport nibbled away, with noise and concrete, at the old Italian-American urban village of East Boston and helped to drive the New Haven Railroad into receivership. Urban programs of state and federal governments are now directed at saving the rail services and devising methods of reviving the characteristics of the urban village in Boston's inner-city neighborhoods.

Across the nation (from the Pacific to the Atlantic on U.S. 80), beef moves in half-empty trucks (the other half is cold air), which often return totally empty, raising the price of food relative to what it might have been if Robert Young of the Chesapeake and Ohio had won his 1930s crusade for two-and-a-half-day rail service from shore to shore. At one of the beef sources, the Lower Colorado River Authority dams were conceived to control floods, to transform subsistence farms into commercial operations. They were supported by hydroelectric power plants. The power distributed from those dams stimulated construction booms in the beautiful Highland Lakes district north of Austin, Texas, where developers built expensive subdivisions and vacation homes. This growth, fostered by available power, water, and recreation facilities, consumed more electric power than the river could supply (through expanded hydroelectric plants). Authority operations then reached out to meet the need, generating new power by using steam plants that burn gas or coal fuel (pressing costs and rates upward) and planning atomic power plants. To cope with mounting threats to lake and ground water quality from the profusion of septic tanks and power plants, the same authority then became the local pollution control agency, debating with federal environmental protection officials over suitable standards. Authority operations further expanded to operate recreation facilities. These facilities become crowded and now must be rationed by user charges.

The thrust of authority policy biases is in no way unique, of course. It is part and parcel of the country's postwar development. The policy biases of public authorities may be less attributable to their corporate independence than to their total immersion in the bargaining processes of American politics and their natural orientation toward short-run business growth.

There is, unfortunately, no hidden hand that shapes, from the countless small choices made by specialized units pursuing their own short-term interests, ultimate rationality for society as a whole and for its natural environment. The authority system of conducting the public's business is pluralism run rampant, and "the characteristic weakness and failure of pluralistic structure is the formation of dominant centers of power bent on maintaining the status quo in the presumed interest of stability, order and effective goal attainment."[6] The failure is not of the authorities themselves but of the political systems that formed them and the government leaders who have not articulated general theories of public enterprise or defined goals in the public interest that might be reasonably imposed on government corporations or devised balanced or representative structures for running them. The cure lies not in eliminating independent government corporations, which may be useful, effective administrative tools, but in defining, developing, and applying to them some long-range public goals.

In Search of a Social Balance Sheet

We must go beyond a financial balance sheet and beyond statutory statements of corporate mission to devise a framework within which to evaluate the performance of public authorities and to judge the organizational alternatives available to government. The public interest is an ambiguous concept that has been used in myriad ways by different schools of thought, from mercantilists and physiocrats to planners and cost-benefit analysts. It requires at minimum reasonably broad, reasonably forward-looking consideration of the well-being of society as a collective and of its shared resources. With the stimulus of leadership, societies can and do make collective, if subjective, value judgments. As a nation, as state and regional communities, we must make some collective value judgments and harness corporate and bureaucratic activities to them.

Accepting the continued viability of pluralism in American politics, we can tamper with our governmental machinery in an effort to give more weight to long-range, unorganized, and diffuse interests. We must prolong and broaden the scanning processes by which individuals and organizations make decisions. We must increase the number of interests among which there should be trade-offs in the bargaining that leads to authoritative decisions. And we must not only open ourselves up to political leadership but demand it (and refuse to reelect officials who look no further than their immediate sources of support).

The decisions and purposes of public enterprise should be judged on the basis of several kinds of costs and benefits that go well beyond the legislative mission and financial record of a single agency. The conduct of public enterprise has political costs and benefits. Its decision-making process must include consideration of the commitments and constituencies of elected officials; the perceived needs of local communities; the sources of political support for the corporation itself; the maintenance of the goodwill of the available sources of funds (including the bond market, taxpayers, paying customers, and officials of grant-giving governments); and the maintenance of a level of honesty and integrity that sustains public trust.

Financial costs and benefits are undeniably important, but calculations of these costs and benefits must include aspects external to the corporation's financial transactions, taking into consideration financial effects on other organizations, public and private, and on the long-range financial planning for the state or regions. If a corporation increases its revenues at the expense of competing facilities (such as subsidized railroads, competing parimutuel tracks that pay full taxes, competing real estate developments paying full property taxes, competing borrowing capacity of state and local governments), such transfers of resources should at least be considered part of the costs and benefits of the corporation's activities and proposals.

Physical or environmental costs and benefits must also be built into the evaluative framework. The environmental impact statements that are being applied to some types of corporate projects may reflect some of these costs and benefits, but they are too often treated as little more than additional forms to fill out for the government. Public enterprise must make a firm commitment to conserving natural resources, to considering their consumption a real and present cost, if its decisions are to contribute to the long-term public welfare.

The distributive effects of enterprise activity on the economy of a region and localities within it must be considered. For example, port authorities should study not merely the promotion of the port but also the impact on local employment and on private real estate markets, not only person-trips but also the accessibility of transportation for job-producing industries, low-income families, and blue-collar workers. Airport authorities should try to find a site for airport expansion that not only is most efficient (on a narrow calculation) but also minimizes damage to settled communities. More broadly, transportation planners should seek alternatives to airport construction that will serve the needs of long-distance travel with lower political and economic costs.

These kinds of considerations are parts of a social balance sheet that is not ultimately susceptible to quantification.[7] The idea that corporations should no longer be judged by financial returns alone, or even by financial returns plus corporate mission, is not a revolutionary one. Robert Dahl has called the large corporation a social enterprise, a political system with great influence on individuals and society.[8] Daniel Bell has called for the subordination of the corporation in postindustrial society. A business study group proposed a "corporate social audit," and nearly half the industrial leaders surveyed by the Committee for Economic Development found the idea acceptable.[9] In fact, more has been written about the social responsibility of the investor-owned corporation than about the social responsibility of the government-owned corporation. Yet corporations with specific missions and financial needs are unlikely to throw themselves wholeheartedly into broad, social decision making. Improving the internal decision-making processes of corporations cannot be the major emphasis of change. We must focus instead on developing the broad decision-making capabilities of general government and utilizing those capabilities for effective control of public authorities and other agencies intended to serve the public interest.

The obvious and simple solution of this problem is comprehensive, long-range government plans to which public enterprises must conform. But Americans' aversion to mandatory plans is probably irreversible, and many examples from home and abroad demonstrate that even centralized planning is not necessarily efficient. It often lacks or overlooks information on local conditions, on short-term changes, or on individual and community preferences. Moreover, comprehensive planning alone cannot resolve the problem of multiple goals for public programs. Why was the U.S. Postal Service created? To make operations more efficient? To take advantage of modern technology? To change the balance of power in collective bargaining for postal employees? To reduce the influence of congressmen and eliminate party patronage in job distribution? To add to the profits of some underwriters and bond lawyers? To suit the tastes of a new administration imbued with the values and virtues of liberal economics? To reduce the burden on the taxpayer? All of these considerations played a part in the collective decision. There is scarcely a public law, program or project in the United States that was not authorized and supported by a combination of people and groups with disparate goals and incompatible expectations about its achievements. Explicit and formal policy planning can be one source of improvement in decision making, but only one among many. The problems of pluralism require plural solutions.

Some criteria for effective public enterprise nonetheless emerge from these considerations. Effective public enterprise requires the following.

First, *there must be a popular and official acceptance of the enterprise as legitimate government activity to be conducted for explicitly public purposes.* The public purposes should be thoroughly discussed in public debate and in the statutory authorizations of the government corporation. At present, the label "public purpose" is simply attached to any problem for which public officials and financial promoters have negotiated an arrangement. Effective public enterprise requires further definition of the goals or social goods to which the enterprise is expected to contribute.

Second, *the financial policies of the enterprise should be integrated with the government's general financial policies and budget plans.* Government must devise orderly means for allocating subsidies to non-revenue-producing social purposes to be served by public authorities (by transfer among corporate projects or transfer from taxes) and for utilizing operating surpluses from corporate services (the government's dividend). They also must continuously review the effects of authority borrowing on government credit and contingent liabilities in the present and future. Even where fiscal self-support is possible, the operation of a public business should not be divorced from the larger considerations involved in allocating public resources. When special subsidies or government guarantees are involved, the need for policy guidelines and government controls is even more pressing. In effect, the profits of public enterprise are policy profits; they result from prices that government permits to be charged with the purpose of drawing surpluses from specific consumers. Government should exercise firm and unified control over the prices, subsidies, and surpluses of wholly owned public enterprises. The managers of the enterprise should not alone determine how to spend surpluses that might be allocated to price reductions benefiting consumers, to employee benefits, to expansion programs, to other public services, or to social outlays.

Third, *there must be strong leadership by elected officials and their executive officers.* Such leadership requires active and effective strategies of control over enterprises, and such strategies require explicit and balanced sets of purposes or plans.

Fourth, *a system must be devised to facilitate accommodations with other agencies and programs in related policy areas.* Different situations require different coordinating devices—stronger ones where policies are most likely to conflict (such as transportation) and looser ones where supplementary and even duplicative activities may be acceptable (as in housing).

Fifth, *adaptability to changing circumstances, popular demands, and shifts in the policy priorities of elected administrations is needed.* Such adaptability requires, at a minimum, orderly means for altering the structure and missions of statutory corporations.

Sixth, *the public and government must have access to information.* Public authority managements should not be entitled to conduct their business in secrecy. The internal operations of the wholly owned government corporation are as much in the public domain as those of departmental agencies. Even if decreased secrecy brings increased interest rates, as authority managers predict, the advantages to investor and taxpayer alike may be worth the cost. Opening up access will help corporate managements in the long run, particularly if they make an effort to educate the public officials and the press to the technical dimensions of their problems. Once they are used to being subjected to public debate, they are likely to find that the demise of secrecy has actually removed a major public bone of contention. Too much of the typical communication between authorities and the public has been in the nature of public relations and too little in the nature of genuine exchange of views and open debate. Too much of the communication between public authorities and legislatures has been confrontation or investigation. More disclosure and less fear of public argument on the part of authority managements themselves could go far to make these relationships more constructive.

Seventh, *management must be open to representative viewpoints from society.* Openness means listening even to viewpoints that management considers narrow and political. At some point, of course, conflicts must be resolved and decisions made—sometimes arbitrarily—but a representative board of directors can absorb political heat and can forge decisions out of a wide diversity of opinions without undermining competence and expertise in management.

Eighth, *strong and stable executive leadership and continuing emphasis on management improvement, performance controls, and administrative decentralization are needed.* Authorities must have the means to attract good managers and to concentrate adequate management power in their hands. The executive director or general manager (the chief executive officer) must remain strong in internal operations. Boards cannot effectively be involved in day-to-day or even in month-to-month management. Strategies of control for public policy should not rely on proliferation of self-defeating internal procedural controls, such as regulation of personnel systems, details of purchasing and contracting, preaudit, or itemized review of budgets. Overly tight regulation is unlikely to eliminate the abuses that occur in these areas but is likely to undermine important management flexibility and strength in the public sector.

Finally, *there must be steady access to capital funds at a pace and under conditions that reflect fiscal responsibility, careful financial planning, and reasonable public control over burdens on the taxpayer.* The word "steady" is important. It implies both continued attention to the soundness of the municipal bond market as a source of funds from investors and the provision of alternative sources of capital funding for high-risk or high-loss public activities and for use by public corporations when the bond market tightens up. Government must establish public investment banking institutions to provide supplementary funds and to offer alternatives to revenue bonds. It is simply not realistic to expect private investors to support the riskier public projects, nor should public enterprise activities be straitjacketed in order to protect investors from risk. The more baroque arrangements invented in the past fifteen years to finance risky ventures met some real needs, but the same needs would be better met by more forthright methods of public finance. If taxpayers, rather than investors, must bear the burdens that arise, then to some extent the government must control high-risk borrowing and the underwriters must forego the opportunity to profit from it. A contemporary version of the Reconstruction Finance Corporation should operate a program of lending and loan guarantees for corporations. Such a program might also serve to bring order out of the chaos of current aids to investor-owned businesses in trouble.

The present system of public authorities has been generally successful at producing good management and effective operations (with some glaring exceptions). It has been generally unsuccessful at planning and allocating resources equitably. As excess revenues mount up in certain corporations and types of enterprise, overwhelming deficits mount up in others, and we have no orderly method of judging those balances or reordering them. As a start, the right of governments to receive dividends from the net revenues of their corporations should be asserted. (A proposal in Massachusetts would tax Massport's revenues to benefit the city of Boston.)

The primary responsibility for regional and sectoral planning should be shifted from public authorities to representative, general-purpose regional institutions or to state government. Minneapolis and St. Paul offer one approach that is adaptable to other areas: a politically appointed board with a fairly comprehensive perspective supervising a planning staff in the preparation of metropolitan development guides with which regional and municipal corporations must come to terms. Another approach involves strengthening the planning activities of consolidated agencies of state government, such as the Massachusetts Department of Transportation and Construction or the California Department of Natural Resources. Statutes might require that public authorities submit their capital plans, well in advance of bond resolutions or specific project design activities, for review by such a department. Procedures should be spelled out for settling disagreements, probably through arbitration by a special unit of the governor's staff. Problems involving interstate authorities must be reviewed by more than one department and gubernatorial veto powers would have to be relied upon for an ultimate resolution of disagreements. Whatever the specific arrangement (and it must vary from place to place), it should be designed to bring to bear on public authority decision making more forethought, more multidisciplinary study, and a broader range of governmental goals within functional areas: transportation, water resource development, energy development and conservation, economic development, and so forth.

State by state, the various statutes and regulations bearing on public authorities should be codified on the basis of comprehensive studies of public authority organization and management. The states should devise uniform provisions for supervision and financial controls while maintaining enough flexibility of structure and organization to create different types of enterprises to meet different needs and situations. A public authorities law (or, in states where it would be more appropriate, a public authorities and special districts law) should provide for periodic in-depth performance audits by public agencies and for submission of annual reports with specified content to a supervisory unit that would review and summarize them. (The unit might be a regional organization, a treasurer's or comptroller's office, or a governor's staff.) Annual reports should include project-by-project financial results, outlines of pending project plans, explicit discussions of program goals and the social effects of activities, and five-year debt and borrowing projections.

Authority budgets and board minutes should by law be public information available to all legislative and executive officials, the media, community groups, and the financial community. Minutes should include, by law, summaries of decisions taken in committee. The public should have the same access to authority files that it has to those of departmental agencies. Feasibility reports should also be made public information; the law should require that they include a social balance sheet of specified form and content, to be filed with the consultant's report prior to project authorizations or bond resolutions.

The law governing statutory corporations should facilitate flexibility over time. It should provide for a periodic review of enterprise statutes and specify legal procedures for merger, elimination, and other changes, with appropriate means of protecting the specific rights of bondholders. The tested procedures for handling mergers, sales, bankruptcies, and other shifts of control for investor-owned and also nonprofit corporations provide useful precedents. Certainly the investor has the right to know about possibilities for change, but the practice of invoking bondholder rights must be abolished as a means of obstructing all changes in the powers, structure, and scope of a public corporation. Procedures for forming regional and multipurpose conglomerates, with or without consolidated financing, should be devised. And the government that creates a corporation should have the residual right to abolish it, assuming or refinancing debts outstanding.

Most of these provisions can be only as effective as governments make them. In most cases, a small specialized staff unit in a governor's or mayor's office or regional government or planning agency (such as an urban county or metropolitan council) is needed to handle authority reports, to perform other supervisory functions, to draft recommendations to the legislature, to review audits, and to consult with the departmental officials involved in activities related to the enterprise.

Integrated financial planning is probably both the most important requirement of effective public enterprise and the most difficult to effect. Because major cities and nearly all states lack effective long-range budgets and financial plans, there are no coherent targets or projections into which public authority financial plans can be integrated. (The U.S. government is unique among Western industrialized countries in its failure to utilize a capital budget.) New York State in the mid-1970s should be a lesson to the rest of the nation, which is rushing headlong into some of the same practices pioneered there, again without thinking about present priorities or future contingencies. After a state, city, or regional government develops effective techniques of financial planning, it can begin to deal with the financial plans of statutory corporations. Breakdowns of total tax-exempt borrowing within the state—by type of bond, by type of agency, by public service category— should be at least as available to public officials as to bond market analysts. Projections of future debt service responsibilities and of direct and indirect state obligations should be maintained on the basis of varying assumptions about the general state of the economy. (The governor and/or mayor, city manager, or county executive should be required by law to approve revenue bond resolutions with direct or indirect impact on public obligations in the future.)

Financial integration on paper alone, however, will not alter priorities. State government must devise orderly means for actually allocating the excess revenues of some government enterprises and the deficits of others. Some statutory corporations may be required to turn over to the owning government net revenues (after debt service and maintenance of reserves) above a specified rate of return. Other corporations might follow the TVA pattern of providing the government itself with a return on its investment in the corporation. These arrangements can be made only for future financings, for the most part, because many bond covenants and authorizing statutes prohibit government from "taxing" the authority. Most states need to explore the legal possibilities further to find methods to reduce the dependence of the public sector on private investment but keep the goodwill of the investment community, which is essential as long as that dependence lasts.

One simple way around the legal difficulties in a number of cases is to direct the authority with profitable facilities into increased social benefit activities, so that the transfer of revenues is internal. The effects on the borrowing capacity of the corporation need to be objectively estimated and the advantages of the arrangement weighed against its costs in raised interest rates. Such measures also should reduce dependence on the municipal bond market. State and local officials should support proposals for taxable bond options, for federally guaranteed bonds, and for federal credit assistance agencies. The federal government should sponsor studies of state- and municipal-owned banking systems in Europe as examples of public financing approaches that might be tried in this country.

Monitoring subsidies is, of course, the other side of the coin. In the transit field, enormous and, for the most part, underestimated deficits are looming throughout the urban portions of the nation. Federal, state, and local legislatures, led by the U.S. Urban Mass Transportation Agency, are appropriating operating assistance funds that are everywhere below the actual deficits accumulating from a rather motley collection of transportation agencies. Legislators and the public are increasingly fed up with feeding the coffers of agencies whose managements they rightly distrust. Adequate tax sources must be found to finance rail and bus transportation, but only with specific services planning and financial control systems that assure that those funds are well spent. Continuing deterioration of transit services contributes to inner-city unemployment, to dropping suburban property values, to energy waste, to environmental degradation, and to disinvestment in public and private facilities—a wide range of demonstrable and quantifiable costs on the social balance sheet. Common sense calls for major allocations from earmarked gas taxes and highway and bridge tolls. In some cases, transfers from profits of public power facilities also have promise. Merger with regional water supply systems may help. But for practical and theoretical purposes, the subsidized transportation authority must be viewed and structured above all as a public agency. Adequate support will simply not otherwise be reliably forthcoming from distrustful legislators and taxpayers. In some cases, the agencies clearly need restructured boards, building in representatives of legislatures and community groups so as to co-opt allies for the agency's needs. Bankers are not of much use to an agency that cannot borrow funds on the private markets; a transit agency needs business skills in its internal management, not on its board of directors. On its board it needs political skills.

Traditional appointments to all authority boards can be combined with representatives of local and state governments and members of the public affected by the agency's activities. Numerous formulas with precedents can be applied to selecting a board that is representative and yet not stymied by irresponsible adherence to narrow constituencies. Corporations that are dependent upon a single government do not need boards that are divorced from that government; a strong corporate manager could be directly responsible to a board of government executives, in the manner of a number of federal government corporations. Governments can use arrangements for expanding representation flexibly to fit the corporation's jurisdiction; where several levels of government provide aid, voting power on the board might be weighted by contribution.

State governments must take the responsibility for exploring new forms of public enterprise that diverge from the typical public authority model. A state transportation authority, for example, might issue consolidated transportation bonds backed by revenues from a number of different subsidiary corporations (including transit, airport, and toll road enterprises) and from earmarked tax receipts, registration fees, and federal aid. Such an arrangement could preserve preexisting trust agreements covering toll and airport revenues as long as necessary; certain revenues could be deposited in separate funds for those purposes. Similarly, a state department of transportation could issue consolidated transportation revenue bonds with appropriate sinking fund arrangements.

Government constitutions, charters, civil service laws, administrative codes, and budgetary and internal management practices need thoroughgoing reforms. In the absence of these reforms, governments use public authorities to escape from obsolescent legal and financial restraints, from incompetence in the civil service, from obsolete jurisdictional boundaries, and from inequitable elections. Every serious student of government is aware of myriad recommendations for change in government management that make good sense. A leader with the courage to ignore the adage that American politics will not sustain large increments of change might disprove it. Government must take the lead in teaching public authorities how to accept political debate, how to engage in open decision making, but the authorities themselves hold many lessons for government on how to manage, how to get things done expeditiously, how to provide incentives for human skill and initiative to flourish on the job, and how to avoid the paralysis of overbureaucratization. Policy control is not incompatible with good management; in fact, our only hope for effective government is to combine the two.

No people can escape their history, but neither need they be enslaved by it. As the United States enters the third century of its experiment in democracy, it needs desperately to reassess its symbols, slogans, and constitutional strictures and to confront its basic fear of collective action. Without collective goals, we are doomed to endure continuing erosions of our resources and our capabilities.

Appendix: Statistical Measures of Government Corporations

How Many Public Authorities?

None of the available sources of nationwide data precisely defines public authorities or government corporations or provides counts of them. Public authorities are often grouped with "special districts," many of which are simply taxing districts managed and controlled by existing local governments. Others are categorized as dependencies of existing local governments.

According to the most recent published Census of Governments (undertaken at five-year intervals by the U.S. Bureau of the Census), there were 78,269 governmental units in the United States at the beginning of 1972: 15,781 local school districts, 23,885 special districts, 18,517 municipalities, 16,991 townships, 3,044 counties, 50 states, and the federal government.

The total had dropped by nearly 13,000 in the decade, with special districts the only category showing significant increase (from 18,000 to 24,000). There were sharp decreases in number of school districts, reflecting consolidations (from nearly 35,000 to fewer than 16,000).

Twenty-one interstate authorities are categorized as special districts under the states in which their headquarters are located. State and local authorities are more difficult to locate in the data. We can compare the census figures with state inventories of public authorities in two states: Pennsylvania's inventory counts 1,882 public authorities and the Census of Governments attributes 1,777 special districts to that state; New York State counts 230 public authorities and the census attributes 954 special districts to it. In both cases, some but not all organizations considered public authorities (or public benefit corporations) by the states are counted as special districts. A further examination of the census information on special districts within other states confirms that some but not all public authorities are subsumed in those figures.

The functional classification of special districts for the Census of Governments is based upon two types of criteria: the name of the entity (for example, all "housing authorities" are so classified), and the fact that the entity is empowered to perform only specialized limited activities (and therefore cannot be classified as a general local government). Limited functions are determined by mail survey.

Of the 23,885 special districts so classified, 59.3 percent had no debt, and another 14 percent had less than $100,000 debt. In other words, nearly three-quarters are not agencies involved in major investment in public facilities from independently raised capital as are the public authorities described in this book. Of the 23,885 special districts, 65.8 percent have no employees. The taxing tools of existing local governments, run by township, county, or municipal councils, they are little more than methods of collecting earmarked taxes for fire protection, sanitation, mosquito control, and so forth. Another 21.7 percent have five or fewer employees.

Another way to break down the statistics on special districts is by tax powers. Of the special districts listed, 11,581 are empowered by state legislation to levy property taxes (some of these, such as state of Washington public utility districts, do not use that power but operate like standard corporate authorities). The other 12,304 special districts include both those that receive earmarked taxes and assessments (drainage districts, soil conservation districts, some water supply and sewage districts, for example) and those that qualify as public authorities by the definition used in this book.

By such processes of elimination and a check against state estimates (I requested estimates in writing from all states, but most of the responses could not provide a full count) and against specialized studies of specific kinds of authorities, I estimate that no more than 5,000 to 6,000 of the entities classified as special districts are public authorities (or "statutory corporations," as they are classified by the Securities Industry Association) with independent management and borrowing but no active taxing powers.

Some public authorities are not listed within the special district category. The Census Bureau's definition of a separate governmental entity excludes some of them from the count by classifying them as dependencies of a parent government unit. Even an authority with complete financial autonomy is classified as being part of a "parent government" if it has one or more (usually more than one) of the following characteristics:

1. Appointment of agency officers by the chief executive of the parent government, or control of the agency by a board composed wholly or mainly of parent government officials.

2. Control by the agency over facilities that supplement, serve, or take the place of facilities ordinarily provided by the creating government.

3. Provision that agency properties and responsibilities shall revert to the creating government after agency debt has been repaid.

4. Requirements for approval of agency plans by the creating government.

5. Legislative or executive specification by the parent government as to the location and type of facilities the agency is to construct and maintain.

This scheme produces a paradoxical result: many of the most important state public authorities are defined dependencies of the parent government and are not separately counted. Some of these are identified in texts provided by the Census Bureau with state-by-state descriptions. They include turnpike and highway authorities, bridge and tunnel authorities, housing and educational facilities financing authorities, and industrial development authorities. The examples cited in the census documents are not all-inclusive and therefore cannot be translated into an accurate count.

The census definitions are sloppy, in any case. There is no consistent reasoning that explains why the Port Authority of New York and New Jersey and New York's regional market authorities are classified as special districts and the Power Authority of the State of New York and nearly all other state corporations are considered dependencies of state government. Why Alabama's airport authorities, tunnel authorities, housing, water, and sewer authorities are listed as special districts and its building and highway authorities and parking authorities are classified as dependent units remains an enigma. In California, 2,223 special districts are counted, including airport, air pollution, drainage, fire, flood control, hospital, and public utility districts and housing, transit, and tunnel authorities. At the same time, in California, the state Toll Bridge Authority, Water Project Authority, the Transit Authority of Sacramento (only), and county and municipal sewer districts are excluded from the count on grounds of being "subordinate agencies."

In effect, because of criteria for definition that are neither meaningful nor accurate reflections of reality, the data provided in these sections of the Census of Governments (volume 1 of *Governmental Organization*) are of limited use.

The error is rooted in the originally confused concept of "autonomy" promoted by the academic writers on special districts. Continuing the confusion, John C. Bollens, the author of a classic work on the subject—*Special District Governments in the United States* (1957)—declared that authorities are more dependent on parent governments than special districts are. Official definitions continue to use tax powers as a measure of fiscal independence; access to private money markets and to revenue-producing monopoly services is nowhere recognized as a source of independent financial power. An appointed governing board—even with long and staggered terms—is considered an indicator of administrative dependence; a board representing two or more local governments is considered an indicator of administrative independence. Those distinctions contradict the findings of this study and are illogical in light of what we know about bases of organizational power. Unfortunately, with few exceptions, public administration definitions of independence or "autonomy" have avoided questions of power.

The Census Bureau acknowledges the muddle. In fact, the 1972 report made exceptions to the classification that had been in effect since 1957:

Exceptions to strict application of these tests of autonomy have been made in a few instances, for types of entities that were treated as dependent agencies of other governments in the 1957 Census of Governments—i.e., school building corporations in Indiana (formerly counted as adjuncts of school districts); certain New Jersey authorities; and, in particular, the numerous "municipal authorities" in Pennsylvania. These exceptions have been dictated mainly by the difficult problems which the dependent-agency approach involved in these instances for the development of statistics on local government finance. (1972 Census of Governments, *Government Organization*, volume 1, Bureau of the Census, p. 13.)

The Role of Authorities in State and Local Finance

Statistics on authority borrowing are somewhat more enlightening. Data provided by The Bond Buyer's Municipal Finance Statistics categorize debt by special districts. So, too, do the Census of Governments' tables on government finances. Because most taxing districts do not borrow heavily, the figures showing nonguaranteed debt by special districts reflect closely public authority–type borrowing, but major additional segments of public authority borrowing are included in nonguaranteed debt of states and municipalities.

The importance of public authorities as financing devices varies from state to state depending upon, among other things, the extent to which the state resorts to nonguaranteed (and therefore constitutionally unrestricted) debt. The contrast between New York and California in this respect was reflected in table 11.1. Table A.1 shows the importance of nonguaranteed debt of state and local governments in the fifty states. Of all the nonguaranteed state and local debt in the United States reflected in these 1972 data, New York and Pennsylvania account for 23 percent. Adding the states of Washington, Texas, and New Jersey brings the sample to 37 percent of nonguaranteed public enterprise debt in the nation. I selected my case studies accordingly.

The public finance and public authority patterns of individual states can be interpreted with the help of additional information. Pennsylvania's

Table A.1
Nonguaranteed Long-Term Debt: State and Local Governments (Thousands of Dollars)

	1962		1972	
State	Amount	Percent of total debt	Amount	Percent of total debt
Alabama				
State	$ 232,491	81.4%	$ 738,452	88.1%
Local	405,542	57.1	1,088,919	67.8
Alaska				
State			116,366	32.8
Local	35,791	31.1	104,372	27.7
Arizona				
State	18,665	99.9	89,248	100.0
Local	308,521	57.4	328,807	28.6
Arkansas				
State	37,416	38.5	110,734	98.9
Local	88,649	33.6	517,049	64.0
California				
State	183,373	6.6	722,214	11.8
Local	1,477,787	25.7	3,858,099	33.5
Colorado				
State	64,823	100.0	120,151	100.0
Local	120,737	19.5	301,722	25.2
Connecticut				
State	346,900	40.0	273,784	13.6
Local	145,910	18.4	149,186	11.8
Delaware				
State	15,190	7.3	93,541	19.8
Local	34,976	26.2	123,863	40.0
Florida				
State	412,469	100.0	1,121,757	100.0
Local	915,755	58.6	2,220,572	64.8
Georgia				
State	438,339	99.9	984,344	99.9
Local	350,871	45.0	929,602	52.1
Hawaii				
State	87,532	42.6	257,719	33.0
Local	37,875	28.1	47,532	18.3
Idaho				
State	4,893	75.0	35,973	94.8
Local	43,463	35.7	53,832	35.5
Illinois				
State	568,992	64.0	1,278,601	73.6
Local	1,216,912	36.5	1,810,965	36.2

Table A.1 (continued)

State	1962 Amount	Percent of total debt	1972 Amount	Percent of total debt
Indiana				
State	$ 439,795	99.9%	$ 566,246	100.0%
Local	459,108	52.8	966,391	53.2
Iowa				
State	16,011	33.5	111,256	94.5
Local	90,612	19.9	342,280	36.0
Kansas				
State	186,219	90.6	214,581	100.0
Local	160,012	25.6	444,814	43.8
Kentucky				
State	437,750	79.3	1,408,769	77.8
Local	261,915	45.5	837,267	58.8
Louisiana				
State	103,901	26.8	547,037	48.6
Local	265,879	23.8	946,403	41.1
Maine				
State	85,154	61.3	51,199	18.7
Local	41,149	34.7	31,494	14.4
Maryland				
State	455,825	63.2	548,082	38.5
Local	221,309	18.3	371,571	15.2
Massachusetts				
State	559,281	37.5	694,710	31.8
Local	373,349	29.8	296,957	10.8
Michigan				
State	819,045	96.8	882,480	73.9
Local	354,622	17.9	928,057	18.5
Minnesota				
State	26,217	12.6	82,179	13.0
Local	175,342	16.5	391,791	13.9
Mississippi				
State	108,653	49.4	215,327	40.5
Local	82,220	20.3	260,655	34.3
Missouri				
State	27,617	31.4	110,795	79.7
Local	312,716	31.3	989,653	42.7
Montana				
State	49,104	91.4	94,840	99.9
Local	35,737	27.5	63,450	37.1
Nebraska				
State	19,783	100.0	83,176	100.0
Local	437,363	70.1	1,049,142	72.0

Table A.1 (continued)

Nevada				
State	$ 2,020	47.7%	$ 21,978	39.9%
Local	26,359	21.6	124,383	28.8
New Hampshire				
State	1,430	1.6	19,424	12.5
Local	12,691	14.2	29,227	12.3
New Jersey				
State	433,391	47.0	1,127,140	47.6
Local	580,372	32.0	834,936	24.2
New Mexico				
State	42,799	68.9	123,879	88.4
Local	81,623	38.8	111,845	38.0
New York				
State	1,627,027	50.8	5,020,763	63.2
Local	2,357,892	23.9	3,725,046	22.8
North Carolina				
State	16,416	6.3	111,972	20.8
Local	84,747	12.1	248,603	18.9
North Dakota				
State	9,592	62.8	40,998	73.2
Local	16,384	11.2	52,389	27.9
Ohio				
State	744,855	83.3	1,009,739	48.3
Local	459,436	18.1	1,324,571	33.8
Oklahoma				
State	254,621	78.5	567,553	75.3
Local	127,259	22.7	328,793	29.6
Oregon				
State	71			
Local	93,519	25.7	299,453	35.3
Pennsylvania				
State	1,184,706	80.1	2,455,801	57.9
Local	1,775,523	54.7	3,255,476	56.0
Rhode Island				
State	6,821	6.4	78,593	22.8
Local	33,027	16.9	53,998	15.8
South Carolina				
State	62,437	24.0	246,565	46.4
Local	104,391	42.9	359,572	47.3
South Dakota				
State	8,752	100.0	39,629	100.0
Local	7,968	13.5	12,783	14.5
Tennessee				
State	9,651	7.0	209,383	38.2
Local	481,843	41.1	912,491	39.5

Table A.1 (continued)

State	1962		1972	
	Amount	Percent of total debt	Amount	Percent of total debt
Texas				
State	$ 190,728	44.4%	$ 655,168	48.8%
Local	1,009,254	27.5	2,408,434	33.0
Utah				
State	19,551	100.0	56,607	58.6
Local	103,392	41.1	151,533	40.7
Vermont				
State	2,370	4.4	91,143	28.2
Local	3,197	6.7	8,646	6.7
Virginia				
State	203,982	96.4	279,410	80.0
Local	383,779	36.7	487,502	21.4
Washington				
State	428,455	88.4	837,891	85.4
Local	1,382,074	74.4	2,688,826	73.5
West Virginia				
State	173,711	59.9	331,995	48.4
Local	95,013	50.6	162,422	60.2
Wisconsin				
State	115,483	100.0	396,606	49.5
Local	128,946	12.8	217,046	11.0
Wyoming				
State	13,409	100.0	38,180	100.0
Local	32,822	31.6	71,748	65.3

Source: U.S. Bureau of the Census, 1962 and 1972 Census of Governments, Government Finances, Compendiums, tables 40, 46.

municipal corporations, for example, are reflected in that state's proportion of local debt that is nonguaranteed, which is well above average. The importance of public power authorities in Nebraska and Washington shows up in the "special district" debt in those states (which is, in the aggregate, 97 percent nonguaranteed for both those states). The eighteen states in which 75 to 100 percent of state debt is nonguaranteed are, for the most part, states with rigid (and aged) constitutional debt limits and relatively moderate total debt levels.

The census data on government finances also provide information on utilities operated by local governments. The term "utility" includes water supply, electric, gas, and transit systems owned and operated by local government instrumentalities. The debt of public authority–managed utilities is partly reflected in the category "special districts" and partly under "municipal utilities." These figures are shown in table A.2. Those figures reflect the

Table A.2
Finances of Utilities Operated by Local Governments: United States, 1971–1972
(Thousands of Dollars)

	Utility expenditure in one year	Nonguaranteed debt outstanding	Full faith and credit debt outstanding
Water supply	$3,739,651	$ 6,760,356	$4,782,084
Municipalities	2,621,549	4,929,343	2,783,056
Special districts	770,197	1,321,206	1,531,540
Other [a]	347,906	509,806	467,488
Electric power	3,281,198	6,160,275	490,553
Municipalities	2,311,880	3,406,130	149,139
Special districts	909,400	2,746,675	338,764
Other [a]	59,917	7,470	2,650
Transit	2,290,432	481,824	3,297,021
Municipalities	1,175,985	88,008	1,907,549
Special districts	1,096,352	388,796	1,389,472
Other [a]	18,095	5,020	
Gas supply	403,802	202,086	21,008
Municipalities	273,289	97,819	20,368
Special districts	129,425	104,267	485
Other [a]	1,088		155
Total	9,715,083	13,604,540	8,590,666

[a] Includes townships and counties.
Source: U.S. Bureau of the Census, 1972 Census of Governments, Government Finances.

overwhelming dominance of public authority-type finance for governmental electric power generation, its importance for water supply and gas operations, and its failure to provide funds for public transit.

Finally, the Securities Industry Association aggregates data under a classification for "statutory authorities." The category is designed for authorities created by statute with their own borrowing powers, without taxing powers, as I have defined public authorities. The actual coverage is subject to some error because titles have been used to sort out types of entities. Commissions, authorities, boards, and corporations are included (except boards of education with taxing power). If "district" is in the title, the entity is classified as a special district unless special information justifies its shift to authority status. Some nontaxing authorities that are entitled districts may be missing, but the debt reported for "statutory authorities" by SIA's *Municipal Statistical Bulletin* and *Municipal Market Developments* can be considered the closest available measure of authority activity. Tables A.3 through A.11 reflect data produced from SIA's computer in the categories I requested. The years 1963, 1969, 1970, and 1971 are used to permit a view of trends and to provide a three-year sequence to average out single-year anomalies. Tables in the text—particularly in chapter 3—reflect SIA data through 1976.

Table A.3
Municipal Bond Sales by Type of Issue and Type of Issuer, 1963 (Millions of Dollars)

	General obligation		Revenue				New housing authority
	Unlimited tax	Limited tax	Utility	Quasi-utility	Special tax	Rental	
States	$ 928	$ 0	$ 0	$365	$ 6	$ 22	$ 0
Counties	499	69	91	81	1	41	0
Municipalities	1,886	142	845	88	13	68	0
School districts	1,473	79	282	8	0	3	0
Special districts	444	42	322	170	1	9	0
Statutory authorities	87	13	449	827	23	822	248

Table A.4
Municipal Bond Sales by Type of Issue and Type of Issuer, 1969 (Millions of Dollars)

| | General obligation | | Revenue | | | | New housing authority |
	Unlimited tax	Limited tax	Utility	Quasi-utility	Special tax	Rental	
States	$2,910	$ 37	$ 95	$ 113	$42	$ 67	$ 0
Counties	940	50	40	28	0	88	0
Municipalities	1,492	175	459	53	3	107	0
School districts	1,358	119	0	0	0	2	0
Special districts	461	30	47	12	1	4	0
Statutory authorities	145	15	296	1,152	34	926	402

Table A.5
Municipal Bond Sales by Type of Issue and Type of Issuer, 1970 (Millions of Dollars)

| | General obligation | | Revenue | | | | New housing authority |
	Unlimited tax	Limited tax	Utility	Quasi-utility	Special tax	Rental	
States	$3,976	$ 0	$ 0	$ 101	$60	$ 28	$ 0
Counties	1,423	77	15	97	58	78	0
Municipalities	3,073	305	752	254	88	72	0
School districts	2,025	144	8	1	0	9	0
Special districts	498	17	467	200	83	23	0
Statutory authorities	303	14	577	2,127	41	960	131

Table A.6
Municipal Bond Sales by Type of Issue and Type of Issuer, 1971 (Millions of Dollars)

| | General obligation | | Revenue | | | | New housing authority |
	Unlimited tax	Limited tax	Utility	Quasi-utility	Special tax	Rental	
States	$5,515	$ 2	$ 106	$ 304	$36	$ 29	$ 0
Counties	1,577	59	87	100	9	130	0
Municipalities	4,281	306	1,085	173	33	152	0
School districts	2,332	77	104	23	0	74	0
Special districts	776	21	466	1,079	0	286	0
Statutory authorities	258	24	615	2,868	15	942	1,000

Table A.7
Municipal Bond Sales by Type of Issue and Use of Proceeds, 1963 (Millions of Dollars)

	General obligation		Revenue				New housing authority
	Unlimited tax	Limited tax	Utility	Quasi-utility	Special tax	Rental	
Education	$2,067	$95	$ 0	$264	$ 0	$381	0
Elementary and secondary	1,943	78	0	35	0	339	0
Colleges and universities	111	16	0	203	0	42	0
Other	13	1	0	26	0	0	0
Transportation	565	52	5	757	3	0	0
Roads, bridges, tunnels	319	47	5	475	3	0	0
Ports, airports	69	2	0	196	0	0	0
Other	177	3	0	86	0	0	0
Utilities and conservation	830	71	1,303	3	0	2	0
Water, sewer	748	62	696	0	0	1	0
Other	82	9	.607	3	0	1	0
Social welfare	401	20	4	10	0	201	248
Public housing	115	0	0	3	0	198	248
Other	286	20	4	7	0	3	0
Industrial	26	1	0	53	0	58	0
Public services	73	11	0	100	5	2	0
Classified, not listed	249	29	678	255	2	205	0
Unclassified	1,108	66	1	98	32	117	0

Table A.8
Municipal Bond Sales by Type of Issue and Use of Proceeds, 1969 (Millions of Dollars)

	General obligation		Revenue				New housing authority
	Unlimited tax	Limited tax	Utility	Quasi-utility	Special tax	Rental	
Education	$2,074	$130	$ 0	$357	$ 4	$582	$ 0
Elementary and secondary	1,787	116	0	15	4	441	0
Colleges and universities	221	8	0	336	0	118	0
Other	66	6	0	6	0	23	0
Transportation	1,332	54	0	596	22	438	0
Roads, bridges, tunnels	933	44	0	306	15	133	0
Ports, airports	55	5	0	67	0	114	0
Other	344	5	0	223	7	191	0
Utilities and conservation	704	45	926	0	0	13	0
Water, sewer	636	39	494	0	0	7	0
Other	68	6	432	0	0	6	0

Table A.8 (continued)

Social welfare	654	44	0	267	0	101	402
Public housing	64	8	0	70	0	0	402
Other	590	36	0	197	0	101	0
Industrial	10	1	0	0	3	36	0
Public services	165	5	0	26	0	15	0
Classified, not listed	370	29	11	98	51	7	0
Unclassified	1,999	117	0	12	0	2	0

Table A.9
Municipal Bond Sales by Type of Issue and Use of Proceeds, 1970 (Millions of Dollars)

	General obligation		Revenue				New
	Unlimited tax	Limited tax	Utility	Quasi-utility	Special tax	Rental	housing authority
Education	$3,321	$204	$ 6	$ 691	$ 35	$781	$ 0
Elementary and secondary	2,777	187	0	0	4	596	0
Colleges and universities	368	11	6	612	15	51	0
Other	176	6	0	79	16	134	0
Transportation	1,540	58	0	1,403	141	32	0
Roads, bridges, tunnels	1,020	37	0	451	28	0	0
Ports, airports	127	18	0	522	0	30	0
Other	393	3	0	430	113	2	0
Utilities and conservation	1,538	73	1,796	0	55	13	0
Water, sewer	1,449	71	658	0	55	12	0
Other	89	2	1,138	0	0	1	0
Social welfare	822	21	0	516	1	168	131
Public housing	74	1	0	214	0	44	131
Other	748	20	0	302	1	124	0
Industrial	15	2	0	0	0	98	0
Public services	306	30	0	13	0	17	0
Classified, not listed	337	29	16	102	61	61	0
Unclassified	3,419	139	0	54	37	0	0

Table A.10
Municipal Bond Sales by Type of Issue and Use of Proceeds, 1971 (Millions of Dollars)

	General obligation		Revenue				New housing authority
	Unlimited tax	Limited tax	Utility	Quasi-utility	Special tax	Rental	
Education	$3,608	$101	$ 0	$ 974	$ 5	$586	$ 0
Elementary and secondary	3,045	90	0	0	1	499	0
Colleges and universities	280	11	0	969	0	68	0
Other	283	0	0	5	4	19	0
Transportation	2,247	47	0	1,923	25	67	0
Roads, bridges, tunnels	1,770	35	0	792	11	34	0
Ports, airports	64	6	0	579	14	31	0
Other	413	6	0	552	0	2	0
Utilities and conservation	2,517	109	2,403	11	0	168	0
Water, sewer	2,153	96	870	2	0	49	0
Other	364	13	1,533	9	0	119	0
Social welfare	1,157	38	0	1,280	0	303	1,000
Public housing	122	6	0	732	0	35	1,000
Other	1,035	32	0	548	0	268	0
Industrial	19	4	0	0	0	184	0
Public services	378	10	0	186	0	27	0
Classified, not listed	488	43	60	162	1	259	0
Unclassified	4,325	138	1	13	62	19	0

Table A.11
Municipal Bond Sales of Statutory Authorities Only: Type of Issue by State (Millions of Dollars)

	1963		1969		1970		1971	
	General obligation	Revenue	General obligation	Revenue	General obligation	Revenue	General obligation	Revenue
Alabama	$14	$ 49	$13	$ 28	$10	$165	$ 2	$ 133
Alaska	0	8	0	6	0	16	0	4
Arizona	0	1	0	31	0	11	0	4
Arkansas	0	6	0	0	0	13	0	5
California	0	190	0	166	3	282	31	206
Canada	0	0	0	0	0	0	0	0
Colorado	2	1	0	0	0	5	0	0
Connecticut	0	0	0	32	0	0	0	52
Delaware	0	0	0	140	0	20	0	0
District of Columbia	0	0	0	0	0	0	0	0
Florida	0	69	0	55	3	91	0	117
Georgia	0	43	9	64	0	61	1	145
Hawaii	0	0	0	0	0	0	0	0
Idaho	0	0	0	0	0	3	0	5
Illinois	0	102	1	62	0	360	2	210
Indiana	8	40	9	124	19	181	5	128
Iowa	0	0	0	0	0	8	0	7
Kansas	1	1	0	15	0	2	0	18
Kentucky	0	15	0	104	0	71	0	176
Louisiana	5	52	1	5	0	10	13	39
Maine	0	0	2	5	0	3	0	0

Table A.11 (continued)

	1963		1969		1970		1971	
	General obligation	Revenue	General obligation	Revenue	General obligation	Revenue	General obligation	Revenue
Maryland	13	22	13	5	10	5	9	34
Massachusetts	0	0	0	62	67	19	13	90
Michigan	0	10	3	20	0	65	12	122
Minnesota	5	3	8	0	65	2	12	7
Mississippi	0	0	0	1	0	16	0	3
Missouri	0	29	0	4	0	16	0	16
Montana	0	0	0	0	0	5	0	5
Nebraska[a]	0	3	0	0	0	0	0	0
Nevada	0	0	0	0	0	0	0	8
New Hampshire	0	0	0	0	0	0	0	8
New Jersey	0	54	0	406	5	152	1	346
New Mexico	0	5	0	0	0	0	0	3
New York	8	419	81	320	0	826	45	1,072
North Carolina	0	2	0	0	0	5	0	2
North Dakota	0	0	0	2	0	3	0	6
Ohio	0	21	0	7	0	9	4	27
Oklahoma	0	49	0	49	0	23	0	103
Oregon	10	0	0	0	10	0	3	8
Pennsylvania	7	673	3	370	30	512	0	604
Puerto Rico	0	13	14	80	13	246	0	165
Rhode Island	0	0	0	2	0	10	0	1

South Carolina	0	1	0	0	1	5	1	27
South Dakota	0	0	0	1	0	6	0	5
Tennessee	0	105	0	12	4	85	3	8
Texas	12	28	2	68	6	234	85	328
Utah	0	0	0	0	0	0	0	0
Vermont	0	0	3	6	46	2	0	9
Virginia	15	0	0	2	25	66	38	29
Virgin Islands	0	0	0	0	0	20	0	0
Washington	0	104	0	63	0	67	3	140
West Virginia	0	1	0	10	0	5	0	12
Wisconsin	0	0	0	80	0	0	0	0
Wyoming	0	0	0	0	0	0	0	3
Other Territories	0	0	0	0	0	0	0	0

[a]Excludes Nebraska public power districts.

Federal Enterprises

Federal enterprises, like state and local enterprises, cannot be definitively and accurately counted, again because they are not clearly defined and categorized by law or administrative practice.

Chart 2.1 listed federal government corporations, but my choice of what to include and what to exclude was necessarily subjective. (Foundations, institutes, regulatory commissions, interagency councils and committees, advisory boards, administrations, and revolving funds were excluded. So was the board of governors of the Federal Reserve System.) I have also taken some liberties with ownership. For example, the law calls the Corporation for Public Broadcasting "nongovernmental" (because Congress was uneasy about political involvement in television). However, by functional measures, it is wholly owned by the government: its entire board is appointed by the president, and it is financed by federal appropriations. Government-sponsored enterprises in private ownership not listed in chart 2.1 include land banks, home loan banks, intermediate credit banks, banks for cooperatives, the Federal National Mortgage Association, the Home Loan Mortgage Association, the Securities Investor Protection Corporation, and the Student Loan Marketing Association. Such ambiguous distinctions among government-owned, government-sponsored, and government-funded corporations characterize much of the development in federal enterprise since World War II.

Examples of departmental bureaus that perform enterprise activities precisely like those of government corporations are the Federal Insurance Administration, Federal Housing Administration, the Bonneville, Alaska, Southeastern, and Southwestern Power Administrations, and the Federal Railroad Administration. The Federal Housing Administration, for example, was created in 1934 and became part of the Housing and Home Finance Agency in 1947. In 1965, it was transferred to the new Department of Housing and Urban Development, where its activities are now directed by an assistant secretary, who is federal housing commissioner. The original Public Housing Administration followed the same route. Today all such banking functions as insuring mortgages and loans made by private lending institutions for different kinds of housing construction, rehabilitation, and subsidization are clustered in this Housing Production and Mortgage Credit Division of HUD. The Federal Insurance Administration is also housed within HUD. It administers three congressionally mandated property insurance programs: flood insurance, riot reinsurance, and crime insurance.

The power administrations within the Department of the Interior build dams and nuclear power facilities, market electricity to private and public customers, set prices, let contracts, raise capital, and generally conduct their businesses in a manner similar to that of public and private energy-producing utilities. The Bonneville Power Administration is authorized by statute to use operating revenues directly and to raise funds by the sale of revenue bonds through the U.S. Treasury, bypassing legislative appropriations. The Alaska Railroad is managed through the Department of Transportation's Railroad Administration.

Examples of bureaus outside cabinet-level departments that engage in enterprise activities are the Small Business Administration (which extends loans to small businesses, supervises small business investment corporations, and guarantees leases) and the National Credit Union Administration (which charters credit unions and charges premiums for insurance).

Most federal enterprise activities (in or out of corporate structures) are banking and insurance-related activities. Of the twenty wholly owned corporations listed in chart 2.1, only the broadcasting agencies, Panama Canal Company, Federal Prison Industries, TVA, St. Lawrence Seaway Corporation, U.S. Postal Service, and the Legal Services Corporation are engaged in directly distributing goods or nonbanking and insurance services. The banking and insurance activities do not compete with private financial establishments but generally absorb some risks from the private sector and expand markets for private services.

In 1969, the federal government adopted a unified budget. The unified budget documents include listings of public enterprise funds, including expenditures of wholly owned government corporations that are derived from operating revenues (for example, from power sales, loan receipts, and insurance premiums), as well as expenditures derived from appropriations. From 1971 to 1977, however, Congress tended to vote piecemeal exceptions to the unified budget, authorizing so-called off-budget outlays for the Postal Service, the Export-Import Bank, the Rural Telephone Bank, the Federal Financing Bank, the U.S. Railway Association, and the Pension Benefit Guaranty Corporation. Legislation has been proposed by the Office of Management and Budget to bring most of these items back into the executive budget.

The federal government, unlike most state and local governments, does not utilize a separate capital budget. Authorization to borrow is budget authority. Outlays from borrowed funds are indistinguishable in budget summaries from outlays from current appropriations. Appropriations flow to government corporations in several ways: directly to the corporation to support administrative expenses or capital investment; by loans or grants extended by other government agencies; through appropriations to the U.S. Treasury from which credit subsidies may be extended to the corporation; and through earmarked revolving funds (for which there is no fiscal year limitation on budget authority).

In summary, the federal government has developed flexibility in modes of management, finance, and control that go beyond any formula for one type of government corporation. Each program is designed by its particular statute, and the variations and permutations are limitless. The ideas of the orthodox corporatists have had more lasting influence on state and local public authorities than on federal enterprise.

Notes

Chapter 1

1. Public administration literature has long debated the definitional distinctions of the public authority. Most of the accepted definitions do include the characteristics insisted upon here: independent corporate status; no direct levy of taxes; power to raise money from private money markets; wholly owned by government. The experts tend, however, to add on a number of additional definitional traits that are in fact empirical characteristics, sometimes present and sometimes absent ("self-supporting," for example). Unfortunately the sources for data have not settled on meaningful or consistent definitions. See, for example, Harry B. Strickland, *Inside the Trojan Horse: Understanding the Specialized Units of Local Government* (Clarks Summit, Pa.: Logo Publishing Co., 1969); Council of State Governments, *Public Authorities in the States* (Lexington, Ky., 1953); Nathaniel S. Preston, "The Use and Control of Public Authorities in American State and Local Government" (Ph.D. diss., Princeton University, 1960); Robert G. Smith, *Public Authorities, Special Districts and Local Government* (Washington, D.C., 1964); Council of State Governments, *State Public Authorities* (1970); and U.S. Bureau of the Census, *1972 Census of Governments: Governmental Organization* (Washington, D.C.: U.S. Department of Commerce, 1973).

The U.S. Bureau of the Census counts some public authorities in the category of "special districts" (most of which are unincorporated taxing districts controlled by elected local governments) and others in the category of dependencies of state or municipal government. The category that comes closest to reality is that of "statutory authority" used by the Securities Industry Association, but corporations that do not have "authority" in their titles tend to slip through this count, and it excludes those not issuing bonds. See the appendix for a detailed analysis of the data sources.

2. Arnold Toynbee, letter to the editor, *New York Times*, June 15, 1973.

3. CBS-TV, "The Corporation," December 6, 1973. Phillips Petroleum issued a statement in 1974 that $685,000 in corporate funds had been contributed to political campaigns over a decade (including the $100,000 previously admitted by Keeler).

4. Vincent Ostrom, *Institutional Arrangements for Water Resource Development*, Report to the U.S. National Water Commission (Washington, D.C.: National Technical Information Service, Accession No. PB 207314, U.S. Department of Commerce, 1971), p. 34.

5. Ibid., p. 16.

6. Garrett Hardin, "The Tragedy of the Commons," *Science* 162 (December 13, 1968).

7. See, for example, Charles Perrow, *Complex Organizations: A Critical Essay* (Chicago: Scott-Foresman, 1972), and David Rogers, *110 Livingston Street: Politics and Bureaucracy in the New York City Schools* (New York: Random House, 1968).

Chapter 2

1. See Marver Bernstein, *Regulating Business by Independent Commission* (Princeton, N.J.: Princeton University Press, 1955), and Richard Hellman, *Government Competition in the Electric Utility Industry* (New York: Praeger, 1972).

2. Marguerite Owen, *The Tennessee Valley Authority* (New York: Praeger, 1973), p. 25.

3. Statements by William H. Dunham, chief executive of Central Maine Power Company and Maine Yankee Atomic Power Company, before the Public Utilities Committee of the 106th Maine Legislature, April 24, 1973.

4. Adam Smith, *An Inquiry into the Nature and Causes of the Wealth of Nations* (New York: Modern Library, 1936), p. 147.

5. Ibid., pp. 650–651 (emphasis added).

6. Ibid., p. 14.

7. None of the distinguishing features used by economic theorists to identify "public goods and services" accounts satisfactorily for the historical growth of government activities—not monopoly, lack of profit, capital intensity, indivisibility of costs or benefits, and certainly not Keynesian concepts of government intervention to maintain full employment. Government utilities and timberlands are profitable; housing, banking, and higher education are not monopolies; mass transportation is labor intensive; industrial and mortgage finance have divisible benefits; and employment was a central objective of public enterprise only in the 1930s.

8. See, for example, John Paterson Davis, *Corporations: A Study of the Origins and Development of Great Combinations and of Their Relations to the Authority of the State* (New York: G. P. Putnam & Sons, 1905).

9. The quasi-public origins of the corporate form are reflected in legal terminology that designates as a "public corporation" the private sector firm with widely held stock (compared with, for example, the close corporation or partnership). In this book, a public corporation is one owned by government, and a private firm is any nongovernmental business enterprise.

10. William Wordsworth, *Complete Poetical Works* (Boston: Houghton Mifflin, 1932), p. 784.

11. Rev. Sidney Smith, letter to the *London Morning Chronicle*, 1843, quoted in Reginald C. McGrane, *Foreign Bondholders and American State Debts* (New York: Macmillan, 1935), pp. 59–60.

12. A. M. Hillhouse, *Municipal Bonds: A Century of Experience* (New York: Prentice-Hall, 1936), p. 157.

13. Included in this count are states that permit state borrowing without a referendum of only minor amounts (outstanding debt less than $500,000 or similar ceiling expressed as a percent of tax base or appropriations). Virginia, also included in this total, makes an exception for self-liquidating debt approved by two-thirds of the legislature and limited to a proportion of general revenues.

14. Data on state constitutional limitations on state borrowing are given in table 95 of the U.S. Advisory Commission on Intergovernmental Relations, 1973–1974 edition of *Federal-State-Local Finances: Significant Features of Federalism* (Washington, D.C.: Government Printing Office). I have moved Maryland from the category of flexible legislative borrowing to severe limitation because of its fifteen-year term limitation on bonds issued.

15. Eric F. Goldman, *Rendezvous with Destiny* (New York: Vintage, 1956), p. 11.

16. This emphasis on education for ethical behavior departs from Adam Smith's theory of personality in which the individual pursuing his own self-interest unconsciously promotes the interest of society.

17. William Allen White, *The Old Order Changeth* (Milwaukee: The Young Churchman Co., 1910), p. 132. The concept of popular conscience that could be released into public life had roots, of course, in eighteenth-century Enlightenment theories.

18. Message of April 10, 1933, from Franklin D. Roosevelt, House Document 15, 73d Congress, 1st session, quoted in C. Herman Pritchett, *The Tennessee Valley Authority* (Chapel Hill: University of North Carolina Press, 1943), p. 29.

19. Goldman, *Rendezvous*, p. 263.

20. Jesse Jones with Edward Angley, *Fifty Billion Dollars: My Thirteen Years with RFC, 1932–1945* (New York: Macmillan, 1951), pp. 491–492.

21. Rowland R. Hughes, speech to a conference of the National Association of Bank Auditors and Controllers, New York, December 7, 1954.

22. Chamber of Commerce of the United States, *Government Competition: Problem and Perspective* (Washington, D.C., 1954), p. 9.

23. Paraphrase from U.S. Commission on the Organization of the Executive Branch of the Government, Staff Study on Business Enterprises Outside the Department of Defense, 1955, p. 4, "A Policy for Government Business Enterprises." A Budget Bureau circular had stated the Eisenhower administration's policy, going even further: "It is the general policy of the administration that the Federal government will not start or carry on any commercial activity to provide a service or product for its own use if such product or service can be procured from private enterprise through ordinary business channels" (January 27, 1955).

24. U.S. Commission on the Organization of the Executive Branch of the Government, *Business Enterprises: A Report to the Congress*, May 1955, p. xi.

25. Ibid., pp. 109-110, 113.

26. Quoted from cabinet meeting, July 31, 1953, by Emmet J. Hughes, in *The Ordeal of Power* (New York: Dell Publishing Co., 1963), p. 133.

27. Representative Chet Holifield in 1955, quoted in Aaron Wildavsky, *Dixon-Yates: A Study in Power Politics* (New Haven, Conn.: Yale University Press, 1962), p. 310.

28. For assessments of government contracting, see Murray L. Weidenbaum, *The Modern Public Sector: New Ways of Doing the Government's Business* (New York: Basic Books, 1967) and Bruce L. R. Smith, ed., *The New Political Economy: The Public Use of the Private Sector* (New York: John Wiley, 1975).

29. Frank J. Goodnow, *Politics and Administration* (New York: Macmillan, 1914); Woodrow Wilson, "The Study of Administration" (1887), in *Political Science Quarterly* 56 (December 1941): 481-506, and *Congressional Government* (New York: Meridian, 1959).

30. See, for example, Dwight Waldo, *The Administrative State* (New York: Ronald Press, 1948); Paul Appleby, *Policy and Administration* (University: University of Alabama Press, 1949); Harold Stein, ed., *Public Administration and Policy Development: A Case Book* (New York: Harcourt Brace & Co., 1952).

31. Foreword to Robert Moses, *Public Works: A Dangerous Trade* (New York: McGraw-Hill, 1970), p. xi.

32. Robert Smith, *Public Authorities, Special Districts and Local Government* (Washington, D.C., 1964), p. 147. Smith has clarified his assessment in his *Ad Hoc Governments* (Beverly Hills: Sage Publications, 1974), p. 39. Frequently repeated arguments for and against the use of public authorities fall into the following categories:

For Authorities
1. They overcome unrealistic debt limits.
2. They provide needed services and facilities without increasing taxes.
3. They shift cost burdens to the user.
4. They facilitate intergovernmental cooperation.
5. They are divorced from politics and provide for independent, efficient, and businesslike operation.
6. They promote citizen participation.
7. They are convenient and flexible.
8. They raise capital more easily and at no more cost than other municipal methods.

Against Authorities
1. They are unnecessary.

2. They circumvent legal debt regulations and other constitutional provisions.

3. They increase public debt without limits.

4. They are not controlled by the electorate.

5. They are accountable to no one.

6. They add to the fragmentation of the governmental structure.

7. They compete with private enterprise.

8. They cost more to finance than other municipal methods.

Many of the arguments are mutually contradictory—for example, numbers 8 for and 8 against, as well as numbers 6 for and 4 against. Other pairs agree on a point of fact but differ as to whether it is good or bad (such as pairs 5 for and 4 against, as well as 1 for and 2 against). Harry B. Strickland, in *Inside the Trojan Horse: Understanding the Specialized Units of Local Government* (Clarks Summit, Pa.: Logo Publishing and Research, 1969), devised a list like this. He attempted empirical analysis of one factor—cost of financing—with mixed results.

33. C. Herman Pritchett, "The Government Corporation Control Act of 1945," *American Political Science Review* 60 (1946): 495–509, and "The Paradox of the Government Corporation," *Public Administration Review* 1 (1941): 381–389; John McDiarmid, *Government Corporations and Federal Funds* (Chicago: University of Chicago Press, 1937); Marshall E. Dimock, *Government-Operated Enterprises in the Panama Canal Zone* (Chicago: University of Chicago Press, 1934), *Free Enterprise and the Administrative State* (University, Ala.: University of Alabama Press, 1951), and *Developing America's Waterways* (Chicago: University of Chicago Press, 1935); John Thurston, *Government Proprietary Corporations in the English-Speaking Countries* (Cambridge, Mass.: Harvard University Press, 1937); Harold A. Van Dorn, *Government Owned Corporations* (New York: Knopf, 1926); W. F. Willoughby, *Principles of Public Administration* (Washington, D.C.: The Brookings Institution, 1927), and "The National Government as a Holding Corporation," *Political Science Quarterly* 32 (1917): 505–521.

34. From the *Washington Star*, quoted in Harold Seidman, *Politics, Position and Power: The Dynamics of Federal Organization* (New York: Oxford University Press, 1970), p. 215.

35. See, for example, Adolf A. Berle and Gardiner C. Means, *The Modern Corporation and Private Property* (New York: Macmillan, 1948).

36. McDiarmid, *Government Corporations,* p. xii.

37. Robert F. Babcock, *State and Local Government and Politics* (New York: Random House, 1957), p. 251.

38. Daniel L. Kurshan, "Developing Productivity in the Port of New York Authority," An Information Memorandum for the United Nations Working Group on Measures for Improving Performance of Public Enterprises in Developing Countries, Herceg-Novi, Yugoslavia, October 1969.

39. The Port Authority of New York and New Jersey, *Annual Report,* 1975, p. 38. Austin Tobin's description of authority origins is not accurate where he asserts: "Through the conception of the authority, [Governor Alfred E. Smith of New York and Governor Walter Edge of New Jersey] initiated the first government enterprise in this country required to be self-supporting or fail. Thus, the test of the marketplace—ability to attain self-support—was introduced to government in 1921 with the establishment of the Port Authority" ("Acceptance Speech to the American Management Association," Port Authority Press Release, September 25, 1962). In fact, until 1933 the Port Authority received $200,000 operating assistance annually from the two states, the maximum operating subsidy committed to it in the compact. Its construction projects through 1935 were funded by state loans (later liquidated by partial payment and by Public Works Administration loans supplementing revenue bonds. Bonds were nevertheless threatened with default (the Arthur Kill Bridge earned one-tenth its revenue estimates)

until Holland Tunnel revenues were transferred to the authority from the states to maintain debt service on the earlier projects, including the partly completed George Washington Bridge.

40. Pritchett, "Paradox," p. 389.

41. The statutes that established many of the early state and local authorities provided for their demise when their bonds were paid off. The facilities they constructed would then revert to regular government agencies for toll-free operation and maintenance. At this time, such corporations were more often engaged in capital construction than in producing competitive services or products. But most contemporary public authorities, by refinancing and issuing new bonds for new projects, manage to stay in debt, and therefore, in business, in perpetuity. Internally sponsored growth accounts for much of the increase in overall activity of public enterprise since World War II.

42. *New York Times,* February 14, 1962.

43. Moses, *Public Works,* p. 362.

44. Juan Cameron, "Whose Authority?" *The Atlantic Monthly* 204, no. 2 (August 1959): 38.

45. U.S. President's Committee on Administrative Management (Brownlow Committee), *Report of the Committee* (1937); U.S. Commission on Organization of Executive Branch of Government (1949, 1955) (first and second Hoover commissions); U.S. President's Advisory Council on Executive Reorganization (Ash Council) (1971).

46. Frederick G. Mosher et al., *Watergate: Implications for Responsible Government: Report to the Senate Watergate Committee by a Panel of the National Academy of Public Administration* (New York: Basic Books, 1974).

47. Herbert Emmerich, *Essays on Federal Reorganization* (University, Ala.: University of Alabama Press, 1950), p. 63.

48. U.S. Commission on the Organization of the Executive Branch of Government, *Report on Federal Business Enterprises* (1949), p. 95.

49. David E. Lilienthal, *The Journals of David E. Lilienthal,* vol. 1: *The TVA Years, 1939–1945* (New York: Harper & Row, 1964).

50. David E. Lilienthal and Robert H. Marquis, "The Conduct of Business Enterprises by the Federal Government," *Harvard Law Review* (1941): 557.

51. David E. Lilienthal, *TVA: Democracy on the March* (New York: Harper, 1944).

52. There have been exceptions. In the 1940s, Erwin Wilkie Bard expressed some uneasiness over the limited influence state governors had over authority policies (*The Port of New York Authority* [New York: Columbia University Press, 1942]), and Luther Gulick criticized the use of authorities to short-circuit the democratic process ("Authorities and How to Use Them," *Tax Review* 8 [1947]: 47–52). In 1953, Victor Jones concluded that autonomous authorities were unlikely to perform activities with low income-producing value and that they should be subject to legislative debate and budgetary control ("Local Government Organization in Metropolitan Areas: Its Relation to Urban Redevelopment," in Coleman Woodbury, ed., *The Future of Cities and Urban Redevelopment* [Chicago: University of Chicago Press, 1953], p. 585).

53. *A Proposed Plan of Solid Waste Management for Connecticut,* prepared by General Electric in Cooperation with the Department of Environmental Protection, Hartford, Connecticut (1973).

54. President's Commission on Postal Organization, *Towards Postal Excellence, Contractor's Report* (Washington, D.C.: U.S. Government Printing Office, 1968), esp. vol. 1.

55. For example, one audit by the U.S. General Accounting Office concluded that the Postal Service bought land and awarded contracts for the construction of a bulk mail

facility without adequate information on alternative sites, site preparation costs, and contractor prices. Final costs exceeded the initial estimates by significant amounts. The Postal Service had hired a former assistant postmaster general as a private real estate consultant to obtain the site; the land he recommended was owned by the Penn Central Railroad, for which he had also been working. The selection of contractors for architectural and engineering services also lacked apparent competition and involved apparent conflicts of interest. Finally, GAO found that the bulk sorting equipment, the keystone of the new facility, did not function properly. It had been purchased from a company that did not have prior capability for delivery, on the recommendation of a Postal Service program director who had been a management consultant to that company the year before. ("Site Selection and Contract Awards for Construction and Mechanization of the New York Bulk and Foreign Mail Facility," B-171594 [Washington, D.C., 1972].)

56. James D. Thompson summarizes these approaches in *Organizations in Action* (New York: McGraw-Hill, 1967).

57. Philip Selznick, *TVA and the Grass Roots* (Berkeley: University of California Press, 1949).

Chapter 3

1. The difference between the yields of taxable and tax-exempt securities increases as interest rates rise, assuming that investors demand the same after-tax returns on different types of investments. At a 40 percent tax rate, if municipal bond yields are 3 percent, the taxable bond yield equivalent would be 5 percent; if tax-exempt municipal bond yields are 6 percent, the taxable equivalent is 10 percent.

Short-term notes are a different type of investment. Short-term borrowing is not subject to the same controls (constitutional and statutory) as long-term debt, nor is it backed by the same resources. Short-term notes are planned as temporary financings—to be replaced at a later date with long-term bonds of the type described here or—if they are tax anticipation or aid anticipation notes—to be redeemed by subsequent budgetary receipts.

2. Borrowing to accumulate capital to invest in facilities with extended useful life is standard business and government practice that permits the cost of purchase or construction to be derived from subsequent income production or from citizens paying taxes over the years when the facility serves them.

3. Some corporate revenue bonds carry the misleading title of "general obligations" of the agency. Because the statutory corporation lacks taxing powers, the bonds are backed by the consolidated revenues of the corporation rather than by only the revenues of a specific project.

4. Edwin A. Deagle, Jr., *The Little Township Goes to the Market and Cries "Whew" All the Way Home: Report by the Center for the Analysis of Public Issues* (Princeton, N.J., October 1972).

5. Interest rates for different time periods cannot be accurately compared, of course, but this rate was good in its own setting.

6. Many bonds carry coupons that the bondholder removes and mails at specific intervals in order to obtain interest payments from a bank trustee. The owners of these bonds are not registered on the books of the corporations as are stockholders. Whoever tears off a coupon and sends it in to the bank trustee receives interest payments. Other bonds have ownership registered with the trustee.

7. In thirty-eight states, commercial banks receiving state and local government deposits are required by law to have certain percentages of public securities in their portfolios of holdings pledged as collateral for government deposits. Proposed legislation providing

100 percent federal insurance for public deposits was attacked in the Senate, after being approved by the House of Representatives, on the grounds that it would severely disrupt the municipal bond market by eliminating the need for bank portfolios to cover government deposits with government securities. That bill, as finally passed in 1974, insured such accounts only up to $100,000. Proposals for full deposit insurance retain the support of the U.S. Advisory Commission on Intergovernmental Relations.

8. The eleven New York City banks that are leading holders of state and municipal bonds from nationwide sources held $8 billion worth at the end of 1972. Such holdings represented 13 percent of one bank's total assets.

9. The bondholding insurance companies also sell policies to the public corporations. Continental, for example, writes five different kinds of policy for Seattle Metro.

10. When issuers sell bonds by private placement directly to investors—without an underwriter—the investors involved usually are the government's own sinking or pension funds.

11. See George G. Kaufman, "Improving the Structure of Competitive Bidding Regulations for Municipal Bonds" (speech delivered to the 68th Annual MFOA Conference, Las Vegas, Nev., June 5, 1974), for analysis of the drawbacks of public agencies relying on simple net interest cost calculations to evaluate bids. More complex and accurate computations are being increasingly used.

12. Of the general obligation bonds issued in 1971, over 99 percent were sold by competitive bidding. Of revenue bonds issued, just under 50 percent were placed by negotiation. The biggest jump in negotiated sales came in 1972 when these sales increased while competitive volume actually decreased. By 1973, negotiated sales accounted for 49 percent of the total tax-exempt market. These promoted public financings became very important to the multipurpose financial firms, whose other brokerage and corporate investment departments suffered substantial losses that year. Public corporations within New York State, expansion of public power in Nebraska, and industrial pollution control financing accounted for large parts of this growth in negotiated revenue bonds.

13. Arbitrage is involved when monies raised by the issue of tax-exempt securities are invested in higher-yield securities, in effect profiting from the interest rate differential between taxable and tax-exempt bonds. Treasury rules limit this practice through complex regulations of time periods, yields, purposes of investment, and amount of bond proceeds that can be so invested.

14. An exception is John Dawson, a respected elder in the business, who, following his retirement in 1974, entered into helpful correspondence with this author.

15. An earlier attempt on Kraft's part to acquire bond counsel status had been unsuccessful. Kraft had persuaded an underwriter he knew to buy into an issue carrying his legal opinion. but established firms obtained a competitive bidding provision for that deal and drafted prospectus language that ruled out use of the new counsel.

16. Some public utilities are public authorities as I have defined them; others are unincorporated municipal enterprises. Nonprofit corporations can be organized under general state business law and usually do not require specific legislative charters.

17. Center for Analysis of Public Issues, *Local Attorneys' Fees in Bond Issues—Nice Work If You Can Get It* (Princeton, N.J., 1973), p. 12.

18. For no particular reason, they do not use the same grades. Moody's assigns, in descending order: Aaa, Aa, A-1, A, Baa-1, Baa, Ba, B, Caa, Ca, C. Standard & Poor's assigns: AAA, AA, A, BBB, BB, B, CCC. A third source of ratings is Fitch Investors Service, Inc., which has organized a new municipal bond division.

19. Roy M. Goodman, testimony before the Joint Economic Committee, Subcommittee on Economic Progress, Hearings on State and Local Public Facility Needs and Financing, 91st Cong., 1st sess., 1966, 1:18.

20. The bibliography on this subject is growing. It includes U.S. Congress, Joint Economic Committee, *Financing Municipal Facilities,* 91st Cong., 1st sess., 1968, vol. 2; Gerald R. Jantscher, "The Effects of Changes in Credit Rating on Municipal Borrowing Costs" (Investment Bankers Association, Washington, D.C., 1970); *The Rating Game: Report of the Twentieth Century Fund Task Force on Municipal Bond Credit Ratings* (New York: Twentieth Century Fund, 1973); Arthur Levitt (New York State Comptroller), "Who Rates the Raters," *Bond Buyer* (1973); *Government Finance* 1, no. 3 (August 1972); U.S. Bureau of the Census, *Governmental Finance.*

21. The Forum is an association of investment bankers who deal in municipal bonds, investors, public officials, bond attorneys, and financial consultants. Its membership is nationwide. The "New York" of its title reflects the dominance of Wall Street in the municipal bond market.

22. These and numerous similar anecdotes are recounted by Moses in his *Public Works: A Dangerous Trade* (New York: McGraw Hill, 1970). New York's transportation decisions remain deeply imbedded in personal relationships. In 1970, officers of the trustee bank for the Fort Erie Bridge Authority bonds arranged its merger into the Niagara Frontier Transportation Authority, on whose board they sat. In 1973, Theodore Kheel and William Ronan worked out a complicated deal at a New York restaurant. Ronan's Metropolitan Transportation Authority, which lacked a credit base sufficient to float its own bonds, sought to obtain funds through a state general obligation transportation bond issue. Two years earlier, Kheel's active opposition to a similar bond issue had contributed to its defeat. In exchange for Kheel's support on a new bond issue referendum, Ronan promised: a Port Authority resolution to the effect that certain surplus revenues of that authority were exempt from 1962 bond covenants and therefore could be spent on transit; a letter of support from Governor Nelson A. Rockefeller in one legal case brought by Kheel against the Port Authority; and Rockefeller opposition to the application for a fare increase on the Port Authority's Hudson Tubes. All of these actions were opposed by Port Authority management and most of its board (of which Ronan was a member). That this deal was outlined on a napkin may be apocryphal, but the offer prompted Kheel to reverse an earlier stand and support the state's transportation bond issue. Subsequently the Port Authority board refused to pass the resolution, and both the authority's fare increase and the state bond issue were defeated.

Chapter 4

1. Since 1956, the federal interstate system has provided a more successful alternative, offering to bear 90 percent of costs, using revenues from gasoline taxes to build highways that must by law remain free. But New Jersey has been one of the slowest states in the nation to complete its share of the free interstate system. Its low-tax profile limits even highway matching funds. Prior to 1956, it had created three separate toll highway authorities, which control its major revenue-producing routes (in addition to the Highway Authority are the New Jersey Turnpike Authority and the New Jersey Expressway Authority).

2. The guarantee made the state "unconditionally liable" for payment of principal and interest should the authority fail to pay them when due. This liability was upheld in a benchmark legal case, *Behnke* v. *N.J. Highway Auth.,* 13 N.J. 14, 97 A. 2d 647 (1953), a taxpayer's suit challenging the establishment of the authority. The suit delayed the issue, so the authority began construction with short-term bank loans and an advance from the state.

3. The 1962 issue was designed by Lehman Brothers as "junior revenue bonds." The sale to institutional investors, was negotiated through Lehman. Buyers included three banks also serving as trustee and paying agent for the bonds. These were term bonds, requiring

no periodic amortization but only semiannual payment of interest until after the redemption of "senior bonds."

4. Federal legislation was required in this case by the terms of the original federal aid for construction of the state portions of the parkway. The federal government has generally taken a dim view of authority toll roads replacing free arteries of the interstate system. Georgia has unsuccessfully attempted to gain federal approval for a revenue bond issue so that it can complete its portion of the interstate system.

5. This spur project was subsequently taken over by the New Jersey Turnpike Authority and renamed the Alfred E. Driscoll Expressway after the former governor, who also was chairman of the Turnpike Authority. Incoming Governor Brendan Byrne requested that the project be abandoned in 1974, and a court ruled that the authority had filed a misleading environmental impact statement for it. Yet the authority, headed after Driscoll's death by a former political supporter of Byrne, persisted with the project, spending over $20 million on it before abandoning it in 1977 under pressure from Chase Manhattan Bank, the bond trustee.

6. Letter from Richard J. Hughes to James S. Hauck and Annmarie H. Walsh, May 9, 1973.

7. Throughout this book, "the Port Authority" refers to the Port Authority of New York and New Jersey; other port authorities are designated by full title.

8. The predecessor firm, Thomson, Wood & Hoffman, had been bond counsel for the Port Authority's earliest issues and defended their tax exemption successfully when it was first challenged—in a suit brought by the federal government (*Helvering* v. *Gerhardt*, 304 U.S. 405 [1938]). Port Authority Commissioner Alexander Shamberg was both a bondholder and a defendant in that case.

9. With the encouragement and aid of the Reconstruction Finance Corporation, bridge authorities based on the Port Authority financing model spread throughout the country during the 1930s and 1940s. In 1949, St. Louis's Bi-State Development Agency was patterned after the Port Authority but has always had financial difficulties. See William N. Cassella, Jr., "Governing the St. Louis Metropolitan Area" (Ph.D. diss., Harvard University, 1952).

10. At the same time, the authority established the Consolidated Bond Reserve Fund. This additional reserve fund, for which there is no statutory requirement, amounted to $62 million at the end of 1975.

11. Port Authority of New York and New Jersey, *Annual Report*, 1973, p. 57.

12. Report to the New Jersey Special Senate Investigating Committee, under Senate Resolution No. 7 of 1961, p. 13.

13. L.F. Rothschild & Co., *Municipal Bond Report*, June 14, 1973.

14. The Port Authority Trans-Hudson Corp. operates the former Hudson Tubes, a deficit-ridden rail link between downtown Manhattan and northern New Jersey, acquired by the authority at the state's insistence when the World Trade Center project was approved in 1962.

15. The purchase of PATH and Trade Center land and their purposes were approved jointly by the state legislatures and considered jointly by courts reviewing condemnation proceedings (*Courtesy Sandwich Shop, Inc.* v. *Port of New York Authority*, 12 N.Y. 2d. 379, 190 N.E. 2d 402, 375 U.S. 960 [1963]). Abraham Stein (in "The Fiction That P.A.T.H. Is a Deficit-Ridden Or Loss Operation," Pace College School of Business Administration, mimeographed, 1971) argues that the Port Authority Trans-Hudson subway and World Trade Center—which is on land leased from PATH—should be treated as one financial entity. The New York State auditors argue that the authority's allocations

of bond and loan proceeds and revenues and its deficit calculations lead to an underestimation of Trade Center deficits and an overestimation of PATH deficits.

16. See Michael N. Danielson, "Commuter Politics in the New York Region" (Ph.D. diss., Princeton University, 1962).

17. This is Tobin's own description of the meeting, in U.S. Congress, House of Representatives, Hearings Before Subcommittee No. 5, Committee on the Judiciary, 86th Cong., 2d sess., pt. 1, 1960, p. 31.

18. Ibid., p. 32.

19. 47, I.C.C. 643-749, December 19, 1917.

20. Erwin Wilkie Bard, *The Port of New York Authority* (New York: Columbia University Press, 1942), p. 23.

21. The first request to the Port Authority for help with railroad problems came from New Jersey in 1926 and was discouraged by New York. In 1931, the authority announced that it had dropped consideration of a suburban rail program because of declining traffic forecasts. In 1946, the local governments and Governor Alfred E. Driscoll asked the authority to consider a rail connection to Newark Airport and purchase of the Hudson Tubes. Then the Port Authority commissioners responded that any program requiring recourse to subsidy "would destroy the entire concept and character of the Authority." In the mid-1950s, when the states created the Metropolitan Regional Transit Commission, the New Jersey legislature threatened to refuse to authorize any new Port Authority projects unless it would finance the MRTC study. Tobin replied that such financing was ruled out by covenant restrictions on the purposes of authority expenditure. Later, after hard bargaining, he found a way, claimed the MRTC as a valuable asset of the Port Authority, and managed to weaken the recommendations of its final report.

22. Hence the Port Authority's 1973 report concluded: "Whether additional trans-Hudson rail capacity will be required, desirable or financially feasible in the future [is] . . . difficult if not impossible to assess fully at this time." *Annual Report*, 1973, p. 7.

23. Under the "special fund doctrine" that allowed municipalities to treat the finances of their own utilities separately, legislative authorization for revenue bonds incorporated indenture covenants. This practice was discontinued after 1935 because it restricted management flexibility. Public authorities have been permitted to reinstate it.

24. Exemption from property taxes has been a persistent source of contention with local governments, particularly the cities of New York, Newark, and Hoboken. The growth of commercial use of Port Authority properties, including airports, marine terminal areas, and the World Trade Center, raises the number of private tenants who escape property taxes. The authority negotiates some substitute payments ("in lieu of taxes") at substantially lower levels.

25. Port Authority executives say that the authority intended to carry out the project with a combination of federal aid and what it would call, for accounting purposes, expenditure on airports. Tobin, who retired shortly before the plan was adopted, acknowledges that it was unfeasible as well as unwise. "Grandstand play" is his phrase. Five years after the announcement, the plan remained a paper commitment.

26. *New York Times*, November 24, 1972.

27. *Dartmouth College* v. *Woodward*, 17 U.S. 629 (1819) did provide that the constitutional prohibition against impairing contracts (article I, section 10 of the United States Constitution) was not intended to restrain states in the regulation of their civil institutions: "All general laws and special acts . . . may be altered from time to time or repealed."

28. *Barron's*, May 6, 1974, p. 7.

29. *Weekly Bond Buyer*, May 6, 1974, p. 1.

30. *United States Trust Company of New York* v. *New Jersey et al.*, Appeal from the Supreme Court of New Jersey, Slip Opinion, 75-1687, June 1977. The New Jersey Superior Court had ruled in May 1975 that repeal of the covenants was valid. That opinion was unanimously upheld by the New Jersey Supreme Court, and the counterpart case in the New York courts was pending. The first ruling came in the consolidated cases of *United States Trust Company of New York, etc.* v. *The State of New Jersey* and *Daniel M. Gaby* v. *The Port of Authority, et al.* (*Gaby*, argued by Theodore Kheel, challenged the original covenants.) Judge Gelman concluded that there was no showing that repeal of the covenants had anything but a temporary effect on the market for Port Authority bonds (in fact, there was evidence that fear of losses from the World Trade Center caused more concern on Wall Street). Reviewing previous contract cases, Gelman concluded that under the contract clause, a state acting under its reserved police powers may alter its remedial processes and thereby diminish contractual security as long as it does not destroy the quality of the security as an acceptable investment for a rational investor. Repeal of the covenants did not destroy investment quality. The Securities Industry Association submitted a brief in support of the argument against covenant repeal.

31. See Marver H. Bernstein, *Regulating Business by Independent Commission* (Princeton, N.J.: Princeton University Press, 1955); Richard Hellman, *Government Competition in the Electrical Utility Industry* (New York: Praeger, 1972); William E. Mosher and Finla G. Crawford, *Public Utility Regulation* (New York: Harper & Bros., 1933).

32. Moses, *Public Works: A Dangerous Trade* (New York: McGraw-Hill, 1970).

33. Unlike TVA and the Bonneville Power Administration, which treat public retailers as preference customers, the Power Authority of New York State sells most of the power it generates to private industry and investor-owned utilities.

34. Through June 1971, TVA had paid to the U.S. Treasury a total of $909 million from power proceeds, including $65 million for the payment of interest and the retirement of bonds held by the Treasury. Payments from chemical plant operations and miscellaneous receipts raised the total payments to Treasury to almost $950 million. By the same date, some $2.5 billion had been appropriated by Congress to support all activities, including flood control, navigation, research and development in fertilizer production, mapping water quality, forestry, and recreation. The major portion of the appropriations predates 1948.

35. It costs TVA on the average 83 cents to produce 100 kilowatt hours of electricity exclusive of capital costs and taxes. TVA sales include a 35 percent markup. The average private utility generates power for $1.32 per kilowatt hour and sells it at a 55 percent markup.

36. Tennessee Electric Cooperative Association to U.S. Congress, Hearings Before a Subcommittee of the Committee on Appropriations, House of Representatives, pt. 5, TVA, 1973, p. 368.

37. The story illustrates the ways in which the financial holding company structure had drained the power industry. Officials of two subsidiary companies testified that they had been forced by Insull superiors to enter into contracts to purchase power from the Lower Colorado project at costs higher than those at which they could generate it themselves.

38. Unlike the New York Power Authority, LCRA did not need Federal Power Commission permits because the river is wholly intrastate.

39. Other multipurpose basin agencies around the nation that do not have energy functions show a preference for water supply functions—their prime moneymaker. Indeed LCRA is now engaged in a legal and political battle over a planned contract (approved by the Texas Water Rights Commission) under which an investor-owned company will pay LCRA for the water the company draws from the river for cooling at a nuclear plant.

LCRA plans to use revenues from this cost-free water supply sale to subsidize the price of power that it sells. The investor-owned companies are protesting the arrangement.

Chapter 5

1. *Business Review*, March 1958, p. 1. The bank's attempt to correlate authority concentration with county characteristics showed a distinctly positive relation with population density.

2. Florida, Georgia, Indiana, and Michigan have established numerous lease-back authorities, and at least twelve other states also use this financing technique. Pennsylvania has by far the largest number of such authorities, and states across the nation have established building authorities to finance and temporarily lease government offices and university buildings patterned after Pennsylvania's General State Building Authority, created in 1949. In 1969, the Wisconsin legislature approved constitutional amendments prohibiting "dummy state corporations" from financing and leasing back certain public works and at the same time eased restrictions on state guaranteed borrowing (permitting the state legislature to authorize bonds for specified amounts up to a percentage of property valuation, less outstanding debt). An Arkansas court has ruled that the state building authority's issuance of revenue bonds backed by state rental payments is an unconstitutional avoidance of requirements for voter approval. Meanwhile the Arkansas legislature has eliminated the requirements of a referendum on industrial lease-back bonds because elections were delaying construction. For an exposition of general legal theories involved, see C. Robert Morris, "Evading Debt Limitations with Public Authorities: The Costly Subversion of State Constitutions," *Yale Law Journal* 68 (1969): 234–268.

3. Among the savings offered by the state authority are its tender offers to bondholders, which have permitted it to repurchase bonds outstanding from the reserves accumulated by the 120 percent lease-rental coverage.

4. The foregoing 1966 figures are derived from Harry B. Strickland, *Inside the Trojan Horse: Understanding the Specialized Units of Local Government* (Clarks Summit, Pa: Logo Publishing Co., 1969).

5. New York's underwriting firms outnumber those in Pennsylvania but mainly by the volume of headquarters offices within New York City. Firms of municipal bond attorneys in Pennsylvania exceed those in New York, even when New York City is included. See the *Directory of Municipal Bond Dealers of the United States*, published by The Bond Buyer, Inc.

6. In *Tranter* v. *Allegheny County Authority*, 316 Pa. 65 (1934), the court held, "It is never an illegal evasion to accomplish a desired result, lawful in itself, by discovering a legal way to do it." Thus the pressures of depression economics brought adaptation around the framework of debt limits from the nineteenth century rather than breaking or altering the framework itself. Authorities were declared entitled to unrestricted borrowing by *Kelly* v. *Earle*, 320 Pa. 449 (1936).

7. *Detwiler* v. *Harfield School District*, 376 Pa. 555 (1954). The New Jersey courts, however, ruled that state's building authority unconstitutional, equating leases with pledges of state credit.

8. H. F. Alderfer, executive secretary of the Institute of Local Government, in a foreword to John H. Ferguson and Charles F. LeeDecker, *Municipally Owned Waterworks in Pennsylvania* (State College, Pa.: Pennsylvania State College, 1948), p. vi.

9. For example, *Lighton* v. *Abington Township*, 336 Pa. 345 (1939) held that a local government that issued "nondebt revenue bonds" violated the Pennsylvania constitutional provision prohibiting delegation to a private corporation of the power to interfere

in a municipal improvement when it covenanted to let a bank trustee manage a sewerage system in case of default. Authorities agree to such provisions regularly. The Lighton decision cast enough doubt on the powers of trustees for municipal issues in case of default to make authority bonds preferred over "nondebt" municipal revenue bonds for the next thirty years.

10. Strickland, *Trojan Horse*, p. 35, quoted from the *Scranton Tribune*, May 4, 1967.

11. Local Government Unit Debt Act 185 (1972).

12. A local government's lease-rental debt that supports authority bonds now adds to the total municipal debt that is regulated, thus ending the sharp legal distinction between borrowing and renting. Provision is made, however, for raising the ceiling on nonelectoral debt to accommodate lease-back authority borrowings.

13. After defeat by the voters of a proposal to guarantee bonds for building the state university system, HFA and the Dormitory Authority began funding that construction with a combination of moral obligation and lease-back bonds. By 1974, the moral obligation pledge appeared in the charters of eleven state corporations and five regional transportation authorities that were not likely to be able to raise private bond financing even with the pledge.

14. Private Housing Finance Law, McKinney's Consolidated Laws of New York Annotated, Chap. 41, section 47 (1) (d).

15. Language included in bond prospectuses of the New York State Housing Finance Agency.

16. The federal housing laws provide that the full faith and credit of the United States is pledged to all amounts that HUD contracts to pay the housing authorities (42 USC 1410 (e), 1970).

17. New York State Constitution, article VII, section 8, and article VIII, sections 1 and 11.

18. *Williamsburg Savings Bank* v. *State of New York*, 243 N.Y. 231 (1926); *Robertson v. Zimmerman*, 268 N.Y. 52 (1935). In 1855, the court had concluded that when there were "claims founded in equity and justice" against the state, "the legislature is not confined in appropriating money or raising taxes to meet those claims" (*Town of Guilford* v. *Board of Supervisors*, 13 N.Y. 143).

19. Quoted in State of New York Temporary State Commission on the Coordination of State Activities, *Staff Report on Public Authorities* (Albany: Williams Press, 1956), p. 27.

20. See article X, section 5, article VIII, section 1, and article XVI. The first provides: "Neither the state nor any political subdivision thereof shall at any time be liable for the payment of any obligations issued by such a public corporation heretofore or hereafter created, nor may the legislature accept, authorize acceptance of, or impose such liability upon the state or any political subdivision thereof; but the state or a political subdivision thereof may, if authorized by the legislature, acquire the properties of any such corporation and pay the indebtedness thereof." This provision—together with the gift and loan provisions—sets the limits of legal liability. State or city guarantees of authority obligations and gifts or loans to corporations are thus prohibited by specific constitutional amendments.

21. As is generally true in the municipal bond market, bond counsel have committed themselves more often orally than in writing. While Mitchell drafted the moral obligation clause for HFA and supported its viability, his firm's formal legal opinion accompanying HFA's first bond prospectus in 1961 represented only that it was of the opinion that the agency had validly covenanted and would take all reasonable steps necessary to deliver to the governor and director of the budget the appropriate statement certifying need for fill-up of reserves. The opinion made no representations as to the legality or likelihood of

the state's transfer of such funds. Thirteen years and $3.7 billion later, an HFA 1974 prospectus carried a legal opinion by the successor firm that was pure boilerplate, repeating its 1961 counterpart nearly word for word.

22. HFA's net interest costs fell between those incurred for general obligation bonds of the state and the city. State bonds carried slightly lower interest rates, but the state's voter-approved bonding capacity was low by comparison to HFA's legislatively authorized capacity.

23. *Weekly Bond Buyer*, November 5, 1973, p. 5.

24. Federal income tax law provided substantial depreciation and tax write-offs to partners investing in limited-profit housing projects. Development corporations form subsidiary partnerships, of which the shares are marketed as tax-shelter investments by brokers. These development corporations then finance their projects by selling mortgages to UDC or other agencies at rates supported by those agencies' tax-exempt bonds.

25. HDC's bonds have two layers of government backing. The moral obligation clause in HDC's statute calls for fill-up of its reserves by the city government. And if the city should fail to fill up HDC reserves, the corporation would be the direct recipient of state aid otherwise due the city.

26. Charles J. Urstadt resigned as state commissioner of housing to take over the post of chairman of the separate Battery Park City Authority, which absorbed some of HFA's bonding authorization and issued its own securities at substantially higher interest rates. HFA's assistant director, Lee Goodwin, moved into Urstadt's vacated commissionership.

27. *Moody's Bond Survey*, September 17, 1973, p. 568.

28. Alan Bautzer, "Nation Experiences Boom in Costly Sports Facilities," *Weekly Bond Buyer*, May 6, 1974.

29. In one example similar to state moral backup arrangements, the city of Pittsburgh pays part of the debt service costs of the Pittsburgh Stadium Authority plus an annual appropriation to its reserve funds. Rentals from the company that owns the Pittsburgh Pirates do not cover half the salaries of the two authority staff members and legal and accounting fees.

30. Philip Iselin, the late president of Monmouth Park, had come into conflict with Sonny Werblin, chairman of the Sports Authority, in the 1960s, when they were both associated with the New York Jets. Iselin remained a major Jets stockholder; hence the Sports Authority competed with both his racing and his football interests.

31. The former treasurer of the state of New Jersey and ex officio board member of the Sports Authority, Joseph M. McCrane, Jr., is the son-in-law of Eugene Mori, the principal owner of the Garden State track. McCrane subsequently was convicted of illegal financing practices in Governor Cahill's 1970 campaign. The Garden State track and the engineering firm that held the design contract for the Sports Authority complex also were indicted along with McCrane for campaign finance practices unrelated to the Sports Authority. The racetrack had allegedly made illegal contributions to Cahill's campaign, channeled through an advertising agency and deducted from the track's federal income taxes.

32. *N.J. Sports & Exposition Authority* v. *McCrane*, 119 N.J. 427 (1971).

33. Governor Nelson Rockefeller had just proposed, and New York's legislature had immediately passed, a bill restructuring racing in New York to improve that state's competitive position (regarding racing dates and parimutuel finances) relative to New Jersey. Rockefeller had moved with similar swiftness in earlier years to defeat New Jersey's proposed Market Authority by development of the Hunt's Point Market in the Bronx and to stave off a threatened move across the river by the Stock Exchange.

34. Wisconsin Statutes, chap. 234, section 234.15. In 1973, after challenge in *State ex rel. Warren* v. *Nusbaum* (59 W. 2d 391, 208 N.W. 2d 708), the Wisconsin Supreme Court upheld the constitutionality of this legislation. With managing underwriters from New York City and a board chairman from a Wisconsin bank, the Wisconsin HFA began raising capital in 1974.

35. *Barron's*, June 3, 1974, p. 5.

36. Industrial revenue bonds are sometimes designated industrial development bonds. By either designation they are revenue bonds that pay tax-exempt interest and are issued by public agencies to help private firms.

37. Theoretical economic analyses have concluded that the financial cost burdens of reducing pollutants and of reducing the social costs to the public imposed by private industrial processes should be borne by the polluting industry, not by the taxpayer. But in practice, it is difficult to get industry to make timely improvements when businesses claim inadequate capital and threaten to relocate or to close particular plants.

38. Quoted by Pamela Archbold, "Pollution Control Financing Grows Up," *Corporate Financing* (July–August 1972).

39. To illustrate, by mid-1974, Bethlehem Steel had received about $100 million for pollution control equipment from public authority issues, saving $40 million to $50 million in long-term interest costs, according to the company. It planned to raise another $300 million in that manner. Additional savings are accumulated by interim investment of the funds, borrowed at less than 6 percent, in higher yield securities, such as bank certificates of deposit paying up to 9 percent. The company also benefits from exemption from SEC registration for this method of raising capital (thereby saving substantial legal fees normally incurred for registration statements); tax deductions, which vary with the structure of the lease or installment purchase arrangement; and sometimes exemption from sales taxes on the purchase of equipment.

40. Because these issues have private corporate backing, their covenants have been unrestrictive. The financial community puts a higher level of trust in the private sector and applies simpler economic standards of credit evaluation to it than to the public sector. But in fact, defaults are more common in this mixed sector than in the wholly public sector of bonds. When the firm cannot meet its lease payments to the public authority, the authority, in turn, must delay interest payments on its bonds outstanding.

41. In the state of Washington, the highest court has held that the port districts violated the state constitutional prohibition against lending public credit to private companies by issuing pollution control IRBs. The court found the leasing arrangement indistinguishable from a loan of credit (Washington Supreme Court, No. 43139, 1974). As of the end of 1976, this decision stood alone in the fifty states.

42. "Editor's Corner," *Weekly Bond Buyer*, December 31, 1973.

Chapter 6

1. Robert Caro, *The Power Broker: Robert Moses and the Fall of New York* (New York: Alfred A. Knopf, 1974), p. 551.

2. *Weekly Bond Buyer*, December 11, 1972, p. 4. The quote is from an open letter to St. Louis by Hollis P. Nichols of H. P. Nichols & Company of Boston.

3. *Business Week*, June 9, 1973, p. 78. The price paid by the authority was established in court, determining the amounts to be distributed to bondholders.

4. *Christian Science Monitor*, February 21, 1964.

5. North Carolina and Virginia use alternative procedures whereby the state acts as a

sales agent for local government bonds (mandatory in North Carolina), dating from 1931 and 1950, respectively. This procedure does not add to aggregate underwriting and legal business but tends to cut municipal financing costs.

6. C. Lowell Harris, "Constitutional Restrictions on Property Taxing and Borrowing Powers in New York," Citizens Tax Council, 1967.

7. Interview with W.M. Thackara, of A.G. Becker & Company, elected in November 1972 to the Red Bank, New Jersey, Town Council.

8. The reporter is Bess Durchsclag of the *Courier Post*, Camden, New Jersey (October 3, 1972).

Chapter 7

1. Charles Adrian, *State and Local Government*, 3d ed. (New York: McGraw-Hill, 1972), p. 327.

2. The founders of the Port Authority were part of a business elite with personal interests in resolving the interstate port problems in favor of New York, as well as political reformers supporting fusion tickets. Outerbridge had been chairman of the chamber of commerce's committee on shipping. His colleague, Irving Bush, was founder of Bush Terminal, a major port facility in Brooklyn. Bush's lawyer, William C. Breed, recommended Cohen to them for fighting New Jersey's petition to the ICC for charges to be imposed on freight movements across the Hudson River and the harbor. Charles Whitman, another of their personal friends, who was then governor of New York, saw to it that Cohen was appointed to represent the state. Cohen went on to draft the Port Authority legislation and to serve as its general counsel until 1942. For an insider's view of these events, see Julius Henry Cohen, *They Builded Better Than They Knew* (New York: Messner, 1946).

3. Ibid., p. 24. New Jersey's Democratic governor vetoed the compact, but the Republican-controlled legislature overrode the veto and appointed the first commissioners by statute.

4. In a few cases, the management of an authority has been sufficiently weak and the politics surrounding its decisions and patronage sufficiently intense that confirmation by the legislature of appointments to the board can make a substantial difference. For example, for eight years, the Delaware River Port Authority reflected the political struggle between the Democratic governor of New Jersey and the Republican-dominated state legislature. Governor Meyner had difficulty getting his nominees for the New Jersey seats confirmed by his own legislature, and he concluded in time that hiring a strong executive director on the model of the Port Authority of New York and New Jersey was the only solution. The governor and the legislature were stalemated for two more years on the appointment of a director, but once he took office, the state government began to relinquish power over the agency in order to cool down the conflicts surrounding its activities.

5. *New York Times*, March 9, 1947.

6. Cohen, *They Builded*, p. 310.

7. "The Port of New York Authority, Guardian of the Toll Gates," *The Reporter*, September 9, 1953, p. 26.

8. *Newark Evening News*, March 12, 1961.

9. Charles E. Landon, *The North Carolina State Ports Authority* (Durham, N.C.: Duke University Press, 1963).

10. From 1921 through 1972, seventy-three commissioners served on the Port Authority board. Thirty-three of them were directors or officers of banks. Twenty-nine were directors or officers of insurance companies or brokerage houses. (The categories overlap;

thirteen commissioners were directors of both banking and insurance institutions.) Ten were corporate lawyers. Eight were chief executive officers of business corporations without banking or insurance directorships. Two former professors and one college president were included. Thirteen commissioners had held local government office (one Westchester County engineer; one Jersey City finance officer; one Hoboken city attorney; one Brooklyn borough president, who served from 1921 to 1924; one member of the New York City Board of Estimate, who served from 1938 to 1949; and several suburban mayors who were also bankers or lawyers). Eight commissioners held state office (including Governors Alfred E. Smith and Charles S. Whitman of New York, one congressman, and one senator).

11. Only twice were local transportation interests represented between 1921 and 1972. Frank J. Taylor (1938-1949) was president of the American Merchant Marine Institute and a member of the New York City Board of Estimate. The warehousemen's association persuaded Governor Herbert A. Lehman to appoint Eugene F. Moran (1942-1959), chairman of the Moran Towing and Transportation Company, headquartered in Brooklyn, and also a commissioner of the New York Transit Authority.

12. Marvin Maurer, "The Role of the Board of Commissioners of the Port of New York Authority in Policy Formation" (Ph.D. diss., Columbia University, 1966), p. 91.

13. Massport's controversial airport expansion is described in Dorothy Nelkin, *Jetport* (New Brunswick, N.J.: Transaction Books, 1974).

14. Erwin Wilkie Bard, *The Port of New York Authority* (New York: Columbia University Press, 1942), p. 290.

15. Austin Tobin, "Administering the Public Authority," *Dun's Review* 60 (June 1952).

16. The only other local Hudson County Democrats to serve on the Port Authority commission were John Milton (1933-1939) and Raymond Greer (1939-1945).

17. Amitai Etzioni, *A Comparative Analysis of Complex Organizations* (New York: Free Press, 1961), p. 141.

18. Paul Tillet and Myron Weiner, *The Closing of Newark Airport*, Inter-University Case Program, No. 27 (University, Ala.: University of Alabama Press, 1955), p. 38.

19. U.S. Congress, House of Representatives, Hearings Before Subcommittee No. 5, Committee on the Judiciary, 86th Cong., Serial No. 24, pt. 1, 1960, p. 627.

20. For a thorough discussion of interstate river basin organizations, see Martha Derthick, *Between State and Nation: Regional Organizations of the United States* (Washington, D.C.: The Brookings Institution, 1974).

21. The first survey is in Nathaniel S. Preston, "The Use and Control of Public Authorities in American State and Local Government" (Ph.D. diss., Princeton University, 1960). In Pennsylvania, a 1970 Butcher & Singer survey of municipal authorities found board members engaged as follows: 10 percent in professions; 15.9 percent as business executives; 22.8 percent self-employed (many of those in real estate); 5 percent as bankers; 11.5 percent as engineers and manufacturers; and 35 percent retired or in miscellaneous occupations. An earlier survey of Pennsylvania municipal corporations concluded that the composite description of an authority board member would show him to be a well-educated businessman about fifty years of age, white, Republican, and middle income. That 1951 survey by Paul A. Pfretzschner of Lafayette College, himself a vice-chairman of a housing authority in 1957, covered the boards of 147 Pennsylvania municipal corporations. Twenty-eight percent of the board members were businessmen; 12.8 percent merchants; 10.1 percent engineers; and 9.7 percent bankers. Despite the fact that many of these authorities were of the lease-back type, providing financial services for local governments, only 3.7 percent of the board members were public officials.

22. The 1934 act creating LCRA provided for the original board to serve until its stag-

gered terms were up. Law provided thereafter for the powers, rights, privileges, and functions of the district to be exercised by a board of twelve directors consisting of at least one from each of the counties named in the LCRA act, except Travis, which has two directors, appointed by the governor with the advice and consent of the senate for a term of six years. It made ineligible any person who had during the preceding three years been employed by an electric power and light company, telephone company, or any other utility. Each director was to receive a fee of $25 per day for each day spent in attending to the business of the authority. This fee was subsequently raised to $40.

23. Newer corporations in New York City have overlapping directorates with city government. The Housing Development Corporation chairman is head of the Housing and Development Administration of the city government, and the board includes the city's finance administrator and budget director. This board also included four public members—two appointed by the mayor and two by the governor. In 1972, the four public members included Thomas E. Dewey, Jr., a general partner of Kuhn, Loeb & Co., investment bankers, and Fredericka C. Hein, a partner in a prominent New York City law firm. In contrast, the two public members appointed by the mayor, rather than the governor, included the former assistant commissioner of buildings and a former corporation counsel. Overlapping government and authority leadership to coordinate the complex of housing and housing-related agencies in the city and state has spread. The first chairman of the Housing Development Corporation had been deputy commissioner of the New York State Division of Housing and Community Renewal, as well as president of the National Housing Association of Housing and Redevelopment Officials. The executive director of HDC had been in the New York City Housing and Development Administration and in the New York State Housing Finance Agency and continued as an official of the Battery Park City Authority. The housing field has numerous agencies and corporations that tap multiple sources of financing. It is—unlike power, water, sewerage, and transportation—not a monopoly function but rather an activity in which a number of enterprises can operate independently or in conjunction to increase supply or reduce the costs of housing.

New York City's Health and Hospitals Corporation is another example, and not a very satisfactory one. The chairman of its board is by law the city's health administrator. The fifteen-member board selects the president of the corporation, who serves as the sixteenth member. Five of the board's votes are cast by members of the mayor's cabinet. Five others are public members named by him, and five more are appointed by councilmen. This board has achieved neither vigorous leadership nor easy agreement, but it has been no less successful in these respects than New York City government generally. Inadequate management systems and overcentralized administration plague both.

24. In the first decade of the twentieth century, New York City financed the construction of the subway lines and leased them to private operators. Fearing that the city would reduce the fare as profits mounted and showing a lack of foresight typical of transportation management, the operating companies made the five-cent fare part of their contracts with the city. By the 1920s, the five-cent fare was a burden rather than a benefit, and the companies went into receivership, with transit deficits assumed by the city. (The city was getting special legislative permission to go outside its debt limits in order to borrow for extension of the subway lines.)

Republican and Progressive reformers led the movement to transfer the system to a public authority; they sought to cut into the influence of local Democratic political machines. Headed by Republican leader Paul Windels, former counsel to the Triborough Bridge and Tunnel Authority, a transit reform group urged an increase in the fare and ultimately recommended the creation of a transit authority to lift the fare and other financial decisions out of the city administration. They blamed the too-low price structure on "politics." In fact, the price structure was set by the private managers.

The New York City Transit Authority Act, finally passed in 1953, set up an authority to lease the system from the city, which retained formal ownership of and continued to pay for the capital plant. With over 40,000 regular employees and assets well over $1 billion, the Transit Authority was a major extension of the use of the authority device, although it has no independent borrowing power. Confronting increasing operating deficits, the need for capital construction, and rider resistance to fare increases, the Transit Authority has always had financial problems.

The original Transit Authority board included two gubernatorial appointees and two mayoral appointees; foreseeing stalemate, the legislation called for the chairman of the Port of New York Authority to serve as the fifth member if the sitting members were unable to agree on someone else for the appointment. As it happened the four could seldom agree on anything, and the fifth was an uncomfortable refugee from the relative peace of the Port Authority. The Transit Authority act was then amended to reduce the membership to three—one appointed by the governor, one by the mayor, and a third selected by the other two.

The new three-member board was modeled on the TVA directorate. The members were full-time salaried executives of the authority rather than part-time directors. This three-headed management structure was not very satisfactory in the Transit Authority (or, indeed, in TVA where conflicts among strong personalities in the early years led to crisis in the president's office, and ultimately forced the resignation of one of the original directors). When taken over by the MTA in 1968, the Transit Authority board members became senior executive officers, and the MTA board became the directors, with Ronan as chairman and chief executive. The city pays over $250 million operating subsidies and reimbursements annually to a badly managed system over which it has little effective control.

25. New York State, Temporary State Commission on Coordination of State Activities, *Staff Report on Public Authorities* (Albany, 1956), p. 53.

26. In the New York region, for example, airports, bridges, rail transportation, shipping, major highways, housing finance, university construction, and hospital construction finance are all encapsulated in corporations created by state legislation. Virtually all the public services with any chance of financial return except water supply have been carved out of city government in this way. And the state has proposed the transfer of the city water supply system to a regional corporation. The shift in New York government is from locally controlled agencies to relatively independent corporate enterprises—increasingly multipurpose conglomerates, subject to growing state influence. MTA took over: TBTA, which had absorbed the Triborough Authority (created in 1933), Henry Hudson Parkway Authority (1934), Marine Parkway Authority (1934), and Midtown Tunnel Authority (1936); the Long Island Rail Road (investor-owned); the Transit Authority (quasi-independent city authority, previously a direct municipal enterprise); and bus companies (some private, some city). Financing of City University construction was absorbed through an incorporated construction fund (CUCF) to the state Housing Finance Agency. Municipal hospital management was shifted to the city Hospitals Corporation, and their finance to the state HFA. Urban redevelopment shifted to the state-sponsored Urban Development Corporation. The Port Authority absorbed city airports, docks, and downtown development functions. The state's Job Development Authority, Dormitory Authority, Medical Facilities Authority, and Housing Finance Agency sponsor a variety of projects in New York City.

Partial responsibility for financing electric utility expansion, previously the province of investor-owned Con Edison, is shifting to the Power Authority of the State of New York, continuing the trend. Finally, in the midst of fiscal crisis, city borrowing was shifted to a corporate creature of the state: the Municipal Assistance Corporation (Big Mac).

27. Luther Halsey Gulick, *Metro: Growth and Problems of Government in the Metro-*

politan Areas of the United States (Washington, D.C.: Governmental Affairs Institute, 1957).

28. Norton Long, "Recent Theories and Problems of Local Government," in *Public Policy: A Yearbook*, ed. Carl Friedrich and Seymour Harris (Cambridge, Mass.: Harvard University Graduate School of Public Administration, 1958), pp. 285, 292.

29. The Municipal League with one hundred members and eighteen standing committees was actively involved in local elections through its candidates' investigating committee and public information efforts during campaigns. The nonpartisan campaigns otherwise depend on a small circle of the candidate's friends and the local press. So strong is the advantage to incumbents that councilman jobs often resemble tenured appointments.

30. Ellis was president of the Municipal League, a member of the state Board of Regents, the National Water Commission, the U.S. Urban Transportation Advisory Council, and the state Planning Council, and chairman of the Mayor's Rapid Transit Commission.

31. Price Waterhouse, *Survey of the Municipality of Metropolitan Seattle*, vol. II (1972), p. 5.

32. The symbolic themes of referenda on metropolitan government of the time were similar across the nation. Opposition typically portrayed regional government as un-American, radical, "supergovernment," potentially spendthrift, and leading to "taxation without representation."

33. Until 1971, costs did not exceed the minimum charge by contract of $24 per year per residential customer. The minimum rate was raised to $33 per year per residential customer in 1971, so Metro can continue to collect excess revenues by holding down costs. Like most other successful operating authorities, Metro also garners profits from investment of reserves in U.S. government securities.

34. Typical Metro contracts require that the town pay its sewage disposal charges to Metro out of gross revenues of the sewage collection system and keep collection charges of that system high enough to cover these fees to Metro, plus its own local system debt service. In this way, Metro eliminates risks for its bondholders and avoids dependence on local council tax revenues as a source of fees.

With Wainwright & Ramsey as financial advisers and using competitive bidding for underwriting, Metro raised $165 million by eleven sewer revenue bond issues from 1961 through 1971. Metro's performance was then well enough established in the national bond market to permit it to use a local firm. Foster & Marshall, Seattle investment bankers, took over as advisers and handled the first issue of tax-backed transit bonds sold by Metro in 1973, by competitive bidding, to a syndicate headed by Halsey, Stuart (New York City) and First National Bank of Chicago.

Metro's bond covenants require that Metro hire outside consultants to contribute to its planning and management, including preparation of an annual report to the bondholders, in which engineering-management contractors report on their own performance. In 1972, Metro's net revenues covered debt service and sinking fund requirements by 1.43, without state or federal aid. Its covenants call for a coverage of 1.15. The balance is allocated to six reserve funds defined in indentures.

35. The one area of public responsibility that Metro seems reluctant to shoulder is industrial pollution control, an omission that is not surprising given the support that Metro receives from business sources. The position of industrial waste engineer was kept vacant from 1967 to 1969 for "budgetary reasons," and Boeing and the metal finishing industries enjoyed a grace period while Metro began a serious study of the problems of reducing industrial chemical inputs in Metro's sewerage system.

36. A legislative covenant promises the bondholders that tax authorization shall not be withdrawn while bonds issued with maturities until 1981 are outstanding. And in 1975, the Washington Supreme Court ordered that the legislature must appropriate to Metro

the full amount of the tax so collected for its transit program. This covenant and this decision raise some of the same questions that arise from the Port Authority transit covenants but in a more logical form. First, the state legislature leaves itself the option of reconsideration after a certain period. Second, the pledge relates to revenues rather than to expenditures. Limitation of expenditures, given adequate revenues, seems difficult to justify when reserves are more than adequate for debt service over the foreseeable future.

37. The role played by James Ellis in Seattle was played in the Twin Cities by Milton Honsey, head of the Hennepin County Municipal League. Honsey visited Toronto and initiated a study of regional approaches for the Twin Cities. A businessman and former mayor, he became a key promoter of regional reform, coordinating business and civic groups to support the change. When the new arrangement took effect, he became chairman of the Waste Control Commission.

38. Dean Lund, executive director of the League of Minneapolis Municipalities, Urban Action Clearinghouse, Case Study No. 20, *Twin Cities Metropolitan Council Anticipates and Supplies Orderly Urban Growth* (Chamber of Commerce of the United States, 1972).

39. The Metropolitan Council covers about half of its own operating costs by direct levy of a metropolitan property tax; the balance comes mainly from federal grants, including grants for housing, urban development, health planning, programs for the aging, for manpower training, and for transit research. The council can levy taxes for debt service of the metropolitan disposal system without limitation of rate or amount. In addition, it can levy taxes directly on any governmental unit that defaults on payment of charges to the Waste Control Commission. The bonds issued by the council ("unlimited tax bonds") are backed by the full faith and credit of the seven-county metropolitan area. But the council does not expect to levy taxes for debt service, and thus far the sewer charges imposed by the commission have covered the costs and financing of that system. Unlike Seattle Metro, however, the commission does not require its municipal customers to pay their fees out of user charges; a portion of the fee comes from municipally raised taxes.

40. The ratings represent some peculiarities, however; Metro Council bonds carry AA; the Sanitary District bonds issued by Minneapolis carried AAA; those by St. Paul, AA; and preexisting suburban sanitary districts also absorbed by the Waste Control Commission–Metro Council structure had been rated BA or BAA.

41. Melvin B. Mogulof, *Governing Metropolitan Areas* and *Five Metropolitan Governments* (Washington, D.C.: The Urban Institute, 1971 and 1972).

42. That a single chairman has served since the beginning of Seattle Metro and that the nonpartisan local elections in the area generally provide extended terms for local politicians who serve on the Metropolitan Council have definitely helped produce this result. In areas of intense partisan politics with rapid turnover of leadership, representative boards might have to be designed differently to limit friction and instability.

43. Ruth Howell, *Handbook for Housing Commissioners* (Chicago: National Association of Housing Officials, 1950), p. 65.

44. The New Jersey State Investigating Commission reported to Governor Brendan Byrne that Ralph Cornell, chairman of the Delaware River Port Authority board, benefited as owner or principal in companies that received about $3 million in authority-awarded contracts between 1954 and 1973 and made $1.9 million profits from selling land planned for authority use, including land he owned in Gloucester County when he voted to extend the authority's Lindenwold Rapid Transit Line. Cornell refused to resign, but Byrne replaced the New Jersey members of the board at expiration of their terms.

45. Harold Seidman, *Politics, Position and Power* (New York: Oxford University Press, 1970), p. 207.

46. Pennsylvania municipal corporations provide countless illustrations of the mix of status satisfactions and business success to which directorships of even small authorities contribute. Lower Bucks County Joint Municipal Authority (water and sewers) has had, for example, the same chairman for twenty-one years. A high school graduate, he is in the business of selling construction supplies. He also serves as a member of the county industrial development corporation and has been president of the Pennsylvania Municipal Authorities Association.

47. Thomas M. Whalen, director of cash management, New York State Comptroller's Office, quoted in Martin Tolchin and Susan Tolchin, *To the Victor . . . : Political Patronage from the Clubhouse to the White House* (New York: Random House, 1971), p. 106.

Chapter 8

1. Letter of March 21, 1974, from Alfred Driscoll to James S. Hauck and Annmarie H. Walsh.

2. By 1934, Moses was simultaneously New York City parks commissioner (a position he retained until 1959), president of the Long Island Park Commission, chairman of the Bethpage and Jones Beach Park authorities, and chairman of the State Council on Parks (holding the latter post until 1963).

3. Jesse Jones with Edward Angley, *Fifty Billion Dollars: My Thirteen Years with RFC* (New York: Macmillan, 1951), p. 164, and Robert Moses to Annmarie H. Walsh, August 11, 1975. Robert Caro, *The Power Broker: Robert Moses and the Fall of New York* (New York: Alfred A. Knopf, 1974), mistakenly states that Moses and Jones never met. Their relationship was one of mutual admiration. Moses reports that he thought Jones "one of the really good men of his time," from whom Moses heard "many a mouthful on and off-the-record" (letter of August 11, 1975, from Robert Moses to Annmarie H. Walsh).

Jones and Moses shared an animosity for Franklin Roosevelt and an apparent ability to defy his wishes. When President Roosevelt asked Jones not to sell LCRA bonds without consulting him, Jones, concluding "some moocher" was trying to get an inside deal, sold the bonds to another group of bidders without informing the president.

4. Many of Robert Moses's writings are packaged in a monumental potpourri of correspondence, speeches, newspaper columns, and acerbic comments, *Public Works: A Dangerous Trade* (New York: McGraw-Hill, 1970). On the cover, Moses is pictured astride a construction beam high over New York City, himself several times the size of the background skyscrapers.

5. If and when TBTA had liquidated its debts, all authority rights and properties would have passed to the city of New York. As of December 31, 1971, TBTA had issued approximately $716 million in bonds and $100 million in notes. The outstanding bond balance was $265 million in 1975.

6. Moses, *Public Works*, p. 261.

7. Moses had tapped additional Washington sources, including PWA grants for the Queens Midtown Tunnel and for the Triborough Bridge, slum clearance grants for the Coliseum, an RFC write-off of $6 million to the New York City Tunnel Authority during the war, a Civil Works Administration grant to the Bethpage Park Authority, and an RFC write-off of a loan to the Hayden Planetarium.

8. Robert Moses to Governor Thomas E. Dewey, July 13, 1954, in Moses, *Public Works*, p. 343.

9. Letter of October 27, 1954, from F. D. Roosevelt, Jr., to Robert Moses, in Moses,

Public Works, p. 348. The agreement to limit sales to the bus-bar meant that the Power Authority would not compete with the private utilities in distributing power but would generate power and sell it cheaply to the existing industries and utilities. The major distribution of wholesale power went to Niagara Mohawk Power Corporation, Alcoa, and Reynolds Metals.

10. Ibid.

11. Moses's influence over appointments and employment extended beyond his own agencies. From the positions of chairman of the city's Slum Clearance Committee and construction coordinator, he had no formal power over the New York City Housing Authority. Yet several members of that board owed their positions to Moses, and the Housing Authority generally accepted most of his proposals on site selection and appointments. Housing projects were located near Moses-developed parks so that housing development funds could be allocated to part of the recreation facility expenditures.

12. Moses, *Public Works*, p. 85.

13. Among Moses's most durable alliances were those with Harry Van Arsdale, head of New York City's Central Labor Council, and Peter Brennan, head of the Construction Trades Council.

14. Letter from Robert Moses to Charles Hand, secretary to Mayor Wagner and commissioner of borough works of Manhattan, October 20, 1950, in Moses, *Public Works*, p. 58.

15. Ibid., p. 410.

16. Ibid., p. 420.

17. Ibid., p. 438.

18. Ibid., p. 394.

19. Ibid., p. 87.

20. Ibid., p. 374.

21. Ibid., p. 523.

22. Matthias E. Lukens, "Practicing Management Theory," *Public Administration Review* 18 (Summer 1958).

23. Daniel L. Kurshan, "Developing Productivity in the Port of New York Authority" (An Information Memorandum for the United Nations Working Group on Measures for Improving Performance of Public Enterprises in Developing Countries, Herceg-Novi, Yugoslavia, October 1969), p.4.

24. In fact, they had cooperated to produce the region's most comprehensive arterial plan, of which most components were built by TBTA, the Port Authority, and—for the nonpaying portions—federal, state, and local government agencies.

25. U.S. Congress, House of Representatives, Hearings Before Subcommittee No. 5, Committee on the Judiciary, 86th Cong., 2d sess., pt. 1, 1960, p. 644.

26. Although trained in public administration, Ronan was a capable political strategist and a loyal policy adviser (according to Nelson Rockefeller) but not a great manager. He failed to integrate management of MTA's subsidiaries or to plan for improvements in staffing, performance, or productivity there. From 1968 to 1973, according to a state performance audit, no substantial improvements in operations took place in the Transit Authority under MTA, and costs increased while riders decreased.

27. Paul Hoffman, *Tiger in the Court* (Chicago: Playboy Press, 1973), describes the investigations and prosecutions in New Jersey led by U.S. attorneys Fred Lacey and Herbert Stern. When Tonti resigned as executive director of the NJHA in February 1971, slightly over one year before he was indicted, according to the corporate minutes the

commissioners praised his management. Press reports had already indicated that he was under investigation by the U.S. attorney's office. Chief Engineer Philip S. May was retained in his job for seventeen months beyond indictment.

Chapter 9

1. Charles Beard, *Public Policy and the General Welfare* (New York: Farrar & Rinehart, 1941), p. 148.

2. See, for example, Wallace S. Sayre, ed., *The Federal Government Service* (Englewood Cliffs, N.J.: Prentice-Hall, 1965), and John W. Macy, *Public Service: The Human Side of Government* (New York: Harper & Row, 1971).

3. Eighteen states mandate collective bargaining for state and municipal employees. The U.S. Bureau of Labor Statistics estimates that from 1968 to 1974, 1.5 million government employees joined unions or employee associations, most of them in state and local government, raising the organized state and local government employment to 3.9 million.

4. Chris Argyris, "Organizations of the Future," in Willis D. Hawley and David Rogers, eds., *Improving the Quality of Urban Management* (Beverly Hills, Calif.: Sage, 1974), p. 350.

5. There are, of course, exceptions to the authority's general record of good internal management. Many of the badly run authorities are those that are no longer building, expanding, or innovating, particularly bridge, parkway, and turnpike authorities that have paid for their original facilities, which should now, in most cases, be turned over to regular governments. The Nassau County Bridge Authority in New York State, for example, manages (badly) and collects tolls from one small bridge. Its ambitions to survive are leading it into beach developments that it is ill suited to undertake. A number of small municipal corporations in other states are undersized and understaffed for effective operations. And the experience of weak management and deteriorating finances in transit is common to both private and public sectors. Finally, where statutory corporations have absorbed government operations, and with them rigid personnel systems, over-centralized administrative processes, and baroque rules, the transfer has not cured the problems (New York City's Health and Hospitals Corporation is a case in point).

6. Marion B. Folsom, *Executive Decision Making: Observations and Experience in Business and Government* (New York: McGraw-Hill, 1962).

7. Marguerite Owen, *The Tennessee Valley Authority* (New York: Praeger, 1973).

8. Austin Tobin, "Management Structure and Operating Policies in Public Authorities: The Port of New York Authority" (speech delivered to the CIOS Triannual Management Congress, New York, September 1963), p. 3.

9. "Staff" and "line" are categories originally developed in military organizations. Luther Gulick applied them to civilian management, in Gulick and L. Urwick, eds., *Papers on the Science of Public Administration* (New York: Institute of Public Administration, 1937). These terms have since been used in business and government studies of formal organization. Line organization is differentiated by rank, and its members have authority directly over production processes or service operations; they are the doers. Line organization is what people typically think of as hierarchy. Staff organizations are professional, collegial, and usually function in planning, research, and advisory capacities. In certain types of organizations line and staff roles are reversed, however. In a university or hospital, for example, the professional staff discharges the major institutional function, and the line administrators look after the auxiliary functions (including maintenance, registration, billing and payrolls, and so forth). Today Gulick concludes that the line and staff distinction does not work well in government agencies.

10. Port Authority Instructions, 10-1, February 21, 1962.

11. For an extensive discussion of multiple meanings of decentralization, see my *The Urban Challenge to Government* (New York: Praeger, 1969), chap. 5, and "Decentralization for Urban Management," in Hawley and Rogers, *Improving the Quality of Urban Management.*

12. Peter Drucker, *Concept of the Corporation* (Boston: Beacon Press, 1946), and Alfred P. Sloan, *My Years with General Motors* (New York: MacFadden-Bartell Co., 1965).

13. The Port Authority's personnel system has been considered a model for public corporations around the nation. It contains three management ranks: junior, middle, and executive. Promotions within executive ranks are based exclusively on performance as judged by supervisors and peers, who counsel those whose performance they find inadequate to leave the organization. In consultations with each line operating division, the personnel department (a staff unit) prepares specific qualification lists and testing procedures for promotion. An active recruitment and testing program is directed to college trainees who are brought into the junior management rank. A mobility scheme encourages employees to accept one-year assignments in different units both inside and outside the authority. Management recruits are given experience in various activities, including a speakers' bureau through which junior staff members can address community groups. Employees in the management ranks are periodically reported on by their supervisors. The reports are consolidated and edited as the information proceeds up to the executive director's weekly report.

Five major employee organizations have collective bargaining rights with the Port Authority (including seven locals of the Building and Construction Trades Council). In addition, eleven labor unions have contracts with PATH.

14. In the early years of World War II, a private power combine challenged TVA to compete on completion schedules for comparable new hydroelectric plants. The race became known as the "Ebasco fiasco" (Ebasco being the private project in which construction lagged considerably behind TVA's).

15. Issues of unionism and collective bargaining were central to the reorganization of the U.S. Postal Department into the Postal Service Corporation. The National Association of Letter Carriers saw the shift from general government to corporate form as an opportunity to shift their negotiations from legislative politics to collective bargaining. As labor legislation in the public sector often does, the Postal Service legislation failed to specify either legislative bargaining or collective bargaining as the preferred forum for resolving employment issues; hence unions utilize both systems. The National Association of Letter Carriers has urged congressional committees to oppose operational changes undertaken by the Postal Service in the name of efficiency.

16. Tobin, "Management Structure," p. 4. This paper largely echoes an earlier article by Matthias E. Lukens, "Practical Management Theory," *Public Administration Review* 18 (Summer 1958).

17. Originally presented as a speech to staff, December 1955, by Daniel L. Kurshan, director of administration.

18. Tobin, "Management Structure," p. 5.

19. Both remarks are quoted in Owen, *Tennessee Valley Authority*, p. 77. Owen was a long-time employee of TVA, and her book is a spirited tribute to the authority.

20. See, for example, the works of Peter Drucker; the Committee for Economic Development's 1971 policy statement, "Social Responsibilities of Business Corporations"; and Lyle C. Fitch, "Increasing the Role of the Private Sector in Providing Public Services," in Hawley and Rogers, *Improving the Quality of Urban Management.* Contracting out has been most useful in medium-sized and small cities (under 100,000) seeking economies of scale in services with high technical and capital requirements.

21. See M. Weidenbaum, *The Modern Public Sector* (New York: Basic Books, 1969),

and Bruce Smith, "The Not-for-Profit Corporations," *The Public Interest* (Summer 1967): 127–142.

22. Overcentralization of administration in urban government is dramatized by realization of scale. New York City's Sanitation Department alone would rank in *Fortune's* inventory of the largest five hundred firms if it were an independent corporation.

Chapter 10

1. One state review group had the contradiction built into its title: "The New Jersey Autonomous Authorities Study Commission" was charged with reviewing state controls over the public corporations.

2. Daniel L. Kurshan, "How Should Authorities Be Controlled" (address before the Governmental Research Association), *GRA Reporter* 5–6 (1953).

3. Nathaniel S. Preston, "The Use and Control of Authorities in American State and Local Government" (Ph.D. diss., Princeton University, 1960), p. 284.

4. In 1975, New York State enacted a new Public Transportation Operating Assistance Program, appropriating $103 million, of which $94 million was allocated to authorities. The state's Department of Transportation projected cash needs from state appropriations of over $400 million for 1976–1977. By one reliable estimate, debt service for UDC would require $650 million in state tax revenues in the decade 1976–1985.

5. New York, Office of the State Comptroller, *Statewide Public Authorities: A Fourth Branch of Government?* (Albany, November 1972).

6. Testimony of Nelson A. Rockefeller to the New York State Moreland Act Commission on the Urban Development Corporation and Other State Financing Agencies, transcript, p. 2354. The governor relied on the underwriters and bankers working with authority boards to exercise fiscal judgment. He admits to little personal interest in how the bills would get paid, and his staff and advisers showed scant concern for financial planning or control. Enthusiastic about politics and contemporary architecture, Rockefeller has little personal interest in banking and high finance. (Interview with Nelson A. Rockefeller, January 12, 1976.)

7. Preface by Nelson A. Rockefeller to Sidney D. Goldberg and Harold Seidman, *The Government Corporation: Elements of a Model Charter* (Chicago: Public Administration Service, 1953), p. viii.

8. Ronan had been director of research for the Hults Commission review of state government, which produced a compendious report on public authorities in 1956, including recommendations for state limitations on authorities that Ronan subsequently, in his new role as authority entrepreneur, resisted. The report noted the "self-perpetuating and imperialist tendencies" of authorities (The Temporary State Commission on Coordination of State Activities, *Staff Report on Public Authorities in New York State* [Albany, 1956], p. 26).

9. Joseph Murphy, a personal associate of Rockefeller, also served as commissioner of taxation, chairman of the Local Government Advisory Board, and a member of the state Board of Equalization and Assessment. In 1967, Rockefeller made him a cash loan of $20,000, which was declared a gift in 1970.

10. Richard Aldrich received $18,167 in 1965.

11. HFA was put into the university construction business when the Dormitory Authority was reluctant to use moral obligation financing.

12. Monies from the Taconic state parkway system and the Westchester parkway systems are held by the state comptroller as the authority's agent. The Westchester system was transferred to the authority through an agreement with county officials.

13. Chapter 648, 1972 Session, Laws of New York. The authority takes title to parts of highways repaired by it and leases those parts back to the state for rentals to cover debt service.

14. The report by Governor Wilson's task force inexplicably failed to reflect any symptoms of the impending cash shortfall that put UDC in temporary default on short-term loan payments a few months later (Richard L. Dunham to Governor Wilson, memorandum, December 26, 1974).

15. Part of the complicated financing of MTA projects involved double and triple layers of authority transactions. By 1975, TBTA was transferring nearly $70 million annually to the Transit Authority and Long Island Rail Road within the MTA framework. At one point, the state appropriated funds to MTA to cover payments on cars that were being leased to the Long Island Rail Road by the Port Authority, which had purchased them with its own bonds issued with a special New York State guarantee.

16. Senator Samuel Greenberg, "New York State First Instance Advances," memorandum, Senate Committee on Finance (Minority), February 27, 1970. The Democratic minority of this committee attempted, without success, to call for brakes on authority financing by the Rockefeller administration. See also New York Senate Committee on Finance, "Minority Report on Public Authority Debt: Catalyst or Cancer?" July 12, 1971.

17. MTA was permitted to establish its own fares, budgets, and collective bargaining agreements. Municipal laws conflicting with the powers granted to MTA did not apply to the authority. MTA was permitted to mortgage its properties or subsidiaries (an atypical power; most authorities are not permitted to mortgage public property). The operating and maintenance costs of all stations, platforms, and land are borne by the city of New York or the county within which a specific facility is located; MTA merely certifies the yearly cost to the locality, which must pay, although it has little control over costs or rates.

18. Some commentators ascribe the lease to Port Authority greed; in fact, the governor used the lease to obtain financing for this large-scale project. As originally planned by the Port Authority (and authorized by the legislatures), the World Trade Center was to consist of six million square feet available only to firms engaged in international trade. Governor Rockefeller approved expansion of the plan to ten million square feet; construction on this scale required generous state rental participation to establish financial feasibility. When the $800 million project was opened, the office space vacancy rate in downtown Manhattan was 11 percent and rising. The Port Authority relaxed its rules about tenant involvement in world trade for the nonstate portions in order to get total rentals up to 78 percent by early 1975. By early 1976, eight million square feet of office space were vacant in lower Manhattan (of which two million were in the World Trade Center). After hard bargaining between agents of the governor and the authority, and without review by the comptroller, the state's Office of General Services executed the lease. It includes a rent escalator provision (linked to the construction costs index and interest rates on Port Authority bonds) and provides for state sharing of common operating and maintenance costs for the South Tower, as well as of some common costs of the whole World Trade Center complex. The amounts billed for common costs in the first year of state occupancy were three times the original estimates. The state comptroller disputed the billings. (The Port Authority was not absorbing the common costs of unrented space, and its allocation of costs to construction and maintenance was questionable.)

19. The law was amended as follows: the state commissioner no longer was required to approve UDC use of HFA money; UDC was allowed to lease or purchase services from any public agency; the permissible investments for UDC funds were extended; and finally, as close to impending disaster as June 1973, its bonding capacity was expanded

to $2 billion. The charter required no legislative approval for individual UDC projects or those of its subsidiaries. In order to get the bonding increase passed, the governor had to make the first major concession on UDC: an amendment that permits the governing bodies of towns and villages to bar UDC residential projects.

20. New Jersey Governor William Cahill's candidacy for reelection was crippled by the charges. Joseph M. McCrane, Jr., New Jersey state treasurer and board member of the Sports and Exposition Authority, was convicted of tax fraud for arranging to permit businesses, including firms subsequently working on the Sports Authority complex, to take illegal deductions for campaign contributions. A previous state treasurer, John A. Kernack, who served under Governor Richard J. Hughes, pleaded guilty to collecting kickbacks from contracts to do work for the New Jersey Highway Authority. Cahill also came under fire when the Turnpike Authority shifted its restaurant franchise from Howard Johnson Inc. to Marriott Inc., a company associated with President Nixon's campaigns. (That shift accompanied a transfer of the authority's business to the law firm in which Nixon and John Mitchell had been partners.)

In 1970, Oklahoma Governor David Hall received $25,000 in postelection contributions from Loeb Rhoades & Co., which firm he then recommended as managing underwriters for a $74 million bond issue by the Oklahoma Turnpike Authority. The firm's revenues from that issue amounted to $1,961,000, according to testimony developed for a series of court proceedings. (Hall was subsequently convicted on four counts of bribery and extortion in connection with investment of state retirement funds, and several of his aides were indicted for taking kickbacks on contracts for work on state agency projects.) In 1973, Illinois Governor Daniel Walker authorized an investigation of contributions to his campaign from underwriters and contractors for the Illinois Toll Highway Authority.

21. Comments by Beadleston and Gallagher were made to and reported by the press and reiterated in interviews with James S. Hauck.

22. Governor Hughes sought state approval to pledge Turnpike Authority revenues to a state transportation bond issue, without success. This proposal was attacked by organizations throughout the state, from the Republican party to the AFL-CIO, the chamber of commerce, the League of Women Voters, and taxpayer associations. Moreover, because of the different terms of the law creating the Highway Authority, although it could build the Garden State Arts Center without any legislative authorization, the governor could not even put to popular vote a proposal that it should support the transportation bond issue.

Governor Cahill's effort to create a "super transit agency" also was directed toward breaking down rigid barriers around financial resources in the transportation field. The authorities were building new traffic lanes that competed with subsidized rail transportation. Cahill's bill, to authorize use of surplus toll road revenues for mass transportation programs, was confronted by heavy opposition from truckers and highway user groups and went into political oblivion with his administration.

Governor Brendan T. Byrne tried to halt construction of the Driscoll Expressway (the turnpike's spur from South Brunswick to Toms River), postponed turnpike toll increases, and opened an investigation of its management.

23. The U.S. Advisory Commission on Intergovernmental Relations concluded, for example, that the appointing governments in Pennsylvania did not effectively monitor authorities and that once operative with bonds outstanding, the municipal corporations were practically independent ("The Problem of Special Districts in American Government," Washington, D.C., May 1964). It particularly cited the strong partiality of authorities to administrative secrecy.

24. *Skinner and Eddy Corp.* v. *McCarl*, 275 U.S. 1 (1927).

25. In accrual accounting, income is recorded when it is earned rather than when it is actually received, and expenses are recorded when the goods or services are used. Costs

of building and equipment are charged to expenses over the useful life of the asset rather than in a single year when construction takes place. Values are also set up for inventory of goods on hand. In cash-flow accounting, income is recorded when received, and expenses, including capital expenses, are charged to the year when actual payment is made, even though the life of the asset extends over a long period of time. Revenues may be charged to a current budget even though they are, in effect, committed to expenditure in the subsequent year's budget.

26. Letter of transmittal from the Bureau of the Budget to the Honorable Sam Rayburn, Speaker of the House of Representatives, 85th Cong. 2d sess., House of Representatives Background Materials on H.R. 8332, Committee Print, Committee on Government Operations, February 1958, p. 5.

27. Comptroller General of the United States, *Standards for Audit of Governmental Organizations, Programs, Activities and Functions,* June 1972.

28. In the case of New York, the comptroller's office has specified that reports should include project-by-project financial results, but state law does not require authorities to comply. The comptroller can order a special audit—to supply project-by-project financial figures for the Port Authority of New York, for example—but he has not been able to persuade the authority to include these figures in its annual reports. The comptroller's office prepares analytical summaries of authority reports in the form of brief memoranda, which are more accessible to the public and to elected officials than the cumbersome annual reports. Other powers of the New York State comptroller include a statutory responsibility to cut off state aid payments in case of some local authority defaults; appointment powers to two statewide authorities (the Dormitory Authority and the Bond Bank); and approval over interest rates. Comptroller Arthur Levitt used his approval powers over interest rates to force the Housing Finance Agency to use competitive bidding on one major issue in 1974. But shortly thereafter, HFA returned to negotiated financing. Levitt points out that unless a procedure is specifically illegal, he can do little but approve the transaction, particularly if the state's attorney general is not willing to challenge it in the courts. The comptroller's preexpenditure review of vouchers applies only to authority expenditures of funds that are designated as state (not corporate) monies. These include state bond funds—such as those spent by MTA—but not start-up loans ("first-instance appropriations") to the corporation.

29. GAO's handbook on auditing has attempted to specify methods of incorporating nonfiscal goals into the auditing process. The Council of State Governments, International City Managers Association, and Municipal Finance Officers Association also publish manuals that provide guidelines for evaluations by audit.

30. Instances in which a legislature has failed to create a bond-issuing corporation recommended by a governor are rare, regardless of political relationships between the two.

31. Chapter 154, Laws of New York, 1921, as amended; Chapter 151, Laws of New Jersey, 1921, as amended.

32. In Preston's survey of 122 state and local authorities ("Use and Control of Authorities"), fifty-two had full powers over new projects without governmental authorization.

33. After the Garden State Arts Center was developed, a legislative investigation resulted in an amendment of the authority's charter stating that "the Authority shall not engage in the construction or operation of any facility or activity not directly related to the use of an expressway project except as may be specially authorized by law" (statutes of New Jersey, 27B-51, C348, section 2, and C441, section 1 [1968]).

34. The appellate division of the state supreme court delayed the construction of the Driscoll Expressway on these grounds. The governor previously had asked the authority to postpone construction, but it had argued that its bond counsel advised that it had no legal recourse but to honor the bond covenants and proceed with construction. The proj-

ect was subsequently delayed by court actions until 1977, when the bank trustee for the bond issue requested that the project be killed and the debt be refinanced. What the governor could not achieve, the bond trustee did. Authority management ceased work on the spur with $20 million sunk in it.

35. U.S. Congress, House of Representatives, Public Works for Water and Power Development, and Atomic Energy Commission Appropriation Bill 1974, Hearings Before a Subcommittee of the Committee on Appropriations, 93d Cong., 1st sess., pt. 5.

36. David E. Lilienthal, *The Journals of David E. Lilienthal* (New York: Harper & Row, 1964), 1:15.

37. When Elizabeth, New Jersey, residents opposed the Port Authority's position on Newark Airport management after a series of plane crashes in that city, local officials got nowhere in their direct dealings with the authority. The conflict was resolved through congressional investigation in Washington. See Paul Tillet and Myron Weiner, *The Closing of Newark Airport* (University, Ala.: University of Alabama Press, 1955).

38. Port Authority staff members charged in interviews that the Celler committee used improper methods to investigate personal activities of Port Authority executives. The charges could not be documented. The court ruled that, under terms of the congressional resolution authorizing the investigation, Tobin was not in contempt.

39. U.S. Congress, House of Representatives, Hearings Before Subcommittee No. 5, Committee on the Judiciary, 86th Cong., 2d sess., pt. 1, 1960, p. 641.

40. In 1971, when the Postal Service bonds were issued, Kidder Peabody had handled only two government agency bond issues, both of them after Nixon had taken office. In addition to Gordon's contributions, other Kidder Peabody personnel contributed a total of $47,893 to various Republican campaign committees in 1968, according to data at the Citizens Research Foundation.

41. U.S. Congress, House of Representatives, Committee on Post Office and Civil Service, *A Report on the Circumstances Surrounding the Proposed Sale of U.S. Postal Service Bonds* (Washington, D.C., September 27, 1971). (Hargrove later returned to Tetco and began negotiating, again through Peter Flanigan, for government approval of gas pipeline routes.)

42. For example: U.S. General Accounting Office, *Site Selection and Contract Awards for Construction and Mechanization of the New York Bulk and Foreign Mail Facility* (B-171594, 1971); *Review of Contract Award for Des Moines, Iowa Bulk Mail Facility* (171594, 1974); *Cost of Furnishing Postmaster General's New Office* (114874, 1974); *Airmail Improvement Program Objectives Unrealized* (114874, 1974); *Observations on Sole Source Procurement and Overruns* (GGD-75-81, 1975); *Forecast of Postal Service's Self Sufficiency Potential* (GGD-75-58, 1975); *Observations and Questions on the Development of the New National Bulk Mail System* (GGD-75-31, 1975).

In his nationally syndicated column of June 20, 1974, Jack Anderson reported that Postmaster General Elmer Klassen collected nearly $23,000 in management consulting fees from a Postal Service contractor while he was a member of the Postal Service Board of Governors. Klassen conceded receipt of the fees. The management by Klassen and other executives he brought with him from American Can Company came increasingly under fire from Congress, the General Accounting Office, and users' groups. Klassen retired from the post in February 1975.

To remove the Postal Service from politics, its business-oriented management had taken the portraits of the president out of local post offices, but according to GAO audits (and the conviction of Congressman Frank Brasco for bribery in connection with a post office trucking contract in 1974), it had not removed favoritism from the allocation of benefits.

43. Clinton Rossiter, *The American Presidency* (New York: Harcourt Brace, 1960), p. 242.

44. Judge Charles S. Desmond's dissent, Court of Appeals, *New York Post* v. *Robert Moses.* The case held that the records of the Triborough Bridge and Tunnel Authority did not have to be opened to the public under general state legislation requiring public access to government agency documentation. The majority ruling was that the Triborough Authority "is not an arm of the city of New York nor an arm or the agency of the state" (10 N.Y. 2d 199, 207, 176 N.E. 2d 7 [1961]).

45. *Tranter* v. *Allegheny County Authority,* 316 Pa. 65 (1934).

46. *Jackson* v. *Pennsylvania Housing Finance Agency,* 453 Pa. 329, 309 A. 2d 528 (1973).

47. Washington Supreme Court, No. 43139 (1974).

48. See, for example, *New Jersey Sports & Exposition Authority* v. *McCrane,* 119 N.J. Super. 457, 292 A 2d 580 (L. Div. 1971); *State ex rel. Warren* v. *Nusbaum,* 59 Wis. 2d 391, 431, 208 N.W. 2d 780, 804 (1973); *Massachusetts Housing Finance Agency* v. *New England Merchants Bank,* 356 Mass. 202, 249 N.E. 2d 599 (1969); *State ex rel. West Virginia Housing Development Fund* v. *Copenhaver,* 153 W.Va. 636, 171 S.E. 2d 545 (1969); *Maine State Housing Authority* v. *Depositors Trust Co.,* 278 A 2d 699, Me. (1971); *New Jersey Mortgage Finance Agency* v. *McCrane,* 56 N.J. 414, 267 A 2d 24 (1970).

49. This leverage is not always sufficient, of course. The Port Authority broke ground for the third tube for the Lincoln Tunnel when approval had been withheld by the township of Weehawken in Hudson County, New Jersey, even though the tunnel plan called for the utilization of Weehawken's streets and property, and arguments over the prices to be paid to purchase property and the relocation of local streets remained unsettled. The city's hand was forced as the shovel dug into the streets.

Chapter 11

1. George B. Hamilton, speech delivered at the 39th Annual Convention of the National Association of State Auditors, Comptrollers and Treasurers, 1954 ("Report," p. 119). The supreme court of Georgia, like that of Pennsylvania, had declared lease-back bonds constitutional, even though they were explicitly backed by property taxes in case of default—an early local version of moral obligation.

2. Robert Dahl, *Preface to Democratic Theory* (Chicago: University of Chicago Press, 1956), pp. 72–73.

3. For information on referenda, see, for example, Lester Milbrath, *Political Participation* (Chicago: Rand McNally, 1965); Howard Hamilton, "Direct Legislation," *American Political Science Review,* March 1970; Robert Crain, Elihu Katz, and Donald Rosenthal, *The Politics of Community Conflict: The Fluoridation Decision* (Indianapolis: Bobbs Merrill, 1969); A. Boskoff and Harmon Ziegler, *Voting Patterns in a Local Election* (Philadelphia: Lippincott, 1964).

4. *Salyer Land Co.* v. *Tulare Lake Basin Water Storage District,* 410 U.S. 719 (1973).

5. California contains nearly nine hundred special districts with separate corporate indebtedness or tax levies. Water utility districts operate under 52 different statutory authorizations; 184 different authorizations apply to all kinds of districts. The boards of supervisors of various counties double as governing boards for some 33 districts; city councils govern 2 districts; separate boards of elected or appointed members govern 741 districts. The degree of independence from existing local governments varies widely from district to district. Of the guaranteed local debt in California (backed by full faith and

credit of a taxing jurisdiction), 33 percent represents borrowings by special districts (exclusive of school districts). The comparable figure in New York is 2 percent. See, for example, Institute for Local Self Government, *Special Districts or Special Dynasties?* (Berkeley, 1970).

6. Harvey Katz, *Shadow on the Alamo: New Heroes Fight Old Corruption in Texas Politics* (Garden City, N.Y.: Doubleday, 1972), p. 164.

7. Ibid., p. 173.

8. See, for example, Crain, Katz, and Rosenthal, *Politics of Community Conflict;* and Morris Janowitz et al., *Public Administration and the Public* (Ann Arbor: Institute of Public Administration, University of Michigan, 1958).

9. The source of bond election data is the Securities Industry Association.

10. In fact, the trends in state constitutional reform and legal change have been in the direction of less restrictive debt provisions. States that have recently revised the general debt provisions of their constitutions provide for legislative approval of their bond issues by governments, without special elections.

11. Instances of revenue bonds that require voter approval are widely varied and include industrial development bonds in Arkansas; municipal power project bonds in Texas; water, sewer, and transportation bonds in Colorado.

12. This discussion of public corporations in West Germany is largely based upon information provided in a field report prepared by Guenther F. Schaefer in response to my outline.

13. Accelerated write-off justifies higher prices and provides operating revenues for investment in new plants. This technique is similar to financial planning by the Port Authority of New York and New Jersey, which has over the years capitalized a significant portion of its operating revenues. The accelerated depreciation by German public corporations reduces the profits that must be turned over to the governmental owner and increases the profits that are poured into depreciation reserves for new investments. In the United States, none of the profits are turned over to the governmental owner.

14. The full title in Italian is Istituto per la Recostruzione Industriale.

15. When public authorities began to proliferate in the 1950s, the Treasury Department similarly challenged their right to share in state and municipal tax exemption, but the federal courts followed precedents that had held the Port Authority and TBTA to be political subdivisions (*Commissioner* v. *Shamberg's Estate*, 144 F.2d 998 [1944] and *Commissioner* v. *White's Estate*, 144 F.2d 1019 [1944]). For such purposes as debt limits, referenda requirements, and personnel systems, state courts have not held authorities to be political subdivisions of the state. Similarly, authority bonds that invoke the moral obligation of the state are held not to be legal liabilities under state law but are considered legal obligations of the state under federal banking regulations. Fundamental inconsistencies between federal and state law are common in this field and go unchallenged largely for pragmatic reasons. The tight restrictions on taxpayer suits, standing to sue requirements, and fragmented judicial jurisdictions protect these inconsistencies.

16. *McCulloch* v. *Maryland*, 18 U.S. 316 (1819); *Collector* v. *Day*, 78 U.S. 113 (1870); *Pollock* v. *Farmers Loan and Trust Company*, 157 U.S. 429 (1894).

17. The language carried in the Internal Revenue Code is that gross income "does not include interest on the obligations of a State, Territory, or a possession of the United States, or any political subdivision of any of the foregoing, or the District of Columbia" (26 USCA, section 103a).

18. Robert Moses, *Public Works: A Dangerous Trade* (New York: McGraw-Hill, 1970), p. 261.

19. As one senior member of the House Committee on Ways and Means put it in 1973 hearings on the taxable bond option, "Mrs. Dodge is the reason we are in this problem in the first place. . . . If we have not cured the problem of Mrs. Dodge, why are we going through all these antics?" (U.S. Congress, House of Representatives, Hearings Before the Committee on Ways and Means on the Subject of General Tax Reform, 93d Cong., 1st sess., pt. X, 1973, p. 4319).

20. Internal Revenue Code (26 USCA, section 103a), amended by the Revenue Expenditure Control Act, P.L. 90-364, 1968.

21. Tax-exempt issues of up to $5 million can also be provided for a private firm if the recipient is limited to capital spending of that amount in any one location over a six-year period.

22. Statement issued by John M. Nash, first executive of the Institute for the Retention of Tax Exempt Bonds, December 1972. The views of most interested groups can be found in the 15-volume *Tax Reform: 1969* (U.S. Congress, House of Representatives, Hearings Before the Committee on Ways and Means, 91st Cong., 1st sess., 1969).

23. Like most techniques of public enterprise, the taxable bond option was not invented by the government. The idea is variously attributed to Daniel Goldberg, former Port Authority counsel, who later regretted his contribution; John E. Petersen, former director of the public finance division of the Securities Industry Association; Harvey Galper of the Urban Institute; and Frank Morris, president of the Federal Reserve Bank of Boston and a former staff member of the Securities Industry Association. Analysis of the option is provided by Robert P. Huefner, "Taxable Alternatives to Municipal Bonds," Federal Reserve Bank of Boston Research Report No. 53 (no date).

24. A 50 percent interest subsidy would provide a sufficient net advantage to the public issuer to minimize the use of tax-exempt bonds. A 33 percent rate would shelter a substantial amount of tax-exempt financing. Refusal to accept the taxable bond option on the part of many of their state and municipal clients shakes many of the tentative supporters of the compromise among investment brokers. In 1977, the taxable bond option was submitted in Senate Bill 261 with a 40 percent interest subsidy.

25. Glass-Steagall Act (Banking Act of 1933, section 21; 12 USCA, section 378).

26. Ross M. Robertson, *The Comptroller and Bank Supervision* (Washington, D.C.: Office of the Comptroller of the Currency, 1968), p. 151. Technically the comptroller had achieved his purpose by promulgating a regulation defining "general obligations of any state or any political subdivisions thereof" as including any obligation payable from "a special fund," even if the obligation is not backed by general taxing power.

27. *Baker, Watts & Company et al. v. Saxon, Comptroller of the Currency,* D.D.C. 19 97-66 (1966).

28. The Municipal Securities Rule-Making Board is comprised of representatives of investment bankers, dealer banks, and brokers. See 15 U.S.C., section 780-4(b) (1-2), 1975.

29. The general manager of the Community Development Corporation is appointed by the president. The head of the five-man board is the HUD secretary, who also makes the other appointments to the board. The secretary has fairly tight policy control of the corporation. HUD's regular staff provide the operating services of the corporation. In effect, then, the corporate device in this case (like the Commodity Credit Corporation) provides for special fund financing and a board to review project plans.

30. William Simon, representing Salomon Brothers and the Securities Industry Association, took the lead in lobbying against several of the federal financing authority proposals shortly before he joined the Nixon administration. Congressmen told the investment bankers that either federal financing authorities or taxable bond options were needed, and if the industry did not like the former, it had better rally to the latter.

See U.S. Congress, Senate, Committee on Banking, Housing and Urban Affairs, *Federal Financing Authority Hearings* (92d Cong., 2d sess., May 1972).

Chapter 12

1. David E. Lilienthal, *The Journals of David E. Lilienthal* (New York: Harper & Row, 1964), 2:179.

2. Woodrow Wilson, *The New Freedom* (New York: Doubleday Page, 1918), pp. 133, 263, 270.

3. Even such true believers as Presidents Wilson, Eisenhower, and Nixon have from time to time found corrective actions necessary to increase the efficiency of the economic system in times of war, to cope with cyclical tendencies, and to restrain the effects of corporate growth, monopoly, and control of public necessities. Wilson's New Freedom, of course, was to be based upon trust busting.

4. Gary Wills, *Nixon Agonistes* (Boston: Houghton Mifflin, 1969), p. 467.

5. Port of New York Authority, "Dynamic Planning for the Metropolitan Region" (mimeographed), August 23, 1955.

6. W. V. Heydebrand, *Hospital Bureaucracy: A Comparative Study of Organizations* (New York: Dunellen, 1973), p. 329.

7. The traditional approach to efficiency—achieving specified objectives at the lowest cost or obtaining the maximum amount of objective for a specified amount of resources —is quantifiable. But the desirability of certain objectives in the first place may depend on the costs of achieving them. The choice of objectives is not in the realm of the technician but in that of the policy analyst. In policy analysis, ends and means, resources and objectives must be traded off (or discounted) simultaneously. See Ruth P. Mack, *Planning on Uncertainty* (New York: John Wiley, 1970). Government agencies use such techniques as extended cost-benefit analysis, systems analysis, and program budgeting to put some quantities into this type of analysis. These techniques are useful to supplement and inform the political bargaining processes into which they are mixed, but they suffer from the absence of, and cannot supply, central priorities, agreed-upon goals, and commitments to some concept of the public interest.

8. Robert Dahl, "A Prelude to Corporate Reform," *Business and Society Review*, no. 1 (Spring 1972): 17–23.

9. John J. Corson and George A. Steiner, *Measuring Business's Social Performance* (Washington, D.C.: Committee for Economic Development, 1973).

Bibliography

Books and Reports

Alesch, D. J., and Dougharty, L. A. *Economies-of-Scale Analysis in State and Local Government.* Prepared for California Council on Intergovernmental Relations. Santa Monica, Calif.: The Rand Corporation, May 1971.

————. *Feasibility of Economies-of-Scale Analyses of Public Service.* Prepared for California Council on Intergovernmental Relations. Santa Monica, Calif.: The Rand Corporation, May 1971.

American Society of Planning Officials. Planning Advisory Service. *Authorities for the Financing and Administration of Public Improvements.* Information Report No. 35. Chicago, 1952.

Andrews, Burton. *The Law of Public Corporations: The Leading Cases in New York and Annotations.* New York: Matthew Bender, 1951.

Appleby, Paul H. *Policy and Administration.* University: University of Alabama Press, 1949.

Asseff, Emmett. *Special Districts in Louisiana.* Baton Rouge: Governmental Research, University of Louisiana, 1951.

Babcock, Robert F. *State and Local Government and Politics.* New York: Random House, 1957.

Baldinger, Stanley. *Planning and Governing the Metropolis: The Twin Cities Experience.* New York: Praeger, 1971.

Barber, James D. *Power in Committees: An Experiment in the Governmental Process.* Chicago: Rand McNally, 1966.

Bard, Erwin W. *The Port of New York Authority.* New York: Columbia University Press, 1942.

Berle, Adolf A., and Means, Gardiner C. *The Modern Corporation and Private Property.* New York: Macmillan, 1948.

Bernstein, Marver H. *Regulating Business by Independent Commission.* Princeton, N.J.: Princeton University Press, 1955.

Bird, Frederick L. *Local Special Districts and Authorities in Rhode Island.* Research Service No. 4. Kingston: Bureau of Governmental Research, University of Rhode Island, 1962.

————. *The Management of Small Municipal Lighting Plants.* New York: Municipal Administration Service, 1932.

————. *The Municipal Debt Load in 1935: Cities of over 50,000 Population.* New York: Dun & Bradstreet, Municipal Service Department, 1935.

————. *A Study of the Port of New York Authority.* New York: Dun & Bradstreet, 1949.

————. and Ryan, Francis M. *Public Ownership on Trial: A Study of Municipal Light and Power in California.* New York: New Republic, 1930.

Blau, Peter M. *Formal Organization.* San Francisco: Chandler, 1962.

Bollens, John C. *Special District Governments in the United States.* Berkeley: University of California Press, 1957.

Bond Buyer's Directory of Municipal Bond Dealers of the United States. New York, annual.

Boskoff, A., and Ziegler, Harmon. *Voting Patterns in a Local Election.* Philadelphia: Lippincott, 1964.

Bourjol, Maurice. *Les districts urbains.* Paris: Editions Berger-Levrault, 1963.

Branning, Rosalind L. *Pennsylvania Constitutional Development.* Pittsburgh: University of Pittsburgh Press, 1960.

Brilliant, Eleanor. *The Urban Development Corporation.* Lexington, Mass.: Lexington Books, 1975.

Bromage, Arthur W. *Political Representation in Metropolitan Agencies.* Ann Arbor: Institute of Public Administration, University of Michigan, 1962.

Butcher & Sherrerd (Investment Bank). *A Record of Municipal Authority Financing in Metropolitan Communities.* Philadelphia, 1967.

————. *A Record of Municipal Authority Financing in Pennsylvania Communities.* Philadelphia, 1965.

Calvert, Gordon L., ed. *Fundamentals of Municipal Bonds.* Washington, D.C.: Investment Bankers Association of America, 1959.

Caro, Robert. *The Power Broker: Robert Moses and the Fall of New York.* New York: Alfred A. Knopf, 1974.

Case, Harry L. *Personnel Policy in a Public Agency: The TVA Experience.* New York: Harper, 1955.

Center for Analysis for Public Issues. *Local Attorneys' Fees in Bond Issues—Nice Work If You Can Get it: A Report.* Princeton, N.J., 1971.

————. *The Doctor Is Out: A Report on the Newark, New Jersey, Division of Health.* Princeton, N.J., 1972.

————. *Microcosm of a Billion Dollar Headache: This Little Town Goes to the Bond Market and Cries 'Whew' All the Way Home.* By Edwin A. Deagle, Jr. Princeton, N.J., 1972.

Chamber of Commerce of the United States of America, Committee on Economic Policy. *Government Competition: Problem and Perspective; Report.* Washington, D.C., 1954.

————. *Re-privatizing Public Enterprise.* Washington, D.C., 1952.

Chatters, Carl H., and Millhouse, Albert M. *Local Government Debt Administration.* New York: Prentice-Hall, 1939.

Cohen, Julius H. *They Builded Better Than They Knew.* New York: J. Messner, 1946.

Committee for Economic Development. *Social Responsibilities of Business Corporations.* New York, 1971.

Coombes, David. *State Enterprise: Business or Politics.* London: Allen & Unwin, 1971.

Copeland, Melvin T., and Towl, Andrew R. *The Board of Directors and Business Management.* Cambridge, Mass.: Harvard University Press, 1947.

Copeland, Morris A. *Trends in Government Financing.* Princeton, N.J.: Princeton University Press, 1961.

Corson, John J., and Steiner, George A. *Measuring Business's Social Performance.* Washington, D.C.: Committee for Economic Development, 1973.

Council of State Governments. *State Public Authorities.* Lexington, Ky., 1970.

————. *Public Authorities in the States: A Report to the Governors' Conference.* Chicago, 1953.

Crain, Robert; Katz, Elihu; and Rosenthal, Donald. *The Politics of Community Conflict: The Fluoridation Decision.* Indianapolis: Bobbs-Merrill, 1969.

Daland, Robert T. *Some Aspects of Municipal Utility Administration in Alabama.* Montgomery: Alabama League of Municipalities, March 1954.

Danhof, C. H. *Government Contracting and Technological Change.* Washington, D.C.: The Brookings Institution, 1968.

Davis, Harmer E.; Moyer, Ralph A.; Kennedy, Norman; and Lapin, Howard S. *Toll Road Developments and Their Significance in the Provision of Expressways.* Research Report No. 11. Berkeley: Institute of Transportation and Traffic Engineering, University of California, January 1953.

Davis, John Paterson. *Corporations: A Study of the Origin and Development of Great Combinations and of Their Relation to the Authority of the State.* New York: Putnam & Sons, 1905.

Davis, Joseph D., and Jones, Charles H., Jr. *Motor Vehicle Toll Facilities.* New York: Wood, Struthers & Company, 1958.

Davis, Joseph S. *Essays in the Earlier History of American Corporations.* Cambridge, Mass.: Harvard University Press, 1917.

DeGraw, Ronald. *The Red Arrow: A History of One of the Most Successful Suburban Transit Companies in the World.* Haverford, Pa.: Haverford Press, 1972.

Derthick, Martha, with Gary Bombardier. *Between State and Nation: Regional Organizations of the United States.* Washington, D.C.: The Brookings Institution, 1974.

Dimock, Marshall E. *Developing America's Waterways: Administration of the Inland Waterways Corporation.* Chicago: University of Chicago Press, 1935.

————. *Free Enterprise and the Administrative State.* University: University of Alabama Press, 1951.

————. *Government-Operated Enterprises in the Panama Canal Zone.* Chicago: University of Chicago Press, 1934.

Directory of Municipal Bond Dealers of the United States. New York: The Bond Buyer, annual.

Downing, Donald A. *The Role of Water and Sewer Extension Financing in Guiding Urban Residential Growth.* Report No. 19. Knoxville: Water Resources Research Center, University of Tennessee, 1972.

Downs, Anthony. *Urban Problems and Prospects.* Chicago: Markham, 1972.

Drake, Alvin W. *Analysis of Public Systems.* Cambridge, Mass.: MIT Press, 1972.

Drucker, Peter. *The Age of Discontinuity.* New York: Harper & Row, 1968.

————. *Concept of the Corporation.* New York: John Day, 1946.

duPont, Pierre. *Moyens d'accroître l'efficacité des entreprises publiques.* Report presented at the International Institute of Administrative Sciences Round Table. Oxford, July 11–15, 1955.

Edelman, Murray. *The Symbolic Uses of Politics.* Urbana: University of Illinois Press, 1964.

Emmerich, Herbert. *Essays on Federal Reorganization.* University: University of Alabama Press, 1950.

Epstein, Edwin M. *The Corporation in American Politics.* Englewood Cliffs, N.J.: Prentice-Hall, 1969.

Etzioni, Amitai. *A Comparative Analysis of Complex Organizations.* New York: Free Press, 1961.

Fabricant, Solomon. *The Trend of Government Activity in the United States Since 1900.* New York: National Bureau of Economic Research, 1952.

Fainsod, Merle; Gordon, Lincoln; and Palamountain, Joseph C., Jr. *Government and the American Economy.* 3d ed. New York: Norton, 1959.

Fair, Marvin L. *Port Administration in the United States.* Cambridge, Md.: Cornell Maritime Press, 1954.

Ferguson, John H., and LeeDecker, Charles F. *Municipally Owned Waterworks in Pennsylvania.* State College: Institute of Local Government, Pennsylvania State College-Pennsylvania Municipal Public Service, 1948.

Fesler, James W. *Area and Administration.* University: University of Alabama Press, 1949.

Folsom, Marion B. *Executive Decision Making: Observations and Experience in Business and Government.* New York: McGraw-Hill, 1962.

Fowler, John F., Jr. *Revenue Bonds.* New York: Harper, 1938.

Freidman, Burton D. *The Quest for Accountability.* Chicago: Public Administration Service, 1973.

Friedmann, W. *The Public Corporation: A Comparative Symposium.* Toronto: Carswell, 1954.

Friedmann, W., and Garner, J. F., eds. *Government Enterprise: A Comparative Study.* New York: Columbia University Press, 1970.

General Electric Company. *A Proposed Plan of Solid Waste Management for Connecticut.* Prepared by the General Electric Company, Corporate Research and Development in Cooperation with the State of Connecticut, Department of Environmental Protection. Hartford, 1973.

Georgetown University, Public Services Laboratory. *Services to People: State and National Urban Strategies.* Washington, D.C., 1973.

Ginzberg, Eli; Hiestand, Dale L.; and Reubens, Beatrice G. *The Pluralistic Economy.* New York: McGraw-Hill, 1965.

Goldberg, Sidney D., and Seidman, Harold. *The Government Corporation: Elements of a Model Charter.* Chicago: Public Administration Service, 1953.

Goldman, Eric F. *Rendezvous with Destiny.* New York: Vintage Books, 1956.

Goodnow, Frank J. *Politics and Administration.* New York: Macmillan, 1914.

Goodrich, Carter; Crammer, Jerome H.; Rubin, Julius; and Segal, Harvey H. *Canals and American Economic Development.* New York: Columbia University Press, 1961.

Goodrich, Carter, ed. *The Government and the Economy: 1783–1861.* Indianapolis, Ind.: Bobbs-Merrill Co., 1967.

Gordon, R. A. *Business Leadership in a Large Corporation.* Washington, D.C.: The Brookings Institution, 1945.

Gulick, Luther Halsey. *American Forest Policy: A Study of Government Administration and Economic Controls.* New York: Duell, Sloan and Pearce, 1951.

———. *Metro: Growth and Problems of Government in the Metropolitan Areas of the United States.* Washington, D.C.: Governmental Affairs Institute, 1957.

Gulick, Luther Halsey, and Urwick, L., eds. *Papers on the Science of Administration.* New York: Institute of Public Administration, 1937.

Hanson, Albert H. *Parliament and Public Ownership.* London: Cassell, 1961.

———, *Enterprise and Economic Development.* London: Routledge & Kegan Paul, 1958.

———, ed. *Public Enterprise: A Study of Its Organization and Management in Various Countries.* Brussels: International Institute of Administrative Sciences, 1955.

Harriss, C. Lowell. *Constitutional Restrictions on Property Taxing and Borrowing Powers in New York.* Prepared for the Citizens Tax Council, Inc. New York: Columbia University Press, 1967.

Hartman, S. W. "Florida and the State and Local Bond Market." Boca Raton: Florida Atlantic University, mimeo., n.d.

Hawley, Willis D., and Rogers, David, eds. *Improving the Quality of Urban Management.* Beverly Hills, Calif.: Sage, 1974.

Hayes, Gary G. *Institutional Alternatives for Providing Programmed Water and Sewer Services in Urban Growth Areas: A Case Study of Knoxville-Knox County, Tennessee.* Report No. 18. Knoxville: Water Resources Research Center, University of Tennessee, 1972.

Heilbroner, Robert I. *Between Capitalism and Socialism.* New York: Vintage Books, 1970.

Heins, A. James. *Constitutional Restrictions against State Debt.* Madison: University of Wisconsin Press, 1963.

Hellman, Richard. *Government Competition in the Electrical Utility Industry.* New York: Praeger, 1972.

Herring, E. Pendleton. *Public Administration and the Public Interest.* New York: McGraw-Hill, 1936.

Heydebrand, Wolf V. *Hospital Bureaucracy: A Comparative Study of Organizations.* New York: Dunellen, 1973.

Hickman, W. Braddock. *Corporate Bond Quality and Investor Experience.* Princeton, N.J.: Princeton University Press, 1958.

Hillhouse, A. M. *Municipal Bonds: A Century of Experience.* New York: Prentice-Hall, 1936.

Hirsch, Werner Z. *The Economics of State and Local Government.* New York: McGraw-Hill, 1970.

Hobday, Victor C. *Sparks at the Grass Roots.* Knoxville: University of Tennessee Press, 1969.

Hoffman, Paul. *Tiger in the Court.* Chicago: Playboy Press, 1973.

Hofstadter, Richard. *The American Political Tradition and the Men Who Made It.* New York: Knopf, 1948.

Holland, Stuart, ed. *The State as Entrepreneur: New Dimensions for Public Enterprise and IRI State Shareholding Formula.* White Plains, N.Y.: International Arts and Sciences Press, 1972.

Howell, Ruth. *Handbook for Housing Commissioners.* Chicago: National Association of Housing Officials, 1950.

Hoy, Terry; Hudson, Barbara; McCarty, John F.; and Scott, Stanley. *The Use of the Port Authority in the United States: With Special Reference to the San Francisco Bay Area.* 1959 Legislative Problems, No. 2. Berkeley: Bureau of Public Administration, University of California, 1959.

Huefner, Robert P. *Taxable Alternatives to Municipal Bonds.* Research Report No. 53. Federal Reserve Bank of Boston, n.d.

Hughes, Emmet J. *The Ordeal of Power.* New York: Dell Publishing Co., 1963.

Hutchins, Wells A.; Selby, H. E.; and Voelker, Stanley W. *Irrigation-Enterprise Organizations.* Circular 934. Washington, D.C.: U.S. Department of Agriculture, 1953.

Ickes, Harold L. *Back to Work: The Story of PWA.* New York: Macmillan, 1935.

Institute for Community Development. *State Review of Local Borrowing: The Michigan Municipal Finance Commission.* Michigan State University, January 1963.

Institute for Local Self Government. *Special Districts or Special Dynasties? Democracy Denied.* Berkeley, Calif., 1970.

Institute for Policy Studies. *New York City's Municipal Hospitals: A Policy Review.* Washington, D.C., 1967.

Institute of Public Administration. *Consolidation of Port and Airport Functions in the Jacksonville Port Authority.* New York, 1968.

Ittner, Ruth. *Special Districts in the State of Washington.* Report No. 150. Seattle: Bureau of Governmental Research and Services, University of Washington, 1963.

Jantscher, Gerald R. *The Effects of Changes in Credit Ratings on Municipal Borrowing Costs.* Washington, D.C.: Investment Bankers Association, 1970.

Jones, Jesse, with Edward Angley. *Fifty Billion Dollars: My Thirteen Years with RFC, 1932-1945.* New York: Macmillan, 1951.

Kahn, Robert, and Boulding, Elise, eds. *Power and Conflict in Organizations.* New York: Basic Books, 1964.

Katz, Harvey. *Shadow on the Alamo: New Heroes Fight Old Corruption in Texas Politics.* Garden City, N.Y.: Doubleday, 1972.

Kaufman, Herbert. *Politics and Policies in State and Local Governments.* Englewood Cliffs, N.J.: Prentice-Hall, 1963.

Knappen, L. S. *Revenue Bonds and the Investor.* New York: Prentice-Hall, 1939.

Kuhn, Tillo E. *Public Enterprise Economics and Transport Problems.* Berkeley: University of California Press, 1962.

Landis, James M. *The Administrative Process.* New Haven, Conn.: Yale University Press, 1938.

Landon, Charles E. *The North Carolina State Ports Authority.* Durham, N.C.: Duke University Press, 1963.

Lechner, Alan B. *Industrial Aid Financing.* New York: Goodbody, 1965.

Legates, Richard T. *California Local Agency Formation Commissions.* Berkeley: Institute of Governmental Studies, University of California, 1970.

Leiby, Adrian C. *The Hackensack Water Company, 1869-1969.* New Jersey: Bergen County Historical Society, 1969.

Lent, George E. *The Ownership of Tax-Exempt Securities, 1913-1953.* New York: National Bureau of Economic Research, 1955.

Lilienthal, David E. *Big Business: A New Era.* New York: Harper, 1952.

———. *The Journals of David E. Lilienthal.* 2 vols. New York: Harper & Row, 1964.

———. *TVA: Democracy on the March.* New York: Harper, 1944.

Maass, Arthur. *Muddy Waters: The Army Engineers and the Nation's Rivers.* Cambridge, Mass.: Harvard University Press, 1951.

McDiarmid, John. *Government Corporations and Federal Funds.* Chicago: University of Chicago Press, 1939.

McGrane, Reginald C. *Foreign Bondholders and American State Debts.* New York: Macmillan, 1935.

Mack, Ruth. *Planning on Uncertainty.* New York: John Wiley, 1970.

Macy, John W. *Public Service: The Human Side of Government.* New York: Harper & Row, 1971.

Makielski, Stanislaw J., and Temple, David G. *Special District Government in Virginia.* Charlottesville: Institute of Government, University of Virginia, 1967.

Mann, Bettie. *State Constitutional Restrictions on Local Borrowing and Property Taxing Powers.* Albany, N.Y.: Governmental Affairs Foundation, Inc., 1965.

Mansfield, Harvey C. *The Comptroller General.* New Haven, Conn.: Yale University Press, 1939.

Martin, Roscoe C., ed. *TVA: The First Twenty Years.* University: University of Alabama Press, 1956.

Maxwell, James A. *Financing State and Local Governments.* Washington, D.C.: The Brookings Institution, 1969.

May, Eleanor G. *Bond Banks.* Charlottesville: Tayloe Murply Institute, University of Virginia, 1973.

Milbrath, Lester. *Political Participation.* Chicago: Rand McNally, 1965.

Moak, Lennox L. *Administration of Local Government Debt.* Chicago: Municipal Finance Officers Association, 1970.

Monat, William R., ed. *Current Problems and Alternatives in Financing Pennsylvania Governments: 1960-1970* (Papers presented at the 26th Annual Pennsylvania Finance Officers Workshop conducted by the Institute of Public Administration, November 1961). University Park: Pennsylvania State University, 1962.

Moore, John R., ed. *The Economic Impact of TVA.* Knoxville: University of Tennessee Press, 1967.

Morris, Peter R. *State Housing Finance Agencies.* Lexington, Mass.: D.C. Heath, 1974.

Moscow, Warren. *What Have You Done for Me Lately? The Ins and Outs of New York City Politics.* Englewood Cliffs, N.J.: Prentice-Hall, 1967.

Moses, Robert. *Public Works: A Dangerous Trade.* New York: McGraw-Hill, 1970.

———. *Working for the People.* New York: Harper & Brothers, 1956.

Mosher, Frederick G., and others. *Watergate: Implications for Responsible Government: Report to the Senate Watergate Committee by a Panel of the National Academy of Public Administration.* New York: Basic Books, 1974.

Mosher, William E., and Crawford, Finla G. *Public Utility Regulation.* New York: Harper, 1933.

Municipal Yearbook. Washington, D.C.: International City Managers Association, annual.

Musolf, Lloyd D. *Public Ownership and Accountability: The Canadian Experience.* Cambridge, Mass.: Harvard University Press, 1959.

———. *Mixed Enterprise: A Developmental Perspective.* Lexington, Mass.: D.C. Heath, 1972.

National Association of State Auditors, Comptrollers and Treasurers. *Report of the Thirty-ninth Annual Convention, December 1-4, 1954, New Orleans, La.* Chicago, 1954.

National League of Cities. *Capital Improvements Programming: A Guide for Small Cities, Towns, Boroughs and Counties.* Department of Urban Studies. Staff Report 68-2. Washington, D.C., June 1968.

———. *Credit Problems of Small Municipalities.* Department of Urban Studies. Staff Report 67-1. Washington, D.C., April 1967.

National Tax Association. *Proceedings of the Fiftieth Annual Conference on Taxation, 1957.* Fifth Roundtable. Harrisburg, Pa., 1958.

New York Law Journal. *Practical Problems of Municipal Finance: A Two-Day Specialty Conference.* C. Willis Ritter, Chairman, 1973.

Olson, James C. *History of Nebraska*. Lincoln: University of Nebraska Press, 1966.

Ostrom, Vincent. *Institutional Arrangements for Water Resource Development*. Report to the U.S. National Water Commission. Washington, D.C.: National Technical Information Service (Accession No. P.B. 207314), U.S. Department of Commerce, 1971.

————. *The Intellectual Crisis in American Public Administration*. University: University of Alabama Press, 1973.

Ott, David J., and Meltzer, Allan H. *Federal Tax Treatment of State and Local Securities*. Washington, D.C.: The Brookings Institution, 1963.

Owen, Marguerite. *The Tennessee Valley Authority*. New York: Praeger, 1973.

Owen, Wilfred, et al. *Financing Highways. Symposium conducted by the Tax Institute, November 8–9, 1956*. Princeton, N.J., 1957.

Pechman, Joseph. *Federal Tax Policy*. Washington, D.C.: The Brookings Institution, 1971.

Perrow, Charles. *Complex Organizations*. Chicago: Scott, Foresman, 1972.

Posner, M. V., and Woolf, Stuart J. *Italian Public Enterprise*. London: Duckworth, 1967.

Peterson, Lorin W. *The Day of the Mugwump*. New York: Random House, 1961.

Port of New York Authority. *Dynamic Planning for the Metropolitan Region*. New York, August 23, 1955.

Practicing Law Institute. *Municipal Bonds Workshop, 10th*. New York, 1974.

————. *Tax Exempt Financing of Industrial Development and Pollution Abatement Facilities*. New York, 1973.

————. *Tax Exempt Financing of Industrial Development and Pollution Abatement Facilities*. New York, 1974.

Pritchett, C. Herman. *The Tennessee Valley Authority: A Study in Public Administration*. Chapel Hill: University of North Carolina Press, 1943.

Pryke, Richard. *Public Enterprise in Practice*. London: MacGibbon and Kee, 1971.

Public Power Directory. Washington, D.C.: American Public Power Association, annual.

Pugh, Olin S. *Industrial-Aid Bonds as a Source of Capital for Developing Regions*. Columbia: Bureau of Business and Economic Research, University of South Carolina, 1971.

Ramanadham, Venkata V. *Problems of Public Enterprise: Thoughts on British Experience*. Chicago: Quadrangle Books, 1959.

Ratchford, B. U. *American State Debts*. Durham, N.C.: Duke University Press, 1941.

Raymond, William L. *State and Municipal Bonds*. 2d ed. Boston: Financial Publishing Company, 1932.

Report of Arden House Conference on Metropolitan Area Problems. New York: Columbia University, September 1957.

Rivlin, Alice. *Systematic Thinking for Social Action*. Washington, D.C.: The Brookings Institution, 1971.

Robertson, Ross M. *The Comptroller and Bank Supervision*. Washington, D.C.: Office of the Comptroller of the Currency, 1968.

Robinson, Roland I. *Postwar Market for State and Local Government Securities*. Princeton, N.J.: Princeton University Press, 1960.

Robson, William A. *Nationalized Industry and Public Ownership*. London: Allen & Unwin, 1962.

————, ed. *Problems of Nationalised Industry*. London: Allen & Unwin, 1952.

Sayre, Wallace S., ed. *The Federal Government Service*. Englewood Cliffs, N.J.: Prentice-Hall, 1965.

Sayre, Wallace S., and Kaufman, Herbert. *Governing New York City: Politics in the Metropolis*. New York: Norton, 1965.

Schubert, Glendon A. *The Public Interest: A Critique of the Theory of a Political Concept*. Glencoe, Ill.: Free Press, 1961.

Scott, Stanley. *Metropolitan District Legislation: Some Problems and Issues*. Berkeley: Bureau of Public Administration, University of California, 1958.

Scullin, George. *International Airport: The Story of Kennedy Airport and U.S. Commercial Aviation*. Boston: Little, Brown, 1968.

Securities Industry Association. *Fundamentals of Municipal Bonds*. 9th ed. New York, 1973.

Seidman, Harold. *Politics, Position and Power: The Dynamics of Federal Organization*. New York: Oxford University Press, 1970, 1975.

Selznick, Philip. *T.V.A. and the Grass Roots*. Berkeley: University of California Press, 1949.

Shepherd, William G. *Economic Performance Under Public Ownership: British Fuel and Power*. New Haven, Conn.: Yale University Press, 1965.

Shepherd, William G., and Gies, Thomas G., eds. *Utility Regulation: New Directions in Theory and Policy*. New York: Random House, 1966.

Sloan, Alfred P. *My Years with General Motors*. New York: MacFadden-Bartell, 1965.

Smith, Adam. *An Inquiry into the Nature and Causes of the Wealth of Nations*. New York: The Modern Library, 1936.

Smith, Bruce L. R., ed. *The New Political Economy: The Public Use of the Private Sector*. New York: John Wiley, 1975.

Smith, Robert G. *Ad Hoc Governments: Special Purpose Transportation Authorities in Britain and the United States*. Beverly Hills, Calif.: Sage Publications, 1974.

————. *Public Authorities, Special Districts and Local Government*. Washington, D.C.: National Association of Counties, Research Foundation, 1964.

————. *Public Authorities in Urban Areas*. Washington, D.C.: National Association of Counties, Research Foundation, 1969.

Social Science Research Council, Committee on Public Administration. *Research in the Use of the Government Corporation*. New York, 1940.

Stein, Harold, ed. *Public Administration and Policy Development: A Casebook*. New York: Harcourt Brace, 1952.

Stern, Philip M. *The Great Treasury Raid*. New York: Random House, 1964.

Strickland, Harry B. *Inside the Trojan Horse: Understanding the Specialized Units of Local Government-Municipal Authorities*. Clarks Summit, Pa.: Logo Publishing and Research, 1969.

Tax Foundation. *Controlling Government Corporations*. New York, 1955.

Taylor, Frederick W. *The Principles of Scientific Management*. New York: Harper, 1911.

Thompson, James D. *Organizations in Action: Social Science Bases of Administrative Theory*. New York: McGraw-Hill, 1967.

Thompson, James D., ed. *Approaches to Organizational Design*. Pittsburgh, Pa.: University of Pittsburgh Press, 1966.

Thurston, John. *Government Proprietary Corporations in the English-Speaking Countries.* Cambridge, Mass.: Harvard University Press, 1937.

Tillett, Paul, and Weiner, Myron. *The Closing of Newark Airport.* Inter-University Case Program, No. 27. University: University of Alabama Press, 1955.

Tolchin, Martin, and Tolchin, Susan. *To the Victor . . . : Political Patronage from the Clubhouse to the White House.* New York: Random House, 1971.

Trull, Edna. *Borrowing for Highways.* New York: Dun & Bradstreet, Municipal Service Department, 1937.

Turvey, Ralph. *Economic Analysis and Public Enterprises.* Totowa, N.J.: Rowman and Littlefield, 1972.

————, ed. *Public Enterprise.* Baltimore, Md.: Penguin, 1968.

Twentieth Century Fund. Power Committee. *Electric Power and Government Policy: A Survey of the Relations Between the Government and the Electric Power Industry.* New York, 1948.

————. Task Force on Community Development. *CDC's: New Hope for the Inner City.* New York, 1971.

————. Task Force on Securities Markets. *The Rating Game.* New York, 1974.

Urban Survey Corporation. *Directory of Special Districts in the United States.* Boston, Mass., 1964.

Van Dorn, Harold A. *Government Owned Corporations.* New York: Knopf, 1926.

Vennard, Edwin. *Government in the Power Business.* New York: McGraw-Hill, 1968.

Waldo, Dwight. *The Administrative State.* New York: Ronald Press, 1948.

Wallace, L. T., and O'Connell, T. B. *Survey of California Water Service Organizations.* Berkeley: Agricultural Extension Service, University of California, 1966.

Wallace, Schuyler C. *Federal Departmentalization.* New York: Columbia University Press, 1941.

Walsh, Annmarie Hauck. *The Urban Challenge to Government: An International Comparison of Thirteen Cities.* New York: Praeger, 1969.

————. *Urban Government for the Paris Region.* New York: Praeger Special Studies, 1968.

Warne, William E. *The Bureau of Reclamation.* New York: Praeger, 1973.

Warner, Kenneth, ed. *Developments in Public Employee Relations: Legislative, Judicial, Administrative.* Chicago: Public Personnel Association, 1965.

Waters, Harry L., and Raines, William H. *Special Districts in Kentucky.* Research Report No. 48. Frankfort, Ky.: Legislative Research Commission, July 1968.

Weidenbaum, Murray L. *The Modern Public Sector: New Ways of Doing the Government's Business.* New York: Basic Books, 1969.

Weinberg, Arthur M., and Weinberg, Lila, eds. *The Muckrakers: The Era in Journalism That Moved America to Reform, the Most Significant Magazine Articles of 1902–1912.* New York: Simon and Schuster, 1961.

Weintraub, Tina V., and Patterson, James D. *The "Authority" in Pennsylvania: Pro and Con.* Philadelphia: Bureau of Municipal Research, May 1959.

White, Leonard D. *Introduction to the Study of Public Administration.* New York: Macmillan, 1939.

White, William Allen. *The Old Order Changeth.* Milwaukee, Wisc.: The Young Churchman Co., 1910.

Wildavsky, Aaron. *Dixon-Yates: A Study in Power Politics.* New Haven, Conn.: Yale University Press, 1962.

Willoughby, W. F. *Principles of Public Administration.* Washington, D.C.: The Brookings Institution, 1927.

————. *The Reorganization of the Administrative Branch of the National Government.* Baltimore, Md.: Johns Hopkins Press, 1923.

Wills, Gary. *Nixon Agonistes.* Boston: Houghton Mifflin, 1969.

Wilson, Woodrow. *Congressional Government.* New York: Meridian, 1959.

————. *The New Freedom.* New York: Doubleday, Page, 1918.

Articles

Alderfer, Harold F. "Is Authority Financing the Answer?" *The American City* 70 (February 1955).

Archbold, Pamela. "Pollution Control Financing Grows Up." *Corporate Financing* (July–August 1972).

Bachrach, Peter, and Baratz, Morton S. "The Two Faces of Power." *American Political Science Review* 56 (1962).

Baldwin, Simeon Eben. "Private Corporations, 1701–1901." In *Two Centuries' Growth of American Law.* Yale Bicentennial Series. New York: Scribner's, 1902.

Bauer, John. "Metropolitan Utility Supply and Organization." *Public Administration Review* 5 (Spring 1945).

Bland, F. A. "Some Implications of the Statutory Corporation." *Public Administration* (London) 15 (October 1937).

Bollens, John C. "When Services Get Too Big." *National Municipal Review* 38 (November 1949).

Bradley, Joseph F., and Bowlin, Oswald D. "Industrial Aid Bonds—A Device for Attracting New Industry." *Municipal Finance* 33 (May 1961).

Brazer, H. E.; Suits, D. B.; and Converse, N. W. "Municipal Bond Yields." *National Tax Journal* 15 (March 1962).

Bromage, Arthur W. "Political Representation in Metropolitan Areas." *American Political Science Review* 52 (June 1958).

Brown, Elizabeth Gaspar. "Obligations of a State-Created Authority: Do They Constitute a Debt of the State: Comment." *Michigan Law Review* 53 (January 1955).

Browne, Alan K. "The Prospective Market for Municipal Bonds." *Municipal Finance* 31 (August 1959).

Brownlow, Louis. "Reconversion of the Federal Administrative Machinery from War to Peace." *Public Administration Review* 4 (Spring 1944).

Cameron, Juan. "Whose Authority?" *Atlantic Monthly* 204 (August 1959).

Canaday, Siesel. "Constraints on the Municipal Bond Market." *Municipal Finance* 43 (August 1970).

Chatters, Carl H. "Is Authority Financing the Answer? Another Point of View." *The American City* 70 (February 1955).

"Constitutional Objections to the Creation of State Authorities: Comment." *University of Chicago Law Review* 21 (Autumn 1953).

Cottrell, Edwin A. "Problems of Local Governmental Reorganization." *Western Political Quarterly* 2 (December 1949).

Crouch, Winston W. "The Government of a Metropolitan Region." *University Law Review* 105 (February 1957).

Dahl, Robert. "A Prelude to Corporate Reform." *Business and Society Review* 1 (Spring 1972).

Davis, Horace A. "Borrowing Machines." *National Municipal Review* 24 (June 1935).

Dimock, Marshall. "Government Corporations: A Focus of Policy and Administration." *American Political Science Review* 43 (October and December 1949).

————. "Principles Underlying Government-Owned Corporations." *Public Administration* (London) 13 (January 1935).

Duzan, Hugo C., et al. "Recent Trends in Highway Bond Financing." *Public Roads* 27 (October 1952).

Easter, C. W. "Maintaining a Market for Your Bonds." *Municipal Finance* 34 (August 1961).

Eastman, Joseph B. "A Plan for Public Ownership and Operation." *Annals of the American Academy of Political and Social Science* 159 (January 1932).

Edelstein, Mortimer S. "The Authority Plan—Tool of Modern Government." *Cornell Law Quarterly* 28 (January 1943).

Feldman, Mark B., and Jassy, Everett L. "The Urban County: A Study of New Approaches to Local Government in Metropolitan Areas: Note." *Harvard Law Review* 73 (January 1960).

Finer, Herman. "State Activity Before Adam Smith." *Public Administration* (London) 10 (April 1932).

Foley, E. H., Jr. "Revenue Financing of Public Enterprises." *Michigan Law Review* 35 (November 1936).

Fox, Annette Baker. "The Local Housing Authority and the Municipal Government." *Land Economics* 17 (August 1941).

Gabler, L. Richard. "The Financing of State and Local Government Activities in the Postwar Period." *Monthly Review: Federal Reserve Bank of New York* 47 (September 1965).

Galper, Harvey, and Petersen, John. "An Analysis of Subsidy Plans to Support State and Local Borrowing." *National Tax Journal* 24 (June 1971).

————. "A Troubled Time for Capital Financing." *Nation's Cities* 8 (March 1970).

Garvey, John, Jr. "Marketing City Services: Step Right This Way." *Public Management* 52 (February 1970).

"Getting the Government Out of Business—A Start." *Newsweek*, July 26, 1954.

Goldstein, Sidney. "The Port of New York Authority." *Journal of Public Law* 5 (Fall 1956).

Goldstein, Stephen R. "Interdistrict Inequalities in School Financing: A Critical Analysis of Serrano v Priest and Its Progeny." *University of Pennsylvania Law Review* 120 (January 1972).

Gottlieb, M. "Cyclical Timing of Municipal Bond Issues." *Quarterly Review of Economics and Business* 1 (May 1961).

Guild, Frederic H. "Special Municipal Corporations." *National Municipal Review* 18 (May 1929).

Gulick, Luther. "Authorities and How to Use Them." *Tax Review* 8 (November 1947).

————. "Politics, Administration and the New Deal." *Annals of the American Academy of Political and Social Science* 169 (September 1933).

Haar, Charles M. "Where Shall the Money Come from?" *Public Interest*, no. 18 (Winter 1970).

Hamilton, Howard. "Direct Legislation." *American Political Science Review* 64 (March 1970).

Hardin, Garrett. "The Tragedy of the Commons." *Science* 162 (December 13, 1968).

Hein, Clarence J. "The Function and Finances of Special Districts in Rural Areas." *Agricultural Finance Review* 22 (September 1960).

Hirsch, Werner Z. "Administrative and Fiscal Considerations in Urban Development." *Annals of the American Academy of Political and Social Science* 352 (March 1964).

Hovde, B. J. "The Local Housing Authority." *Public Administration Review* (Winter 1941).

Inger, Charles W. "Are Public Controls over Authorities Adequate?" *National Tax Association Proceedings of Fiftieth Annual Conference on Taxation, October 21–25, 1957, Columbus, Ohio.* Harrisburg, Pa., 1958.

"Insuring the Payoff to Help Sell [Municipal] Bonds." *Business Week*, January 8, 1972.

Jaffee, Lee K. "Public Relations—The New Government Service." *Public Relations Journal* 11 (October 1955).

James, George. "Health for the City." In *Agenda for a City: Issues Confronting New York.* Edited by Lyle C. Fitch and Annmarie H. Walsh. Beverly Hills, Calif.: Sage Publications, 1970.

Jones, Victor. "Local Government Organization in Metropolitan Areas: Its Relation to Urban Redevelopment." In *The Future of Cities and Urban Redevelopment.* Edited by Coleman Woodbury. Chicago: University of Chicago Press, 1953.

————. "The Withering Away of the City." *Public Management* 32 (December 1960).

Key, V. O., Jr. "Government Corporations." In *Elements of Public Administration.* Edited by Fritz Morstein-Marx. New York: Prentice-Hall, 1946.

Kochan, James L. "The Market for State and Local Government Bonds." *Economic Review: Federal Reserve Bank of Cleveland* (August–September 1972).

Kurnow, Ernest. "The Nonguaranteed Debt of State and Local Government." *National Tax Journal* 15 (September 1962).

Kurshan, Daniel L. "Developing Productivity in the Port of New York Authority." An Information Memorandum for the United Nations Working Group on Measures for Improving Performance of Public Enterprises in Developing Countries. Herceg-Novi, Yugoslavia (October 1969).

————. "How Should Authorities Be Controlled?" *GRA Reporter* 5 (September–October and November –December 1953).

Kushell, C. J., Jr. "Operating Aspects of Revenue Bond Financing." *Journal of Finance* 10 (May 1955).

Lee, Eugene C. "Use of Lease-Purchase Agreements to Finance Capital Improvements." *Municipal Finance* 24 (November 1951).

LeeDecker, Charles F. "Device for Operating Utilities." *National Municipal Review* 34 (June 1945).

Levitt, Arthur. "Who Rates the Raters." *Bond Buyer*, Special Conference Issue, 1973.

Lewis, Robert S. "A Study of Local Government Finance." *Pennsylvanian* (May 1969).

Lilienthal, David E., and Robert H. Marquis. "The Conduct of Business Enterprises by the Federal Government." *Harvard Law Review* 54 (1941).

Lindsay, George G. "The Municipal Authority in Pennsylvania; Note." *Dickinson Law Review* 55 (January 1951).

Long, Norton E. "Recent Theories and Problems of Local Government." In *Public Policy: A Yearbook.* Edited by Carl Friedrich and Seymour Harris. Cambridge, Mass.: Graduate School of Public Administration, Harvard University, 1958.

Lukens, Matthias E. "Practicing Management Theory." *Public Administration Review* 18 (Summer 1958).

McDiarmid, John. "California Uses of the Government Corporation." *American Political Science Review* 34 (April 1940).

McLean, Joseph E. "Threat to Responsible Rule." *National Municipal Review* 40 (September 1951).

————. "Use and Abuse of Authorities." *National Municipal Review* 42 (October 1953).

Mitchell, John N. "Municipal Industrial Aid Bonds." *Municipal Finance* 33 (May 1961).

Moses, Raphael J. "Irrigation Corporations." *Rocky Mountain Law Review* 32 (June 1960).

"The Municipal Finance Officer and Financial Consultants." A series of three articles reprinted from *Municipal Finance*, February 1954. Chicago: Municipal Finance Officers Association.

National Institute of Municipal Law Officers. "Report of Committee on Municipal Bonds." *NIMLO Municipal Law Review* 37A, pt. 5 (1974).

"New Ways to Sell Municipal Bonds." *Business Week*, January 16, 1971.

Nottage, Raymond. "Reporting to Parliament on the Nationalised Industries." *Public Administration* (London) 35 (Summer 1957).

O'Donnell, John L. "The Tax Cost of Constitutional Debt Limitation in Indiana." *National Tax Journal* 15 (December 1962).

Ostrom, Vincent. "State Administration of Natural Resources in the West." *American Political Science Review* 47 (June 1953).

"Pennsylvania's Billion Dollar Babies: The Story of Our Mushrooming Municipal Authorities." *Business Review: Federal Reserve Bank of Philadelphia* (March 1958).

Peterson, George E., and Galper, Harvey E. "Tax-Exempt Financing of Private Industry's Pollution Control Investment." *Public Policy* 23 (Winter 1975).

Pincus, William. "Shall We Have More TVA's?" *Public Administration Review* 5 (Autumn 1946).

Pogue, Thomas F. "The Effect of Debt Limits: Some New Evidence." *National Tax Journal* 23 (March 1970).

Pritchett, C. Herman. "The Government Corporation Control Act of 1945." *American Political Science Review* 40 (June 1946).

————. "The Paradox of the Government Corporation." *Public Administration Review* 1 (Summer 1941).

"Public Authorities." (Special Issue.) *Law and Contemporary Problems* 26 (Autumn 1961).

Reader, F. Eugene. "Financing Municipal Sewage Treatment Facilities in Pennsylvania by Use of Municipality Authorities." *Dickinson Law Review* 55 (1950-1951).

Reilly, William K., and S. J. Schulman. "The State Urban Development Corporation: New York's Innovation." *The Urban Lawyer* 1 (Summer 1969).

"Report of the Annual Convention of the National Association of State Auditors, Comptrollers and Treasurers." Providence, R.I., annual.

Ritter, C. Willis. "Federal Income Tax Treatment of Municipal Obligations: Industrial Development Bonds." *The Tax Lawyer* 25 (Spring 1972).

Robinson, Susan R. "Industrial Development Bonds: They're Not What They Used To Be." *Business Review: Federal Reserve Bank of Philadelphia* (March 1969).

Robson, William A. "National Industries in Britain and France." *American Political Science Review* 44 (June 1950).

Sayre, Wallace S. "Trends of a Decade in Administrative Values." *Public Administration Review* 11 (Winter 1951).

Schnapper, Morris B. "Our New Municipal Landlords." *National Municipal Review* 28 (June 1939).

Seidman, Harold. "The Government Corporation: Organization and Controls." *Public Administration Review* 14 (Summer 1954).

————. "The Theory of the Autonomous Government Corporation: A Critical Appraisal." *Public Administration Review* 12 (Spring 1952).

Shestack, Jerome J. "The Public Authority." *University of Pennsylvania Law Review* 105 (February 1957).

Shore, William B. "Developments in Public Administration." *Public Administration Review* 61 (Winter 1961).

Smith, Bruce L. R. "The Not-for-Profit Corporations." *The Public Interest* (Summer 1967).

"Some Observations on the New York City Transit Authority; Legislation." *St John's Law Review* 28 (December 1953).

Staats, William F. "Taking Aim at Tax-Exempts." *Business Review: Federal Reserve Bank of Philadelphia* (September 1969).

Steiner, Gilbert Y. "A State Building Authority: Solution to Construction Needs?" *Current Economic Comment* 17 (February 1955).

Stiles, Lynn A. "Economic Effects of Authority Operations and Financing." In *National Tax Association Proceedings of the Fiftieth Annual Conference on Taxation, October 21–25, 1957, Columbus, Ohio.* Harrisburg, Pa., 1958.

Stober, William J., and Laurence H. Falk. "Industrial Development Bonds as a Subsidy to Industry." *National Tax Journal* 22 (June 1969).

"Tennessee Valley Authority: The Yardstick with Less Than 36 Inches." *Forbes Magazine*, April 1, 1975.

Thompson, Arthur A. "Business Experience with Industrial Aid Bonds as a Source of External Financing: Some Empirical Evidence." *California Management Review* 13 (Winter 1970).

Tobin, Austin J. "Administering the Public Authority." *Dun's Review* 60 (June 1952).

————. "Authorities as a Governmental Technique." Address before the Third Annual Institute, the Place of Authorities in the Life of New Jersey Citizens, sponsored by the New Jersey Council for Social Studies and Bureau of Governmental Research, Rutgers University, March 26, 1953.

————. "Management Structure and Operating Policies in Public Authorities: The Port of New York Authority." Address before CIOS Triannual Management Congress, New York, September 1963, p. 3.

————. "The Port of New York Authority." *State Government* 20 (September 1947).

————. "The Private Side of a Public Business." *Challenge* 7 (April 1959).

"Toll Roads and Toll Authorities." *State Government* 26 (June 1953).

Wagner, Richard E. "Optimality in Local Debt Limitation." *National Tax Journal* 23 (September 1970).

Walker, Mabel. "The Authority Device for Financing Public Works." *Tax Policy* 25 (December 1958).

Wallace, David W. "Organization of an Authority's Accounts." *GRA Reporter* 3 (November–December 1951).

Walsh, Annmarie Hauck. "Decentralization for Urban Management: Sorting the Wheat from the Chaff." In *Improving the Quality of Urban Management.* Edited by Willis D. Hawley and David Rogers. Beverly Hills, Calif.: Sage Publications, 1974.

Warren, Robert. "A Municipal Services Market Model of Metropolitan Organization." *Journal of American Institute of Planners* 30 (August 1964).

Westmeyer, Troy R. "Authorities: An Escape from Debt Limitations?" *GRA Reporter* 6 (Fourth quarter, 1954).

Wildavsky, Aaron. "TVA and Power Politics." *American Political Science Review* 55 (September 1961).

————. "The Political Economy of Efficiency." *The Public Interest* (Summer 1967).

Willoughby, W. F. "The National Government as a Holding Corporation: The Question of Subsidiary Budgets." *Political Science Quarterly* 32 (December 1917).

Wilson, Woodrow. "The Study of Administration" (1887). In *Political Science Quarterly* 56 (December 1941).

Wiltse, Charles M. "Representative Function of Bureaucracy." *American Political Science Review* 35 (June 1941).

Wood, David M. "Legal Aspects of Revenue Bond Financing." *Journal of Finance* 10 (May 1955).

————. "Special Authorities." *Municipal Finance* 25 (May 1953).

Ylvisaker, Paul W. "Growing Role of State Government in Local Affairs." *State Government* 41 (Summer 1968).

Government Publications

California. Assembly. Interim Committee on Municipal and County Government. *Special District Problems in the State of California.* Sacramento, 1961.

Colorado. Legislative Council. *Regional Service Authorities; Report to the Colorado General Assembly.* Research Publication No. 176. Denver, November 1971.

Connecticut. Laws and Statutes. *An Act Concerning Establishment of a Connecticut Resources Recovery Authority.* (Public Act 73-459.) Hartford, 1973.

Denver Regional Council of Governments. *An Approach to Regional Services: The Colorado Service Authority Act of 1972.* Denver, 1972.

Florida. Legislative Service Bureau. *Florida Special Districts: Statutory Authority, Membership, Terms, Method of Selection and Tax and Finance Provisions.* Tallahassee, February 1970.

Illinois. Commission on Local Government. *Report to Governor . . . and Members of the 76th Illinois General Assembly.* Springfield, March 1969.

Louisiana. Office of the Treasurer. *Would You Believe?* Baton Rouge, 1969.

Massachusetts. *Special Commission Relative to the Finances and Operation of the Massachusetts Bay Transportation Authority.* Interim Report. Boston, July 1969.

Massachusetts Bay Transportation Authority. *Report of . . . Authority Relative to Mass Transportation Within the Commonwealth.* (Senate No. 1270.) Boston, March 1969.

Memorandum in Opposition to Certain Bills Relating to Public Authorities Submitted by Bethpage Park Authority, Jones Beach State Parkway Authority, Power Authority of the State of New York, Triborough Bridge and Tunnel Authority. New York, February 23, 1959.

Memorandum Opposing Certain Bills Relating to Public Authorities Submitted by Bethpage Park Authority, Jones Beach State Parkway Authority, Nassau County Bridge Authority, Power Authority of the State of New York, Triborough Bridge and Tunnel Authority. New York, February 10, 1958.

Memorandum Opposing Certain Bills Sponsored by Temporary State Commission on Coordination of State Activities Submitted by Bethpage Park Authority, Jones Beach State Parkway Authority, Nassau County Bridge Authority, Power Authority of the State of New York. New York, February 28, 1957.

New Jersey. County and Municipal Government Study Commission. *Beyond Local Resources: Federal/State Aid and the Local Fiscal Crisis.* Trenton, April 1971.

―――. *Creative Localism: A Prospectus.* Trenton, March 1968.

―――. *Solid Waste: A Coordinated Approach.* Trenton, 1972.

New Jersey. Joint Legislative Autonomous Authorities Study Commission. *Public Hearings before the Commission, held May 14, June 19, October 30, 1968.* 3 vols. Trenton, 1968.

―――. *Public Hearings before the Commission, held March 3, 1969.* Trenton, 1969.

―――. *Public Hearings before the Commission and the New York State Assembly Committee on Corporations, Authorities and Commissions, held March 5 and 12, 1971.* 2 vols. Trenton, 1971.

―――. *Report.* Trenton, 1972.

New Jersey. Senate. Special Investigating Committee. *Report of . . . Committee under Senate Resolution No. 7 of the Year 1961.* Trenton, June 28, 1963.

New York City. Temporary Commission on City Finances. *Transportation Authorities; Fiscal and Organizational Relations with the City of New York.* Staff Paper 7. New York, July 1966.

New York State. *Five-Year Projection of Income and Expenditures: General Fund (Fiscal Years 1974–75 Through 1978–79).* Albany, 1974.

―――. *Preliminary Staff Report on a Proposal for the Regionalization of Existing Highway and Bridge Authorities.* Legislative Doc. No. 24. Albany, 1955.

―――. Department of Audit and Control. *Audit of New York State, New York City and Public Authorities.* Albany, 1973.

―――. *Audit Report on the Financial Statements and Practices of the Port of New York Authority.* Albany, 1969, 1974.

―――. *Debt-Like Commitments of the State of New York.* Albany, January 1973.

―――. *Financial Report.* Albany, annual.

―――. *Principles of Accounting and Standards of Reporting for Public Authorities.* Albany, October 1970.

―――. *Report on Audit of Certain Financial and Operating Practices Triborough Bridge and Tunnel Authority, New York, N.Y.* Report No. NY 25–67. Albany, 1965.

————. *Statewide Public Authorities: A Fourth Branch of Government?* Albany, November 1972.

————. *Statewide Public Authorities: Individual Authority Summaries.* 2 vols. Albany, 1972.

New York State. Joint Legislative Committee on Metropolitan and Regional Areas Study. *Coordinating Governments Through Regionalism and Reform.* Vol 2: *Fiscal Crisis and Local Government Manpower Opportunities: Letting Necessity Mother Invention.* Legislative Doc. No. 19. Albany, 1971.

New York State Metropolitan Transportation Authority. *The Ten-Year Program at the Halfway Mark.* New York, 1973.

New York State Charter Revision Commission for New York City. "Public Benefit Corporations in New York City." Mimeo., 1973.

New York State Moreland Act Commission on the Urban Development Corporation and Other State Financing Agencies. *Restoring Credit and Confidence: A Reform Program for New York State and Its Public Authorities. (Report to the Governor, March 31, 1976.)* Albany, 1976.

New York State Senate. Committee on Finance (Minority). *New York State First Instance Advances.* Albany, February 27, 1970.

New York State Study Commission for New York City. (Scott Commission.) *Health Care Needs and the New York City Health and Hospitals Corporation.* New York, 1973.

New York Temporary State Commission on Coordination of State Activities. *Staff Report on Public Authorities Under New York State, March 21, 1956.* Albany: Williams Press, 1956.

New York, New Jersey Port and Harbor Development Commission. *Joint Report with Comprehensive Plan and Recommendations.* New York, 1920.

Pennsylvania. Governor's Management Review Task Force. *Commonwealth of Pennsylvania: The Governor's Review, 1972.* Harrisburg, 1972.

Pennsylvania Constitutional Convention, 1967-1968. *Local Government.* Reference Manual No. 4. Harrisburg: The Preparatory Committee, 1967.

Pennsylvania Department of Community Affairs. *Directory of Municipal Authorities in Pennsylvania—1972.* Harrisburg, n.d.

————. *Equalization of School Support.* Harrisburg, February 1972.

————. *Local Government Unit Debt Act (Act 185 of 1972).* Harrisburg, July 1972.

Pennsylvania Economy League. *Where the Money Comes from: A Study of the Financing of Local Government in Pennsylvania.* Report No. 4—Local Debt Limits and Borrowing Procedures. Prepared for the Local Government Commission and the Department of Community Affairs of the Commonwealth of Pennsylvania, September 1970.

Sause, George E. *Municipal Authorities: The Pennsylvania Experience.* Harrisburg: Department of Internal Affairs, Commonwealth of Pennsylvania, 1962.

Schroeder, Werner W. *Metropolitan Transit Research Study.* Chicago: Chicago Transit Authority, n.d.

United Nations. Department of Economic and Social Affairs. Public Administration Division. "Handbook on Public Enterprise." (Mimeo.) New York, 1972.

U.S. Advisory Commission on Intergovernmental Relations. *Alternative Approaches to Governmental Reorganization in Metropolitan Areas.* Report A-11. Washington, D.C., June 1962.

————. *Factors Affecting Voter Reactions to Government Reorganization in Metropolitan Areas.* Report M-15. Washington, D.C., May 1962.

————. *Federal Approaches to Aid State and Local Capital Financing.* Report A-37. Washington, D.C., September 1970.

————. *Federal-State-Local Finances: Significant Features of Federalism.* Washington, D.C., 1973–1974.

————. *Industrial Development Bond Financing.* Report A-18. Washington, D.C., June 1963.

————. *Performance of Urban Functions: Local and Areawide.* Report M-21, rev. Washington, D.C., September 1963.

————. *The Problem of Special Districts in American Government.* Report A-32. Washington, D.C., May 1964.

————. *State Constitutional and Statutory Restrictions on Local Government Debt.* Washington, D.C., September 1961.

————. *State and Local Finances: Significant Features, 1966 to 1969.* Report M-43. Washington, D.C., 1968.

————. *State and Local Finances: Significant Features, 1967 to 1970.* Report M-50. Washington, D.C., 1969.

————. *State and Local Finances: Significant Features and Suggested Legislation.* Report M-74. Washington, D.C., 1972.

————. *State Technical Assistance to Local Debt Management.* Report M-26. Washington, D.C., 1965.

U.S. Bureau of the Census. *1972 Census of Governments.* Washington, D.C., 1974. Vols 1, 4.

————. *Special District Governments in the United States.* State and Local Government Special Studies No. 33. Washington, D.C., January 6, 1954.

U.S. Commission on Organization of the Executive Branch of the Government (Hoover Commission). *Business Enterprises: A Report to the Congress.* Washington, D.C., May 1955.

————. *Staff Study on Business Enterprises Outside the Department of Defense.* Washington, D.C., 1955.

————. *Task Force Report on Lending Agencies. Appendix R to Report on Federal Business Enteprises.* Washington, D.C.: U.S. Government Printing Office, 1949.

U.S. Congress. House of Representatives. Committee on the Judiciary. Subcommittee No. 5. *Hearings on the Port of New York Authority.* 86th Cong., 2d Sess. Washington, D.C., 1960.

————. House of Representatives. Committee on Post Office and Civil Service. *A Report on the Circumstances Surrounding the Proposed Sale of U.S. Postal Service Bonds.* Washington, D.C., September 27, 1971.

————. House of Representatives. Committee on Ways and Means. *Tax Reform, 1969: Hearings.* 91st Cong., 1st Sess. Washington, D.C., 1969. 15 vols.

————. House of Representatives. Committee on Ways and Means. *Hearings on the Subject of General Tax Reform.* 93rd Cong., 1st Sess. Washington, D.C., 1973. 10 vols.

————. Joint Committee on the Investigation of the Tennessee Valley Authority. *Hearings.* 75th Cong., 3rd Sess. Washington, D.C.: U.S. Government Printing Office, 1939.

————. Joint Committee on Reduction of Nonessential Federal Expenditures. *Reduction of Nonessential Federal Expenditures. Additional Report of the Joint Committee on Reduction of Nonessential Federal Expenditures, Congress of the United States, Pursuant to Section 601 of the Revenue Act of 1941. Government Corporations . . .*

78th Cong., 2d Sess., Senate Doc. 227. Washington, D.C.: U.S. Government Printing Office, 1944.

———. Joint Economic Committee. *Financing Municipal Facilities.* 91st Cong., 1st Sess. Washington, D.C.: U.S. Government Printing Office, 1968. 2 vols.

———. Joint Economic Committee. *State and Local Public Facility Needs and Financing.* 89th Cong., 2d Sess. Washington, D.C.: U.S. Government Printing Office, December 1966. 2 vols.

———. Senate. *Reference Manual of Government Corporations.* 79th Cong., 1st Sess., Senate Doc. 86. Washington, D.C.: U.S. Government Printing Office, 1945.

———. Senate. *Supplement I to the Reference Manual of Government Corporations.* 80th Cong., 1st Sess., Senate Doc. 74. Washington, D.C.: U.S. Government Printing Office, 1947.

———. Senate. Committee on Banking and Currency. *Development Corporations and Authorities.* (Revised December 2, 1959.) 86th Cong., 1st Sess. Washington, D. C.: U.S. Government Printing Office, 1959.

———. Senate. Committee on Banking and Currency. *Financial Control of Government Corporations; Report.* (To Accompany H.R. 3660) 79th Cong., 1st Sess., Senate Report 694. Washington, D.C.: U.S. Government Printing Office, 1945.

———. Senate. Committee on Banking, Housing and Urban Affairs. *Federal Financing Authority Hearings.* 92d Cong., 2d Sess. Washington, D.C., 1972.

———. Senate. Committee on Government Operations. *Audit Reports of Government Corporations and Agencies; Report.* Washington, D.C.: U.S. Government Printing Office. Annual.

———. Senate. Committee on Government Operations. *Senate Action on Hoover Commission Reports; Report.* 82d Cong., 2d Sess. Washington, D.C.: U.S. Government Printing Office, 1952.

U.S. Department of Agriculture. *A Selected Bibliography on Special Districts and Authorities in the United States; Annotated.* Misc. Publication No. 1087. Washington, D.C., 1968.

———. Economic Research Service. *Evaluating Enabling Laws for Special Districts: A Case Study in Oklahoma.* (ERS 281.) Washington, D.C., 1966.

U.S. Department of Transportation. *Final Report on Basic National Rail Passenger System.* Washington, D.C., January 28, 1971.

U.S. Environmental Protection Agency. *National Capital Region Water and Waste Management Report.* Washington, D.C., April 1, 1971.

U.S. General Accounting Office. *Auditing: Operational Management, Performance Effectiveness; A Compendium.* Washington, D.C., June 1972.

———. *Charges for Use of Federal Electrical Power Transmission Lines Should Be Reevaluated.* B-114858. Washington, D.C., September 1971.

———. *Cost of Furnishing Postmaster General's New Office.* Washington, D.C., 1974.

———. *Evaluating Governmental Performance: Changes and Challenges for GAO.* Washington, D.C.: U.S. Government Printing Office, 1975.

———. *Forecast of Postal Service's Self Sufficiency Potential.* Washington, D.C., 1975.

———. *Observations and Questions on the Development of the New National Bulk Mail System.* Washington, D.C., 1975.

———. *Site Selection and Contract Awards for Construction and Mechanization of the New York Bulk and Foreign Mail Facility.* B-171594. Washington, D.C., October 1971.

————. *Standards for Audit of Governmental Organizations, Programs, Activities and Functions.* Washington, D.C., 1972.

U.S. President's Commission on Budget Concepts. *Report.* Washington, D.C.: U.S. Government Printing Office, 1967.

U.S. President's Commission on Postal Organization. *Towards Postal Excellence.* Contractor's Report. Washington, D.C.: U.S. Government Printing Office, 1968.

U.S. President's Committee on Administrative Management. *Report. Submitted in Accordance with Public Law 739.* 74th Cong., 2d Sess. Washington, D.C.: U.S. Government Printing Office, 1937.

Wilkes College, Institute of Municipal Government. *New Developments in Long-Term Financing. Proceedings of 27th Annual Meeting of Pennsylvania Municipal Finance Officers.* Wilkes-Barre, Pa., 1963.

Vermont Statutes. Chapter 93, 1970. Municipal Bond Bank.

Dissertations

Ball, Richard E. "The Significance of the Government Corporation in Administrative Theory." Ph.D. dissertation, Notre Dame University, 1955.

Cassella, William N., Jr. "Governing the St. Louis Metropolitan Area." Ph.D. dissertation, Harvard University, 1952.

Clay, Comer. "The Lower Colorado River Authority: A Study in Politics and Public Administration." Ph.D. dissertation, University of Texas, 1948.

Danielson, Michael N. "Commuter Politics in the New York Region." Ph.D. dissertation, Princeton University, 1962.

Diamond, Arnold H. "The New York City Housing Authority: A Study in Public Corporations." Ph.D. dissertation, Columbia University, 1954.

Foster, John F. "Theoretical Foundations of Government Ownership in a Capitalistic Economy." Ph.D. dissertation, University of Texas, 1946.

Kimmelman, W. M. "Local Agency Formation Commissions in Southern California, 1963-1970." Ph.D. dissertation, Claremont Graduate School, 1971.

Maurer, Marvin. "The Role of the Board of Commissioners of the Port of New York Authority in Policy Formation." Ph.D. dissertation, Columbia University, 1966.

Mitchell, William E. "The Use of Nonguaranteed Debt to Circumvent State and Local Government Legal Debt Limitations." Ph.D. dissertation, Duke University, 1967.

Preston, Nathaniel S. "The Use and Control of Public Authorities in American State and Local Government." Ph.D. dissertation, Princeton University, 1960.

Stuart, Richard K. "Public Improvement Financing by the State of Maine." Ph.D. dissertation, University of Pennsylvania, 1956.

Todd, J. D. "The Risk Management Concept Applied to Municipal Government." Ph.D. dissertation, University of Wisconsin, 1968.

Van Dohlen, Gerard N. "The Investment Decision Making Process of the Port of New York Authority: A Benefit-Cost Study." Ph.D. dissertation, Columbia University, 1970.

Index